D0886277

Little is known of the enigmatic gentle aut
gentle author is their intimate confidante ar
stories of the remarkable people to be found .

www.spitalfieldslife.com
@thegentleauthor

'For a unique insight into everyday life in the East End, let blogger The Gentle Author take you on a journey into Spitalfields' street life, art, markets, houses and culture'. – *Evening Standard ES magazine*

'In an Olympic year awash with books about London, no work came close to the eccentric charm and warmth on offer in Spitalfields Life by the anonymous "Gentle Author". This deadpan blogger's encounters with East Enders old and new, now transformed into a sumptuous volume, built into an irresistible group portrait of modern metropolitans and their overlapping histories . . . rather like WG Sebald'. – Boyd Tonkin, *Independent*

'This fine collection includes many memorable episodes on the history and heritage of the area, and many colourful characters such as a rhyme collector, street artist, rapper, mudlark and a master bell founder'. – *The Times*

'For the brief time of reading, one steps into the skin of the subject, and inhabits them. Inherits them, perhaps.' – *Evening Standard*

Spitalfields Life points you to London's hidden gems'. – *Stylist*

'A joy to read, whether you know Spitalfields or not . . . It's not for nothing that the author's observational skills and ability to convey them to the reader have led some to liken them to Pepys and Dickens . . . Some places have a heart and a soul, a special something, and if it touches you it will grip you and hold you and captivate you. Spitalfields is such a place . . . An unusual book that's pure joy, a tribute to life'. – *We Love This Book*

Spitalfields Life

'IN THE MIDST OF LIFE
I WOKE TO FIND MYSELF
LIVING IN AN OLD HOUSE
BESIDE BRICK LANE IN
THE EAST END OF
LONDON'

*Illustrations by Mark Hearld,
Lucinda Rogers and Rob Ryan*

THE
GENTLE AUTHOR

First published in Great Britain in 2012 by Saltyard Books
An imprint of Hodder & Stoughton
An Hachette UK company

This paperback edition first published in 2013

1

A CIP catalogue record for this title is available from the British Library

ISBN 978 1 444 70396 2

Printed and bound by T J International, Cornwall, England
Typeset in Miller by Nicky Barneby & David Pearson

Hodder & Stoughton policy is to use papers that are natural, renewable
and recyclable products and made from wood grown in sustainable forests.
The logging and manufacturing processes are expected to conform
to the environmental regulations of the country of origin.

Hodder & Stoughton Ltd
338 Euston Road
London NW1 3BH
www.saltyardbooks.co.uk

CONTENTS

INTRODUCTION

*'In the midst of life I woke to find myself living in an old
house beside Brick Lane in the East End of London.'*

A new life began for me when I came to live here in a corner of London I had visited for many years, but where I knew no one except Sandra Esqulant – landlady of the Golden Heart in Commercial Street. Spitalfields always held an allure for me as the authentic heart of old London, a mythic place of incredible history, existing as a vast repository of untold stories, and I was drawn by the exuberant chaotic life of this ancient neighbourhood bordering the City of London.

Two thousand years ago, the Romans built their villas outside the City walls, beside Ermine Street, the main road north from London. A thousand years later, Walter Brunus opened St Mary's Hospital as a refuge for the sick and the poor who could not sustain themselves within the confines of the City. In doing so, he gave the name to the place, as St Mary's Hospital Fields became *Spitalfields* in common parlance and, even today, older people still refer to it as 'the fields'. Most importantly, he established Spitalfields as a place of refuge, defining the nature of this location as a bright field of possibility where the wealth of the City meets the poor of the Tower hamlets.

In the twelfth century, Jewish people started a market here when they could not trade in the City, and this market, which still exists in Petticoat Lane, initiated the vibrant culture of street trading that fills Spitalfields every Sunday. Similarly, in the sixteenth century, theatres were built in Shoreditch when they were not permitted in the City and it was there William Shakespeare's early plays were first performed.

These fields served as a rural retreat for Elizabeth I and the Earl of Essex, who both had houses near Aldgate. Market gardens and pleasure gardens flourished, and newly woven woollen cloth was stretched to dry upon the tenter grounds. In 1538, Henry VIII turned the precincts of St Mary's Hospital into an artillery ground. A century later, Charles I signed the charter for a market in Spitalfields. Daniel Defoe came to report upon the victims of the Great Plague and Samuel Pepys sought refuge here from the Fire of London in 1666.

Huguenot silk weavers arrived from France and Belgium to escape religious persecution after the Revocation of the Edict of Nantes in 1685, building fine houses in the fields and bringing a sophistication and flair to the textile industry that was to occupy Spitalfields for subsequent centuries. They were followed by migrant workers from Kent and East Anglia who came in search of employment at the looms, and then Irish refugees too, escaping the famines and seeking a better life.

Asserting the supremacy of the Church over this mixed neighbourhood of migrants and foreigners, Nicholas Hawksmoor's Christ Church was built in Spitalfields between 1714 and 1729. An epic, disproportionate masterpiece, it looms above the marketplace and dwarfs all other human endeavour.

In the nineteenth century, thousands of Jewish families came – fleeing for their lives from Russian pogroms. Many travelled steerage, hoping to get to New York, but when they arrived at the Port of London they settled for Spitalfields instead. Meanwhile, the overcrowded city sprawled eastwards to create the place known pejoratively at the end of the nineteenth century as the 'East End'. It was a location that became emblematic of the worst of urban degradation and criminality, and – even today – the sensationalist violent histories that accompanied this vision often obscure the lives of the ordinary working people of the territory.

Yet my discovery is that the history of poverty in the East End has engendered a parallel history of resourcefulness – as, driven by necessity, people devoted themselves to invent ingenious and often creative ways of seeking a living. In my work, I never came across any of the feckless Cockneys of popular lore but I met plenty of self-respecting people from modest backgrounds with a desire to improve their lot – and that of others too – through embracing education and work.

As Jewish people left Spitalfields after the Second World War to seek better housing in the suburbs, more immigrants came from Asia – Sikhs, Pakistanis and then Bengalis. Many were sea captains and sailors who worked in the clothing factories that they eventually took over, and opened canteens to feed themselves which subsequently became the curry restaurants of Brick Lane today.

Even to describe these major waves of immigration neglects to include the numberless people who came from every country in the world through the London docks, Afro-Caribbeans, Maltese, Germans, Scandinavians, Italians, Somalis, Thais and Filipinos, Latin Americans, Nigerians, Ghanaians and more. Today there are also those who have come from North America and the Antipodes, whose ancestors emigrated from here long ago.

No one can deny there has been a history of conflict in the East End, accompanying the turbulence of changing industries and population. But this has always been counter-balanced by a strong egalitarian spirit, nurtured in a society where, of necessity, people learn to live alongside each other and thereby come to understand each other. It was a spirit that became manifest in the Battle of Cable Street in 1936 – a definitive moment, when three hundred thousand people formed a human chain to prevent Fascists entering Whitechapel.

A lifetime's interest in the East End taught me something of the vast nature of the subject, enough to recognise that it is beyond the capacity of any writer to create a definitive account. In approaching it myself, I realised that I could not write more than one story a day and thus the idea was born to write about a different person each day.

Charles Dickens, Henry Mayhew, Robert Louis Stevenson, Jack London and George Orwell all came to the East End to write stories of the people that make this place, providing me with inspiration and a range of examples that I was able to follow in writing my own pen-portraits describing the qualities of those who live and work here today.

The loss of human stories that go unrecorded when people die is a matter of grief to me, initially brought to mind by the death of my parents and the recognition that although I was left with the photographs, I could never fully know their stories. I first recognised this emotion upon seeing family photo albums for sale in markets. It filled me with alarm at the loss of the affectionate histories which accompanied these once treasured artefacts. And so it was as a consequence of these sentiments that I set out to devote my experience as a writer to writing down people's stories and publishing them, often with their own photographs as illustration.

At first, I interviewed people in Spitalfields as if I were a journalist, but very quickly the boundaries came down – because these are the people who live in the place I inhabit. Before long, the writing project that began as *Spitalfields Life* quite simply became my life. It made me look at people differently as I grew to understand their motives better and the result is that the city has become a more human place for me.

Sometimes I was asked, 'What are you going to do when you run out of stories?' but it was clear from the start that there would be no problem finding material, the only difficulty is to choose what to write of each day because the possibilities are almost infinite. Truly all of human life is here in Spitalfields. My frequent experience is that each interviewee tells me of others I should write about and readers write in with suggestions too, so that even as I cross off names from the top of my list, more are added to the bottom, and the endlessly expanding possibilities can engender a sense of vertigo. I can readily imagine how Noah must have felt, thinking, 'How am I going to fit everyone in?'

In the course of my interviews, I met a ninth-generation silk weaver and a sixth-generation umbrella maker – not to mention a paper bag seller, bellfounder and poulterer, all fourth generation in their trades. In this book, you will find Richard Lee, a bicycle seller, whose family has been trading from the same market stall off Brick Lane each Sunday, since 1880. In these pages, you will also find a flower seller named Albert Dean – through four successive generations, great-grandfather, grandfather, father and son, all sharing the same names, each Albert Dean has been selling flowers on the same corner of Columbia Road for more than a century. One of my most astonishing discoveries is

Stanley Rondeau, who works as a volunteer guide in Christ Church on Tuesdays where his Huguenot ancestor John Rondeau was Sexton, eight generations and more than three hundred years previously.

The one thing that everybody tells me is, 'Spitalfields has changed,' yet my investigation has revealed that, even though there has been major rebuilding and movement of people, there are plenty who still carry the culture and stories of this place stretching back over centuries. Not only is Spitalfields alive, but the cultures of the past coexist and commingle with those brought by more recent immigrants, and by all the young people who have also come to the East End, drawn by instinctive curiosity. Today, the cultural mix that is the outcome of the history of Spitalfields has made it a fashionable destination as visitors from all over Europe descend in their hundreds of thousands every weekend to explore the markets and experience the street life.

In Spitalfields now, change is accelerating and I have taken on the responsibility to record this transformation day by day, retelling the most compelling stories of the past, and exploring the human losses and reinventions, as the monstrous whirlwind of time roars through Brick Lane turning everything on its head.

Like those writers in fourteenth-century Florence who discovered the sonnet but did not quite know what to do with it, we are presented with the new literary medium of the blog – which has quickly become omnipresent, with many millions writing online. For my own part, I respect this nascent literary form by seeking to explore its own unique qualities and potential. In spite of its novelty, there are several venerable precedents. Firstly, in the diaries and journals that people have always written to make a single narrative from the chaos of life. Secondly, in the epic collections of stories such as *The Arabian Nights, The Decameron* and *The Canterbury Tales*, constructed to reveal a multi-dimensional picture of human nature. Thirdly, in the distinguished literary form of the pen-portrait, which had its former flowering in the newspapers that languished when the internet came along.

These three currents of literature converge in the wide river of writing, with its many tributaries and backwaters, that for want of a better name is termed 'the blog'. The stories you find collected here in this book were selected from my first eighteen months of writing a story online each day, and you can follow my continuing progress daily at www.spitalfieldslife.com.

Once I was concerned that writing was an overly solitary activity to pursue as a lifetime's occupation, yet *Spitalfields Life* has led me out into the world and I have met more people since I started this work than I had done in the whole of my life up to that point.

When I get home from an interview and open my notebook to look at my notes, I always think, 'How can I do justice to this person?' Without all the individuals who have opened their hearts to me, these stories could not exist, and any success *Spitalfields Life* has won must be attributed to their qualities alone, while I personally must claim responsibility for the flaws as indicative of my own limitations.

One day, I shall throw a big party in Spitalfields for all the subjects of my pen-portraits and invite you, my readers, to come and meet them. But in the meantime, as I gather my thoughts and sharpen my pencil to continue, I hope, through the practice of my work, to become better at this endeavour, in order to be more worthy of my subjects – since there are so many more things I must show you and more people I want to introduce.

YOUR LOYAL SERVANT
THE GENTLE AUTHOR

SPRING BULBS AT BOW CEMETERY

Plant Life

WHEN UNSEASONABLY WARM SUNSHINE brought temperatures of ten degrees to the East End and the promise of an early spring, I decided to visit Bow Cemetery to see if the bulbs were showing yet. Already I have snowdrops, hellebores and a few primroses in flower in my Spitalfields garden, but at Bow I was welcomed by thousands of crocuses of every colour and variety spangling the graveyard with their gleaming flowers. Beaten and bowed, grey-faced and sneezing, coughing and shivering – the harsh winter has taken it out of me, but feeling the warmth of the sun and seeing these sprouting bulbs in such profusion restored my hope that benign weather will come before too long.

Some of my earliest crayon drawings are of snowdrops, and the annual miracle of bulbs erupting out of the barren earth never ceases to touch my heart – an emotion amplified in a cemetery to see life spring abundant and graceful in the landscape of death. The numberless dead of east London – the poor buried for the most part in unmarked communal graves – are coming back to us as perfect tiny flowers of white, purple and yellow, and the sombre background of grey tombs and stones serves to emphasise the curious delicate life of these vibrant blooms, glowing in the sunshine.

Here within the shelter of the old walls, the spring bulbs are further ahead than elsewhere in the East End and I arrived at Bow Cemetery just as the snowdrops were coming to an end, the crocuses were in full flower and the daffodils were beginning. Thus a sequence of flowers is set in motion, with bulbs continuing through until April, when the bluebells will come leading us through to the acceleration of summer growth, blanketing the cemetery in lush foliage again.

Created by act of Parliament as the growing population of London overcrowded the small parish churchyards, and extending to twenty-seven acres, the City of London and Tower Hamlets Cemetery (as it was formally called) opened in 1841, and within the first half-century alone around a quarter of a million were buried here. By the end of the nineteenth century the site was already overgrown, though burials continued until it was closed in 1966.

Today, where death once held dominion, nature has reclaimed the territory and a magnificent broadleaf forest has sprung up, bringing luxuriant growth that is alive with wildlife. Now the tombstones and monuments stand among leaf mould in deep woods, and I found myself alone in the vast cemetery save for a few magpies, crows and some errant squirrels chasing each other around. Walking further into the woodland, I saw yellow winter aconites gleaming bright against the grey tombstones and, crouching down, I discovered wild violets in flower too. Beneath an intense blue sky, to the chorus of birdsong echoing among the trees, spring was making a persuasive showing.

Stepping into a clearing, I came upon a red admiral butterfly basking upon a broken tombstone, as if to draw my attention to the text upon it, 'Sadly Missed', commenting upon this precious day of sunshine. Butterflies are rare in the city in any season, but to see a red admiral, which is a sight of high summer, in February is extraordinary. My first assumption was that I was witnessing the single day in the tenuous life of this vulnerable creature, but in fact the hardy red admiral is one of the last to be seen before the onset of frost and can emerge from months of hibernation to enjoy single days of sunlight. Such is the solemn poetry of a lone butterfly in winter.

It may be over a month yet before it is officially spring, but we are at the beginning now.

JOAN NAYLOR OF BELLEVUE PLACE

THIS IS JOAN NAYLOR, photographed in the garden of her house in Bellevue Place, a terrace of nineteenth-century cottages in Stepney entirely hidden from the street behind a green door.

Joan moved into Bellevue Place with her husband, Bill, in 1956, when they were first married, and they brought up their family there. 'When we first moved in it was known as "Bunghole Alley" and no one wanted to live there,' she recalled with a shrug. Origin-ally it was part of a crescent of cottages around a green which served in the Victorian period as tea gardens, until Charrington built a brewery on the site, lopping the terrace in half, constructing a wall round it and using the cottages for their workers. Enclosed on all sides, there is a door in one wall that led directly into the brewery, which remains locked today, now the brewery has gone.

Joan's husband, Bill, was a load clerk

whose job it was to devise the most efficient delivery routes and loads for the draymen on the rounds of all the Charrington's pubs in the East End. When Joan arrived, the brewery workers started early, commencing each day with a few pints in the taproom before beginning work, and Bill was able to pop home through the door in the wall at nine o'clock to enjoy breakfast with Joan.

'If you looked out of the bedroom window, you could see a pile of wooden barrels 100 foot high, and the smell of stale beer permeated the air,' said Joan, recalling her first impressions. 'Nothing had been changed in the house. The brewery brought in the decorators but we still had a tiny bathroom off the kitchen and an outside loo. It didn't bother me. When you think we brought up six of us in that house – I remember the ice on the inside of the window! We used to cut up old barrels to light the fire and they'd burn really well because they had pitch in them.'

It is with pure joy that Joan remembers the days when there were around a dozen children, including her own, living in Bellevue Place. They all played together, chasing up and down the gardens, an ideal environment for games of hide-and-seek, and there were frequent parties when everyone celebrated together on birthdays, Christmas and Bonfire Night. 'There was always a party coming up, always something to look forward to,' explained Joan, because it was not only the children who enjoyed a high old time in the secret enclave of Bellevue Place.

Since everyone knew each other through working together at the brewery, there was a constant round of parties for adults too. It was the arrival of Stan, the refrigeration engineer and famous practical joker, to live in the end cottage, that Joan credits as the catalyst for the golden age of parties in Bellevue Place.

When all the children were safely tucked up asleep ('We had children, we couldn't go out'), the residents of Bellevue Place enjoyed lively fancy-dress parties, in and out of the gardens, and each other's houses too. 'The word would go out from Stan and we would go round the charity shops to see what we could find, but no one would tell anyone what their outfit was going to be. It was lovely. Everybody had fun and nobody carried on with each other's wives,' Joan told me.

Let us not discount the proximity of the brewery in our estimation of the party years at Bellevue Place, because I have no doubt there was never any shortage of drinks. Also, No. 1, the large house at the beginning of the terrace, was empty and disused for many years, and the brewery even gave the residents a key, so it could become the social venue and youth club, with a snooker table, and a rooftop that was ideal for firework parties. With all these elements at their disposal, the enterprising party animals of Bellevue Place became expert at making their own entertainment.

There is a bizarre twist to Joan's account of the legendary parties at Bellevue Place, because she was born on 29 February, which means she only has a birthday every leap year. So, when she did have a birthday, Joan's neighbours organised parties appropriate to the birthday in question, and she was given a Yogi Bear annual as a present for her seventh birthday when she was twenty-eight years old. I hope Joan will not consider it indiscreet if I reveal to you that she has now at last reached her twenty-first birthday.

It is apparent that the mutual support Joan enjoyed among the women in her terrace, who became her close friends, and the camaraderie shared by the men, who worked together in the brewery – all surrounded by the host of children who played together – created an exceptionally warm and close-knit community in Bellevue Place that became in effect an extended family. Even though they did not have much money and lived together in a house that many would consider small for six, Joan's memories of her own family life are framed by this rare experience of the place and its people in these circumstances, and it is an experience that many would envy.

By the time Joan moved out of Bellevue Place for good, she had become the resident who had lived there the longest and remains the living repository of its history. I visited her in sheltered housing in Bethnal Green, where she told me her beautiful stories of the vibrant social life of this modest brewery terrace, while her son John, who is a regular visitor, worked on his hand-held computer in the corner of the room.

'We were very lucky to have lived down there to bring up the family,' said Joan, her eyes glistening with happiness as she spread out her collection of affectionate and playful photographs, cherishing the events which incarnate the highlights of her existence in Bellevue Place. She may have first known it as Bunghole Alley, but for Joan Naylor Bellevue Place lived up to the promise of its name.

Joan (holding the glass) with her neighbours

THE WORLD OF
THE EAST END CAR WASH

Street Life

CAR WASHES come and go in the East End, opening up in vacant railway arches or disused petrol stations, enjoying a brief flowering and then vanishing as unexpectedly as they appeared. Yet within the mutable world of the car wash, business goes on relentlessly, because as quickly as

vehicles are cleaned, the traffic and the weather and the mud restore the necessity for it to be done all over again. Teams of men work ceaselessly in shifts, twenty-four hours a day, at a job that requires astounding stamina and patience.

Let me admit, it gives me the shivers just

to imagine the lot of a car washer, working outside through the damp and cold of a London winter, so I was humbled by the goodwill that I encountered from these men, demonstrating resilience and tenacity in circumstances that few would envy. When I arrived at T2 Car Wash under the railway arches at the western extremity of Cable Street, beneath the main line coming out of Fenchurch Street Station, the car washers welcomed me into their cosy cubbyhole off the main working area, a den where they enjoyed a bowl of porridge and watched satellite TV, toasting their toes by the heater during a rare break from the everlasting parade of taxis which pass through here night and day.

Yet once a vehicle pulled up, they were all over it with preternatural dexterity and speed. Working in concert, they were spraying shampoo, mopping it with sponges – one in each hand – then rinsing it down and polishing it up with chamois leathers – again one in each hand – until the customer received his charge back, gleaming and spotless. And then the car washers moved on to the next in line with undiminished enthusiasm. While one team attended to the exterior, others were hoovering and cleaning out the interior, and everyone worked round each other – like some elaborate dance in which the moves kept shifting as everyone accommodated to everyone else in the constant imperative to keep things moving. These men are expert at what they do and show grace in their warmth and mutual respect, excelling in an endeavour which to others might be of little consequence.

Mohaimenul Islam, car washer

All this spectacle takes place within a whitewashed arch lit by fluorescents, open to daylight at either end, where, in a glacial mist, every surface glistens with damp and the floor is awash with water and soap suds draining away through culverts. For the most part these men do not wear gloves, even working with wet sponges and wringing them out in cold water, but when I asked, 'Don't you get cold?' the answer was automatic, 'We don't feel the cold when we're working, and when we're not working we're in by the heater.'

At the car wash, I always seek human details – the Christmas baubles, or the plastic birds, or the bunting, or the odd chairs scattered around, or the newspaper cuttings stuck to the wall, indicating that the employees have taken possession of their space. Be aware, the car wash is an arena we enter as guests, because the car washers are rulers of their soapy domain and customers must understand the decorum which requires a retreat to the waiting room, or to use the facilities, or to stand outside at a respectful distance from the centre of activity.

Alone in the den at the T2 Car Wash, a room excavated into the thickness of the old brick vault, where I was privileged to warm myself, I realised that I had found the inner sanctum in which the car washers came to regroup, sitting upon the worn couch and office chairs, whiling away the long dark nights and bolstering each other's resolve to make it through another winter. In the face of this arduous repetitive work, a group of Ghanaians and Romanians had banded together to make the best of it under an arch in Cable Street.

You might say that washing cars is a pointless activity, since the vehicles get dirty again at once, yet, as with many human occupations, the nobility lies not in the nature of the task or even in the reward, but in the manner of its execution. And there on the wall in the den, I saw the medal for car washing, awarded to the team for the ever-growing number of customers each month, objective evidence – if it were necessary – of the otherwise unacknowledged heroism of the proud car washers of the East End.

The champion car washers of Cable Street

MOLLY THE SWAGMAN

MAKE NO MISTAKE, Molly is a swagman. It is a title that carries its own raffish assertion of independence. There are no swagwomen, only swagmen, and Molly is a proud swagman. She told me it all began with her great-grandfather, who was a swagman on Petticoat Lane, and he lived to be ninety-nine. And now I shall expect no less from Molly herself – because there is no doubt that, as a fourth-generation

swagman, she is the shrewd inheritor of the good-humoured perseverance which is required to achieve longevity in market life.

Although I always knew the word 'swag' from comic books, where masked burglars have it written on their sacks, it was Molly herself who first explained to me that 'Swag is when you are selling a variety of goods, from clothes to jewellery – anything you can find.' And she gave me a significant glance of complicity, which led me to assume there might be a shady history, before returning to her plate of bacon and egg, accompanied by a pile of toast, that formed the primary focus of her attention at that moment. We were enjoying a hearty breakfast in Dino's Café in Commercial Street, huddled together round a small table at the back with Molly's old friend Jimmy Cuba, the dealer in Latin music, and Ellen, her loyal associate from the market, completing the party.

'My first market was down the lane,' Molly confided in tender reminiscence, pushing the empty plate to one side and lifting her mug of tea. 'I was about three, toddling around on my first day in Petticoat Lane, where we lived. The house where I was born, it was in Leyden Street, No. 6. My

Jimmy Cuba and Molly

in backchat to accompany it. 'If they say, "You've got to give me a discount,"' recounted Molly, raising her eyebrows in delight and assuming a hoity-toity voice, 'I say, "Why? Do I know you?"' Then she chuckled to herself, recalling another recurring dialogue. 'Those yuppies, they ask, "If I buy this, can I get this free?" So then I put on my best cockney voice,' she continued, placing a hand on my forearm and assuming an archly demure manner, 'and I say, "Here, love, come back next week, when you've got a bit more money."' Chuckling again, and launching into a raucous self-parody, 'They've got to be hedge-ucated!' she declared with a triumphant grimace, pressing the ball of her hand on the table in response to the general mirth of those of us who comprised her audience.

great-grandfather had the pitch and it went down through the family – that's how it was in those days. Anything you could sell, he would sell it. He was a dodgy dealer, he used to do deals. My grandfather, my father and my uncle were all in it too. Uncle Bob and Grandad used to front the stall, while my father was the money behind the scenes. My father had the advantage of going to school. My grandmother was in films, so she sent her two sons to boarding schools. He was a very snappy dresser, when he had some money he used to go and get two new suits made. He had the whole look, the cufflinks and the polished shoes. "You have to dress up to do business," he said. Grandad sold linens off the back of the van and Uncle Bob was the one with china – he threw it up in the air. And I used to take the money. It's where I learned to add up.'

Molly's pedigree as a swagman imparts a singularity of attitude which balks no condescension, and graces her with a sharp line

I learned that Molly's experience is not restricted to market life, because for five years she worked as Girl Friday to Peter Grant, the manager of Led Zeppelin. As we sipped tea and digested our breakfasts, she regaled Jimmy, Ellen and me with her tales of the rock 'n' roll years. 'The boys used to call me "ma",' she revealed shyly. 'I knew them all, Mickie Most, Adam Faith and the rest. They all came down to the country, where I used to cook breakfast for the guests, walk them round the house and make up these fantastic ghost stories. When I was down there, I treated them just like anybody else. One day this tall blond guy came down with his laundry, so I showed him how to work the machine – that was Robert Plant.' At this point, Jimmy Cuba could contain himself no longer, interposing, 'This was when Led Zeppelin were the biggest band on the planet!' and Molly smiled bashfully, blushing a little to recall her days as a rock chick.

Each Wednesday, Thursday and Friday, you will see Molly stalling out in the Spitalfields Market with Ellen at her side, the lone swagman with her modest swag spread out before her on the table. Even after all these years Molly cannot predict each day's trading – market life is akin to gambling in that way. The two self-effacing women preside like sentinels, whispering together about the ceaseless spectacle passing before them. For Molly, it is a fleeting show, because she is the living representative of the three swagmen who came before her and it gives her a unique sense of perspective. Market life has made her circumspect and she would not tell me her full name or even reveal the name of her great-grandfather who lived to be ninety-nine. Yet I was honoured to speak with her because Molly is an extraordinary woman, dignified, witty and with great strength of character, and she is the last of the Spitalfields swagmen.

GARY ARBER

PRINTER

Human Life, Past Life

I SET OUT EARLY from Spitalfields, crossing the freshly fallen snow in Weavers' Fields, towards the premises of W. F. Arber & Co. Ltd at 459 Roman Road. Once I rang the bell, Gary Arber appeared from the warren of boxes inside, explaining that he did not have much time because he had to do his accounts.

'I'm here under duress, because I'd rather be flying a Lincoln bomber,' protested Gary, explaining that he took over the business, sacrificing his career as a pilot when his father died, since his mother relied upon the income of the printing works. 'I left the beautiful air force in 1956,' he revealed wistfully. It is not hard to envisage Gary as a handsome flying ace; he has that charismatically nonchalant professionalism. He retains the air force moustache over half a century later, so you only have to imagine a flight suit in place of the overalls to complete the picture. There is no doubt Gary saw life before he swapped the flight suit for overalls and vanished into the print shop. He was there at Christmas Island to witness one of the first nuclear tests, though he was not one of those pilots who flew through the dust cloud to collect samples. 'We were guests of the day, watching from a boat. We had bits of dark glass and they

told us to shut our eyes when the count-down reached two and open our eyes to look through the glass when it reached minus five – but you saw it through your eyelids. Then you felt the shock, the turbulence and the heat. It was great fun.' Mercifully, Gary appears to have suffered no ill-effects, still running the shop today at seventy-eight, driving daily from his home in Romford.

These days, Gary's shop has become something of a destination for artists who love his old-school letterpress printing, but, as a sole operator, Gary now only under-takes these jobs 'under pressure'. 'The quality is rubbish,' he says, grabbing a pad of taxi receipts and turning one over to reveal the impress of the type, embossed into the paper – the only way he can get a clear print from the worn type now. 'It should be smooth,' he sighs, running a single finger across the reverse of the page before tossing it back on to the pile. I was concerned on Gary's behalf until he dis-armed me, 'I don't make any money. I'm just pottering about and enjoying myself!' he confided gleefully. Owning his premises,

Gary enjoys complete security and has the freedom to carry on in his own sweet way.

Gary's grandfather Walter Francis Arber first opened the shop in 1897, as a printer and stationer who also sold toys. The business was continued by Gary's father, who was also called Walter Francis Arber, and it is this name that remains on the stationery today. I heard a rumour that the Suffragettes' handbills were printed here and Gary confirmed this. 'My grandmother, Emily Arber, was a friend of Mrs Pankhurst and she wouldn't let my grandfather charge for the printing. A ferocious woman, she ruled everyone. The women – my grandmother and aunt – ran the toys side of the business.' And although the toys side was wrapped up long ago, when Gary's aunt (also called Emily) died, the signs remain. Lift your eyes above the suspended fluorescents and you discover there are beautifully coloured posters produced by toy manufacturers pasted to the ceiling. 'If I removed those the roof would probably collapse!' quipped Gary with a grin. Then, indicating the glass-fronted cases that were used to display dolls, he said proudly, 'All the shopfittings are a hundred years old. Nothing's been touched.' He pointed to an enigmatic line with scruffy ends of string hanging down, each carrying more dust than you would have thought possible. 'Those bits of string had board games hanging from them once.'

Moving a stack of boxes to one side, Gary uncovered some printing samples for customers to select their preferred options. What a selection! There was a ration card from a butcher round the corner, a dance

ticket for 30 December 1939 at Wilmot Street School, Bethnal Green, and one for an ATS social with the helpful text 'You will be informed in the event of an air raid', just in case you got seduced by Glenn Miller and did not hear the siren. There is a crazy humour about these things being here. I turned to confront an advert for a Chopper bicycle portraying a winsome lady with big hair exhorting me to 'Be a trendy shopper'. I turned back to Gary. 'This is a shop not a museum,' he said sternly. You could have fooled me.

Aware that I was keeping Gary from his chores, I was on the brink of taking my leave when he confessed that he was no longer in the mood for doing accounts. Instead he took me down to the cellar, where six printers worked once. 'This is where it used to happen,' he announced, as we descended the wooden staircase into a subterranean space where six oily black beasts of printing presses crouched, artfully camouflaged beneath a morass of waste paper, old boxes and packets, with the occasional antique tin toy, left over from stock, to complete the mix. Here was a printing shop from a century ago, an untidy time capsule where the twentieth century passed through like a furious whirlwind, demanding printing for the Suffragettes and printing for the government through two world wars, and whisking Gary away to Christmas Island to witness a nuclear explosion. And *this* was what was left. I was overawed at the spectacle, as Gary began removing boxes to reveal more of the machines, explaining their qualities, capabilities and operating systems. He pointed out the two that were used for the Suffragettes' handbills and I stood silent a moment in reverence before the historical significance of these old hulks, a Wharfedale and a Golding Jobber.

Gary made a beeline for the Heidelberg, the only one that still works, and began tinkering with the type that he used to print the taxi receipt I saw earlier. This was the heart of it all. I joined him and, standing together in the quiet, we both became absorbed by the magic of the press. Gary was explaining the technical names for the parts of the printer's pie when an unexpected wave of emotion overcame me there in this gloomy cellar, on a cold morning in February, up to my ankles in rubbish, surrounded by historic printing presses. 'Will you print something for me?' I blurted out, and although he claimed he only did this 'under pressure', Gary consented at once.

I needed some correspondence cards and Gary kindly agreed to print them for me (in Perpetua, my favourite typeface) as a memento of his wonderful printing shop. Once we agreed on the nature of the job, another customer arrived. So I said my goodbyes, secure in the knowledge that I now had reason to go back and continue our conversation, once the proofs were ready.

I doubt very much that Gary did his accounts that day, but Gary is a sociable man with a generous spirit (even if he strikes an unconvincingly gruff posture occasionally) and if you choose to pay a visit yourself, then it is highly possible that you will learn (as I did) about the Roman sarcophagus that was discovered in the Roman Road, or the woman who was the inspiration for the character of Eliza Doolittle in *Pygmalion*, or Gary's adventures on steam trains in India, or when Gary was invited to the National Physics Laboratory in the 1950s to see an early computer, as big as four houses, that could play chess.

One word of caution – 'Printers are either highly religious or wicked,' says Gary, adding, 'and I don't go to church!' So if you go round, be sure to pay him the courtesy of buying something, however small. Bear in mind, as you purchase your box of paperclips, that Gary is there under duress – and then, once your subterfuge is achieved, it is appropriate to widen the nature of discourse.

AT THE ANNUAL
GRIMALDI SERVICE

Past Life, Spiritual Life

THE FIRST SUNDAY in February is when all the clowns arrive in east London for the annual service to honour Joseph Grimaldi (1778–1837), the greatest British clown – held since 1946 at this time of year, when the clowns traditionally gathered in the capital prior to the start of the circus touring season. Originally celebrated at St James's, Pentonville Road, where Grimaldi is buried,

the service transferred to Holy Trinity, Dalston, in 1959, where the event has grown and grown, and where there is now a shrine to Grimaldi graced with a commemorative stained-glass window.

By mistake, I walked into the church hall, which served as the changing room, to discover myself surrounded with painted faces and multicoloured suits. Seeing my

disorientation, Mr Woo (in a red wig and clutching a balloon dog) kindly stepped over to greet me, explaining that he was a veteran of forty years' clowning, including a stint at the Bertram Mills Circus with the legendary Coco the Clown – before revealing it was cut short when he fell over and fractured his leg. He illustrated the anecdote by lifting his trouser to reveal a savagely scarred shin bone. 'He's never going to win a knobbly knees contest now!' declared Uncle Colin – with alarming levity – Mr Woo's performing partner in the double act known as the Custard Clowns. 'But what did you do?' I enquired, still concerned by Mr Woo's injury. 'I got a comedy car!' was Mr Woo's response, accompanied by an unnerving chuckle.

Reeling from the tragic ambiguity of this conversation, I walked around to the church, where fans were gathering for the service, and there in the quiet corner chapel dedicated to Joseph Grimaldi I had the good fortune to shake hands with Streaky the Clown, a skinny veteran of sixty-three years' clowning. There is a poignant dignity to old clowns such as Streaky, with face paint applied to wrinkled skin, because the disparity between the harsh make-up and the infinite nuance of the lined face beneath cannot fail to make a soulful impression.

At first, the presence of the clowns doing their sideshows to warm up the congregation changed the meaning of the sacred space, as if the vaulted arches were tent poles and we had come to a show rather than a church service, but both were reconciled in the atmosphere of celebration that

prevailed. Yet although the children delighted in the comedy and the audience laughed at the gags, I must admit that (as I always have) I found the clowns more funny peculiar than funny ha-ha. But it is precisely this contradiction that draws me to them, because I believe that through wholeheartedly embracing such grotesque

self-humiliation they expose an essential quality of humanity – that of our innate foolishness, underscored by our propensity to take ourselves too seriously. We need to be startled, or even alarmed, by their extreme appearances, their gurning and their dopey japes, in order to recognise our true selves. This is the corrective that clowns deliver with a cheesy grin, confronting us with a necessary sense of the ridiculous in life.

'This is the best job I ever had – to make people smile and get them to laugh,' declared Conk the Clown, once he had demonstrated blowing bubbles from his saxophone. 'How did you start?' I asked. 'I got divorced,' he replied. And everyone within earshot laughed, except me. 'I had depression,' Conk continued with a helpless smirk, 'so I joined the amateur dramatics.

But I was no good at it, so I thought, "I'll be a clown!"' Twelve years later, Conk has no apparent cause to regret his decision, as his mirthful demeanour confirmed. 'It's something inside, a feeling you know – everyone's got laughter inside them,' he informed me with a wink, before he disappeared up the aisle in a cloud of bubbles, pursued by laughing children.

Turning around, I found myself greeted by Glory B., an elegant lady dressed in tones of turquoise and blue, sporting a huge butterfly upon her hat. Significantly, her face was not painted and she described herself as a 'children's entertainer' rather than a 'clown'. 'Sometimes children are scared of clowns,' she admitted, articulating my own thoughts with a gentle smile, 'so I work with Mr Woo as a go-between, to comfort them if they are distressed.'

Once the clown organist began to play, everyone took their seats and the parade of clowns commenced, old troupers and young goons, buffoons and funsters, jokers and jesters, enough to delight the most weary eyes and lift the spirits of the most downhearted February day. They filled the church with their pranking and japes and their high-wattage personalities. The intensity of an army of clowns is a presence that almost defies description, because even when they are at rest there is such bristling potential for misrule which might be unleashed at any moment.

In their primary-coloured parodic suits, I could recognise the styles of many periods from the nineteenth and twentieth centuries, and when a clown stood up to carry the wreath to lay in honour of 'Joey Grimaldi', I saw he was wearing an eighteenth-century clown suit. At the climax of the service, the names of those clowns who had died in the year were read out and, for each one, a child carried a candle down the nave. After the announcements of Sir Norman Wisdom, Buddi, Bilbo and Frosty, I saw a faint light travel through the crowd, to be lost at the rear of the church, and it made tangible the brave purpose of clowning – that of laughing in the face of the darkness which surrounds us.

ABDUL MUKTHADIR

WAITER

Culinary Life, Human Life

THE CHARISMATIC Abdul Mukthadir – widely known as Muktha – is a born storyteller, blessed with a natural eloquence, as I quickly discovered when I sat down with him in the brief stillness of the afternoon, while the last diners emptied out of Herb & Spice Indian Restaurant in White's Row. The businessmen were still finishing off their curry in the other half of the restaurant, while in a quiet corner Muktha produced a handful of old photographs and discreetly spread them out on the table to begin. Our only interruption was a request for the bill and, once it had been settled, in the silence of the empty restaurant, Muktha's story took flight.

'I came to Spitalfields in 1975, when I was ten years old. My father got married one day when he went back home to Bangladesh – it was an arranged marriage. At the time I was born, he was working in this country.

He didn't see me until two years later, when he came back again and stayed for three months. I have another two sisters, and a brother born here.

'My father missed his family, so once he got his British citizenship and he had the right to stay in this country, he made a declaration to bring us over and my mother had a big interview at the British Consulate in Dhaka. When we came we had nowhere to stay, my father shared a room with three others in Wentworth Street. The other gentlemen moved into the sitting room and gave one room for us all to live there. After three weeks, my father went to the GLC office in Whitechapel and they gave us a one-bedroom flat in the same street without a bathroom, and a loo in the passageway shared by two households, for one pound fifty a week. My father worked as a presser in the tailoring industry, and sup-

porting a family was really difficult. On Saturday, he gave us each ten pence and we used to go to the Goulston Street Public Baths. They gave you a towel, a bar of soap and a bottle of moisturiser, and you could change the bath water as often as you liked. Six hundred people used to line up. It was very embarrassing for the Asian ladies, so one day my mother called all the ladies in the building into our flat. She said, 'We can buy a tin tub so we can bath ourselves at home.' Everyone contributed, and they bought a long tin bath and took it in turns. But there was no hot water, so they worked out a rota and eight ladies put their kettles on at the same time. They put the bath up on the flat roof, and sent the smallest boys round to collect all the kettles and fill the bath. Only the women could do this.

'We were not allowed to play outside alone, because of the racists. The skinheads used to prowl around the area. We could not go out to play football in the Goulston Street playground until after the English boys had gone home, but even then we had to watch out for their return – because anyone might come and snatch our ball or beat us up. One day, my mum came out swearing at them in Bengali, "Leave my boy alone! Let them play!" We had that sort of problem every week, and that was the only playground we had. Although we were not allowed out after dark, we used to go to evening classes in Bengali on Saturday and Arabic on Sunday. At that time, there was a man who went round with a sack and if he found anyone, he would capture them and ask for a ransom. There were one or two incidents. One day he pounced upon our neighbour's daughter as she was coming from Arabic. He caught her and tried to put her in the sack and carry her away. She was screaming and we were all at home. Everyone came outside and I saw. We saw this three or four times. Between the English kids and the man following us to rape or take us, fourteen was very tough. My people were scared in those days. At that time you couldn't even go out – it wasn't safe.

'We had to move because they were expanding the Petticoat Lane Market. It was really famous then. So the GLC offered my dad a flat in Limehouse, but my father thought it wasn't safe because there were no other Bangladeshis. Then he refused Mile End, even worse for a Bangladeshi family. Finally, he was offered a flat in Christian Street off Commercial Road. It had four bedrooms and a bathroom, and he fell in love with it. This was in 1979, after the six of us had lived in a one-bedroom flat for four years. He was over the moon. I can remember the day we moved. He moved all the furniture in an estate car in five or six trips.

'That was how we lived in England in those days. It was tough, but it was fun and everyone was more sincere, people spoke to each other. No one worked on Saturday and everyone used to invite each other round, saying, "Come to my home next Saturday. My wife will cook!"

The first of Muktha's family came to Britain in the 1940s to work in the Yorkshire cotton mills and he married an English-woman. A sailor lured by tales of Tower Bridge, the miraculous bridge that rose up to let the ships pass through, when he returned to East Pakistan, crowds followed him, shouting, 'He comes from England. Wow!' They nicknamed him Ekush Pound, because he earned twenty-one pounds a week as a foreman at a cotton mill in Keighley. At the request of the mill owner, he sponsored eight men to return with him. Thus Muktha's father and uncle came to Britain, setting in train the sequence of events that led to Muktha working today in Herb & Spice Indian Restaurant in Spitalfields, serving curry to City businessmen.

A waiter since the age of fifteen, Muktha is distinguished by a brightness of spirit that makes him a popular figure among regular customers, who all hope that he will join their table at the end of service and regale them with his open-hearted stories. He becomes enraptured when speaking of Spitalfields, because the emotional intensity of his childhood experiences here have bound him to this place for ever.

'I have hundreds of stories because this is my playground. I belong here. I have so many memories – where I played and where I practised football. If I see a mess in this street, I clear it up because it matters to me. I am a poor man. If I was a millionaire I would do something here, but I am just a waiter, working to pay my mortgage.'

THE PUMP OF DEATH

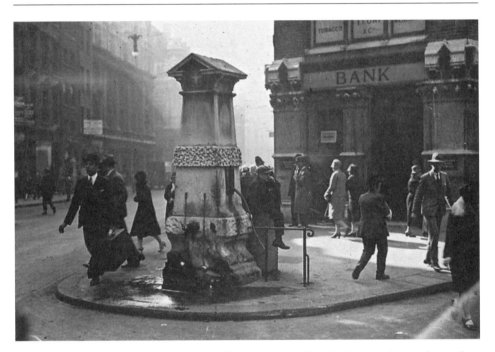

SEE THESE PEOPLE come and go at the junction of Fenchurch Street and Leadenhall Street in the City of London in 1927. Observe the boy idling in the flat cap. They all seem unaware that they are in the presence of the notorious 'Pump of Death'. Switched to mains supply fifty years earlier, in 1876, the water began to taste strange and was found to contain liquid human remains that had seeped into the underground stream from cemeteries.

Hundreds died in the resultant Aldgate Pump epidemic from drinking polluted water – though this was obviously a distant memory by the 1920s, when Whittard's tea merchants used to 'get the kettles filled at the Aldgate Pump so that only the purest water was used for tea tasting'.

Yet before the Aldgate Pump transferred to a supply from the New River Company of Islington, its spring water was appreciated by many for its abundant health-giving mineral salts, until it was discovered that the calcium in the water had leached from human bones.

This bizarre phenomenon quickly entered popular lore, so that a bouncing cheque was referred to as 'a draught upon Aldgate Pump' and in rhyming slang 'Aldgate Pump' meant to be annoyed – 'to get the hump'. The revelation confirmed widespread preju-dice about the East End, of which Aldgate Pump was a landmark defining the beginning of the territory. The 'Pump of Death' became emblematic of the perceived degradation of life in east London and it was once declared, with superlative partiality, that 'East of Aldgate Pump, people cared for nothing but drink, vice and crime.'

Today this sturdy late-eighteenth-century stone pump stands as the battered reminder of a former world, no longer functional, and lost among the traffic and recent developments of the modern City. No one notices it any more and its gruesome history is almost forgotten, despite the impressive provenance of this ancient landmark, from where all mileages east of London are calculated.

Aldgate Well was first mentioned in the thirteenth century – in the reign of King John – and referred to by the sixteenth-century historian John Stowe, who described the execution of the Bailiff of Romford on the gibbet 'near the well within Aldgate'. In *The Uncommercial Traveller*, Charles Dickens wrote, 'My day's business beckoned me to the East End of London, I had turned my face to that part of the compass ... and had got past Aldgate Pump.' And before the 'Pump of Death' incident, music-hall composer Edgar Bateman, nicknamed 'the Shakespeare of Aldgate Pump', wrote a celebratory ballad including the lyric 'I never shall forget the gal I met near Aldgate Pump ...'

The pump was first installed upon the well head in the sixteenth century and subsequently replaced in the eighteenth century by the gracefully tapered and rusticated Portland stone obelisk that stands today, with a nineteenth-century gabled capping. The most remarkable detail to survive to our day is the elegant brass spout in the form of a wolf's head – still snarling ferociously – put there to signify the last of these creatures to be shot outside the City of London.

In the photo from 1927, you can see two metal drinking cups that have gone now, leaving just the stubs where the chains attaching them were fixed. Tantalisingly, the brass button that controls the water outlet is still there, yet, although it is irresistible to press it, the water ceased flowing in the last century. A drain remains beneath the spout where the stone is weathered from the action of water over centuries and there is an elegant wrought-iron pump handle – enough details to convince me that the water might return one day.

FRED

THE CHESTNUT SELLER

Culinary Life, Human Life, Market Life

ALMOST AS MUCH of a familiar landmark in Spitalfields as the church or the market, Fred has been standing in his flat cap and selling chestnuts from a can of hot coals on a barrow every Sunday at the corner of Bell Lane and Wentworth Street for over half a century.

I heard a rumour that chestnut sellers were secret millionaires who put their feet up all summer, but he was eager to disabuse me of this notion. 'The idea that you get rich quick is not true!' Fred swore to me in his singsong voice, glowing with animation, while expertly turning over the hot chestnuts with his blackened fingers. 'For the past six weeks, I didn't cover my expenses. I get up at half five, leave the house at a quarter to six, then I am here from eight until four, and by the time I get home it's eight o'clock. So if I didn't love this job, I wouldn't be here now.'

When Fred began, in the heyday of Petticoat Lane, Wentworth Street was a parade of Jewish delis, and it was this cultural identity which permitted the existence of the market when laws restricted other Sunday trading in London. 'This used to be the best market in London. You couldn't walk through it,' recalled Fred with author-

ity, his eyes focused in concentration as he stepped over to stir the peanuts that he was caramelising in a pan to one side. Remarkably, while the market has changed beyond all recognition around him, Fred has simply continued roasting chestnuts.

'I was fourteen and a half when I started. My dad sold chestnuts and I used to go and help him up the West End – Greek Street and then down in Leicester Square – until I got a licence here about fifty years ago. I used to have a casual licence. It was so busy then, you couldn't get a pitch unless someone else didn't turn up. I was on this corner at fifteen before I got married – my wife is English and now I've been married fifty years.

'The selling business is in the blood. My dad's family were all chestnut sellers in Malta and my grandfather came from Sicily. King George gave the Maltese people a medal for bravery in the war. We fought the Turks. Everybody wanted a piece of Malta.

'My father came over here in the 40s from Malta. I was born there and came to London in 1957, helping my dad. He came here to try a different life. Plumber's Row in Whitechapel, that's where we lived at first. It was all prostitutes in those houses in

them days. I asked my dad who these ladies were. He said, "They're all film stars." Then we moved down to live in Christian Street. It was all Maltese down there. The East End was a nice place to be. We used to buy our chestnuts in the Spitalfields Market, but nowadays I have to go further afield.

'I've always loved selling chestnuts. I've been like this since I was a kid. I've never been to school – I just wanted to do this. This is about making your customers feel good. With this game, you've got to know how to go with people, otherwise don't come in the market. My dad designed the can. After two or three years, you have to make a new one. It only takes me half an hour to get the coals hot, with some bits of wood and a spot of paraffin. I work from October until March or April, only three to four months, and as soon as I have finished my year's stock of chestnuts, it's over. I'll ease up now, and I won't come up if the weather's bad one Sunday.

'I'm going to Malta next week to visit my mum and dad. He went back thirty years ago. If it wasn't for my grandchildren and my kids, I'd move back to Malta too. But I reckon I'll be here a few more years.

'They should give me a medal for service to the English people.'

As Fred spoke, a stream of eager customers carried off bags of chestnuts. Many were regulars on first-name terms and others were tourists who Fred seduced with repartee, inveigling his way into their holiday snaps. As well as chestnuts, Fred sells monkey nuts and freshly caramelised and roasted peanuts, while his son-in-law Lee fries hamburgers and hot dogs on the other side of the pitch, and Fred's little grandson runs around excitedly in a flat cap drumming up business. Quite a drama for a street corner.

I asked Fred if he likes chestnuts and he smiled. 'I eat them all the time. If I start I can't stop,' he admitted, picking up a stray chestnut and putting it in his mouth absentmindedly. 'They're good for your cholesterol – any doctor will tell you,' he added, chewing and nodding his head in emphatic confirmation.

It is a delicious thing to buy a bag of hot chestnuts on a cold day and peel them in the street – a timeless seasonal ritual. So, as much as I long for the spring to come, I shall miss Fred on the corner of Bell Lane when he disappears. But I shall be waiting for his return in October, with his buoyant humour, bringing a whiff of the new season's chestnuts from Italy roasted on hot coals, as a time-honoured harbinger of the changing year in the East End – the legendary chestnut seller of Petticoat Lane.

SOME FAVOURITE PIE AND MASH SHOPS

Culinary Life

I HAVE GROWN SO SKINNY these past months at the end of winter – chasing stories around Spitalfields – that I decided to undertake a tour of my favourite pie and mash shops in order to explore all the delights on offer and put some meat on my bones.

Pie and mash shops have a special place in my affections because they originated in east London and are inextricably bound up

with the cultural and historical identity of this place – destinations where people enjoy pilgrimages to seek sustenance for body and soul, paying homage to the spirit of the old East End incarnated in these tiled, steamy temples dedicated to the worship of hot pies. Let me admit, it is a creed I can subscribe to wholeheartedly.

Taking my cue from that golden orb in the sky, I decided to commence in the east and work my way west across the territory, beginning with G. Kelly, established since 1937 at 526 Roman Road. Here I had the privilege to be welcomed by the lovely Sue Venning – resplendent in her white uniform – the proprietor who greets everyone with a brisk yet cheery, 'Yes, love?' – commonly reciprocated by, 'Hello, gorgeous.' It was a delight to walk into this sympathetic, clean and bright interior, adorned with daffodils and lined with marble and tiles, gleaming under the globe lamps.

'My Aunt Theresa on my father's side married George Kelly, who opened this in 1937,' explained Sue, introducing the intricate web of relations that connects this establishment to the two other pie and mash shops by the name of Kelly, all independently run today by increasingly distant relatives as the generations pass by. 'Samuel Robert Kelly opened up originally in Bethnal Green in 1915. He had three sons – Samuel, who took over in Bethnal Green, Joe, who opened in Bonner Street, and George, who came here to the Roman Road. My father, Bill (George Kelly's brother-in-law), ran this with my mother, Bea, until he died in 1969, and then I took over from her in 1990.' She outlined all this with a relaxed smile and a practised efficiency that left me reeling.

Arriving with the first customers of the day, I was fascinated to discover that my fellow diners were from Suffolk and Kent, and had gone out of their way to be there. This couple from East Anglia were up to visit their nan who lived nearby, and Sue confirmed that many of her customers were those who had once moved out of the East End, for whom a trip to her pie and mash shop was an opportunity to revisit a taste of home. Yet Sue retains a solid constituency in the Roman Road. 'People know each other here,' she confirmed fondly. 'You know their orders when they come in. They don't need to ask.'

I hit the rush at G. Kelly, 414 Bethnal Green Road (an independent business connected only genealogically to G. Kelly, Roman Road), where Matt Kelly, proprietor for the last fifteen years, baker and third-generation pie man, had his work cut out in the kitchen to meet the lunchtime demand for pie and mash and liquor, £2.65. Diners here eat off elegant cast-iron tables beneath framed portraits of local boxing heroes of yesteryear and everyone is at home in one of this neighbourhood's cosiest destinations.

At the head of the lunch queue was Mrs Julia Richards. 'I'm going to be ninety-eight,' she bragged with a winsome grin, the picture of exuberance and vitality as she carried off her plate of pie and mash hungrily to her favourite corner table, pursued by her sprightly seventy-year-old daughter Patricia – both living exemplars of the sus-

taining qualities of traditional East End meat pies. 'I've been coming here over fifty years,' revealed Patricia proudly. 'I've been coming here since before it opened!' teased Julia, her eyes shining with excitement as she cut into her steaming meat pie. 'They used to have live eels outside in a bucket,' she continued, 'and you could pick which one you wanted to eat.' I left them absorbed in their pies, the very epitome of human contentment, beneath a hand-lettered advertising placard proclaiming 'Kelly for Jelly'.

Up at F. Cooke in Broadway Market, once I had emptied my plate of some outstandingly delicious pies, I enjoyed a quiet after-lunch cup of tea with the genial Robert Cooke – 'Cooke by name, cook by nature' – whose great-grandfather Robert Cooke opened a pie and mash shop at the corner of Brick Lane and Sclater Street in 1862. 'My father taught me how to make pies and his father taught him. We haven't changed the ingredients and they are made fresh every day,' explained Robert plainly, a fourth-generation pie maker sitting proudly in his immaculately preserved café, which offers the rare chance to savour the food of more than a century ago.

'My grandfather, Robert, opened this shop in 1900, then he left to open another in the Kingsland Road, Dalston, in 1910 and Aunty May ran this one until 1940, when they shut it after a doodlebug hit the canal bridge,' he recounted. 'My mother, Mary, came over from Ireland in 1934 and worked with my grandfather in Dalston, alongside my father, Robert, and Uncle Fred. And after they got married in 1947, my grandfather said to my parents, "Here's the keys. Open it up," and they returned here to Broadway Market, where I was born in 1948.'

It was a tale as satisfying in its completeness as eating a pie, emphasising how this particular cuisine and these glorious shops are interwoven with the family histories of those who have run them and eaten at them for generations. Yet beyond the rich poetry of its cultural origin, this is good-value wholesome food for everyone, freshly cooked without additives, and meat pies, vegetable pies, fruit pies and jellied eels comprise a menu to suit all tastes. Reluctantly, after three pie and mash shops in one day, I was finished – but even as I succumbed to the somnolence induced by my intake of pies, I took consolation in dreamy thoughts of all those pleasures that await me in the other pie and mash shops of the East End I have yet to visit.

COLUMBIA ROAD MARKET I

Plant Life, Market Life

I WOKE in the night several times to the sound of rain falling and, sure enough, I found myself walking up the road to the market in the wet early the next morning. The market was the emptiest I had ever seen it, with just the stallholders huddling under their canopies, clutching cups of hot tea after a long night loading their vans, travelling and setting up in the pouring rain. I was admiring all the additional herbs on sale, when I saw the herb women shivering and congratulated them on their courage in making it here. 'We've got no choice – this is our living,' they replied brightly. 'Let's hope we get some brave customers today!'

This is the season when stalling out becomes a gamble against the weather for the traders. They are prepared to stand for hours outdoors in the cold in the hope that the rain will not drive away custom and send them home empty-handed after all their work. Yet there are always a few empty pitches in the market at this time, when some cannot countenance the risk of a wasted day at the expense of so much effort.

Certainly, the prices were as ridiculous as the weather, with cut flowers at four bunches for a fiver. Anyone who braved the rain that day could have bought armfuls of flowers for just a few pounds. I came home with four pots of tiny lustrous winter aconites (*Eranthis hyemalis*) and replanted them in a bowl to place on my old dresser while I await the spring flowers in my garden.

HOLMES & WATSON
SPITALFIELDS PIGLETS

Animal Life

I HOPE you will forgive me if I admit that I chose to keep a discreet silence over the peaceful death of Itchy, the old sow at the Spitalfields City Farm, and instead share my delight in beginning this new year by introducing these two beloved young squealers, Holmes & Watson.

When I went along to pay a visit on Holmes & Watson in the sty that serves as their approximation to 221B Baker Street, I did not know which was which. But it soon became apparent that the smaller, darker one possessed the keener eye and more remarkable faculties in general,

and that one was Holmes. Helen Galland, the pink-haired farm manager who plays the role of Mrs Hudson, providing food and housekeeping for these two bachelors, said she spotted the disparity when they first arrived at their new lodgings three months earlier. 'They like play-fighting, pushing each other out of the way to discover who is dominant – and seemingly it is the smaller one!' she told me with a grin of astonishment.

'When I tried training them by whistling and giving rewards if they came, Watson didn't understand the game at all but Holmes deduced it at once – "If I do this I get food!"' explained Helen with custodial affection. 'They have a love-hate relationship over food. When I scatter the vegetables in the pen and they run around finding them, the smaller one always gets more than the bigger one, which is strange. Maybe he's hiding them somewhere?'

Holmes & Watson are officially registered Kuni Kuni pigs, like Itchy before them, hailing from New Zealand and descended from just sixteen hardy survivors when the breed came close to extinction in the 1960s. Born at a rare-breeds farm near Ipswich, they were weaned early when their mother died of a spinal abscess. But in spite of this early tragedy, both piglets have embraced life wholeheartedly, as Helen proudly explained to me. 'They love people, because they know people bring them food, and if you tickle their bellies they lie down – it's an instinctive response.'

Little else is known of their early months,

yet on the basis of these ominous words overheard from Holmes while they were at the trough, we can only assume they are relieved to find themselves in Spitalfields, 'It is my belief, Watson, founded upon my experience, that the lowest and vilest alleys in London do not present a more dreadful record of sin than does the smiling and beautiful countryside.' Subsequently, I was surprised to hear Watson confess, 'I naturally gravitated to London, that great cesspool into which all the loungers and idlers of the Empire are irresistibly drained. There I stayed for some time at a private hotel in the Strand, leading a comfortless, meaningless existence, and spending such money as I had, considerably more freely than I ought.' Let us be thankful that Holmes & Watson have found a satisfactory home now at the City Farm.

I certainly enjoyed my brief opportunity to share the serenity of their existence while visiting the piglets in their pen, although I did become frustrated that they barely took their snouts out of the mud, until Helen helpfully explained that this is called 'the investigative instinct'. When she conjured this phrase, I could not help recalling the unfortunate break-in and abduction of a ferret at the farm a year earlier and I wondered if this event might have proved a factor in the decision to bring in Holmes & Watson. Yet at just six months old, it seemed premature to enquire about the crime-busting potential of these piglets. May it suffice to know that Holmes & Watson have ended up in clover.

STEVE BROOKER

MUDLARK

Human Life

IN LONDON, the Thames has always been the natural receptacle for concealing and disposing of things, creating a miry hoard of secrets, all just waiting for Steve Brooker, the mudlark, to come along and snaffle them up. Over the last seventeen years while he has been searching, the mud has been eroded by wash from the Thames clippers, exposing unprecedented numbers of finds that compel Steve to come mudlarking several times each week at low tide and be the first to see what has been newly revealed.

Steve is widely known as the Mud God – which seemed a little far-fetched to me until I saw him striding towards me eagerly in his chest-high bespattered waders, clutching his yellow plastic bucket and trowel. Over six feet tall with a grizzled beard and intense, glittering eyes, he was as excited to get down on to the beach as a child on the first day of the summer holiday. Only someone with Steve's natural authority can carry off such unmediated enthusiasm naturally. He is a man who is confident of his place in the world, and that place is the foreshore of the Thames.

We came down the slipway as the tide fell towards its lowest ebb. The day was mild yet occluded, and my heart lifted as I was released from city streets into a vast open space, the domain of water and sky. The territory of the Mud God. He understands the idiosyncrasies of the tide, and the nuances of the mudbanks and the riverbed. As well as coins and buttons, he finds Roman shoes, medieval pins, eighteenth-century witches' bottles, nineteenth-century lovers' tokens, twentieth-century voodoo dolls, live bombs and new guns – and sometimes he finds human bodies too. He knows where to look and he does not need a metal detector because he has sharp eyes.

When Dame Helen Mirren lost her ring throwing her grass clippings over the river wall from her Wapping garden, it was Steve who found it for her in the river. When villains throw handguns and sawn-off shotguns into the river at Woolwich to lose them for ever, it is Steve who collects them and hands them to the police – he found fifteen recently.

Mudlarks tend to work in pairs for safety's sake on this hazardous river. I had the privilege to be Steve's partner in slime for a day and I was happy to be in his company, because Steve is a member of the Society of Thames Mudlarks, has a licence from the Port of London Authority and has the

necessary experience to judge the treacherous movement of the tide against the access points to the shore.

On the beach, Steve used his trowel to indicate where the mud had been washed away, revealing a fresh bed of stones beneath, suggesting the type of location worthy of searching. Scraping away the top layer, he scanned for objects and passed me a medieval pin – a sign that other personal or domestic artefacts might be present. Thus the pattern was established of walking,

scanning and pausing to scrape at promising sites. We continued until Silvertown, where thousands of bullets mysteriously litter the foreshore, an unexplained military dump from the Second World War. All around the Isle of Dogs, we walked upon a shore littered with the metalwork of the shipbuilding industry that was once here. Eighteenth-century iron splitters once used for breaking up tree trunks into planks, to build ships sunk long ago, now lay redundant.

At low tide, we reached Mast Point, where Steve finds whole clay pipes – pipes that once fell from a stevedore's hand and sank into the mud without breaking. Here I saw impacted layers of eighteenth- and nineteenth-century riverbed, now exposed by erosion, with tantalising fragments of white pipe protruding. We squatted down to peer at the tiny bowl of a pipe, washed from the mud by the waves that very day and exposed for the first time. In the shape of a lady with a wide skirt, which formed the bowl of the pipe, it was a tiny sculpture with a presence all of its own, and we were the first to touch it since whoever dropped it 200 years ago. Steve's eyes popped because he'd never seen one like it before. Moments like this are what keep bringing Steve back, because he knows he will always find something, but he never knows what it will be.

We walked miles along the water's edge in the centre of London and the only others we met were two friends of Steve's, also searching the shore. I forgot entirely about

the city on the river bank above us, because I was down in the riverbed in the land of the mudlarks. All of the history of London was present with us – you just had to look. It was a magical place to be.

BRICK LANE MARKET I

WIRY, AGILE and full of vitality, Dennis Major has been dealing in toiletries, cut-price chocolate and general hardware in the market for more than thirty-five years. 'When I first started, I was down the other end of Cheshire Street,' he explained to me. 'They used to sell dogs and cats then, and sometimes I took sickly kittens home that were abandoned in the gutter, but they always died. There was a stall that sold chickens – they would wring their necks and pluck them for you before your eyes. We were next to the bird man, who would go crazy because everybody would be all over the birdcages, and the birds made such a racket. We did have some laughs.'

Even though he is retired now, Dennis cannot break the habit of Sunday in Brick Lane, because the same customers keep coming back to greet him after all these years. While we were talking, a senior market gardener from Cambridgeshire with hardy features and straggly white hair, who has been travelling down on the bus each Sunday for more than fifteen years in search of 'something fresh to see', popped by to have his weekly chat with Dennis. 'There's no end of villages where I come from,' he informed me, hinting at the workaday nature of his rural life.

When the market gardener departed, in a brief lull, Dennis pointed across Cheshire Street and confided to me quietly, 'One Sunday, I came down when Ginger Marks was killed outside the Carpenter's Arms. There was a bullet hole in the wall and they'd roped it off where he'd been shot, but they never found the body. If you lost a bike in south London you could always find it here next Sunday. This was a good market. People off the boats in the docks would come here and you could sell them all sorts of things. There was a fellow who sold train sets. Most of them have died. There's not so many like me down here any more.'

'I'VE BEEN coming here since I first visited with my father to buy canaries for our shop in Woking. That was sixty-two years ago,' revealed Arthur Benham with the relaxed, genial air of one entirely at home in the market, for whom doing deals and taking money off a string of customers is second nature. 'I've always been at this end of the street, since I started as a very young lad fly-pitching with a pram full of bits and pieces,' he recalled enthusiastically. 'And I have been on this spot as a licensed trader for at least twenty-five years. I took over from Frank Fisher, who'd been here many moons before me. He was a Smithfield meat porter. This little area was packed then. It was a job to get a pitch – they used to fight over them. Ever since I could drive, it's been a weekly ritual coming into London on Sunday.'

Such is Arthur's trustworthy reputation that local people will confidently buy used electrical gadgets from him. 'I always offer a refund on anything electrical,' he assured me as an African lady delightedly carried off a food processor in her bag for twenty pounds. 'I remember what I buy and sell and I know the price of everything. Sometimes I keep things in the interests of future prosperity, and I've got a nice rug as a future heirloom. Once I bought a lion with its foot on the globe for fourteen shillings, then sold it for fifty shillings to a lady named Sylvia. It turned out to be early-eighteenth-century Capodimonte and went for 2,000 pounds at auction – but when she died ten years ago, she left me a thousand pounds in her will.'

Arthur buys at house clearances and jumble sales, hoping to shift a quarter of the stock that he keeps in his van and top it up again each week. 'My father bred canaries and showed them at Crystal Palace. He used to buy the birds up here in the market because he had the experience to know what he was buying. I remember the first thing I ever sold, a BSA Bantam motorbike in Club Row when I was seventeen, and I still can't keep away today,' Arthur confessed to me with an amiable, modest grin, hooked by the endless cycle of market life – appreciating this as a place of commerce and equally as an important location of social life and collective memory.

MARIA PELLICCI

COOK

Culinary Life, Human Life

THE WEATHER was unremitting and my shoes were leaking, so I went round to E. Pellicci, the Italian café at 332 Bethnal Green Road, where Maria Pellicci, the head cook, proprietor and beloved matriarch, cooked me a generous dish of steaming hot spaghetti with freshly made bolognese sauce, which Salvatore, Maria's nephew, topped off with some Parmesan and ground black pepper. As I wolfed it down, I could feel my spirits reviving. Overcome with the intense culinary experience afforded by the tangy tomato sauce and the sweet spaghetti that was of perfect consistency, I was barely aware of the enthusiastic lunch crowd arriving and filling every seat in this historic, perfectly proportioned café, lined with exquisite Italian marquetry by Achille Capocci in 1946.

As the multiple conversations around me accumulated symphonically, it was like sitting in the centre of an orchestra and hearing all the different instruments playing at once. Yet I felt quite comfortable enjoying my solitary meal peacefully in the midst of this gregarious friendly crowd of locals and regulars, some of whom – Nevio, Maria's son, told me – have been coming for lunch for more than four generations now, ever

since Pellicci's opened in 1900. Justifiably, this café is a legend in its own lunchtime – a lunch service that has now extended over 110 years. There is room for thirty customers and there are five waiting staff, which means that everyone gets attention paid to them, and Anna (Maria's daughter), Nevio, Salvatore and their colleagues have time to enjoy relaxed conversations with their guests, while keeping the service running efficiently with deceptive ease.

Peering out through the graceful ballet of customers coming and going, and drinks and meals being served, all accomplished through the ingenious collective manoeuvres that have evolved in this confined space over a century of use, I could just make out the sleet falling in the blue light outside and took comfort in being inside among this happy community of diners. There is a constant debate about whether the East End spirit still exists, but all that is required is a visit to Pellicci's to experience the egalitarian human spirit for yourself.

In that moment when you have finished eating, peek back through the hatch at the rear of the café and you will see Maria busy in the kitchen, where she has worked six days a week since 1961, from six in the morning until seven at night (from four in the morning originally), ever since she first came to Bethnal Green, leaving the small Tuscan village of Casciana that was her birthplace. Taking a glance through from the café into the kitchen, you will not be ignored, you will not be met with indifference, Maria will raise her Sophia Loren brows to meet your gaze with her glittering eyes and the gentle smile that you recognise from all those Tuscan paintings of the early Renaissance.

Consequently, it was with some humility that I accepted the honour of Maria's invitation to visit her there in her kitchen, whence she presides over her entire domain. 'Mamma Maria' the children call her, when their parents bring them to the café where they also came to eat as children once upon a time. If these children can show themselves well behaved throughout their meal, as a reward they are sometimes permitted to visit Mamma Maria in the kitchen, where she might dispense a sweet treat if they are especially good.

With her strong features, deep chestnut eyes and exuberant nature, Mamma Maria immediately had me under her spell. She showed me her hands, with which she has been cooking her whole life, beautiful working hands, nimble and strong and graceful. She wears the gold ring that her husband, Nevio Senior, gave her. It was Nevio Senior's father, Priamo Pellicci, who began here in 1900, but he died young and left his wife, Elide, to run the business and bring up seven children, which she did with great success. Elide Pellicci was the E. Pellicci

whose name is still upon the Grade II listed façade today. Her son Nevio, who was born above the café in 1927, took over from her until his death in 2008, leaving Maria as the head of the family business, supported in the café by Nevio Junior, Anna and Salvatore.

Maria Pellicci cooks every dish on the menu herself, all the meat pies, speciality pasta dishes and traditional desserts, prepared from scratch using fresh ingredients each day. She even cuts every chip personally by hand, a feat that recently won her an award for the best in London. She is keen to emphasise that she takes exceptional pride in her cooking and is always eager to respond to the requests of her customers. Scrupulous, Maria orders her meat from the nearby butcher, making regular small orders so that food never hangs around, and she has a rigorous cleaning regime too, so everything is left spotless at the end of each day.

'There is no secret here,' declared Maria, gesturing playfully around her immaculate kitchen, once she had outlined the nature of her work. The fact is the Pelliccis love their café and their loyal customers reciprocate the affection, inspiring a passionate human tradition that thrives today as it has done over so many years. It is a rare haven of kindness, appreciated as it deserves.

I kissed Maria's hand as I left the kitchen and I was just shaking hands with Nevio before I stepped outside when Maria appeared unexpectedly through the stained-glass door that leads to the kitchen and flashed her huge eyes, holding up a tinfoil parcel for me. It was my sweet treat.

As I walked along the Bethnal Green Road and crossed Weavers' Fields in the dark, on my way back to Spitalfields in the gathering blizzard, I could not resist opening the parcel, discovering two slices of bread pudding in there. Let me confess, I ate them both before I got home. My shoes were still leaking but I was warm inside, thanks to Mamma Maria.

AT GOD'S CONVENIENCE

Past Life, Spiritual Life

Slovenliness is no part of Religion. Cleanliness is indeed close to Godliness.
John Wesley, 1791

OFTENTIMES, ON MY WAY between Spitalfields and Covent Garden, I walk through Bunhill Fields, where – in passing – I pay my respects to William Blake, Daniel Defoe and John Bunyan, who are buried there. Sometimes I also stop off at John Wesley's Chapel in the City Road to visit the underground shrine of Thomas Crapper, champion of the flushing toilet and inventor of the ballcock.

It seems wholly appropriate that here, at the mother church of the Methodist movement, is preserved one of London's finest historic toilets, still in perfect working order. Although it was installed in 1899, over a century after John Wesley's death, I like to think that if he returned today Wesley would be proud to see such immaculate facilities provided for worshippers at his chapel – thereby catering to their mortal as well as their spiritual needs. The irony is that even those, such as myself, who come here primarily to fulfil a physical function

cannot fail to be touched by the stillness of this peaceful refuge from the clamour of the City Road.

A sepulchral light glimmers as you descend beneath the chapel to enter the gleaming sanctum, where, on the right-hand side of the aisle, eight cedar cubicles present themselves, facing eight urinals to the left, with eight marble washbasins behind a screen at the far end. This harmonious arrangement reminds us of the Christian symbolism of the number eight as the number of redemption – represented by baptism – which is why baptismal fonts are octagonal.

Never have I seen a more beautifully kept toilet than this. Every wooden surface has been waxed, the marble and mosaics shine, and each cubicle has a generous supply of rolls of soft white paper. It is both a flawless illustration of the rigours of the Methodist temperament and an image of what a toilet might be like in heaven. The devout atmosphere of George Dance's chapel, built for John Wesley in 1778 and improved in 1891 for the centenary of Wesley's death (when the original pillars made of ships' masts were replaced with marble from each country in the world where Methodists preached the gospel) encourages solemn thoughts, even down here in the toilet. And the extravagant display of exotic marble, some of it bearing an uncanny resemblance to dog meat, complements the marble pillars in the chapel above.

Sitting in a cubicle, you may contemplate your mortality and, when the moment comes, a text on the ceramic pull invites you to 'Pull & Let Go'. It is a parable in itself – you put your trust in the Lord and your sins are flushed away in a tumultuous rush of water that recalls Moses parting the Red Sea. Then you may wash your hands in the marble basin and ascend to the chapel to join the congregation of the worthy.

Yet before you leave and enter Methodist paradise, a moment of silent remembrance for the genius of Thomas Crapper is appropriate. Contrary to schoolboy myth, he did not give his name to the colloquial term for a bowel movement, which, as any etymologist will tell you, is at least of Anglo-Saxon origin. Should you lift the toilet seat, you will discover 'The Venerable' revealed upon the rim, as the particular model of the chinaware, and it is an epithet that we may also apply to Thomas Crapper (1836–1910). Although of humble origins, Crapper, the son of a sailor, rose to greatness as the evangelist of the flushing toilet, earning the first royal warrant for sanitary ware from the Prince of Wales in the 1880s and creating a business empire that lasted until 1963.

Should your attention be entirely absorbed by this matchless parade of eight Crapper's Valveless Waste Preventers, do not neglect to admire the sparkling procession of urinals opposite by George Jennings (1810–82) – celebrated as the inventor of the public toilet. Some 827,280 visitors each paid a penny for the novelty of using his

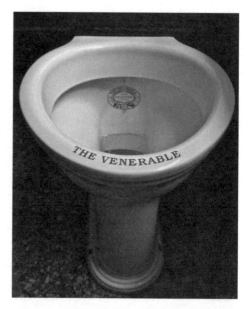

Monkey Closets in the retiring rooms at the Great Exhibition of 1851, giving rise to the popular euphemism 'spend a penny', still in use today in overly polite circles.

Once composure and physical comfort are restored, you may wish to visit the chapel to say a prayer of thanks or, as I like to do, visit John Wesley's house, seeking inspiration in the life of the great preacher. Wesley preached a doctrine of love to those who might not enter a church, and campaigned for prison reform and the abolition of slavery, giving more than 40,000 sermons in his lifetime, often several a day and many in the open air – travelling between them on horseback. In his modest house, where he once ate at the same table as his servants, you can see the tiny travelling lamp that he carried with him to avoid falling off his horse (as he did frequently), his nightcap, his shoes, his spectacles, his robe – believed to have been made out of a pair of old curtains – the teapot that Josiah Wedgwood designed for him, and the exercising chair that replicated the motion of horse-riding, enabling Wesley to keep his thigh muscles taut when not on the road.

A visit to the memorial garden at the rear of the chapel to examine Wesley's tomb will reveal that familiar term from the toilet bowl, 'The Venerable', graven in stone in 1791 to describe John Wesley himself, which prompts the question whether this was where Thomas Crapper got the idea for the name of his contraption, honouring John Wesley in sanitary ware.

Let us thank the Lord if we are ever caught short on the City Road, because, due to the good works of the venerable Thomas Crapper and the venerable John Wesley, relief and consolation for both body and soul are readily to hand at God's convenience.

John Wesley excused himself unexpectedly from the table ...

KING SOUR DA MC

RAPPER OF BETHNAL GREEN

Human Life, Literary Life, Street Life

'I'M MORE OF A RAPPER THAN A POET, though it's because of poetry that I became a rapper. Since I was nine – after listening to hip hop – I wanted to rap, but before that I used to be writing poetry. It made me happy, putting words together, even just a couple of lines. I wouldn't call it a talent, I would call it "practice makes perfect". Ever since I understood what life was about, when I was about seven, I have always wanted to help people out. You could say I'm a helper, a healer. I want to see people get treated equally in this world. Music is the remedy of hatred. People usually respond well to music and poetry, and my lyrics are short and to the point.'

These are the words of Yasin Ahmed, aka King Sour DA MC, spoken as we sat together one afternoon, sheltering from the rain beneath the canopy of the bandstand in Arnold Circus, at the heart of the tightly woven web of streets that he knows intimately. Blessed with an astonishing gift of eloquence, at just sixteen years old Yasin has already established a reputation in the neighbourhood through his performances here in the bandstand and an appearance at the O2 Arena, as a finalist in a competition out of 21,000 under-sixteens. Yet in spite of demonstrating the strength of character needed to stand up and perform in public – sometimes extempore – Yasin possesses a self-effacing personality, speaking thoughtfully under his breath and pausing frequently for thought. A contemplative character who does not make eye contact when he is thinking, he lights up when speaking passionately of poetry and rap.

'At first, my school didn't realise I was taking it that seriously,' he explained, talking about his evolution as a writer, 'but I have Miracle MC, Naga MC and Chinx MC. They're only a year older than me but they've helped me develop lyrically, and Chinx he helped me to stand up again, every time I had the grief.' Yasin is referring here to lapses of courage when inventing poetry spontaneously for a live audience, a testing and definitive requirement of his chosen medium. With quiet determination, Yasin is pushing the boundary of his own ease in order to become stronger. 'It helps me to think out of the box, to learn to be calm and control my anger,' he informed me in a perfectly relaxed tone that demonstrated the self-evident truth of his statement.

Yasin is vividly aware of the social politics of the world he has grown up in – east London and beyond – a situation defined by the conflicts and controversies in the wake of 9/11. 'Religion is important to me because religion gets stereotyped, when it is important to me to respect all religions,' declared Yasin, thinking out loud as we both sat gazing at the falling rain. 'People need to be open-minded and live together, because our life in this world is short.' And Yasin was not talking in abstractions, because he was eyewitness to the violence provoked by the presence of the racist

English Defence League outside the East London Mosque in Whitechapel.

Yasin prefers to speak of literature, especially of the works of John Steinbeck and William Shakespeare that he is studying, though it brings him back again to the same subjects. Reading Steinbeck's account of characters struggling at the time of the Great Depression has an obvious resonance for Yasin, while the works of Shakespeare reflect back on the tensions that he experiences daily in Bethnal Green. 'I have lived in these streets and I know the codes, so I do feel comfortable to a certain extent, because I have friends that look out for me,' said Yasin, apprising me of the situation. 'It's not as bad as *Romeo and Juliet*, but it could be.' Yasin told me he plans to go to performing arts college, and in ten years' time he sees himself living in Canada or Portugal – because he wants to experience other cultures.

My conversation with Yasin led me to appreciate the epic scale of the world he inhabits, even when he is walking through the small streets of Bethnal Green. Yasin looks over his shoulder and carries his unknowable ancestry that connects him to Bangladesh and beyond back to Kenya. Yasin looks around and he sees the crisis of the current moment in global politics, and chooses to address it personally through embracing the aesthetic challenges of rhetoric and verse. Yasin looks forward and he has hopes for the future. Yasin has got presence of mind. Yasin finds joy in words. Yasin wants to talk about human dignity and he has a story to tell.

Meeting Yasin gave me hope too because, resisting alienation, he has fought to retain an open mind and an optimistic temperament, channelling his thoughts and abilities into finding a creative voice, and discovering a sense of moral clarity in the process. It confirms my faith that young people will always recognise the emotional truth of a situation intuitively, open-heartedly seeking freedom for everyone, when their seniors can too readily be clouded by prejudice.

AT THREE COLTS LANE

Street Life

SITUATED MIDWAY between Spitalfields and Bethnal Green lies Three Colts Lane. Although many years have passed since there were colts here, today there are many other attractions to make this a compelling destination, especially if you are having problems with your car – because Three Colts Lane is where all the motor repair garages are to be found, gathered together in dozens and snuggled up close in ramshackle order. Who can say how many repair shops there are in Three Colts Lane, since they inhabit the railway arches in the manner of interconnected troglodyte dwellings carved into a mountain, meaning no one can ever tell where one garage begins and another ends.

Three Colts Lane is where the lines from the east and the north converge as they approach Liverpool Street Station, providing a deep warren of vaulted spaces, extended by shambolic tin shacks and bordered with scruffy yards fenced off with corrugated iron. Here in this forgotten niche, while more fences and signs are added, few have ever been removed, creating a dense visual patchwork to fascinate the eye. Yet even before I arrived in Three Colts Lane, the commingled scents of engine oil and spray paint were drawing me closer with their

intoxicating fragrance, because, although I have no car, I love to come here to explore this distinct corner of the East End that is a world of its own.

Each body shop presents a cavernous entrance, from which the sounds of banging

and clanging and shouting emanate, every one attended by the employees, distinguished by their boiler suits and oily hands, happily enjoying cigarettes in the sun. Yet standing in the daylight and peering into the gloom, it is impossible to discern the relative size and shape of these garages, which all appear to recede infinitely into the darkness beneath the railway arches.

A cheerful spirit of anarchy presides in Three Colts Lane, revealed by the senior mechanic, with his upper body under a taxicab, who, when I asked gingerly if I might enter the extravagantly vaulted narrow old repair shop deep beneath the arches, declared, 'It's not my garage. Do as you please! Make yourself at home!' To outsiders, these dark grimy spaces might appear alien, but to those who work here it is a zone where everyone knows everyone else, and where you can spend your working life in a society with its own codes, hierarchy and respect, only encountering the outside world through the motorists and cabbies who arrive needing repairs. My father was a mechanic and I recognise the liberation of filth, how being dirty in your work sets you apart from others' expectations. The layers of grime and dirt here – in an environment comprised almost exclusively of small businesses where no one wears a white collar – speak of a place that is a law unto itself.

Starting at the eastern end of Three Colts Lane, the first person I met was Lofty, proprietor of the A1 Car Centre, who proved to be a gracious ambassador for the territory.

'Some garages, they just want to take the money,' Lofty declared in wonder, his chestnut-brown eyes glinting with righteous ire at the injustice – like a sheriff denouncing outlaws – before he pledged his own personal doctrine of decency. 'But I believe it's how you treat the customers that's the most important thing. That's why we are still here after twenty-five years.' And proof that Lofty is as good as his word was evident recently when 700 customers signed a petition saving the garage from developers who threatened to build student housing on the site.

Under the railway bridge and down the road, I came upon Erdal and his nephew at Repairs R Us, where I marvelled at the monster engine from a Volvo truck that Erdal rebuilt and today keeps as a trophy by the entrance of his tiny arch. Further down, I met Ahmed, a native of Cyprus who grew up above the synagogue in Heneage Street and has run his garage here for twenty-eight years. At the corner, across from Bethnal Green Station, I was greeted by Ian and Trevor, two softly spoken brothers who have been here twenty years, repairing taxis in a former scrap yard that still retains its old weighbridge. We all squinted together at the drainpipe head dated 1870 with the initials of the Great Eastern Railway upon it, declaring the history of the site in Gothic capitals, before Ian extracted a promise from me to come back once I had discovered the origin of the name Three Colts Lane.

Apart from calendar girls adorning the walls, the only women I glimpsed were those who restricted themselves to answering the telephone – barely visible in tiny cabins of

domestic comfort, sheltering their femininity against the barbaric male chaos of the machine shops. But then, strolling down a back lane and passing one of the governors in a heated altercation with a quivering cabbie who had innocently scraped his Daimler, thereby providing the catalyst for an arresting display of bullish masculinity, I met Ilfet. With a triumphant mixture of self-assurance and sharp humour, she has won the respect of her male colleagues in the body shop, wielding a spanner as well as the next man. She is a bold pioneer in her field and a sterling example to others. I was proud to shake the hand of Ilfet, the only – or rather the first – female mechanic in Three Colts Lane.

PAUL GARDNER

PAPER-BAG SELLER

Human Life, Past Life

RECENTLY, I have taken to dropping in to the premises of my new friend Paul Gardner, the paper-bag seller at 149 Commercial Street, to observe the constant parade of long-standing customers that pass through, creating the life of this distinctive business. One morning, I called round at six thirty, opening time, to enjoy a quiet chat before the rush and Paul explained that his great-grandfather James Gardner began trading here in this same building as a scale maker when it was built in 1870 – which means Paul is a fourth-generation market sundriesman and makes Gardners' the longest-established family business in Spitalfields.

Paul still has his great-grandfather's accounts from the end of the nineteenth century, when as scale makers they serviced the scales for all the traders in the fruit and vegetable market on a regular basis. Turning the pages and scanning the lines of James's fine copperplate handwriting your eye alights upon the names, Isaac, Isaiah and Ezekiel, indicative of the Jewish population that once defined the identity of Spitalfields. There is an ancient block of wood with three scoops carved out that are smoothed with wear, it has been in use since the days of Paul's great-grandfather. Then his son Bertie (Paul's grandfather) used it, then Bertie's son Roy (Paul's father) used it and Paul still keeps his cash in it today. As the twentieth century wore on, each of the successive Mr Gardners found that customers began to expect to buy their produce in a paper bag (a trend which is now reversed) and so the trade of dealing in bags supplanted the supply of scales entirely over four generations.

Turn your back on the traffic rattling down Commercial Street and stand for a moment to contemplate the dignified Brunswick-green frontage of Gardners' Market Sundriesmen. An old glass sign reads PAPER & POLYTHENE BAG MERCHANT and, sure enough, a variety of different-coloured bags are festooned on strings like bunting. Below them are some scales, hinting at the origins of the business, and then your attention is distracted by a mysterious wooden sieve, a memento of Paul's grandfather. Enter the shop to be confronted by piles of bags of every variety in packets stacked up on either side and leaving barely any room to stand. Only two routes are possible: straight ahead, leading into the dark recesses where the stacks grow taller and closer together in the gloom, or turn right to the makeshift counter, improvised from an old counter-top supported upon yet more packets of bags. Beneath the fluorescent glow, the dust of ages is settling upon everything. You think you have entered a storeroom, but you are wrong, because you neglected to notice Paul sitting at the counter in a cosy corner, partly concealed by a stack of bags. You turn to greet him and a vista appears with a colourful display of bags and tags and tapes and those old greengrocer's signs that say 'Today's price 2/8' and 'Morning gathered' – which creates a pleasant backdrop to the figure of Paul Gardner as he stands to greet you with a genial, 'Hello!'

With his wavy grey locks, gentle face, sociable manner and innate decency, Paul could have stepped from another age and it is a joy to meet someone who has successfully resisted the relentless imperative towards haste and efficiency at any cost that tyrannises our age and threatens to enslave us all. When you enter the shop, you enter Paul's world and you discover it is a better place than the one outside.

Paul was thirteen when his father, Roy, died unexpectedly in 1968, creating a brief interregnum when his mother took over for four years until he came of age. 'I came here the first day after I left school at seventeen,' says Paul. 'It was what I wanted to do. After the first year, my mother stopped

Paul's grandfather Bertie Gardner, standing with Paul's father Roy Gardner as a child outside the shop around 1930

Roy, now a grown man, standing outside the shop after the Second World War, around 1947

coming, though my nan used to live above the shop then. I haven't had a day off since 1972. I don't make much money. I will never become a millionaire. To be honest, I try to sell things as cheap as I can while others try to sell them as expensive as they can. I do it because I have done it all my life. I do it because it is like a family heirloom.'

Paul Gardner's customers are the stall-holders and small businessmen and women of east London, many of whom have been coming for more than twenty years. Especially loyal are the Ghanaian and Nigerian people, who prefer to trade with a family business. Paul will sell small numbers of

bags while others only deal in bulk and he offers the same price per bag for ten as for 100. Even then, most of his customers expect to negotiate the price down, unable to resist their innate natures as traders. Paul explained to me that some have such small turnovers they can only afford to buy ten carrier bags at a time.

In his endeavours, Paul supports and nurtures an enormous network of tiny businesses that are a key part of the economy of our city. Many have grown and come back with bigger and bigger orders, selling their products to supermarkets, while others simply sustain themselves, like the Nigerian woman who has a stall in Brixton Market and has been coming regularly on the bus for twenty-three years to buy her paper bags here. 'I try to do favours for people,' says Paul, and, in spontaneous confirmation of this, a customer rings with the joyous news that they have finally scraped enough money together to pay their account for the last seven years. Sharing in the moment of triumph, Paul laughs down the phone, 'What happened, did you win the lottery or something?'

Paul has the greatest respect for his customers and they hold him in affection too. In fact, Paul's approach could serve as a model if we wish to move forward from the ugliness of the current business ethos. Paul only wants to make enough to live and builds mutually supportive relationships with his customers over the long term based upon trust. His is a more equitable version of capitalism tempered by mutual respect and a belief in the essential goodness rather than the essential greediness of people. As a fourth-generation trader, Paul has no business plan. He is guided by his beliefs about people and how he wants to live in the world. His integrity and self-respect are his most precious possessions. 'I have never advertised,' says Paul. 'All my customers come because they have been recommended by friends who are already my customers.'

However, after Gardners' survived two world wars and the closure of the market, there has recently been a new threat as the landlord seeks to increase the annual rent from 15,000 to 25,000 pounds. 'I earn 250 pounds a week,' reveals Paul with frank humility. 'If I earned 500 pounds a week, I could give an extra 250 towards the rent, but at 250 pounds a week, the cupboard is bare.'

Ruminating upon the problem, 'They've dollied up the place round here!' says Paul quietly, in an eloquently caustic verdict upon the situation in which his venerable family business finds itself, after 140 years, in a fashionable shopping district with a landlord seeking to maximize profits. We must support Paul by sending more business his way, because Paul is a Spitalfields legend we cannot lose. But more important than the history itself is the political philosophy that has evolved over four generations of experience. It is the sum of what has been learned. In all his many transactions, Paul unselfconsciously espouses a practical step-by-step approach towards a more sustainable society. Who would have expected that the oldest-established trader in Spitalfields might also turn out to be the model of an ethical business pointing the way to the future?

SHAKESPEARE IN SPITALFIELDS

Literary Life, Past Life

A NINETEENTH-CENTURY Staffordshire figure of Shakespeare stands on my chimney piece in Spitalfields to remind me of the writer I love best. On the right is Sarah Siddons as Lady Macbeth and on the left is her brother John Philip Kemble as Hamlet.

Coming across William Shakespeare's younger brother Edmund's tombstone in Southwark recently and learning that some of William's plays were first performed in our neighbourhood set me wondering about whether he was actually here in Spitalfields.

According to a memo by fellow actor Ned Alleyn, in 1596 Shakespeare lived 'near the Bear Garden in Southwark'. London Bridge was the only bridge across the Thames in those days, so Shakespeare must have walked up and down Bishopsgate (he knew it as Bishoppes gate streete) whenever he made his way between Southwark and Shoreditch, while his plays were being performed at the Theatre and the Curtain Theatre here on Curtain Road.

Maybe he got sick of trudging to and fro, commuting across the City, because in 1598 there is a William Shakespeare listed by the tax collector as resident in the parish of St Anne's, Bishopsgate, though we cannot be certain if this was our man. We know

he was lodging on Silver Street (at the south of the Barbican) in 1604, based on the words of a maid – 'one Mr Shakespeare laye in the house' – and a court deposition signed by Shakespeare when his landlord was challenged with not paying his daughter's dowry.

For years I lived in the Highlands of Scotland and I remember the Gaelic weavers' working songs, so it touched a chord with me when in the First Folio of Shakespeare's plays I came across Falstaff's line from *Henry IV Part One* in a scene at the Boar's Head, Eastcheap, in the City of London, 'I would I were a weaver. I could sing all manner of songs.' Wool was a primary industry in Shakespeare's day and in Spitalfields we have Tenter Ground, where once pieces of newly woven woollen cloth were staked out to dry. Surely the weavers sang at their work here just as those in the Hebrides still do today. Shakespeare could have heard them singing when he walked through Spitalfields.

I was further intrigued to discover that in the earlier Quarto edition of 1598 the line reads, 'I could sing psalms or anything.' Many of the wool weavers in Shakespeare's time were Calvinist exiles from Flanders who fled the Duke of Alva and were known

for their love of psalmody. Scholars believe the line was altered in the First Folio to avoid any politically sensitive anti-Protestant reading.

I rest my case with a line from Shakespeare's fellow playwright and drinking pal Ben Jonson, whose character Cutbeard in *The Silent Woman* has the line, 'He got his cold with sitting up late and singing catches with clothworkers.'

So there you have it, Shakespeare knew Spitalfields and it is no stretch of the imagination to envisage him and Jonson enjoying late-night singing sessions with the weavers here, just like the guys who come on all-night benders to the clubs in Brick Lane nowadays. And of course, Shakespeare portrayed a weaver in the character of Bottom in *A Midsummer Night's Dream*. Is it possible he met the prototype in Spitalfields?

COLUMBIA ROAD MARKET II

Human Life, Market Life

THERE WAS JUST ME and the lonely fox on the streets of Spitalfields before seven in the morning as I made my way up to Columbia Road to have a chat with Anthony James Burridge. He is the first member of this celebrated family I have spoken with, whose story is interwoven with that of the flower market here over several generations – the Columbia Road aristocracy. 'They might not all be called Burridge but there's quite a lot of us working here, brothers, cousins, sisters and uncles,' explained Anthony with a cheery grin that belied the chilly morning, while at the next stall his son, also Anthony James, who started three weeks ago selling winter bulbs, shivered in the cold.

Anthony started trading in Columbia Road twenty-eight years ago at the age of twenty-two. 'When I left school I was a marble fitter, but then I joined the family business,' he explained. 'My dad had a stall at the end and this pitch became available. My dad and all his brothers were in the business. It goes back to my nan, who died fifteen years ago – she was here up to sixty years ago.' Anthony first came to Columbia Road when he was five. 'My dad would get me up and bring me down here in the summer,' he told me, casting his eyes up and down the road affectionately. 'In the 60s and 70s, this market used to be seasonal and we only traded twenty-five to thirty weeks of the year. Then it was only English produce, but the variety of plants has been extended by bringing them from overseas.' He added with a shrug of droll bemusement,

ifers, camellias and topiary, though I spotted some interesting bedding plants, including a special favourite of mine, gentians. Over the years, he has learned what plants work best in the small gardens of the East End. When I asked Anthony how he dealt with the cold, he told me that he keeps the house plants in the van until it is time to sell them so they do not get spoilt by the frost, without realising that I was enquiring about his own welfare. 'You get used to it. You put on an extra coat and an extra couple of jumpers. You pull your hat down over your ears and get on with it!' he declared with sparkling eyes of anticipation, looking up to the beautiful clear sky of dawn breaking over us and in hope of a sunny spring day that will bring plenty of eager customers to the flower market.

'People no longer know the seasons for plants any more, now that everything's available all the time.'

Shrubs and small trees are Anthony's speciality, including evergreen shrubs, con-

THE ALTERATION TAILORS
OF THE EAST END

Human Life

THE ALTERATION TAILORS go unregarded for the most part – no one notices them. It is almost as if they have mastered the art of invisibility, for they can sit in the window of a dry cleaner's or a shoe repair business while the customers come and go to the counter without even casting a glance at them working placidly at a sewing machine in the most conspicuous position in the shop. From this privileged location facing on to the street, all of existence passes like a charade before the eyes of the alteration tailor, screened by the plate-glass window and the collective amnesia of the populace.

Yet there comes a moment when they occupy the focus of attention, when life cannot continue because your trousers split or you discover your hem is showing, and your need of an alteration tailor is burning. Then, like a superhero lurking in the margin of your consciousness, they step to the fore and you thank the heavens you can rely upon them in your hour of need. A brief conversation is all that is required and, with the mere exchange of a few pounds, your self-esteem is restored.

Such is my fascination with the paradoxical existence of the alteration tailors that I set out to make a study of these ethereal beings in the hope of bringing them further into visibility. Superficially, it might seem that these stitchers are inferior to the tailors who actually make clothes, yet it is my perception that the work of the alteration tailor is a subtler art, one of accommodation to flawed humanity, since the two arenas of endeavour for these tailors are those of repair and adjustment and, commonly, both are indicators of fallibility.

In Bethnal Green, at the Ironing Parlour, there is an eye-catching display of old irons in the window which Hussein, the proprietor, told me he inherited from the previous owner, symbolic tokens of gratitude offered on the altar of the modest alteration tailor. And it explained a certain self-respecting ease, even a mild swagger common to all the alteration tailors I met, acknowledging that they appreciate that what it costs to expend their skill is so much less than what it means to us. As Mohammed Abdul Mannan at Needlepoint in Barnet Grove put it succinctly, 'I think it is nice job. People like us because they need us.' Consequently, although it was a source of embarrassment for me when a fellow customer came in to get his wife's dress repaired and negotiated a price reduction from eight to five pounds, while also seeking assurances that it would be done well, the alteration tailor reacted with admirable restraint. 'I will do my best for you,' was his response, accepting the mean-spirited reduction with grace. 'You're always going to make a living, but you're never going to make a fortune in this trade,' was the ambivalent summation – accompanied by a weary smile – repeated by several of my subjects of enquiry.

Yet there is little intrinsic melancholy in the lives of the alteration tailors, because the line of the needy is always balanced by the line of the jubilant, collecting their repairs – while the tailors mediate the space between, working conscientiously at their own pace. When I was in the Ironing Parlour, a senior lady pushing a trolley came in hopefully on the off-chance to check if there was anything for her to collect, only to leave disheartened when they explained politely that she had brought nothing in for repair. After searching carefully, just to make sure, Shabaz and Chris, who work here, looked at each other in disappointment at sending her away empty-handed.

As Vaida, who does the repairs at Classi Clean in the Liverpool Street Arcade, confirmed with a shy smile, 'I like it. I've been doing it from when I was a child.' This week, she is busy letting out the waists for her City gents, as she usually does at winter's end, just as she will expect to take them in again next summer, when they lose weight for the beach. Vaida came here from Vilnius eight years ago, when she lost her job in a clothing factory after manufacturing transferred to China, and Mr Patel, who has run this store for twenty-five years, prizes her for her nimble work. 'We were struggling to find a competent seamstress. 'They don't teach it here. Young people in this country can't even sew on a button.' It did not seem appropriate to tell him of young Ali at Needlepoint in Barnet Grove, six months into the profession with dexterous fingers and an eager personable manner.

Back in Bethnal Green, a different Mr Patel, my old friend at Smarty Pants, did his best to live up to the name of his shop. 'This is what you call philosophical,' he declared, rolling his eyes ironically while seated behind his machine, patching a pair of jeans. 'The poor man's necessity is the rich man's hobby. Here people eat less to lose weight – in the poor countries, they lose weight because they can't afford to eat. Here people have a Rolls-Royce but they prefer to walk – in the poor countries, people walk because they can't afford the bus. Here people pay to get their old jeans patched – in the poor countries, they can't afford to buy new ones.' It was a glimpse of the sly wisdom of the alteration tailor, observing weakness and vanity, yet bringing a quick needle and a compassionate sensibility to supply our needs.

MARK JACKSON AND HUW DAVIES
PHOTOGRAPHERS

Human Life, Market Life, Night Life

IN THE LAST EIGHTEEN MONTHS of the Fruit and Vegetable Market in Spitalfields, young photographers Mark Jackson and Huw Davies set out to record the life of the market that had operated on this site for over three centuries, before it closed for ever in 1991. Recent graduates, Mark was working in a restaurant at the time and Huw was a bicycle courier. Without any financial support for their ambitious undertaking, they saved up all their money to buy cameras and rolls of film, converting a corner of their tiny flat into a darkroom.

'It was quite a struggle,' Mark Jackson confided when I spoke to him, 'because we weren't earning a lot. But Spitalfields fired our imaginations. We caught the last tube to Liverpool Street and spent the night there taking photographs, before heading into work next morning.' The result of their passionate labours is an unparalleled archive of more than 4,000 images and it was my privilege to have the first glimpse of this photographic treasure trove.

I have the greatest respect for anyone who sets out to pursue idealistic projects such as this at great cost to themselves. In this case, I am equally impressed by the

quality of Mark and Huw's photographs as distinguished social documentary, unsentimental yet infused with affectionate poetry too. Today, we are the fortunate beneficiaries of their selfless enthusiasm over all those months when they stayed up each night to take pictures and worked each day to buy film.

The market traders warmed to the young photographers, respecting the commitment that Mark and Huw demonstrated, turning up night after night, and this accounts, in part, for the relaxed, intimate nature of some of these images.

These pictures take us on a cinematic journey from the busy nocturnal world, when the market was active, through dawn into the early morning, when the drama subsided. Mark and Huw photographed a dignified gallery of traders and homeless people, who were drawn by the fire that had burned to alleviate their discomfort ever since the market was granted its charter. We no longer see any of these characters in Spitalfields. Theirs are soulful faces from a universe that is gone. When I walk through the market at night now, it feels like an empty theatre, lacking the performance of the nightly drama that ran from 1638, when

Charles I signed the licence to commence trading.

Even though Mark and Huw took their pictures only twenty years ago, they portray a society that feels closer to the world Dickens knew than our own present tense, early in the twenty-first century. These photographs were to be the first of a series documenting all the markets of London that might have been a lifetime's vocation for Mark and Huw. It was not to be. Life intervened, Mark became a writer and Huw is now a teacher. They both have lives beyond their nascent photographic enterprise, but they deserve to be proud of these vital pictures, because they are an honourable contribution to the canon of British documentary photography.

SANDRA ESQULANT

QUEEN OF SPITALFIELDS

Human Life, Night Life

EVERYONE IN THE NEIGHBOURHOOD knows Sandra Esqulant, beloved landlady of the Golden Heart in Commercial Street, sometime hula-hoop dancer, darling of the contemporary art world and the un-crowned monarch of Spitalfields. Before taking this picture, I asked Sandra to 'show me the Manet' and she graciously assumed the pose from *Bar at the Folies-Bergère*. Born just round the corner in Wentworth Street, Sandra has kept the Golden Heart for us since 1977, through the lean years and the good. She and her husband, Dennis, pre-sided here together until he died in 2009, and now she reigns alone. If Spitalfields were a tall ship, with all the residents as its crew, we should have an effigy of Sandra hewn from oak as our figurehead and know that we could sail through all the vicissi-tudes of life's great ocean with confidence, with her as our inspiration and spiritual guide.

ROA

STREET ARTIST

Street Life

IT WAS LAST AUTUMN that Roa the Belgian street artist's squirrel in Redchurch Street first caught my eye, and now, as you can see from this tall bird that appeared at the junction of Hanbury Street and Brick Lane just recently, Roa is back again, and he has taken the opportunity to further populate our neighbourhood with his distinctive, finely drawn creatures.

I was walking down Hanbury Street when, unexpectedly, I looked up to see Roa hard at work painting on the top of a motorised cherry picker, high above my head. I craned my neck, watching as he used strokes of the spray can to make each of the individual marks that characterise his highly recognisable style. From the cradle of the cherry picker, at arm's reach from the wall, Roa could only see directly in front of him, so in his left hand he clutched a sketch that allowed him to envisage the entire figure, while he wielded the spray can in his right.

Roa's intention had been to paint a heron but, after being asked if it was a crane by Bengali people – for whom the crane is a sacred bird – he morphed his bird into a crane to best complement its location on the wall of an Indian restaurant. Roa always asks before painting his creatures on to walls and has discovered that many owners are receptive to having large paintings enhance their buildings, which can become landmarks as a result. The truth is that since these paintings take four to eight hours to complete, it is not an option to create them as a hit and run operation, especially if you want them to last.

Roa's fine draughtsmanship sets him above other street artists and I particularly admire the vivid sense of life that he imparts to his creatures, which transfix you with their wide eyes. The anatomical detail is lovingly achieved, yet they are portraits of feral beasts that demand respect, resisting our simple affection. Their looming scale and piercing gaze can be challenging – charged with tension, their eyes always follow you. Similarly, any human figure you see in the vicinity of these paintings unavoidably exists in relation to them, a measure of their fierce intensity.

For the most part, Roa places his animals in unloved, unrecognised corners of the cityscape that are the natural home for scavengers and vermin. But once these spaces are inhabited, the creatures become the familiar spirits of their locations, living embodiments of these places, and our relationship with them parallels our feelings about the streetscape itself. Their powerful presence does not permit us to remain indifferent.

THE RETURN OF JOAN ROSE

Human Life, Past Life

THIS GRACIOUS LADY with the keen grey eyes is Joan Rose, standing in the doorway of Leila's Shop in Calvert Avenue on the spot where her father was photographed, around 1900, more than a century ago. Joan's grandfather Albert Raymond opened the greengrocer's shop that year, running it with the assistance of her father, Alfred Raymond, who continued the business until it closed when he died in 1966. Much to Joan's delight, in recent years Leila McAlister has picked up where Alfred Raymond left off and the place is once again filled with a quality selection of fresh fruit and vegetables for sale.

Joan is a remarkably spirited person

with an exceptional recall for names and places throughout her long life. An educated woman and former teacher, she can place anyone within London by their accent. Although unsentimental about the past, she talks affectionately about her happy childhood in Arnold Circus. In 1951 she left to get married and live in Becontree, but the emotional memory of her time in Shoreditch remains vivid to her. 'I am here,' she said to me when I met her for tea at Leila's Café, and I understood what she meant, even if today she lives on the other side of London.

When she was growing up in the 1930s, Joan told me, she helped her grandfather in the shop and he called her 'Tangerine' because she always stole tangerines, even though she could have as many as she wanted. 'I used to sit on his lap in the corner of the shop and he told me all these stories about the neighbourhood and I thought they were all nonsense – but later I found they were all true. He had a set of Shakespeare in the flat up above the shop and he said, "There's a plaque to Shakespeare in St Leonard's, Shoreditch." After he died, I found the plaque and I cried, because I had never believed him.'

Joan was very close to her grandfather Albert, who taught her the exact science of stacking fruit and vegetables in tall pyramids (stalks up for apples, pears, plums and tomatoes, eyes up for oranges), and when he went to Spitalfields Market in the dawn to buy new stock, he took her with him and they had breakfast together at one of the pubs that opened in the early morning. He kept a pony and trap in the yard at the back of the shop and took Joan for rides around Arnold Circus – that was when she learned that eight times round the bandstand was a mile.

Joan was born in 1926, the youngest of four daughters, Lily, Vera and Doris being the names of her sisters. Joan's family lived in a series of different flats in the Boundary Estate as she was growing up, moving at one point from 20 Shiplake Buildings (eighteen shillings and sixpence a week) to 10 Laleham Buildings (twelve shillings and sixpence a week) to save money.

'Although we had a shop here, my mother went out working as a furrier's machinist. We never realised that things were hard for our parents. My mother made our clothes and Mr Feldman made our winter coats. It was a system of favours, you deal off me, I'll deal off you. People were poor but proud. They ate the cheapest food – monkfish or a pig's head as a Sunday roast. My father hated Christmas because he saw people buy the best of everything and toys for their children, when they could barely afford a loaf of bread, and he knew they would end up in debt, running round to the pawnbrokers in Boundary Passage.'

Joan never felt that she was disadvantaged by her origins until she and her sisters went up to the West End to dances and met boys who asked where they came from. 'If you said you were from Shoreditch, that was the last you saw of them,' Joan admitted to me. 'We used to say we were from Arnold Circus, because they didn't know where it was.' Occasionally, charabancs of out-of-towners would slow down outside Raymond's greengrocer's shop and the driver would announce to the passengers, 'And these are the slums,' much to her grandfather's ire.

Joan's father was disappointed that he never had a son to carry on the business in his family name, but he changed his opinion when the Second World War came along, declaring he was grateful to have four daughters and not to have a son to send to war. Yet there was a hidden irony to this statement, because he had an illegitimate son, Terry Coughlan, who turned up in the shop once to buy an apple when Joan was serving and her father was out. In a youthful impulse and, to Joan's eternal regret, she said to her father when he returned, 'Your son was here!' Alfred went into the back of the shop, talked with her mother, then came out and said, 'I spoke to the boy.' That was the last that was ever said of it and Joan never met her younger brother again. Now Joan would like to find him. He will be seventy years old if he lives.

Joan describes the burning of London in 1940, when the warden knocked on all the doors in the Boundary Estate, telling the residents to take refuge in the crypt of St Leonard's, Shoreditch. She was not scared at all until she got down into the crypt and saw the priest in his black robes walking among the hundreds of silent people sitting in the gloom. It was this eerie image that filled her with fear.

Although her grandfather refused to leave London during the Blitz, Joan's father took the family to Euston and made the spontaneous choice to buy tickets to Blackpool, where he quickly found an empty shop to open up as a greengrocer, and they lived there until the war ended. As they left Euston, the sisters sat crying on the train and the other passengers thought a member of their family had been killed in the bombing, when in fact the four girls were weeping for their wire-haired terrier, Ruff, that had been put down on the morning they left London.

We leave Joan in that railway carriage travelling north, knowing that she will come back to London, get married, have children, become a teacher, have grandchildren, have great-grandchildren and live into the new millennium, to return to Arnold Circus and discover that the greengrocer's opened by her grandfather in 1900 has reopened again and life goes on and on.

When she speaks, telling her stories, Joan fingers the broad gold ring made from her grandmother Phoebe and mother Lily's wedding rings. Once, it had the initials JR, standing for Joan's maiden name Joan Raymond, and it was on her husband's finger but now that he has gone and the initials have been worn away, Joan wears it as a simple gold band to contain all the memories that she carries of her family and of this place. To many of us born later, even familiar history can appear as unlikely fiction, but meeting someone with Joan's generosity of spirit, eloquence and grace brings the big events of the last century vividly alive as reality. Joan does not bear grievances or carry complaints, she has not been worn down or made in the least cynical by her life. She is an inspiration to us all.

GIOVANNI GROSSO is a charismatic chatty young Italian who sells immaculately fine gloves, hand-made in the 1950s by his father, Alberto, the renowned glove maker of Naples – a rare opportunity, since Alberto ceased glove making in the 1970s. Giovanni himself is a talented sculptor who showed me some tiny cameos he has carved with astonishing skill into seashells. Currently serving an apprenticeship in stonecarving with Raniero Sambuci, Giovanni explained to me that he came to London because 'in Naples, unless you compromise with the mafiosi you leave'.

LINDA LEWIS has been a dealer in kitchenalia, vintage china and glass for twenty years. With enviable stamina, she gets up at four thirty to drive here in all seasons from her home in north Essex. 'My partner is a banker, so this is just part-time,' Linda whispered discreetly, adding, 'But now he's been made redundant, maybe I'll have to go back to doing it full-time.' Yet, demonstrating her appealingly buoyant nature, Linda qualified this by saying, 'I love it, I wouldn't do it otherwise, and because I like it so much, it doesn't seem like work.'

MY PAL BILL is a dignified market stalwart who deals in coins, whistles, gramophone needles, souvenir thimbles, magic-lantern slides, trading tokens, small classical antiquities and prehistoric artefacts. 'I sell quite a few things, but on a low margin,' he admitted, speaking frankly. 'I'm here for enjoyment really. I was a shy person before, but it's made me more confident, having a stall.' Bill comes each week with all his stock in a backpack and large suitcase – practical, economic and an added incentive to sell.

RISHI SHAH from Bethnal Green and Thomas LaRoche from Paris are two pale young gentlemen peddling charnel-house chic. 'We came together because we both collect taxidermy and we realised there is a shortage,' explained Thomas, casting an affectionate eye over his depleted collection of animal parts, bones and religious artefacts. 'We sell jars with foetal pigs, chicken embryos, octopus and rats in formaldehyde, all of which have died of natural causes,' revealed Rishi, tenderly displaying a sinister white rodent in a bottle for me to admire.

ROY EMMINS

SCULPTOR

Human Life

AT THE FURTHEST END of Cable Street are the Cable Street Studios, where Roy Emmins has cloistered himself for more than ten years, working six days every week, alone in a tiny workshop. A former porter at the Royal London Hospital in Whitechapel, after more than thirty years' service Roy took early retirement to devote himself to sculpture, and today his studio is crammed to the roof with creations that bear testimony to his prodigious talent and potent imagination.

When Roy opened the door to me, I could not believe my eyes. There were so many sculptures, it took my breath away. With more artefacts than a Pharaoh's tomb, I did not know where to look first. Roy stood and smiled indulgently at my reaction. Not many people make it here to the inner sanctum of Roy Emmins's imagination. He is not a demonstrative man and he has no big explanation – he's not expecting praise or inviting criticism either. In fact, he has no art world rhetoric at all, just a room packed with breathtaking sculptures.

First to catch my attention were large carvings hewn from tree trunks, some in bare wood, others painted in gaudy colours like sculptures in medieval cathedrals and sharing the same vigorous poetry, full of energetic life and acute observation of the natural world. Next, I saw elaborate painted constructions in papier-mâché, scenes from the natural world, gulls on cliffs, fish in the ocean, monkeys in the jungle and more – all meticulously imagined, and in an aesthetic reminiscent of the dioramas of the Natural History Museum but with more soul. I stood with my eyes roving, absorbing the immense detail and noticing smaller individual sculptures in ceramic, bronze and

plaster, on shelves and in cubbyholes. Turning 180 degrees, I faced a wall hung with tabletops, each incised with relief sculptures. I sat on a chair to collect my thoughts and cast my eyes to the windowsill, where sat a menagerie of creatures, all contrived with consummate skill from tinfoil and chocolate wrappers.

The abiding impression was of teeming life – every figure quick with it, as if they might all spring into animation at any moment, transforming the studio into an overcrowded Noah's Ark, with Roy as an entirely convincing Mr Noah. Yet, in his work, Roy emulates the supreme creator, reconstructing Eden – fashioning all the beloved animals, imbuing them with life and movement, and creating jungles and forests and oceans – imparting a magical intensity to everything he touches. There is a sublime quality to Roy Emmins's vision. Roy's sculptures are totems, and his carved tree trunks resemble totem poles, with images that evoke the spirits of the natural world. Even Roy's tinfoil stags possess an emotionalism born of a tension between the heroic dignity of the creature he sculpts so eloquently and the humble material from which each figure is fashioned.

It is a paradox that Roy, an English visionary, exemplifies in his own personality, which is appealingly lacking in ego yet tenacious of ambition in sculpture. Originally apprenticed as a graphic artist, he developed Wilson's disease, which caused him to shake, yet spared him military service. After years attending the Royal London Hospital, a drug was found to treat his affliction but by then, Roy admitted, he preferred the atmosphere of the hospital to the design studio, because it was an environment where he was always meeting new people. Taking a job as a porter, Roy also attended evening classes at Sir John Cass School of Art in Whitechapel, pursuing painting, ceramics, life modelling and woodcarving. Once these closed down in 1984, Roy joined a group of woodcarvers who met at weekends in the garden studio of their ex-tutor, Michael Leman, in Greenford. When the hurricane came in 1987, they hired a crane to collect fallen trees – and one of these became Roy's first tree-trunk carving.

When he took retirement in 1995, Roy was permitted to retain his caretaker's flat in Turner Street, at the rear of the hospital. After a stint at the Battlebridge Centre in King's Cross, where he had a free studio in return for one day a week building flats for homeless people, Roy came to the Cable Street Studios and has been here ever since. Always working on several sculptures at once, Roy often returns to pieces, reworking them and adding ideas, which may go some way to explain the intensity of detail and richness of ideas apparent in all his sculpture.

Looking at Roy's work, I wondered what influence it had on his psyche, wheeling patients around for thirty years at the hospital. The sense of wonder at the natural world is exuberantly apparent, but this is not the work of an innocent either. In a major sculpture that sits outside his door entitled *The Shadow of Man*, Roy dramatises the destructive instinct of mankind, yet it is not a simple didactic work, because the agents of destruction are portrayed with humanity. Again, it brought me back to medieval carving, which commonly subverts its own allegory, picturing villains with charisma, and there was a strange pathos when Roy placed his hand affectionately upon the head of a figure wielding a chainsaw, a contradictory force embodying both destruction and creation.

Roy inherited his love of people from a father who worked his whole life on the railways and ended up manager of the bar on Liverpool Street Station, while Roy's mother was skilled at assembling electrical parts, which she did at home, imparting an ability in intricate work to her son. Each of Roy's three uncles, a master carpenter, a plumber and a builder, was a model maker and Roy's brother makes models too, though, in contrast to Roy, he makes ships and cars – mechanical things.

I am fascinated by the creative skills of working men expressed in areas of endeavour parallel to their working lives. Roy's work exists in the tradition of the detailed handicrafts undertaken by sailors and prisoners, and the model railways of yesteryear, yet in its accomplishment and as a complete vision of the world, it transcends these precedents. Roy is a unique talent and a true sculptor who grasps the essence of his medium.

Showing me a wire and plasticine dancer, with a skirt made from the paper cases manufactured for buns, Roy explained that a figure must have three points of contact with the ground to stand upright. In this instance, the ballerina had one foot pointing forward and a back foot that met the ground at toe and heel. Roy placed the precarious figure on a surface and, just like his spindly tinfoil creatures, it stood with perfect balance.

BEATING THE BOUNDS IN THE CITY OF LONDON

Spiritual Life, Street Life

I JOINED the Portsoken Militia, along with a host of City worthies and the children of Sir John Cass Primary School at the annual Beating the Bounds ceremony, setting out from St Botolph-without-Aldgate to walk the boundaries of the Portsoken ward in the City of London. As we set forth with the Ward Constable in front, followed by the Beadle leading the Portsoken Militia and the Aldermen of Portsoken, ahead of the mass of schoolchildren straggling along at the rear, we made an unlikely procession, but one impressive enough to stop the traffic, cause every office worker to reach for their camera phone and bring the City to a halt around us.

First stop was Mitre Square, where a bunch of tourists on a Jack the Ripper tour had the shock of their lives as we all came round the corner, walking out of history with a mob of children in tow. 'Get your cameras ready!' the Ward Constable called to them, with a smirk of pride, occasioning a dramatic moment seized by Laura Burgess, the Rector of St Botolph, to announce the first stop on our circuit, causing everyone to gather round in a crowd.

There is a curious mixture of civility and anarchy about the Beating the Bounds ceremony. Held annually on Ascension Day, the Rector explained, it dates from a time when maps were rare and the community joined together to mark the boundaries of the parish, and to pray for God's blessing to ward off evil from the territory. Civility is represented by the dignitaries and anarchy is introduced when the children are handed sticks and given liberty to use them. Although, in the absence of boundary stones, lamp posts, bollards, signs, railings and a wall had to stand substitute, none of the children seemed disappointed. Without hesitation, they all embraced the absurdity of this extraordinary moment, in which the adults distributed long sticks and stood around in approval, as the children worked themselves up into a state of great excitement, battering the designated inert objects with gleeful enthusiasm. Everyone present

proudly agreed that the children all played their parts well.

Naturally, there is a certain necessary ritual that precedes this invitation to violence. In each location, as a precursor, the Rector delivered a brief history lecture followed by a quiet prayer. Then the Alderman gave the instruction, 'Now let us beat this boundary!' and everyone chanted, 'Cursed be he that removeth his neighbour's landmark,' and, while wielding their sticks, the children cried, 'Beat! Beat! Beat!'

We moved on swiftly through Devonshire Place, Petticoat Lane, across Aldgate High Street, down to Portsoken Street, St Clare Street and back up the Minories to St Botolph in an hour's circuit, stopping off for the ritual beatings as we went. As the journey progressed, the various constituencies in our procession mingled, acknowledging that we were fellow travellers upon some kind of pilgrimage with our particular chosen purpose, which set us apart from the present-day world around us. During the Rector's history lectures we all nodded in reverence to the waves of immigrants in Petticoat Lane, the memory of Wat Tyler and the Peasants' Revolt, in whose footsteps we trod when in Aldgate High Street, and

William the Conqueror, who entered the City through Portsoken Street and is known to this day here as William I, because he negotiated a truce with the City of London, he did not conquer it.

Arriving back at St Botolph, the children were invited to beat upon the churchyard railings one last time, and then the sticks were summarily removed from their sweaty hands and locked away in a vestry cupboard until next year, before the possibility of any improvised high jinks could occur.

When the children went home, the adults, who were now feeling rather playful – catching the infectious holiday spirit engendered by all the excited children – had their pictures taken on the steps of St Botolph. This was followed by tea and iced cakes inside and, for the duration of the party, the atmosphere was that of a village parish tea. The bounds had been truly beaten for another year. We were celebrating. We all felt we had achieved something, although no one quite knew what. Children and adults together, we had left our daily routines for an hour and shared our delight in the romance of the great city, enacting a ritual that drew us closer to each other and to those who had gone before.

TOM THE SAILOR

Human Life, Past Life, Street Life

IF I WAS TO CHOOSE one person who incarnates the spirit of Brick Lane Market for me, it would be Tom – Tom the Sailor, as he is widely known – who you will find almost every day of the week with his faithful dog Matty, stalling out on the pavement with a few bits and pieces for sale. A distinguished gentleman of soulful character, yet with indefatigable humour and spirit, Thomas Frederick Hewson Finch has been around as long as anyone can remember, although few are aware of his origins or the extraordinary story of how he came to be here.

'In 1941, when the Germans were at war with England, that's when I came along. My father wasn't married to my mother. As far as I know, I was born in Goole in Yorkshire, but I don't know for sure – no one knows, because it was 1941. I don't think anybody cared about me, I was just a problem. I say my mother died when I was born but I don't know, and I don't want to know, because I've had my life now, and I was slung in a home then, which was natural. All I can remember is me lying on a floor and watching a rocking horse.

'That home was St John's in Ipswich. It's not there any more. You went from baby to cots and then you went to beds. In other words you went through the stages. It was a big place. Loads of people like me needed somewhere to go. Why this place was picked was because there was Yanks all around. Although it may not be true, what I say is that my father was American. My mother went out with other people. She was part Gypsy and she had to take care of herself, and naturally she would go with the Yanks, who gave her cigarettes and stockings. Why would a woman want to go with Englishmen that were poor and had nothing?

'When you sit there as an orphan and see other people being given presents, how do you imagine I felt? One child had an electric train set and I nicked it and buried it, but when I went back to get it a year later it was rusty and no good. Why take somebody's train set? It was how I thought. It was wrong, I know this now. I hid above a toilet for three days when they were looking for me, after they thought I had run away. As I got older, they slung me out because I was too unruly, and they put me in a stronger home. It was in East Grinstead, and the one who run it, he was – now he would be locked up in prison – he was very hard. He used to love hitting me. He used the birch, he kept it in vinegar. He put you over a bench for six of the best. It was always me.

'They sent me to a training ship for orphans on the River Medway – the *Arethusa* – where I reached Chief Petty Officer Boy. We slept in hammocks and you had to climb the 170-foot masts every day and slide down the lanyards. It was a sailing ship from Harwich. From there, when you passed out you went to the *Ganges* in Suffolk, where everyone went to go into the Royal Navy. They were training me in Morse code and typing, and I went on HMS *Paladin*. But I went deaf, on account of the cold weather in Iceland when I was drilling ice off a boat. I was invalided out with a pension of six shillings and nine pence a week, which I sold for 250 pounds, and with the money I bought a motorbike – a Super Flash.

'I started working with woodworkers, Hollar Bros. in Hull, where I met my wife. I went in a café in Dagger Lane and the chap was doing no good and he asked me if I wanted the café for fifteen pounds a month, so I thought, "I'll have that." It turned out to be one hell of a place. All the bikers came and it was packed out with motorcyclists from Brighton and all over England. I was open twenty-four hours and it was so busy you couldn't park in the street. From there I ended up with seven nightclubs, and ten other cafés, with casinos above them. I had dogs on the door, and I had one doorman dressed as a fisherman because they knew me and I went to sea with them.

'After that, I was twenty years on the run. I gave up everything when I left. Me and my family, we just walked out. All the others ended up in the nick, but they couldn't catch me and I came down here to the East End to get away. In other words, I was a bit of a villain. I've had a few premises round here, on Great Eastern Street, Boundary Street and two shops on Brick Lane, and in Cheshire Street. I never paid for any of them. I used to have a partner, me and Terry – they called us "Tom and Jerry", cat and mouse. Our first shop on the Hackney Road, we sold the shop window just to get going. We used to sell nicked fireplaces, Victorian ranges and marble. You could get that stuff easy when there was no cameras. We sold them at giveaway prices. Even the police came to buy from us. The shop was given to me by a Jew that was going to America. I was sitting in the Princess one day and he came in and threw the keys on the counter and said, "Take it, it's yours!"

'A camera crew came round once and asked me to show them how to sell a fireplace. We had one marked at fifteen pounds, so they filmed me and I asked for "thirty pounds" and they gave me the cash. Each time I asked more, until it was seventy-five pounds. And when they said, "Can we have our money back?" I said, "It's your fireplace!" You can do anything in a market. Me and Terry closed up and went to the stripper pub on the corner. That's how you sell a fireplace.

'All my family are well off, they all made it. My little boy Andrew, he's my son, he was always with me. He's grown up now too, but I just carry on in my own stupid way. Why does a man do it? I can only do what I've always done. I know it better than anything. I've done it all my life. Old Tom's still an orphan, it's the way I was brought up.'

Larger than life yet of this life, Tom the Sailor is the most charismatic rogue you will meet, with his nautical tattoos, weather-beaten features, white mutton-chop whiskers and an endless supply of yarns to relate. He delights in ruses and fables. With the wisdom and modesty of one who has lived many lives, Tom recognises that the truth of experience is rarely simple, always ambiguous. And if, like me, you are of a similar cast of mind, then there is almost no better way to pass time and learn about the East End than hanging on Old Tom's ear.

THIS BELL WILL RING WHEN THE MONEY RUNS OUT

A SPRING SHIRT
FROM LIBERTY OF LONDON

Past Life

I PULLED this old Liberty shirt out of my cupboard in Spitalfields to celebrate a sequence of bright days that convincingly proposed the notion of spring this week. If you look closely, you can see the collar is wearing through, but this does not diminish my affection for this favoured garment that I have worn for years now, bringing it out just for these early months when the temperature starts to rise. Though I am not a flowery person and most of the few clothes I own are of undecorated design, there is a gentle lyrical quality about this pattern that appeals to me strongly.

When I wear this shirt with a dark grey or blue jacket, the colours really sing and I feel I am doing my bit to participate in the seasonal change. For both men and women, the contrast of formal wear with a Liberty shirt can express a certain dignified restraint while at the same time revealing a romantic attachment to flowers, plants, gardens and nature – a contradiction that I cannot deny in my own personality. I love the conceit of having violets on my shirt when the violets in my garden are in bloom and I enjoy the subtle tones of all the flowers portrayed, which remain as recognisable species while artfully stylised to make an elegant pattern. The evocation of the natural world in this simple design touches a chord for me and, as with so many things that trigger an emotional response, I discovered that my passion for these floral patterns from Liberty goes back a long way.

When I came across this photograph of my mother, Valerie, as a child, I did a double-take when I recognised the pattern on the dress. It was a Liberty print, very similar to this spring shirt of mine which I hold in such affection. In that moment, I recalled that my grandmother once bought fabric at Liberty in London and had it made up into dresses for my mother. This was a gesture which made such an unforgettable impression on my mother that for her whole life she carried her delight in these cotton dresses, which were so magical to her as a little girl in Somerset in the 1930s. Floral prints fed her innocent imagination, nurtured on *The Songs of the Flower Fairies* and by performing

as one of Titania's attendants in a school play.

A generation later, I grew up with the received emotion of this memory, a story my mother must have told me when I was a child. I thought I had forgotten, but I realised it was through an unconscious recollection of the photograph of my mother in the Liberty dress that I was attracted to this beautiful flowery shirt, without understanding the origin of my desire at the time.

The story was confirmed when my uncle Richard moved out of the house where he and my mother grew up, and in my grandmother's dressing table I found a small leather pocket diary from the 1930s recording her London trip with the entry, 'Stayed at Claridge's. Ordered carpet and sideboard at Harvey Nichols and bought materials at Liberty.' My grandmother was the daughter of a diminished aristocratic family who married my grandfather Leslie, a bank manager, and adopted an autocratic manner to compensate for her loss of status. Consequently, my mother, with admirable resourcefulness, ran away from home at nineteen to escape my bossy grandmother and married my father, Peter, who was a professional footballer – an act of social rebellion that my grandmother never forgave.

Nevertheless, the taste I acquired for these elegant old-fashioned designs reflects the fondness my mother held for that special moment in her childhood which she never forgot, when my grandmother showed maternal kindness to her little daughter in the gift of flowery cotton dresses. This act came to represent everything about my grandmother that my mother could embrace with unqualified affection, and she encouraged me to remember the best of people too.

Today, I wear my Liberty shirt as the sympathetic illustration of a narrative which extends over three generations, and as I button my spring shirt, before walking out to celebrate sunshine and a new beginning, I am reminded that I alone carry these emotional stories now, clothing me in the affections of my forebears.

DAN JONES

RHYME COLLECTOR

Human Life

THE AMIABLE Dan Jones has lived down in Cable Street since 1967 and has made it his business to collect children's rhymes, both here and all over the world since 1948. Dan has many hundreds in transcripts and recordings that are slowly yet inevitably converging into a book of around a thousand rhymes that he has been working on for some years, entitled *The Singing Playground*, which will be his magnum opus. He explained that the litany of classic nursery rhymes which adults teach children has barely altered since James Halliwell's collection *The Nursery Rhymes of England* of 1842, when they were already old. In contrast, the rhymes composed and passed on by children are constantly changing and it is these that form the mass of Dan's study.

When you enter the bright red front door of his house in Cable Street, you can barely get through the passage because of a huge mural painted by Dan of the playground of St Paul's School, Wellclose Square, that is about ten feet tall and twenty feet long. Painted on wooden panels, it is suspended from the wall and jutting forward, which

puts you directly at the eye level of many of the children in the painting and, thus confronted, you see that all the figures are surrounded by rhymes. The effect is magical and one reminiscent of Breughel's 'Children's Games'.

As well as collecting rhymes, Dan is a painter who creates affectionately observed murals of children in school playgrounds, all painted in rich natural hues and with such levity and appreciation for the exuberant idiosyncrasy of childhood that I was immediately beguiled. I have always loved the joyful sound of the children playing in the school playground that I can hear from my house, but Dan has found a method to explore and celebrate the specific quality of this intriguing secret world through his scholarship and paintings.

Once you get past the mural, you find yourself in a parlour lined with more paint-ings. Some even protrude from behind the comfortable armchairs, which are arranged in a horseshoe like an old-fashioned doctor's surgery, indicating that Dan lives a very sociable existence and that this room has been the location for innumerable happy gatherings over the last forty years he and his wife, Denise, have lived here. There are shelves brimming over with all manner of books devoted to art and social history, and children's books on the coffee table for the amusement of Dan's grandchildren, who wander in and out as we are talking.

Rhymes spill out of Dan Jones endlessly and I could have sat all day hearing the fascinating stories of the origins of familiar examples and all their different versions over time and in different languages. Dan has a paradoxical quality of seeming both young and old at the same time. While displaying a fine white beard and resembling a patriarch in a painting by William Blake, he also possesses the gentle nature and spontaneous enthusiasm of youth. I can understand why children choose to line up in the playground to tell Dan their rhymes, as they do when he arrives in schools, and why old people too, when Dan puts them on the spot, asking, 'What rhymes do you remember from your youth?', summon whole canons of verse from the depths of their memories for him.

The heartening news from the playground that Dan has to report is that the culture of rhymes is alive and thriving, in spite of all the distractions of the modern age. The endless process of repetition and reinvention goes on with ceaseless vigour. Most rhymes accompany action and melody, which means that while the words may change, other elements – especially the melodies – can remain constant over centuries or across continents, in different languages and cultures, tracing the historical movements of peoples.

Perhaps the most astounding example Dan gave me was *Ching, chang, choller* (paper, scissors and stone), a game used to select a random winner or loser, which was depicted in the tomb of a Pharaoh 4,000 years ago and of which there are versions recorded in ancient Rome, China, Japan, Mongolia, Chile, Korea, Hungary, Sweden, Italy, France and the USA. Dan recorded it being played at Columbia Road Primary School nearby. By contrast, I was especially delighted to learn that 'Twinkle, Twinkle, Little Star' was written by Jane and Ann Taylor of Islington in 1806, and to discover the Bengali version recently recorded by Dan at Bangabandhu School in Bethnal Green.

> *Chichmic chichmic koray*
> *Aka shetay tara*
> *Dolte deco akha chete*
> *Masto boro hera*
> *Chichmic chichmic koray*
> *Aka shetay tara.*

Sometimes, there is a plangent history to a rhyme, of which the children who sing it are unaware. Dan has traced the path of stone-passing games that were carried by slave children in the eighteenth century from West Africa to the Caribbean and then, two centuries later, brought to London by immigrants from the West Indies. Meanwhile, new rhymes constantly arise, as Dan explained. 'Some burst forth just in one particular school playground to blossom like a spring flower for a few weeks and then vanish completely.'

Living in Spitalfields, surrounded by old buildings and layers of history, I am always fascinated to consider who has been here before. You have read the tales of the past I have collected from old people, but Dan's work reveals an awe-inspiring historical continuum of much greater age. There is a compelling poetry to the notion that the oldest thing here could be the elusive and apparently ephemeral games and rhymes that the children are playing in the playground. I love the idea that these joyful rhymes – mostly carried and passed on by girls between the ages of eight and twelve, and marginal to the formal culture of society – have survived, outliving everything else, wars and migrations of people notwithstanding.

COLUMBIA ROAD MARKET III

Human Life, Market Life

GEORGE GLADWELL has been selling plants on Columbia Road longer than anyone else and is the only one left who was there on the very first day of the flower market, just a few years after the war. Over eighty years old, yet still lifting heavy boxes and trading through every winter, George possesses extraordinary vitality. As Chairman of the Columbia Road Traders' Association, he is the spokesman for his fellow traders, which suits him well because he has greater experience of market life than anyone else and knows his own mind too. Softly spoken, although possessing a powerful physical presence, George has staying power and, remarkably, after more than sixty years of early mornings in the frost, he is still smiling.

When I spoke to George, I was eager to learn about that mythic day when it all began ...

'I arrived in this lonely little street in the East End with only boarded-up shops in it at seven o'clock one Sunday morning in February 1949. And I went into Sadie's Café, where you could get a whopping great mug of cocoa, coffee or tea, and a thick slice of bread and dripping – real comfort food. Then I went out on to the street again at nine o'clock, and a guy turned up with a horse and cart loaded with flowers, followed by a flatback lorry also loaded with plants. At the time, I had a 1933 ambulance and I drove that around to join them, and we were the only three traders until someone else turned up with a costermonger's barrow of cut flowers. There were a couple more horse and carts that joined us and, around eleven thirty, a few guys came along with baskets on their arms with a couple of dozen bunches of carnations to sell, which was their day's work.

'More traders began turning up over the next few months until the market was full. There were no trolleys then, everything was on the floor. Years ago, it wasn't what you call "instant gardening", it was all old

gardeners coming to buy plants to grow on to maturity. It was easy selling flowers then, though if you went out of season it was disappointing, but I never got discouraged – you just have to wait.

'Mother's Day was the beginning of the season and Derby Day was the finish, and it still applies today. The serious trading is between those two dates and the rest of the year is just ticking over. In June it went dead, until it picked up in September, then it got quite busy until Bonfire Night. And from the first week of December, you had Christmas trees, holly and mistletoe, and the pot-plant trade.

'I had a nursery and I lived in Billericay, and I was already working in Romford, Chelmsford, Epping, Rochester, Maidstone and Watford markets. A friend of mine – John – he didn't have a driving licence, so he asked me to drive him up on a Sunday, and each week I came up to Columbia Road with him and I brought some of my own plants along too, because there was a space next to his pitch.

'My first licensed pitch was across from the Royal Oak. I moved there in 1958, because John died and I inherited his pitches, but I let the other four go. In 1959 the shops began to unboard and people took them on here and there. That was around the time public interest picked up, because formerly it was a secret little market. It became known through visitors to Petticoat Lane. They'd walk around and hear about it. It was never known as Columbia Road Flower Market until I advertised it by that name.

'It picked up even more in the 1960s when the council introduced the rule that we had to come every four weeks or lose our licences, because then we had to trade continuously. In those days, we were all professional growers who relied upon the seasons at Columbia Road. Although we used to buy from the Dutch, you had to have a licence and you were only allowed a certain amount, so that was marginal. It used to come by train – pot plants, shrubs and herbaceous plants. During the war, agriculture became food production, and fruit trees planted before the war had matured nicely. They sold masses of these at the Maidstone plant auctions and I could pick them up for next to nothing and sell them at Columbia Road for 2,000 per cent profit. Those were happy times!

'In the depression at the end of the 1950s, a lot of nurserymen sold their plots for building land because they couldn't make it pay and it made the supply of plants quite scarce. So those of us who could grow our own did quite well, but although I did a mail-order trade from my nursery, it wasn't sufficient to make ends meet. Hobby traders joined the market then and they interfered with our trade, because we were growers and kept our stock from week to week, but they would sell off all their stock cheap each week to get their money back. I took a job driving heavy haulage and got back for Saturday and Sunday. I had to do it because I had quite a big family, four children.

'In the 70s I was the first to use the metal trolleys that everyone uses now. My associates said I would never make it pay, because I hocked myself up to do it. At the same time, plants were getting plastic containers, whereas before we used to sell bare roots, which made for dirty pitches, so that was progress. All the time we were getting developments in different kinds of plants coming from abroad. You could trade in these and forget growing your own plants, but I never did.

'Then in the 90s we had problems with rowdy traders and customers coming at four in the morning, which upset the residents, and we were threatened with closure by the council. We had a committee and I was voted Chairman of the Association. We negotiated with the neighbours and agreed trading hours and parking for the market, so all were happy in the end.

'It's been fulfilling. What I've finished up with is quite a nice property – something I always wanted. I like hard work, whether physical or mental. I used to sell plants at the side of the road when I was seven, and I used to work on farms helping with the milking at five in the morning before I went to school. I studied architecture and yet, as a job, I was never satisfied with it. I preferred the outdoor life and the physical part of it. Having a pitch is always interesting – it's freedom as well.'

I was captivated by the lyrical tone that

George adopted to tell his story, while equally impressed by his determination and ingenuity in surviving as a plantsman, sticking with what he loves most, cultivating plants at home on his nursery and selling them each week at the market.

George told me that in the spring after the harsh winter of 1963, he was the only trader at Columbia Road with geraniums, which had been decimated throughout the East End by the snow. It was 'a bumper year', he recalled, his eyes gleaming in fond reminiscence, and so, after last winter's cold snap, George Gladwell is anticipating a bumper spring for plant sales at Columbia Road Market.

SHAJEDA AKHTER

PLAYWORKER

Human Life

THIS POISED young woman is Shajeda Akhter, a playworker at the Attlee Community Centre, in the shadow of Christ Church, Spitalfields. Although she may appear at peace now, she endured a long fight to win self-possession as an independent woman and claim the freedom to make her own choices. Yet Shajeda's struggle gave her both the motivation and the experience which enable her to support other young women facing similar pressures today – a responsibility that she has embraced with every particle of her being.

'I came to this country in November 1995 after getting married to my husband, Mujib. I was born and brought up in Debarai in Sylhet, Bangladesh – a lovely village with open fields where I was able to go out and play as a child. We were a very close family and everyone knew everyone, and I still take

my kids back there. I came from a poor background and in my childhood I had freedom, but when I grew older I couldn't go out to study as I wanted to do.

'Ever since I was very young, I saw how my mother went through pain and I didn't want to suffer like that. I asked her, "Why don't you speak up?" and she said, "It's the tradition." So I said to my mother, "But if he leaves you, you have nothing." I realised that you cannot guarantee that your husband will support you. Both parties must be able to earn some money and have the respect they need. The tradition comes second, it has to be me first!

'My husband was my first cousin, born and brought up in London, and he went back on a holiday and met me and we fell in love, and he told his mum and dad that he wanted to marry me. They didn't approve, but he went ahead and married me anyway. My father also disapproved, because he knew that I would have to come and live here – knowing that my husband's side of the family would not accept me. I did not speak English and my husband could not read or write Bengali, but Mujib and I could understand each other, and he got Captain Shiv Banerjee, the Bengali magistrate, to compose his love letters to me.

'We had a secret wedding with a few friends at night in the pouring rain. My husband's family asked him to move out when they learned about it. In London, we had to stay with Shiv until my husband bought a flat in Backchurch Lane in 1996. It was a struggle. I was very lonely without friends and family, but Shiv and his wife, Selina, adopted me as a daughter and slowly I began to make some friends. On my second day here, Shiv said, "I will arrange for you to learn English," but I did not like the classes and I wanted to earn my own money. So, instead of language school, I worked as a volunteer at a community centre in Finsbury Park for a year and my English improved quickly.

'Once my English was better, I searched for a job and got one in a jewellery factory in Kentish Town. But it was difficult there and after six months I offered my services free to a travel agency, if they would pay my daily travel expenses. I did that for a year and a half before I was offered a paid job at an agency in Brick Lane. And I did that for another year until I became pregnant with my first child, working all through my pregnancy and planning to go back to work afterwards. I found myself very isolated at home, and I stayed in and cried until Selina came round and supported me, taking me out for day trips.

'I thought my husband's parents would come when our baby was born but they never visited the hospital. They would not accept me because of my independence and, on the third day, my husband took our daughter to show them, but I have never been allowed to go into their house. They came to this country over forty years ago and, although I do not blame them for their beliefs, I wish I had their support.

'My elder sister, Majeda, was due to give birth on the same day as me, in Bangladesh, but a week passed before I learned she had died the day my daughter was born. Her in-laws did not seek medical attention because they did not want a doctor to examine her body – eventually my family took her to a hospital, but by then it was too late. Once I found out, a week later, I didn't want to go back to work. I didn't want to leave my daughter, Shoma, with anyone else.

'When I became pregnant with my second child, I joined a mother and toddler group at the Attlee Community Centre on Brick Lane. Tanya, the manager, watched me and asked if I had any experience working with children. She told me to put my name down as a volunteer. Later, when my son, Imon, was two years old, she asked if she could put my name forward. I told her I had no experience but she said she would train me. She gave me responsibility and the keys to the building. Eventually she said, "We'll pay you part-time as a sessional worker," but I wouldn't leave my son, so she said, "Bring your children, as long as you can take responsibility for them." I became qualified and I have been here for the past nine years.

'My work is about freedom, enabling young girls growing up to leave the house and be independent. Often I go and pick them up from their homes because they aren't allowed to go out. I go and talk to the parents and persuade them to let their daughters go out, and they agree as long as I take them and bring them home. It was hard work at first, but slowly I have built it up from five girls in Backchurch Lane until now it is about fifteen or twenty girls.

'It is very important they see life beyond family life, because the normal route would be not going out, not becoming Westernised. A lot of girls may still wear headscarves but they have learned to say, "No." One young girl, she's going to university and her parents want her to have education, but there is also pressure, so I am giving her the power to make her own decision, because she must decide what is for her own good, for her own future – and I will support her in whatever she decides. A lot of young girls are under pressure, but slowly we will come out of it. I give them my number and tell them to call me whenever they need support.'

As I listened to Shajeda, speaking in professional fluent English, and with controlled emotion, her moral courage became apparent – a woman caught between worlds, who through strength of character has prevailed in the face of forces larger than herself. With extraordinary independence of mind, she saw beyond the circumstances of her own upbringing and sought her own liberty. Neither complacent nor embittered, Shajeda Akhter has translated her own painful experiences into practical measures to help other women seek their own freedom, ensuring the individual steps that can bring about wider social change. It is a serious remit for one who goes by the deceptively lightweight job description of playworker.

SPINACH AND EGGS
FROM SPITALFIELDS CITY FARM

Animal Life, Culinary Life

THE OLD HAWTHORN at the Spitalfields City Farm was in full blossom under a blue sky to welcome me as I arrived in search of spinach and eggs, in anticipation of one of my all-time favourite lunches. At the far end of the farmyard, I was greeted by Helen Galland, whom I interrupted in the midst of her mucking-out duties to sell me half a dozen freshly laid eggs. I deliberated between hen's and duck's eggs, so Helen kindly gave me three of each, a pound for the lot.

The Spitalfields flock is a mixture of rare breeds (Marsh Daisies and Buff Orpingtons) and rescued chickens, bought by a charity from battery farms that would otherwise destroy the hens after a year's life of producing an egg a day, when they still have another four to five years of life left laying

eggs. 'When they arrive they have to learn to be chickens, because they have never seen anything but the inside of a cage before, so the first thing they do when they arrive is lie in the sun,' explained Helen with maternal sympathy, as the flock ran around our ankles, pecking in the yard. 'In factory farms, they have no nesting materials but they soon get the hang of it here.'

I stowed the half-dozen eggs in my bag and walked over to the other end of the farm, where the vegetables are grown. Here Chris Kyei-Balffour, a community gardener, led me into the humid atmosphere of one of the polytunnels to admire his fine patch of spinach, glowing fresh and green with new leaves in the filtered sunlight. To my delight, Chris picked me a basket of the most beautiful spinach I had ever seen and presented it to me in exchange for a pound. Anyone can buy produce at the City Farm, you just have to go and ask.

Although spinach and eggs is one of the simplest of meals, careful judgement is required to ensure both ingredients are cooked just enough. It is a question of precise timing to ensure the perfect balance of the constituents. I steamed the spinach lightly while I poached the eggs in salted water. The leaves need to be blanched but must not become slushy, because texture is everything with spinach – it needs to be gelatinous yet chewy.

Once the spinach was on, I broke three hen's eggs, slipping them gently into a pan of simmering water, and poached them until the white of the egg was cooked but the yolk remained runny. Be aware, you have to be careful not to break the yolks when you drop the eggs into the water and some concentration is required to master the knack of scooping them out intact too. I have ruined the aesthetics of my spinach and eggs on innumerable occasions with a casual blunder at this stage, though I can assure you the meal still remains acceptable to the taste buds even if you top your spinach with pitiful fragments of poached egg.

I placed a generous serving of my delicious spinach in an old soup dish and – blessed with good luck – balanced all three eggs on top, perfectly intact and wobbling like jellies. With eggs freshly laid that morning and spinach picked half an hour before I ate it, the ingredients could not have been fresher. No vocabulary exists to explain fully why I like this combination so much. It is something about what happens when you recklessly slice through the egg and the hot golden yolk runs down into the slippery seaweed-green spinach. You have to try it for yourself, because the combination of the sweet yolk and almost-bitter spinach is astounding.

Having added a little ground black pepper and grated Parmesan on the top, I carried the spinach and eggs outside into the garden triumphantly, enjoying my lunch in the sunshine for the first time this year. The contrast of eating my meal of ingredients fresh from the local farm here in the secret green enclave of my garden in the heart of Spitalfields only served to amplify the pleasure. It was an unforgettable moment of spring.

BRICK LANE MARKET II

Human Life, Market Life

ON ANY SUNDAY, at the heart of Brick Lane, where the food stalls cluster on the railway bridge, you will find eager players around carrom boards, absorbed in their games, and a crowd of spectators too, mesmerised by this sport from India that is a curious blend of billiards and draughts. Played with discs upon square wooden boards coated in French chalk, the objective is to knock your opponents' counters into the pockets at each corner.

Look closely among the throng and you will spot the genius responsible for this spontaneous flowering of a game that has complete strangers playing together across the table every week. Slight of build, with spidery limbs and lank hair – a man who greets everyone as a friend – this is Carrom Paul, President of the Carrom Association of the United Kingdom.

'One day fifteen years ago, I went to Ealing and I saw these game boards that I'd seen in India, so I bought four and brought them back to the Spitalfields Market and set them up for people to play, but it got so big I had hassle from the other stallholders. I was selling religious artefacts then, and once I sold the carrom boards, I thought I wouldn't get any more. But this old Indian

man came along and explained that the pockets at each corner are the four great religions of the world, Islam, Hinduism, Christianity and Judaism, and when all the religions meet in the centre there will be peace and the moon will turn red, represented by the red counter at the centre.

'So then I decided to buy lots! I moved to the Upmarket in the Truman Brewery

and they gave me the dead stall out the back where no one goes, but I opened the fire exit and played my music and everyone came in from Brick Lane and the place was full of people playing carrom. Eventually they put my rent up from thirty to 190 pounds a week, and squeezed me out of there in 2009. Then the food stalls on Brick Lane invited me to join them and set up my carrom boards, and I've been here ever since. And now, this is my life! It's become my life because I love the game so much. The beauty of it is there is no luck, no chance, only tactics and play. You get lovely people coming to play, no blaggards, drunks or druggies – they can't be bothered. It's a magnet. It's chilled out and it's relaxed.'

Carrom Paul comes up to Brick Lane from Tunbridge Wells every weekend. Now he has a mission to get carrom declared an Olympic sport, and since billiards, which is a derivative of carrom, has already been listed, he has some hopes of success.

It certainly is a beautiful spectacle Carrom Paul has conjured on Brick Lane, an unlikely haven where anyone can sit down and play for free. He paired me with Robbie, a passing white-haired gentleman, to try a friendly game, just to learn the ropes and develop our technique for flicking the counters, and by the end of the game – which I found unexpectedly relaxing – we had become friends. It is a perfect Sunday pastime, civilised and egalitarian, with spiritual overtones.

GEORGE COSSINGTON

STEEPLEJACK

Human Life, Past Life

GEORGE COSSINGTON is on the left of this picture, photographed in the pursuit of his trade as a steeplejack and steel erector, perched on a 150-foot jib during the construction of Paternoster House, next to St Paul's Cathedral, in 1958. Seeing this vertiginous image, you will no doubt be relieved to know that George survives to tell the tales of his daring aerial adventures, still fit and full of swagger today at seventy-seven. 'In my day, you weren't called a steel erector, you were called a spider man. I used to run up a sixty-rung ladder in less than a minute and come down in less than twenty seconds. You just put your hands and feet on the sides and slid down!' he bragged, with a modest smile that confirmed it was the truth.

George's father was a steeplejack who once climbed Big Ben to fix the hands on the clock face and worked as chargehand on the construction of the Bank of England. So in 1947, when George left school at fourteen, there was no question about his future career. 'All my friends were going into the Merchant Navy, but when I came home with the form, my dad said, "No. You're going into my trade so you get a pension."' In fact, three out of the five boys in George's family became steeplejacks, a measure of George's father's confidence in his own profession.

'My father, uncle and my brothers, we all loved it! There was none of this Health and Safety shit then. You learned to be careful. What started coming in was the safety harness, a big belt with a hook on it attached to a rope – we hardly used them. There was no such thing as a crash helmet. Me and my brothers, we used to watch each other to check we put the bolts in correctly. It was all done properly, even without today's safeguards.

'I was apprenticed to Freddie Waite of Stratford. I started off as a tea boy. You watch as the months go by, and then someone else becomes the tea boy and you learn how to adjust swivel bolts, rigging up steel beams, and how to sling a beam for the crane to lift. It takes well over a year before you start going off the ground. You had to learn rigging, slinging, welding, acetylene burning and rope splicing. It takes five years to become a steeplejack. We used to walk the purlins that were four inches wide. You can't do that today. Before scaffolding, we used wooden poles held together with wire bands, like they still do in the Far East. You had to know how to tie the wire bands securely, because it wasn't an easy job going up to forty feet.

'I enjoyed it, but I didn't enjoy it when it was wet or cold. The crane used to take us in a bucket and put us on top of the steel work. In the winter you could freeze. If it was a frosty night, we had a big fire in an oil drum and wrapped the chain around the fire to get the frost out of it, because if you didn't it could snap like a carrot – a fifteen-ton chain.

'The day I fell, I was cutting some steelwork at Beckton Gas Works and it pissed down with rain, so they called us down. When I went back up again later, I cut one end of a beam without realising I had already cut the other end. I was seventeen years old. I was very lucky – my dad couldn't believe it – a corrugated-iron roof broke my fall. I had a few bruises, and a scar to this day. They called an ambulance but I was standing up by the time it came. I think I was only off work for a week, but I knew a couple of fellows that fell to their deaths.

'My dad was still working up high until he was sixty-six. When he was the family foreman, he looked the business in a bowler hat. He taught me splicing and slinging, and he knew every sort of knot there was. He wouldn't let you do anything he couldn't do. He could throw a three-quarter-inch bolt forty feet up for me to catch from a beam. Our last job together was on John Lewis in Oxford Steet. We were 100 feet up in the air and he walked along beams as if they were on the ground.

'I've never had a problem with heights. I've stood on the spider plate at the very top of a crane, 350 feet up without a rope. I did it just for a laugh, but if my dad had seen me he'd have shot me ...'

George retired at forty-five when he was

required to wear a helmet on site, because he belonged to an earlier world that put more trust in human skill than safety procedures. When he spoke of pegging his own ladder to scale a factory chimney, I recognised a continuum with those who once climbed the spires of cathedrals, trusting their lives in the application of a skill which now exists only in the strictly controlled conditions of sport. Thankfully, with the advent of modern cranes and cherry pickers, men are no longer required to risk their lives in this way, but it only serves to increase my respect for George Cossington, his brothers, his father, uncle and all of those in this city who fearlessly undertook these death-defying challenges as part of their daily routine. When you meet a steeple-jack at the fine age of seventy-seven, his very existence confirms his skill and proficiency in his former profession.

Because Freddie Waite bought a camera in 1958 to record the construction of Paternoster House, we are privileged to see George's aerial escapade photographed by one of those who worked alongside him. And while Paternoster House may already be history – demolished for a subsequent development – in the meantime there are enough monumental structures still standing that George worked on, like Shell House, the Chiswick Flyover, the Edmonton Incinerator towers and the chimney at the Bryant & May factory, to remind him of his thirty-year career as a steeplejack and steel erector.

THE WAX SELLERS
OF WENTWORTH STREET

Human Life

ON A RAINY SUNDAY in Spitalfields when everything is grey, I wend my way to Wentworth Street to visit the African textile stores, which glow like multicoloured lanterns illuminated in the dusk – where a troupe of magnificent women preside, each one a shining goddess in her own universe.

Sunday is when it all happens in Wentworth Street, when customers coming from as far away as Aberdeen and the Nether-lands converge to savour its wonders as the international destination for the best Holland wax, French lace, Swiss voile and headties to be found anywhere.

Weaving through the Petticoat Lane Market and pausing in the drizzle to gaze into the shop windows, you will spy the fine ladies of Wentworth Street holding court in their shops to the assembled throng, simultaneously displaying the wit of matriarchs, the authority of monarchs and the glamour of movie stars, and all dressed up to show off the potential of their textiles. Identified upon the fascias by their first names, as Franceskka Fabrics, Tayo Fashions & Textiles, and Fola Textile, many of these women put themselves forward as bold trendsetters, designing their own fabrics, defining the fashion and styling their customers too. In this, the oldest part of Spitalfields, the textile industry which has defined this neighbourhood for centuries is alive and thriving today, thanks to the talents of these shrewd businesswomen of Wentworth Street.

Franceskka Abimbola, Franceskka Fabrics

Franceskka Abimbola, whose business is the longest-established here, welcomed me into her kaleidoscopic shop with mirrored ceiling and walls draped in lush fabrics, just as there was a brief lull in the mid-afternoon trade. 'In the late 80s, I came here from Edinburgh to Petticoat Lane to buy this fabric and I found the dealers were all Jewish who didn't wear it and didn't understand it,' she explained with a humorous frown. 'I spoke to Solomon at Renee's, who introduced me to his supplier. So then I wanted to be the first African woman to open a shop, and I used to buy it and sell it from the back of a car. But when I spoke to the supplier about opening my own place, he said, "You want to open a shop and start selling my fabrics? I'm going to break you into pieces!"'

Undeterred, Franceskka bravely opened her shop in the Kingsland Road – at a respectable distance – and, fourteen years ago, she was one of the very first to open in Wentworth Street, thus initiating this extraordinary phenomenon where now every other shop here sells wax, all competing with their own styles and prices. Thankfully, Franceskka is still in one piece and, as reward for her courage, she is a big success.

'Lots of Nigerian women came at first to buy and ask advice,' she revealed delightedly, 'but then women from Gambia, Senegal, Sierra Leone, Zimbabwe and Ghana came too. Many didn't know how to tie the headtie, so I teach them how to do it.' Franceskka, who has a postgraduate diploma in business studies, controls her international business empire from this tiny shop, extending to two more in Lagos and a third in Abuja. 'I go to the fabric exhibitions in Paris and Spain to get inspiration. I design the fabrics myself and get them manufactured in Switzerland. The French laces are in vogue at the moment and they are very expensive, but if it's for a wedding people will go all out to look beautiful,' she said,

Sheba Eferoghene, Novo Fashions

Onome Efebeh-Atano, Beauty Stones

with a delicate smile and lift of her brow, merely hinting at the razzle-dazzle on offer.

Banke Adetoro at Royal Fashions incarnates the notion of sassy with her extravagant eyelashes, constantly fluttering like butterflies. 'There's nothing you want that you can't get here,' she informed me with an amused gesture of unqualified authority, when I dropped in. 'I get all the latest stuff. I can do as many as twenty buying trips in a year. My shop is the biggest and the most beautiful!' You really need to visit this shop to experience the vast phantasmagoria of patterns on display.

By contrast, across the road at Tayo Fashions & Textiles, I met the alluring Tayo herself in her small shop. 'My mother used to do this back in Africa, and I picked it up,' she confided to me quietly. 'I just started trading at home and through the church, and then I started in a small shop with a little help from the bank. Now I have a shop in Lagos too and I go three times a year.'

Outlining the convenient balance between the trade on both continents, she explained, 'At Christmas it's busy there when it's quiet here, and it's busy here in the summer when it's quiet there.' Tayo's two sons help her out in the shop and I was fascinated that in every single shop I visited these women had their children present. In fact, most had come into it through their families and some already had their children working with them. I found it an interesting contrast to the perceived dilemma between children and career that many European women face.

Betwixt the fabulous fabric shops in Wentworth Street are those selling the accessories to complete the outfit, the gleaming metallic pointy shoes and matching bags in multiple colourways and, of course, the jewellery. My favourite is Beauty Stones, lined entirely with coral necklaces that cascade like a waterfall down the walls to create an environment like a magic cave in a fairy tale. 'Since the beginning of African culture, anyone that wears it will be honoured,' declared Onome, the gentle custodian of the coral. 'In Africa, we believe it is more precious than gold but, in this market, I have realised that lots of other people are in love with it too.' Standing proud, Onome, who is a celebrant in her own tribe, gestured to the coral that surrounded her, feeling its benign presence. 'It's my mother's business,' she continued fondly, 'but when she died ten years ago I couldn't let the business die too.' And today the business is lively, since Onome's nine children work in the shop (two were adopted after her sister's death) and, as we spoke, happy little children ran around our legs, playing with strings of coral beads they were threading. 'It really is lovely to look at – sometimes when I put my hand on a bead, it tells me what to do, how to make the necklace,' Onome admitted, clasping a string of coral in her hand. 'And the children are very good at the beads too – it's in the family.'

Speaking with the wax sellers of Wentworth Street, who taught me the Yoruba concept of 'Aso-Ebi' – using coordinated textiles at a social gathering to express the interrelationships of all the people there – I realised that these small shops contain an entire cultural universe with its own sophisticated language spoken in the vocabulary of textiles. Fashion exists here but, more than this, each decision taken, in both the choice and the combination of fabrics, makes a personal statement which gives every single outfit a vibrant poetry all of its own.

PAUL GARDNER'S COLLECTION

Past Life

I WENT BACK to Paul Gardner's shop at 149 Commercial Street to photograph some of the unique collection of artefacts that have accumulated there since his great-grandfather James Gardner first opened in 1870, trading as a scale maker. We took down some things from the walls and photographed them on the floor, we arranged other items on the worn counter-top and I stood upon Paul's chair to take my pictures.

Coming upon Paul's collection in a museum would be intriguing but not surprising. In a museum these artefacts would be removed from life and arranged. But the only arrangement you see here was created for these photos. Discovering these items still in the workplace where they belong is

enthralling in a different way. In Paul's shop they retain their full functional quality as objects that were once in use, now acquiring meaning as the relics of the three antecedents who pursued the same trade in this place where Paul works today. Quite simply, these are the things that Paul's predecessors James, Bertie and Roy left behind, and their presence lingers in these everyday possessions as the evidence of their working lives and as evocations of the world they knew. Today, Paul is his forebears' unselfconscious living representative and the custodian of their stuff. I do not imagine he thinks twice about his wooden coin tray, worn by four generations of use, unless someone points it out to him. And there is something profoundly beautiful about this.

You will recognise the style of the price labels from the one which Paul was holding up in my earlier portrait of him. I love the varieties and descriptions of apples and pears specified here, Comice, ripe Williams, Dunn's Seedlings, choice Worcesters and

Ellison Orange – names as lyrical as a Betjeman verse. Equally, there is a powerful magic to the simple phrase 'morning gathered' that fills my mind with images of dawn in the orchards, though I do wonder what kind of world it was that could be enticed by the pale allure of 'Worthing grown'.

Most fascinating to me was the daybook begun by James Gardner on 1 January 1892 with some bold calligraphic flourishes. We all recognise that auspicious sense of possibility when you write your name to inaugurate a new book, revealing the future as a sequence of blank pages, ripe with potential. James used this sturdy book with fine marbled endpapers to record all the different East End greengrocers where he serviced the scales on a regular basis. James's elegant italic hand can readily be deciphered to read many familiar addresses in Spitalfields. It is remarkable that he could maintain such poised handwriting when you consider how many customers he visited in a single day, though as business increased through the life of this ledger, his handwriting does become hastier and more excited.

There was so much more I could have shown you – the family Bible, 'Won by the Bugler James Gardner of the 1st Tower Hamlets Rifle Brigade for shooting. Presented by Lady Jane Taylor, December 21st 1882', with the entire family tree over five generations (revealing James's year of birth as 1847 and his birthplace as Thaxted in Essex), the catalogues of scales, the insurance certificates, various family military cards from the different wars, and the modern receipt books with their blue carbon pages that end in 1968 on the day Paul's father, Roy Gardner, died – all the pamphlets and pieces of paper that add up to four generations of trading for Gardners'.

As you know, Paul Gardner's business has been under threat, as the landlord sought to raise his annual rent from 15,000 to 25,000 pounds. For a business with a small turnover, it was an untenable increase. Meanwhile, hundreds of the smallest businesses and market traders, who are the basis of the economy in east London, rely upon Paul – because no one else is prepared to sell such small quantities of bags at a time. However, I am relieved to report that he renegotiated the increase and I hope that in future the managing agents recognise their wider social responsibility to the neighbourhood in their handling of Gardner's, because I am sure they would not wish to become responsible for sending Spitalfields' oldest family business to the wall.

I never want to see Paul Gardner's collection in a museum. I want to see it stay where it belongs, in his shop, scattered among all the different stacks of coloured paper bags and hidden among the tapes and tags, to be discovered on shelves and racks behind the handsome green façade of this celebrated business in Commercial Street.

ALBERT STRATTON

PIGEON FLYER

Animal Life, Human Life

WITH THE PIGEON RACING SEASON commencing shortly I took the opportunity of
an introduction to the sport kindly extended to me by Albert Stratton, secretary
and clock setter of the Kingsland District
Homing Society, which has been established
for over a century. I was delighted to find
Albert in the garden of his house beside
Weavers' Fields in Bethnal Green, where he
has two sheds filled with pigeons, and learn

that the venerable East End culture of
keeping homing pigeons survives, nurtured
by a small group of flyers.

Albert is a powerfully built man who
becomes lyrical when talking about these
familiar birds that are as mysterious as
they are mundane. Commonly considered
pests, pigeons are so ubiquitous as to be
almost invisible, yet if they were rare maybe
we would prize them for their fine plumage
and astounding navigational abilities – just
as Albert does.

'When I was fourteen, growing up in
Shoreditch, I was walking through the flats
one day and there was a pigeon on the floor,
as skinny as you can get. He had a ring
round his foot, so I took him home and my
dad said, "It's a racing pigeon. You've got
to let it go because it belongs to someone."
Then we found it couldn't fly, so he said,
"We'll keep it on the balcony and build it
up until it can fly." But when we did let it go,
it flew up in the air and back into the box –
and after that I became fascinated with
pigeons and how they will stay with you.

'We moved to the Delta Estate and had a
flat on the top floor with a big balcony, and
when I found four Tippler pigeons (which
are fancy pigeons, not racers) abandoned,

I took them home and kept them on the balcony in crates with wire netting on the front. I used to let them go out and fly, and they'd come back. Then, when we bought the house in Bethnal Green, we decided to keep racing pigeons. We built two sheds and had six babies delivered by courier from the Massarella stud in Leicester.

'In 1983 I joined the Kingsland District Homing Society and my first year's racing with them was 1985. I won fourth place in the club, which gets you into the prize money. And you think to yourself, anyone can do this – but you find out later, it's hard. You've got to keep your pigeons healthy and fit – spot on. Sick pigeons can't race. You've got to train them to build up the muscle and the fitness. Pigeon racing is like horse racing – the money is in the breeding, not the racing. You pay to breed from the winners. Studs buy up the winning pigeons and then sell off their young ones.

'We start the season in April at Peterborough. From there to my house is seventy-one and a half miles. After that first race, we carry on in stages of thirty miles between each race point, moving up the country. Newark at 112½ miles is the second race point, and after fifteen weeks we end up in Thurso at 507 miles north of here.

'Before the race, we all go round to the club headquarters in Mr Hamilton's garden, where we mark each pigeon with a numbered rubber band. Then we synchronise our clocks. Once the pigeon arrives home, you take the number off the leg and put it in the clock, which stops the timer. The timing runs from the moment when the pigeons are liberated.

'Pigeons fly at fifty miles per hour with no wind. So, if they are liberating the pigeons at nine o'clock in Peterborough, you check the weather and, if the wind forecast is thirty-five miles per hour from the north, then you estimate it should take approximately two hours, which means the pigeons will arrive in Bethnal Green at eleven. Once you've worked out a time of arrival, you are waiting for them. I've stood at the back door looking to the north and everything that moves in the sky you go, "Come on, come on!" – if it's yours or not. You look at your watch and then back at the sky.

'There's nothing better than seeing one of your birds come out of the sky, when it folds to make itself small to become as fast as possible, because it wants to get home. As soon as it arrives, you go in the garden with peanuts to get his attention, so you can get the rubber band off and put it in the clock.

'Then you go round to the club, where the rubber bands are collected and all the clocks are struck off against the master timer to confirm they are all the same. We know the exact time they left and the exact time they arrived, so we divide the distance by the time to get velocity and the bird that has the greatest velocity wins. We record our first ten birds, which means everyone gets their name published in *The Racing Pigeon*, which covers all the East End clubs.'

I followed Albert into the shed while he cleaned out the shelves and tenderly checked on those birds hatching eggs or nursing chicks, even holding up a tiny blind newborn chick in his large hand to show me, replacing it gently under its mother's breast before it got cold, and then chasing the other pigeons outside to get some exercise.

When Albert joined the Kingsland club in 1983 there were thirty members but now there are eight. The others have died or moved east towards Clacton, Albert says, and Kingsland itself is the only club left in Hackney, where there were once four or five. Today there is one in Stepney Green and another in Wood Green, which is distinguished by its multiracialism. 'Polish people might be the lifeblood needed to save pigeon racing in this country,' commented Albert absent-mindedly from within the shadows of the pigeon shed. 'If people don't mix there'll be no peace in this world.'

It is remarkable how these modest birds can navigate over great distances, and I was touched to observe the passion they draw from Albert whenever the miracle is repeated, each time they fly home to him. Through pigeons, Albert in his small garden

in Bethnal Green is connected to the wide landscape that the pigeons traverse, and through pigeons Albert is also connected to the intense social life of the Federation of Racing Clubs, where the average for every pigeon accumulates through the season and the prize-winning bird can deliver a substantial reward.

While we were talking in the living room, our conversation was interrupted when we saw a cat appear on the roof of the pigeon shed and Albert rolled his eyes. 'Look at that creature! Where's my rifle?' he growled.

THE WIDOW'S BUNS AT BOW

Culinary Life, Spiritual Life

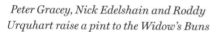

Peter Gracey, Nick Edelshain and Roddy
Urquhart raise a pint to the Widow's Buns

ON GOOD FRIDAY, what could be more appropriate to the equivocal nature of the day than an event which involves both celebration of hot cross buns and remembrance of the departed in a single custom? Such an event is the ceremony of the Widow's Buns at Bow.

A net of hot cross buns hangs above the bar at the Widow's Son in Bow, and each year a sailor comes to add another bun to the collection. Though before you make any assumption based on your knowledge of my passion for buns, I must clarify that no hot cross buns are eaten in the ceremony, they are purely for symbolic purposes. Left to dry out and gather dust and hang in the net for eternity, London's oldest buns exist as metaphors to represent the passing years and as talismans to bring good luck, but, more than this, they tell a story.

The Widow's Son was built in 1848 on the former site of an old widow's cottage, so the tale goes. When her only son left to be a sailor, she promised to bake him a hot cross bun and keep it for his return. But although he drowned at sea, the widow refused to give up hope, preserving the bun and making a fresh one each year to add to the collection. This annual tradition has been continued in the pub as a remembrance of the widow and her son, and of the bond between all those on land and sea, with sailors of the Royal Navy coming to place the bun in the net every year.

Behind this custom lies the belief that hot cross buns baked on Good Friday will never decay, reflected in the tradition of nailing a hot cross bun to the wall so that the cross may bring good luck to the household – though what appeals to me about the story of the widow is the notion of baking as an act of faith, incarnating a mother's hope that her son lives. I interpret the widow's persistence in making the bun each year as a gesture, not of self-deception but of longing for wish-fulfilment, manifesting her love for her son.

When I arrived at the Widow's Son, I had the good fortune to meet Frederick Beckett who first came here for the ceremony in 1958 when his brother Alan placed the Hot Cross Bun in the net, and he had the treasured photo in his hand to show me. Frederick moved out from Bow to Dagenham fifteen years ago, but he still comes back each year to visit the Widow's Son, one of many in this community and further afield who delight to converge here on Good Friday for old times' sake. Already, there was a tangible sense of anticipation, with spirits uplifted by the sunshine and the flags hung outside, ready to celebrate St George's Day.

The landlady, Kathy, proudly showed me the handsome fresh hot cross bun, baked by Mr Bunn of Mr Bunn's Bakery in Chadwell Heath, who always makes the special bun each year – 'Fabulous buns!' she declared, almost succumbing to a swoon as she held up her newest sweetest darling, which would shortly join its fellows in the net over the bar. There were many more ancient buns, she explained, until a fire destroyed most of them fifteen years ago, and the burnt ones in the net today are merely those few that were salvaged by the firemen from the wreckage of the pub. Remarkably, having opened their hearts to the emotional poetry of hot cross buns, at the Widow's Son they even cherish those cinders which the rest of the world would consign to a bin.

The effect of the beer and the unseasonal warm weather upon a pub full of sailors and thirsty locals rapidly induced an atmosphere of collective euphoria, heightened by a soundtrack of pounding rock, and, in the thick of it, I was delighted to meet my pal Lenny Hamilton, the jewel thief. 'I'm not here for the buns, I'm here for the bums!' he confided to me with a sip of his Courvoisier and lemonade, making a lewd gesture and breaking into a wide grin of salacious enjoyment as various Bow belles in off-

the-shoulder dresses, with flowing locks and wearing festive corsages, came over enthusiastically to shower this legendary rascal with kisses.

I stood beside Lenny as three o'clock approached, enjoying the high-spirited gathering as the sailors came together in front of the bar. The landlord handed over the hot cross bun to widespread applause and the sailors lifted up their smallest recruit. Then, with a mighty cheer from the crowd and multiple camera flashes, the recruit placed the bun in the net. Once this heroic task was accomplished, and the landlady had removed the tinfoil covers from the dishes of food laid out on the billiard table, all the elements were in place for a knees-up to last the rest of the day. As they like to say in Bow, 'Another year, another Good Friday, another bun.'

THE RETURN OF AUBREY SILKOFF

Human Life, Past Life, Street Life

TODAY AUBREY SILKOFF returned to Navarre Street, Arnold Circus, to see the brick where he incised his name on 19 April 1950, when he was eleven years old – it is just to the left of his upper arm in the photograph. When I first spoke with Aubrey over the phone, he admitted that he had no memory of carving it, although he con-firmed that he grew up here in Laleham Buildings on the Boundary Estate and Navarre Street was where he played football as a child.

Fortunately for us, 1950 was also the year of the photo craze, when Aubrey and his pals acquired cameras and were able to develop their pictures at the Cambridge and Bethnal Green Boys' Club in Chance Street. As a consequence, we have a photographic record to show a few of the children who wrote their names on the wall of Wargrave Buildings at that time, capturing the spirit and energy of a fleeting moment, and allowing us to put faces to the names incised on the bricks – those who created graffiti of such unlikely longevity.

As we walked down Navarre Street together, I had the strange experience of introducing Aubrey to his long-forgotten graffiti. 'It was something to do while we talked,' said Aubrey, explaining that he and his pals used nails from the wooden scooters they constructed to roam as far as the bombsites in the City and around St Paul's. Yet although Aubrey recognised a few names when he saw them on the wall, together we confronted the limit of his fragmentary memory after so many years. 'I wonder what life held for them?' he said quietly, contemplating the names on the wall, as we stood in the empty street lined with parked cars that once echoed to the noise and shouting of children playing.

'The streets were clear of vehicles, except maybe the odd coal wagon or a fruiterer with a horse and cart. There were few cars because no one could afford one and, if someone bought one, they took all the kids for a ride in it as a novelty,' Aubrey told me, explaining how, as children, they had possession of the streets for their playground, using cans, or laying down jumpers or coats in the road, to create goalposts.

'We were a group of kids that used to know each other and spend all our time to-

gether in the streets because the flats were not conducive to playing in. There was no space for us inside, so we used to be outside, swinging on the railings at the corner of Navarre Street and Arnold Circus. We didn't know anything about girls. The boys had nothing to do with girls. Half the kids were Jewish, but there was no conscious decision to mix with your own kind, although I think we gravitated together because we considered ourselves outsiders. Many kids had lost their fathers in the war and they had background problems.

'You didn't know that you didn't have much money, because it was just not to be found. I had new clothes once a year. I used to have a new suit at Passover. My mother took me down to a place off Brick Lane. There were *schleppers* everywhere on the street – touts for tailors. I remember going back for fittings. There wasn't much ready-made clothing available then. I was ashamed of my parents because I was born late and I thought they were old. On the day of the VE celebrations we came down into the yard with our food on plates and our chipped enamel cups – we didn't have china.

And when the people saw them, they asked in disapproval, "Can we replace them?" That was embarrassing.

'I took the eleven-plus exam, which decided whether I would go to grammar school or secondary modern, which was inferior. I don't know what happened but I never passed or failed, I went to a central school instead. At the end of term we were called on to the stage and divided up between which schools we were going to. I cried because I didn't go to grammar school. It was cruel, because it split friendships up. "What are you doing today? We're doing Latin and logarithmic equations," they said, and I felt a failure because I didn't do any of those things.

'Nothing has been easy for me. Exams were always hard. But I was never at the bottom and never excelled either, I was always in the heap. I was fortunate that in those post-war years there were expanding opportunities open to me, giving me an education and a career, because I had no ambition – I never looked further than my nose. Though I knew I wanted to get out of the East End, because I did not want to work in a tailoring sweatshop as my father and all his friends did. As a greeting, they always asked each other, "Are you working?", because the work was seasonal and people were out of work for long periods of time.

'In 1958 I moved out to a bedsitter in Stoke Newington on my own. I learned to

to buy a ticket but the kiosk person said, "You haven't got enough," so this couple behind me in the queue said, "Do you really want to see it?" and they bought me a ticket. That was *La Bohème* – I wish I could repay that couple today.'

Contemplating the photo of himself at eleven, a crucial moment in his childhood, Aubrey pointed out the spilt food on the 'scruffy' jacket and interpreted his expression as 'sardonic', while I saw self-possession and humour in his youthful visage. 'I'm thinking "Why am I here?"' he said, rolling his eyes with a droll grin. 'Now I look at all these photographs and I wonder, "Did it actually happen?"' he continued, thinking out loud. When he returned to Arnold Circus, he encountered the evidence that it did happen, because sixty years later Aubrey found his name graven into the wall on Navarre Street – 'A Silkoff Wed 19 April 1950'.

look out for myself and be wary of what people are trying to put over you, and as a consequence I've been known as a cynical person throughout my life. But I have no regrets about any of it today, because it gave me a sense of looking at the glass as half empty. I never expected anything wonderful to happen and it has. I have progressed over the years and I feel very lucky indeed.

'I was interested in classical music from a very early age. One day I went over to Sadler's Wells Theatre and offered money

COLUMBIA ROAD MARKET IV

Market Life, Plant Life

I BOUGHT THREE BUNCHES of heavily scented narcissi from Lisa Burridge at Columbia Road for just two pounds. Possessing a pungent musky fragrance that fills my living room and perfectly complements the first flawless blue skies over the East End, they are just one of the many subtly different varieties of English daffodils and narcissi from Spalding Market that Lisa has on sale now, at the peak of the season for spring flowers.

Waking early to sunlight, I am tempted to lie in bed all morning, watching the nesting birds coming and going from the birdhouse outside my bedroom window, but it is a pleasure to rise when the sun offers such promise, and take a stroll up to Columbia Road to visit Lisa Burridge at her stall and

return with an armful of spring flowers for the exchange of a few pounds. With her brightness of manner and sassy hoop earrings, Lisa brings a touch of feminine glamour to the market, and it is always a pleasant diversion to stop by for a chat interspersed by eager customers arriving to carry off flowers in delight. Lisa married into the Burridges – the family that over more than three generations has become such an integral part of the history of this market.

'I started working here for my father-in-law, Herbie Burridge, when I was eighteen, twenty-four years ago,' Lisa confided to me proudly. 'And my kids usually help out, only one's got a driving lesson and the other has a throat infection,' she added with a philosophical smirk, explaining, 'I take care of my family all week and work here on Sunday, and sometimes in the market at Waltham Abbey on Saturday.'

Lisa runs the cut-flower stall on one of the long-established Burridge family pitches for her husband, Pete, while he manages the nursery in Hoddesdon with his brother, dealing in plants that are sold on another pitch. 'It used to be forty stalls out of fifty-two here were Burridges once upon a time, Herbie told me,' commented Lisa in wonder. 'More like twenty-one out of fifty-two,' qualified Pete, with a good-natured shrug, making a more conservative estimate as he arrived to join the conversation – still quite an extraordinary proportion for one family in a market. 'The old man liked to tell a tale,' admitted Lisa to me, flashing an indulgent smile, before she turned back to serve the next customer, reaching for yet another handful of the scented spring flowers that surrounded her in a bower of pale yellow.

AT THE TWEED CYCLE RUN

Street Life

ON A DAY when the light was as you thought only existed in a landscape painting by Gainsborough, 500 dapper gallants on bicycles, dressed up to the nines in tweeds and other fancy gear, set out from St Paul's Cathedral at midday to flaunt their finery in the face of the metropolis's populace. And to see this vast current of stylish cyclists go forth from the great cathedral – launching themselves with a cheer down Ludgate Hill on a flawless spring day – was a joyous spectacle, guaranteed to melt the heart of any foolish misanthrope in a flash.

I never saw so much tweed gathered together in one place as I saw that morning beneath the gleaming dome towering overhead. There were so many plus-fours and suits and jackets and trews and caps and waistcoats and ties that I thought my vision was going awry for all the herringbone pattern crossing my retina. Yet everyone wore tweed differently and everyone had dressed to look their very best, expressive of their relish at being among the first 500 who managed to obtain one of the coveted tickets. The gentlemen had waxed their moustaches and the ladies had primped their perms. Groomed and shining, all were raring to leap astride their mounts and take the city by storm, riding vintage bicycles, penny-farthings and tricycles and tandems and boneshakers. There was even a piano-bicycle with a pianist who kept on pedalling even as he played the keys.

No wonder the magnificent Tweed Run is already a global phenomenon. Beginning with 160 cyclists arrayed in tweed for a turn around London in January 2009, it has now inspired copycat events in sixteen other cities across the world, including New York, Paris, Sydney and Tokyo. The notion of enthusiasts for traditional cycling attire banding together for a beano, enjoying a high old time, lifting the spirits of a city and raising money for bikes for Africa is elegant in its simplicity. The Tweed Run is one of the things we can be proud of giving to the world.

The traffic ground to a halt – horns honked and 500 cycle bells tinkled – and drivers leaned from their windows to gawp in awestruck delight as, like salmon coursing through a great river, the playful cyclists of the Tweed Run teemed through the city streets, spreading innocent amazement, causing pedestrians to stop in wonder and break into laughter at this bizarre event.

Across Westminster Bridge they pedalled, over to the Palace then down the Mall, around Trafalgar Square and up Regent Street – where Saturday shoppers broke into cheers and applause – before veering east to arrive at Lincoln's Inn Fields at two for tea. Remarkably for such a warm day and the ubiquity of tweed, there were few who displayed visible perspiration or reddening of the face, although the queue for a cuppa stretched halfway to the Old Cheshire Cheese and the lawn was littered with those grateful to recline upon the soft green grass in the shade of the heavy blossom and freshly unfurled leaves overhead. Music from the bandstand drifted gently among the trees as photographers took advantage of this colourful *fête champêtre*, while the tweedy cyclists, having become a tribe now, turned gregarious, and since they no longer required any introduction to one another, a spontaneous sense of communal goodwill arose which overflowed the park.

From here, as the afternoon shadows lengthened, it was a straight home run eastward down the Clerkenwell Road to arrive at the Bethnal Green Working Men's Social Club, completing the day's modest ten-mile jaunt. There were singing and tap-dancing, and a lively trade in pints at the bar as parched cyclists quenched their thirst, and

the party soon spilled out on to the green, where new friends swapped contacts as the time for farewells drew near. Lingering late and reluctantly leaving – it was a day of beautiful hullabaloo, already containing the anticipation of fond memories to come.

Later, I realised how rare it was to see so many people relaxed and happy in public, and inhabiting the city streets as if they owned them – which, in fact, we all do. The day was a celebration of our great city, which offers an unsurpassed backdrop to life, and the day was a celebration of native idiosyncrasy and our culture, which delights in imaginative individuality of all kinds, and the day was a celebration of dressing up and having fun, and the day was a celebration of moustaches, and the day was a celebration of cycling, and, naturally, the day was a celebration of tweed – because, in case you did not know it, tweed is sexy again.

FERGUS HENDERSON

BOOKWORM

Culinary Life, Human Life, Literary Life

ALTHOUGH FERGUS HENDERSON is widely celebrated as the presiding spirit and co-founder of St John, the Smithfield restaurant, his literary tendencies are less commonly known. And so, desirous of learning more, I dropped by the restaurant one bright morning, with my City of London library card in hand, to enjoy a steadying glass of Fernet Branca with Fergus and discover how it is that certain books have become the means by which he communicates the ethos of this unique culinary enterprise to his staff. Still windswept and tanned from a recent holiday on the Isle of Tiree, Fergus arrived glowing with all the enthusiasm and energy of a schoolboy returning from summer camp. 'Sometimes I feel that I am not the most clear of chaps,' he confessed to me with a tender grimace – as we each knocked back the bitter liqueur laced with rhubarb and saffron yet possessing an aroma of frankincense and myrrh – adding plainly, 'so I amassed this collection of books to explain.

'It was when I first handed the reins to another chef, Ed Lewis, that I needed some means to convey the essence,' continued Fergus mysteriously. 'I chose *Master and Commander* by Patrick O'Brian, because I think of the kitchen as very much like an eighteenth-century man o' war – a confined space. As chef you have to be everybody's friend, but you must be in charge, so you need to keep yourself at a distance too. My march up and down between the fridges in the kitchen, there's some similarity there with the captain's march up and down the deck, I think,' he said, adopting an unconvincing comic frown of fierce authority as his attempt at a captain of an eighteenth-century man o' war. 'I have given this book to every head chef and sous-chef,' he explained, before raising his eyebrows with a self-deprecatory smile, changing tone as a thought occurred to him. 'Maybe I should ask if they read it?'

His second choice appeared more esoteric, though I quickly became aware of a theme emerging. Fergus chose L. T. C. Rolt's 1957 biography of Isambard Kingdom Brunel, a subjective portrait of the engineer, tracing his triumphs and tribulations to create a narrative that reads like a novel. 'Unlike recent biographies that have been critical, Rolt just loves Brunel and so I love him too. What's so brilliant about Brunel is that he builds the Great Western Railway, which is a feat in its own right, gets to Bristol, notices the Atlantic and says we'll build the SS *Great Britain* and go across it – What a guy!' said Fergus, with an admiring grin, making a lateral connection to St John's next step beyond the restaurant, the hotel in Leicester Square. 'With the hotel, we thought, "We've fed them, now we'll bed them." Not quite as ambitious as spanning the Atlantic but in his spirit,' he outlined with a deferential shrug. I knew that Fergus himself trained as an architect, so it seemed the appropriate moment to ask if he designed his restaurants. 'I am to blame for most of it,' he admitted, drawing a long face of self-parody and casting his eyes around the cavernous white interior.

As we arrived at Fergus's third title, Thomas Blythe, the general manager, walked in, assuming a slow grin when he overheard the subject of our conversation – because he is himself a recipient of these books, and he knew what was coming next, Ian Fleming's *The Man with the Golden Gun*. 'I chose it because I thought Bond and Scaramanga ate whole crabs together and drank pink champagne,' revealed Fergus wistfully, before Thomas confirmed, 'I read the book and it doesn't exist, it wasn't there at all.' They both exchanged a glance of crazy humour. 'That's why we always serve whole crabs on the menu here,' continued Fergus with supreme logic. 'It's a sad story, but Thomas enjoyed the book – who wouldn't enjoy it?' Then they looked at me and smiled in solidarity, like brothers.

This obscure paradox was the ideal introduction to Fergus's fourth title, John Berger's *Ways of Seeing*. 'What I took from this book was the importance of *genius loci*, the sense of place,' admitted Fergus. 'Restaurants are places rich in *genius loci*. There is this chaos that happens twice a day, extraordinarily different people coming together. Also, Berger discusses Leonardo's cartoon that no one was interested to look at until an American offers to buy it for a million dollars and then a line forms. Restaurants can be a good example of this phenomenon too.'

I took this as a cue to probe Fergus about the origin of St John, which has led the renaissance in British cooking in recent years, and is now integral to the identity of both Smithfield and Spitalfields. Explaining that Dickens was appalled by the variety of offal eaten in Spitalfields when he visited in 1851 and that Joan Rose remembers poor people eating a pig's head when they could not afford a Sunday roast in the 1930s, I asked him about his relationship to the food of the past. 'Dickens was narrow-minded and pig's head is delicious!' he retorted with unexpected fervour, eyes sparkling through his horn-rimmed spectacles as he declared his personal manifesto. 'Food is permanent, while fashion just changes, but what was good then is good now. I'm not interested in historical recreations. I am a modernist through and through, yet a pickled walnut is something that has been around for ever and is still a thing of joy. I think of our food as permanent British. Nose-to-tail eating is because it's polite. It is not because of thrift, it's simply because it is delicious.'

So now I hope I understood something. Many of the elements I recognise at St John are present in these books – the acute drama of collective enterprise, the particular glamour of dining incarnated by Bond, and the unadorned presentation of good food that resists fashionable categorisation. A sensibility is at work here that is a synthesis of these literary works, serious yet with levity, and it adds up to the unique quality of tone that characterises St John – which all makes complete sense for a distinctively British restaurant because we are a nation of writers.

TAJ STORES, THEN AND NOW

Human Life, Past Life

THE GENTLEMAN on the right is Abdul Khalique, standing with his shop assistant in the early 1950s outside the very first Taj Stores in Hunton Street, (now Buxton Street, where Allen Gardens is today). Abdul Khalique's brother Abdul Jabbar, the founder of the grocery store, commonly known then as 'Jabber's Shop', was a seaman who came from Bengal (as it was called at that time) to Spitalfields in 1934 after leaving the navy. He worked in textile sweatshops for two years before opening

his store, which he ran with his Irish wife, Cathleen.

These sparse facts, which I learned from Abdul Jabbar's nephew Jamal (who never met his uncle), are all that is known of this brave man who travelled across the world and undertook the risky venture of starting a business in another continent, working hard to build it up until his death in 1969. I think he would be quite amazed to visit the Taj Stores today in Brick Lane and see how his enterprise has blossomed.

I enjoyed a tour of the aisles recently in the company of Jamal (Abdul Quayum), who has been involved in the family business since he was seventeen years old, and now runs the store jointly with his elder brother, Junel (Abdul Hai), and younger brother, Joynal (Abdul Muhith). It is a wonderful experience simply to explore here and savour the rich selection of produce on offer from all over the world in the Taj Stores. I love to study the beautifully organised displays of exotic fruit and vegetables, printed sacks of rice, tall stacks of brightly coloured cardboard packages, cans, bottles and jars – each with their distinctive fragrances. Then there is the cooking equipment, towers of plastic jugs and bowls, steel pots and pans, and scourers. It is a phenomenal feat of organisation that the brothers have pulled off, bringing this huge range of supplies together from the different corners of the globe.

Jamal explained to me how the business is run nowadays between the three brothers. Jamal does the hiring and the paperwork, while Joynal takes care of the day-to-day

buying and selling, and Junel runs the catering supply and wholesale side of the business. 'The beauty of it is we have different responsibilities. We are a modern Muslim family and we treat each other like friends,' says Jamal proudly.

Their father, Alhaj Abdul Khalique, first came to the United Kingdom in 1952 as a student, before becoming involved in running the business with his brother. In 1956 the grocery shop moved to larger premises at 109 Brick Lane (opposite where the Brick Lane Bookshop is now), and then, when Abdul Jabbar died in 1969, Abdul Khalique ran it with his brother Abdul Rahman. The pair are seen here looking every bit the sharp businessmen they were, in this handsome studio portrait taken at that time.

As the Taj Stores prospered, they moved again in the 80s to the current site at 112 Brick Lane and an era ended in 1994, when Abdul Khalique died. Then the family business passed from the brothers who had emigrated to this country into the stewardship of the current generation who were born here.

In recent years the stores have continued to expand with the purchase of the premises next door and the launch of the online business. When I took my portrait of Joynal, Junel and Jamal, the brothers explained to me that they now look back to their roots and, in the tradition of nineteenth-century

businessmen turned benefactors, they are funding a school and a mosque, building social housing and investing in irrigation and two cancer clinics back in Moulvibazar, Sylhet, Bangladesh – the hometown from where Abdul Jabbar set out all those years ago when this story began.

STANLEY RONDEAU

HUGUENOT

Human Life, Past Life

IF YOU VISIT Nicholas Hawksmoor's Christ Church, Spitalfields, on any given Tuesday, you will find Stanley Rondeau – where he works as a volunteer, one day each week, welcoming visitors and handing out guides to the building. The architecture is of such magnificence, arresting your attention, that you might not even notice this quietly spoken white-haired gentleman sit-

ting behind a small table just to the right of the entrance, who comes here weekly on the train from Enfield. But if you are interested in local history, then Stanley is one of the most remarkable people you could hope to meet, because his great-great-great-great-great-great-grandfather Jean Rondeau was a Huguenot immigrant who came to Spitalfields in 1685.

never lived here, I feel I am so much part of the area.'

Jean Rondeau was a serge weaver born in 1666 in Paris into a family that had been involved in weaving for three generations. Escaping persecution for his Protestant faith, he came to London and settled in Brick Lane, fathering twelve children. Jean had such success as a weaver in London that in 1723 he built a fine house, 4 Wilkes Street, in the style that remains familiar to this day in Spitalfields. It is a measure of Jean's integration into British society that his name is to be discovered on a document of 1728 ensuring the building of Christ Church, alongside that of Edward Peck, who laid the foundation stone. Peck is commemorated today by the elaborate marble monument next to the altar, where I took Stanley's portrait.

'When visiting a friend in Suffolk in 1980, I was introduced to the local vicar, who became curious about my name and asked me, "Are you a Huguenot?"' explained Stanley with a quizzical grin. 'I didn't even know what he meant,' he added, revealing the origin of his life-changing discovery. 'So I went to Workers' Educational Association evening classes in genealogy and that was how it started. I've been at it now for thirty years. My own family history came first, but when I learned that Jean Rondeau's son John Rondeau was Sexton of Christ Church, I got involved in Spitalfields. And now I come every Tuesday and I like being here in the same building where he was. They refer to me as "a piece of living history", which is what I am really. Although I have

Jean's son John Rondeau was a master silk weaver and in 1741 he commissioned textile designs from Anna Maria Garthwaite, the most famous designer of Spitalfields silks, who lived at the corner of Princelet Street, adjoining Wilkes Street. As a measure of John's status, in 1745 he sent forty-seven of his employees to join the fight against Bonnie Prince Charlie. Appointed Sexton of the church in 1761 until his death in 1790, when he was buried in the crypt in a lead coffin labelled 'John Rondeau, Sexton of this Parish', his remains were exhumed at the end of the twentieth century and transported to the Natural History Museum for study.

'Once I found that the crypt was cleared, I made an appointment at the Natural

History Museum, where Dr Theya Molleson showed John's bones to me,' admitted Stanley, widening his eyes in wonder. 'She told me he was eighty-five, a big fellow – a bit on the chubby side, yet with no curvature of the spine, which meant he stood upright. It was strange to be able to hold his bones, because I know so much about his history.' Stanley spoke in a whisper of amazement, as we sat together, alone in the vast empty church that would have been equally familiar to John the Sexton.

In 1936 a carpenter removing a window-sill from an old warehouse in Cutler Street that was being refurbished was surprised when a scrap of paper fell out. Once unfolded, this long strip was revealed to be a ballad in support of the weavers, demanding an act of Parliament to prevent the cheap imports that were destroying their industry. It was written by James Rondeau, the grandson of John the Sexton, who was recorded in directories as doing business in Cutler Street between 1809 and 1816. Bringing us two generations closer to the present day, James Rondeau, author of the ballad, was Stanley's great-great-great-grandfather. It was three generations later, in 1882, that Stanley's grandfather left Sclater Street and the East End for good, moving to Edmonton when the railway opened. And subsequently Stanley grew up without any knowledge of Huguenots or the Spitalfields connection, until that chance meeting in 1980 led to the discovery that he is an eighth-generation British Huguenot.

'When I retired twelve years ago, it gave me a new purpose,' said Stanley, cradling the slender pamphlet he has written entitled 'The Rondeaus of Spitalfields'. 'It's a story that must not be forgotten because we were the originals, the first wave of immigrants that came to Spitalfields,' he declared. Turning the pages slowly, as he contemplated the sense of connection that the discovery of his ancestry has given him, he admitted, 'It has made a big difference to my life, and when I walk around in Christ Church today I can imagine my ancestor John the Sexton walking about in here, and his father, Jean, who built the house in Wilkes Street. I can see the same things he did, and when I am able to hear the great eighteenth-century organ, once it is restored, I can know that my ancestor played it and heard the same sound.'

There is no such thing as an old family, just those whose histories are recorded. We all have ancestors – although few of us know who they were, or have undertaken the years of research Stanley Rondeau has done, bringing him into such vivid relationship with his forebears. It has granted him an enviably broad sense of perspective, seeing himself against a wider timescale than his own life. History has become personal for Stanley Rondeau in Spitalfields.

TUBBY ISAAC'S JELLIED EEL STALL, ALDGATE

Culinary Life, Street Life

AT THE FURTHEST EXTENT of Spital-fields, where it meets Aldgate, is Tubby Isaac's Jellied Eel Stall, run today by Paul Simpson, the fourth generation in this cele-brated business founded in 1919, still selling the fresh seafood that was once the staple diet in this neighbourhood. Here, where the traffic thunders down Aldgate High Street, tucked round the corner of Goulston Street, Tubby Isaac's stall shelters from the hurly-burly. And one morning this week, Paul told me the story of his world-famous stall as he set up for the day, while I savoured the salty-sweet seaweed scent of the seafood, and eager customers arrived to eat that famous East End delicacy, jellied eels for breakfast.

'I'll be the last one ever to do this,' Paul confessed to me with pride tinged by melan-choly, as he pulled a huge bowl of eels from the fridge. 'My father, Ted Simpson, had the business before me. He got it from his uncle Solly, who took over from Tubby Isaac, who opened the first stall in 1919. Isaac ran it until 1939, when he got a whiff of another war coming and emigrated to America with his boys, so they would not be conscripted – but then they got enlisted over there instead. And when Isaac left, his nephew Solly took over the business and ran it until he died in 1975. Then my dad ran it from 1975 till 1989, and I've been here ever since.

'I began working at the Walthamstow stall when I was fourteen – as a runner, cleaning, washing up, cutting bread, getting the beers, buying the coffees, collecting the bacon sandwiches and sweeping up. The business isn't what it was years ago. All the eels stalls along Roman Road and Brick

Lane – they were here for a long, long time and they've closed. It's a sign of the times,' he informed me plainly. Yet Paul Simpson is steadfast and philosophical, serving his regular customers daily and taking consolation from their devotion to his stall. In fact, 'Regular customers are my only customers,' he admitted to me with a weary smile, 'and some of them are in their eighties and nineties who used to come here with their parents!'

Understandably, Paul takes his eels very seriously. Divulging something of the magic of the preparation of this mysterious fish, he explained that when eels are boiled, the jelly exuded during the cooking sets to create a natural preservative. 'Look, it creates its own jelly!' declared Paul, holding up the huge bowl of eels to show me and letting it quiver enticingly for my pleasure. The jelly was a crucial factor before refrigeration, when a family could eat from a bowl of jellied eels and then put the dish in a cold pantry, where the jelly would reset, preserving it for the next day. Paul was insistent that he sells only top-quality eels, always fresh, never frozen, and after a lifetime on the stall, being particular about seafood is almost his religion. 'If you sell good stuff, they will come,' he reassured me, seeing that I was now anxious about the future of his stall after what he had revealed earlier.

Resuming work, removing bowls of winkles, cockles, prawns and mussels from the fridge, 'It ain't a job of enjoyment, it's a job of necessity,' protested Paul, turning morose again, sighing as he arranged oysters in a tray. 'It's what I know, it's what pays the bills,

but it ain't the kind of job you want your kids to do, when there's no reward for working your guts off.' Yet in spite of his bluster, it was apparent that Paul harbours a self-respecting sense of independence at holding out against history, after lesser eel sellers have shut up shop. 'When it turns cold, I put so many clothes on I look like the Michelin Man by the end of the day!' he boasted to me with a swagger, as if to convince me of his survival ability.

Then Jim arrived, one of Tubby Isaac's regulars, a cab driver who wolfed a dish of eels doused in vinegar and liberally sprinkled with pepper, taking a couple of lobster tails with him for a snack later. Paul brightened at once to greet Jim and they fell into

hasty familiar chit-chat, the football, the weather and the day's rounds, then Jim got back on the road before the traffic warden came along. 'It's like a pub here, the regulars come all day,' Paul confided to me with a residual smile. And I saw there was a beauty to the oasis of civility that Tubby Isaac's manifests, where old friends can return regularly over an entire lifetime, a landmark of continuity.

It is a testament to Paul Simpson's stubbornness and the quality of his fish that Tubby Isaac's is still here, now that this once densely populated former Jewish neighbourhood has emptied out and the culture of which jellied eels was a part has also vanished. Tubby Isaac's is a stubborn fragment of an earlier world, carrying the lively history of the society it once served now all the other jellied eels stalls in Aldgate are gone and the street is no longer full of people enjoying eels. But leaving all this aside, Paul is open seven days a week selling delicious and healthy non-fattening food, so please seek him out and try it for yourself.

DAVID MILNE
DENNIS SEVERS' HOUSE

Human Life, Past Life

ONCE UPON A TIME, David Milne used to arrange all the old things from his parents' house in the attic of their home to create his own world of play. Today, as curator at Dennis Severs' time-capsule house at 18 Folgate Street, it is his job to arrange things - both in the general sense of maintaining every aspect of the property and also in the specific sense of arranging all the myriad objects which fill these crowded rooms.

Yet the success of David's arrangements renders his labour invisible, since when you come upon the artefacts occupying these rooms, everything appears to have occurred

naturally in the course of the daily life of the fictional inhabitants. But very little is accidental in this house of mysteries, because everything has been arranged to tell a story, and making those arrangements is David's tour de force and his life's passion too.

'I think I have a good understanding of what the life of a servant must have been like, except I am the servant to an imaginary family,' David confided to me after years of cleaning and polishing. He widened his eyes significantly as he qualified his statement, 'though I am a very taxing master, because everything has to be right,' and underlined this with such a stern glance that I almost felt pity for him, suffering under such an exacting, scrupulous employer.

I recognised the glance from when David instructed me to hold silence when I first came to visit during a public opening. It was a look of such gravity that it ensured silence reigned throughout the property, no one daring to utter a word. Yet this hauteur only serves to emphasise the unexpected radiance of his smile when you greet him off duty, because the evocation of fantasy at 18 Folgate Street is a serious business and David understands his responsibility to set a certain tone while at work. It is an onerous duty that magistrates, members of the clergy, footmen and the guards at Buckingham Palace will recognise, and one which David has perfected to an art.

David discovered 18 Folgate Street in his early twenties when was exploring London by following the medieval street plan and he came upon Norton Folgate while walking up through Shoreditch. He peered through the latticework of the dining window and spied the baroque interior. 'Spitalfields at that time was dark and faded, as if the eighteenth-century inhabitants had simply locked their doors and gone, and because I had seen into one of the houses, my imagination created the stories in all the others,' he told me, recalling the moment with delight.

With characteristic rigour, David decided that he would never pay to visit the house, because he knew at once that his involvement had to be more than a tour. Fortuitously, years later, he was invited to a party in the East End and found himself back outside 18 Folgate Street. As he explained to me, 'I came into this house, walked up to the first floor, where Dennis Severs was sitting in the Smoking Room, holding court with his circle of friends, and I asked him, "Whose house is it?" and he said, "It's mine!" And from that moment we were friends, speaking on the telephone every day until two weeks before his death. I never came to this house to strip it down, I never asked questions, I never asked, "Why?" I just accepted it as his beautiful creation.'

David lives in a tiny modern flat built upon the roof of a Victorian stucco mansion block in Earl's Court that he has furnished with seventeenth-century furniture and lit entirely by candlelight – existing in a manner that is completely in tune with the ambience of Folgate Street. 'When you live with candlelight, you learn how to use it,' he told me. 'You don't arrange your candles evenly in the room and all at the same height, as people commonly do. You place them strategically. For example, in the kitchen here, there is a low candle on the table where the cook was studying a recipe book. I like to place things together in the manner of "still life" and I love the light of seventeenth-century paintings. You see it everywhere in this house.'

I realised how unusual it was for David to sit and talk, because his job consists primarily of housework, indicated by the long apron that is his professional uniform. All four storeys, staircases and rooms, are cleaned twice a week, the silver, brass and copper are polished every fortnight, floors and furniture are waxed annually, bed and table linen are laundered and starched regularly, and dusting is a continuous activity. Additionally, the food is prepared daily, with the master's breakfast cooked every morning, and tea and coffee freshly brewed. It takes all day, while the house is closed, to prepare it to open for visitors, and maintain its imaginary inhabitants in the style to which they have become accustomed.

David Milne's involvement in the house is personal, rooted in his friendship with Dennis Severs, which ultimately led to his lifelong commitment to the vision which the house manifests. 'I used to come and stay regularly, and Dennis and I used to play together, cooking meals and taking photographs. I spent twelve Christmases in this house. When Dennis died, I decided to step up and take on the house, because it needed people who understand it. Now I am waiting for the right person to walk through the door one day who can do my job,' said David, getting lost in thought, gazing fondly around the artfully dilapidated Dickensian attic where he stayed when he first came to visit for weekends at Dennis Severs' extraordinary house so many years ago. 'It's a story that's never-ending.'

SHAKESPEARIAN ACTORS
IN SHOREDITCH

Literary Life, Past Life

NOWADAYS, the neighbourhood is full of actors, like moths batting around a flame. Some live here, others drop by. I have only to walk out of my front door and I am tripping over Toby Stephens in Hanbury Street, Damian Lewis in Redchurch Street, Reese Witherspoon shopping in the Spitalfields Market, Gael Garcia Bernal and Eva Green lunching at St John Bread and Wine, Sienna Miller wolfing curry in Brick Lane, Ralph Fiennes reading Dostoevsky in Leila's Café, Julie Christie in Bethnal Green Tesco, Maggie Gyllenhaal in Ryantown, Gwyneth Paltrow dining at Les Trois Garçons or

Jennifer Aniston stepping into Shoreditch House.

In this respect, not much has changed since the sixteenth century, when, before the West End and before the South Bank, this was London's theatre district and most of the actors were residents. The very first playhouse, the Theatre, opened in New Inn Broadway in 1576 and then the Curtain Theatre nearby in Curtain Road in 1577. I have no doubt there were plenty who felt the neighbourhood was going downhill when these new entertainment venues opened up within a year of each other.

If you read my piece about Shakespeare in Spitalfields you will know that many of Shakespeare's plays were first performed here at the Curtain Theatre and you may recall that I came upon the tombstone of Shakespeare's younger brother, Edmund, in Southwark Cathedral last year – he was an actor at the Curtain and his young son was buried in the churchyard of St Leonard's, Shoreditch.

It surprised me, after all these years, to come upon the collecting box with the phrase 'The Actors' Church' when I visited the atmospheric unrenovated St Leonard's recently. In the sixteenth century, it was simply the parish church for local actors, but it has been entirely rebuilt since then and nowadays St Paul's, Covent Garden,

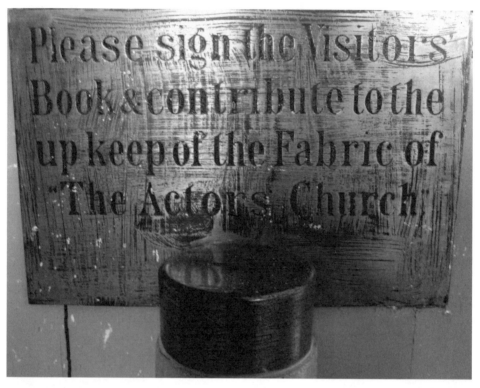

is known as 'The Actors' Church'. However, since I discovered who exactly is buried at St Leonard's, I understand why the church might wish to brag about it.

If you enter the main door of St Leonard's and turn right inside the body of the church, you can go through a pair of double doors to ascend a wide staircase which leads to a space at the top of the stairwell where you will find the monument to all the Shakespearian actors who were once residents of our neighbourhood and are interred here. It is an impressive roll call, taller than a man and graven in marble by the Shakespeare League in 1913, who, I suspect, were also responsible for the phrase on the collecting box.

Top of the list is James Burbage, who trained as a joiner and then became an impresario, building the Theatre, and whose sons became distinguished actors. James was not troubled with explaining the requirements of a theatre to a carpenter, because that was his own trade. He also had an instinct for show business and became a theatrical producer in his own venue. That instinct followed through into the next generation when his son Richard became an actor – the first to play Hamlet.

When I met Ben Whishaw – the most

exciting Hamlet of our own generation – buying his Christmas tree at the Columbia Road Market, I wish I had suggested he walk over to the churchyard of St Leonard's, and maybe take a holly wreath, to admire the wintry flowers growing there nourished by the remains of our very first Hamlet, Richard Burbage, who was buried in 1619. Certainly, I shall never be able to walk down Shoreditch High Street and take the short cut through the churchyard again without thinking that this is where Hamlet lies.

If, like Virginia Woolf's 'Orlando', I could have lived through all these centuries, I might have written 400 years ago that the place was full of theatrical types, like moths batting around a flame – I could not walk out of my front door without tripping over William Shakespeare stepping out of the ale house with Ben Jonson, Edmund Shakespeare mourning his son at St Leonard's, Richard Burbage supping with his father James and brother Cuthbert at the Boar's Head, Richard Tarlton shopping at the market, Gabriel Spencer in Bishoppes gate streete, William Somers in the Spittal Fields, William Sly at the bawdy house and Christopher Marlowe getting arrested in Norton Folgate. The list is endless.

THE BAISHAKHI MELA IN SPITALFIELDS

Spiritual Life, Street Life

THE STREETS were closed off from dawn and, in the cool of early morning, an expectant hush lay upon the neighbourhood. Then, in the distance, came the sound of drumming, which grew and grew until around midday the Baishakhi Mela procession arrived, beneath a transparent blue sky, filling Brick Lane with a joyful chaos of colour and noise and life. The Mela, celebrating the Bengali New Year, is the largest Bengali festival held outside Bangladesh and, for one day, Spitalfields is transported to another continent.

From mid-morning, drummers, dancers, groups of children and fantastic carnival animals gathered on the far side of Spitalfields Market, before lining up in Lamb Street. Once everyone was assembled, the mayor took a photocall and cut a ribbon. Then they all set off past the Golden Heart and into Hanbury Street, before erupting on to Brick Lane, where, among curry-houses, Bangladeshi grocers and in the shadow of the mosque, the whole extravagant drama took on its full meaning. The narrow street and tall buildings intensified

the din of drumming, whistles and horns, while spectators found themselves crowded together and swept along by the infectious sense of carnival that ruled Brick Lane. This annual moment, when the Baishakhi Mela procession passes through Brick Lane, manifests the jubilant apotheosis of Bangladeshi culture, both here in east London and for members of the Bangladeshi diaspora across Britain.

Meanwhile, I was nipping around, in and out of the crowd, climbing on to street furniture and sprinting through the side streets, to catch every detail of the parade. Standing upon a telephone junction box, I found myself eye to eye with those riding the magnificent elephant, and party to spectacular perspectives up and down Brick Lane, of the procession of dancers and drummers stretching in either direction, as far as I could see. The images passing before my eyes added up to a poem, with each carnival float and attendants attired in silk and tinsel, comprising a sequence of verses featuring an owl, butterflies, a giant water lily, an elephant and a turtle. It evoked the imaginative universe of a dream, or a collection of Indian folk tales, or a set of miniature paintings, except it was here now – loud and brash – and in your face in Brick Lane!

I followed the procession as it turned into Old Montague Street, where the atmosphere changed as the crowds ebbed away. In the residential streets, people leaned out of the windows of their houses to wave, and homeless people woke from sleeping on the grass to witness an unlikely vision. From here, it was a short journey to arrive at Weavers' Fields, which held a funfair and a huge concert stage. The parade was merely the catalyst to ignite the festivities and, for the rest of the day, the streets, parks and curry houses of the East End were full of high-spirited revellers enjoying the blessing of the sunshine. Everyone had plenty to celebrate, because it was Bengali New Year and the day summer arrived in Spitalfields too.

JIM HOWETT

DESIGNER

Human Life

IN MY OPINION, Jim Howett is the best-dressed man in Spitalfields – pictured here with a characteristically shy smile – sitting on a 1720s staircase in one of the houses in Fournier Street he is currently restoring for the Spitalfields Trust. He looks entirely at home in this shabby yet elegantly proportioned old house, a specifically localised environment that over time has become his natural habitat and is now the place you are most likely to find him in east London.

For years, I admired Jim's fine artisan clothing whenever I caught glimpses of him, always crossing Commercial Street and disappearing through the market, or off down Folgate Street preoccupied with some enigmatic intent. Then we were introduced and I discovered that Jim sleeps each night in the attic at Dennis Severs' House and crosses the market every day to work at 3 Fournier Street with fellow designer Marianna Kennedy, creating the furniture and lamps that are so distinctive and have become ubiquitous in the houses around Spitalfields. I also learned that Jim is responsible for a significant number of the most appealing shopfronts in the neighbourhood – though I should have guessed that the twill clothing he wears from head to toe and which suits him so snugly is made by Marie Willey and Will Brown at Old Town.

At first, I assumed Jim was Irish on account of his soft vowels and quietly spoken manner, his words, almost whispered sometimes, drawing your attention to both what is said and what is unspoken. Such is the nature of his mind that Jim will begin a sentence and then pursue a digression that leads to another and yet another – though such is the intelligence of the man that when he leads you back to the resolution of the original thought, it acquires a more precise import from all the qualifications and counter-arguments it has received. Without doubt, Jim is a consummate prose talker.

Jim's origins lie in Ohio, in the foothills of the Appalachians, where he grew up in Salem. But his father worked in international development and in the 1960s the family moved to the Congo. His father was then transferred to Vietnam, with the family ending up in London in 1967. Jim studied at the Architectural Association under the tutelage of Dan Cruickshank, subsequently working for a few years in prehistoric archaeology, before deciding to study at the London College of Furniture, which was then in Commercial Road.

Renting a room on Brick Lane, Jim dropped a card to his former tutor, who wrote back to say he had just bought a house in Elder Street full of broken furniture, so Jim set up a workbench in Dan's basement to undertake the repairs. As an undomesticated bachelor living in a romantically shambolic old house, Dan became a magnet for the attentions of women who always arrived bearing hampers of food – an occurrence of such regularity that, as the attractive female benefactors walked through the door, Dan would simply yell down the cellar stairs, 'Jim, dinner's come!'

'Dennis Severs knocked upon the door one day, looking for Dan,' said Jim. 'He said he'd just bought a house round the corner and wanted to do tours, and we thought he was crazy but we helped him set it up. I made the shutters, the partition with the arch in the dining room and I copied the fireplace from one in Princelet Street,' he added, revealing the origin of his own involvement with 18 Folgate Street, where today he is the sole resident. Before long, Jim was sharing a workshop with Marianna Kennedy and ceramicist Simon Pettet in Gibraltar Walk, all of them creating new work inspired by historical models and applying traditional craft skills. They found themselves at the centre of a community focused around the restoration of the eighteenth-century houses, dubbed 'Neo-Georgians' by the newspapers – a moment recorded today in the collection of magazines and photo features, illustrating the renaissance of Spitalfields, that Jim keeps in a box in his workshop.

Jim taught himself furniture making by copying a Hepplewhite chair – constructing four versions until he could get the proportions right – before he discovered that there was no market for them because dealers considered them so dangerously close to the originals as to approach fakes. Yet this irony, which was to hamper Jim's early career as a furniture maker, served as a lesson in the significance of proportion in engaging with historical design.

When Jim won a commission to design an armoire for Julie Christie, he thought he had found the path to success. 'She gave me a tip of half the value of my commission fee and I thought, "This is as good as it gets," but she remains the best client I ever had,' admitted Jim, wistfully recognising the limited market for custom-built new furniture in antique styles. 'I used to make these pieces and have no money left over to buy coffee afterwards,' he declared with a shrug.

Instead, the renovation of Spitalfields gave Jim the opportunity to become one of those who have created the visual language of our streets, through his subtle approach to restoring the integrity of old shopfronts that have been damaged or altered. Perhaps the most famous are Verde & Co. and A. Gold in Brushfield Street, 1 and 3 Fournier Street and Bedell Coram, Andrew Coram's shop in Commercial Street. In these and numerous other examples, through conscientious archival research, Jim has been responsible for retaining the quality of vernacular detail and proportion that characterises this as Spitalfields, rather than any other place. The beauty of Jim's work is that these buildings now look as if they had always been as they are today.

Yet Jim is quick to emphasise that he is not an architect, explaining that his work requires both more detailed knowledge of traditional building techniques and less ego, resisting the urge to add personal embellishments. 'The difference between me and architects working on historic buildings is that I restrict myself to organising the space. I believe if a building has survived for 200 years, it has survived because it has certain qualities. The reason I don't put my finger in the pie is because I can express myself in other things.'

While Jim spoke, he produced file after file of photographs, plans and maps, spreading them out upon the table in his workshop to create a huge collage of Spitalfields, while maintaining an extraordinary monologue of interwoven stories about the people, the place and the buildings. I was fascinated by Jim's collection of maps, spanning the last 500 years in Spitalfields, and I realised that he carries in his mind a concrete picture of how the place has evolved. When I have seen him walking around, he is walking in awareness of all the incarnations of this small parish, the buildings that have come and gone through past centuries.

It fired my imagination when Jim took me into the cellar of 15 Fournier Street, where he was working, and pointed out the path across the yard belonging to the sixteenth-century building that stood there before the eighteenth-century house was built. Converted into a mission hall in the nineteenth century, Jim was restoring it to its original ground plan and recreating a lost eighteenth-century staircase.

Simon Pettet portrayed Jim on one of his tiles as a fly on the wall, reflecting Jim's omnipresence in Spitalfields. 'I think if my father had not taken us to the Congo, I should still be there in Salem, Ohio,' confessed Jim with a weary smile, 'because at heart I am a localist.' Jim showed me the missing finger on his left hand, sliced off while cutting a mitre from left to right, a mark that today he regards as the proud badge of his carpenter's trade. In his work and through his personal presence, Jim has become an inextricable part of the identity of Spitalfields. After more than thirty years, I hope we may now describe him as a local.

THE BREAD, CAKE
AND BISCUIT WALK

I DECIDED to take advantage of the fine afternoon to enjoy a walk through the City of London in search of some historic bakery products to feed my obsession for all the good things that come from the bakery and thereby extend my appreciation of the poetry and significance of this sometimes undervalued area of human endeavour.

Leaving Spitalfields, I turned left and walked straight down Bishopsgate to the river, passing Pudding Lane, where the Fire of London started at the King's Bakery, reminding me that a bakery was instrumental in the very creation of the City we know today.

My destination was the noble church of St Magnus the Martyr, which boasts London's stalest loaves of bread. Stored upon high shelves beyond the reach of vermin, beside the west door, these loaves were once placed here each Saturday for the sustenance of the poor and distributed after the service on Sunday morning. Although in the forgiving gloom of the porch it is not immediately apparent, these particular specimens have been there so many years they are now mere emblems of this bygone charitable endeavour. Surpassing any conceivable shelf life, these crusty bloomers are consumed by mould and covered with a thick layer of dust – indigestible in reality, they are metaphors for God's bounty that would cause any short-sighted, light-fingered passing hobo to gag.

Close by in this appealingly shadowy incense-filled Wren church, which was once upon the approach to London Bridge, are the tall black boards tabulating the donors who gave their legacies for bread throughout the centuries, commencing in 1674 with Owen Waller. If you are a connoisseur of the melancholy and the forgotten, this a good place to come on a mid-week afternoon to linger and admire the shrine of St Magnus, with his fearsome horned helmet and fully rigged model sailing ship – once you have inspected the bread, of course.

I walked west along the river until I came to St Bride's Church off Fleet Street, as the next destination on my bakery products tour. Another Wren church, this possesses a tiered spire that became the inspiration for the universally familiar wedding-cake design in the eighteenth century, after Fleet Street baker William Rich created a three-tiered cake for his daughter's marriage based upon the great architect's design. Dedicated today to printers and those who

work in the former print trades, this is a church of manifold wonders, including the pavement of Roman London in the crypt, an iron anti-resurrectionist coffin of 1820 and, most touching of all, an altar dedicated to journalists killed while pursuing their work in dangerous places around the globe.

From here, I walked up to St John's Gate, where a biscuit is preserved that was sent home from the trenches in the First World War by Henry Charles Barefield. Surrounded by the priceless treasures of the Knights of St John, magnificently displayed in the new museum, this old dry biscuit has

become an object of universal fascination for both its longevity and its ability to survive the rigours of the mail. Even the Queen wanted to know why the owner had sent his biscuit home in the post, when she came to open the museum. But no one knows for sure, and the enigma is the source of the power of this surreal biscuit.

Pamela Willis, curator of the collection, speculates that it was a comment on the quality of the rations – 'Our biscuits are so hard we can send them home in the mail!' Yet while I credit Pamela's notion, I find the biscuit both humorous and defiant, and I

or his wife, but I think we can be assured that it was an emotional moment for Mrs Barefield when the biscuit came through her letter box – to my mind, this is a heroic biscuit, a triumphant symbol of the human spirit, that manifests the comfort of modest necessity in the face of the horror of war.

I had a memorable afternoon filled with thoughts of bread, cake and biscuits, and their potential meanings and histories, which span all areas of human experience. And unsurprisingly, as I came back through Spitalfields, I found that my walk had left me more than a little hungry. After several hours contemplating baked goods, it was only natural that I should seek out a cake for my tea, and in St John Bread and Wine, to my delight, there was one fresh Eccles cake left on the plate, waiting for me to carry it away.

have my own theory about its meaning. In the midst of the carnage of the Somme, Henry Barefield was lost for words, so he sent a biscuit home in the mail to prove he was still alive and had not lost his sense of humour either.

We do not know if he sent it to his mother

COLUMBIA ROAD MARKET V

Plant Life, Market Life

I WOKE IN THE NIGHT to the sound of a downpour, yet when I rose at six the rain had ceased and the air was cool and fresh. By the time I reached the market there was already a brisk trade and the traders were cheerful at the opportune timing of the rain, good for gardeners and good for the market too. The damp air brought out all the fragrances of the flowers and, as one trader wheeled a barrow of sweet peas past me, the scent was intense.

Each year at this time, I buy pinks from Columbia Road to add to my small collection of dianthus. The less-cultivated varieties are my preference, in deep or pale pink. It is the subtle details that speak to me, the pattern of veins and the fine denticulated ends of the petals. And to savour the detail and scent of my new acquisitions, I keep them on the dresser for a few weeks in old pots that I find in the market, before planting them out at the edge of a dry border in the hope of seeing them bloom again next summer.

These distinctive flowers have been in cultivation since the medieval period (Shakespeare calls them 'gilliflowers'). And the verb 'to pink', dating from the fourteenth century and meaning to perforate – as in 'pinking shears' – may be the origin of the

common name, referring to their denticulated petals. In turn, the word 'pink' as a colour may originate from these flowers that come in such a subtle range of tones, from sugared almond to coral, perfectly complemented by their silvery grey-green stems and narrow leaves. Rich in association of many times and places, it lifts my spirits to encounter their subtle clove-like scent when I walk into the room each morning.

ANDREW CORAM

ANTIQUES DEALER

Human Life

FOR SEVERAL YEARS NOW, the most interesting shop window in Spitalfields has been that of Bedell Coram, Andrew Coram's antiques shop at 86a Commercial Street. Every single day, I walk past and always direct my gaze to discover what is new. I am rarely disappointed with lack of novelty, and sometimes I am astonished by Andrew's latest finds and ingeniously surreal displays that are worthy of Marcel Duchamp.

Over a year ago, I admired three yellowed newspaper hoardings in his window – *Evening Standard*: THE PRINCE: TOUCH-ING SCENE, *Evening News*, Late Extra: MAN-HUNT IN LEICESTER SQUARE and *Evening News*, 6.30: LONDON HIGHWAY-MEN ON WHEELS. They were gone as quickly as they appeared. 'Gilbert and George bought them,' Andrew told me discreetly. 'They rang to say they saw them in the window and came round next morning to buy them. They don't usually collect old ones, they just go to the newsagent across the road to get them new.' Clearly, Andrew has a well-deserved following, and as I have gone about my interviews, when I have admired a delft bowl or a corner cupboard in an old house, invariably the owner will say, 'I got it from Andrew.'

Andrew is the youngest of eight children of an antiques dealer from Plymouth who was born in 1900 and died in 1980, when Andrew was still a child. His father began in domestic service and started in the antiques business after the Second World War when the country houses of Devon were being knocked down, creating a vibrant trade in china, furniture and paintings. 'He knew how to speak to those people,'

explained Andrew, vividly aware of the negotiation skills that are key to his profession. When Andrew was growing up, his father was trading from Carhampton, near Minehead in Somerset, and he remembers long summer holidays hanging around the shop. 'I think my poor brother spent all his time polishing my finger marks off the mahogany furniture,' he recalled fondly.

Today, Andrew Coram is a popular figure in Spitalfields, with trenchant humour and a fluent lyricism that he indulges when speaking of his treasured discoveries. He is a poet among antiques dealers, with a melancholy streak that he resists yet exposes when he speaks of his motives. Sitting in a chair wedged between boxes of stock, casting his eyes around at all the beautiful things that he has surrounded himself with in his shop, Andrew revealed almost apologetically, 'It's not about the money, it's about the way that some antiques speak to you. There's a sense of loss every time you sell something you like, which I didn't have when I started. I think I may have lost focus. My father never lost focus, because he had to support six people. It's easy to let the things take over. You hope to do something that continually generates itself, and inspires you, so that, as you are discovering new things, you are learning more and you accumulate knowledge.'

Who cannot sympathise with this conflict? It is the quintessential dilemma that cuts to the heart of the passionate antiques dealer. The modest trader spends his time searching, using his ingenuity to find wonderful things, and learns to appreciate and understand their histories, as Andrew has done. Then he collects his treasures together, and all for the purpose of disposing of them to others.

Even though his father was an antiques dealer and Andrew incarnates his occupation so magnificently that I cannot think of him any other way, he did not set out to follow in his father's footsteps. Impatient of waiting for a lucky break as an artist, Andrew started trading his personal collection in the Spitalfields Market years ago, in the days when it was free to have a stall, and he made seventy-five pounds on the first day. 'When you start out trading, you feel you have achieved something the first time you buy a Georgian chest of drawers or a long-case clock on a hunch and it proves to be right,' said Andrew, relating milestones on the career path. He claims he learned everything as he went along, that he has no conscious memories of the trade from his childhood, but I think Andrew's upbringing accounts for the personal sensibility he brings to everything he does. Andrew's unique sense of tone, his distinctive style of dress that is of no determinate period, his instinct for seeking out such charismatic artefacts and the artful displays he creates, all these attest to his special quality as an antiques dealer, born and bred.

Still ambivalent about how much he chooses to keep, Andrew admitted recklessly, 'There's a part of me that would like to have nothing!' So I asked him what drew him to things that he liked, and he thought for a moment, assuming his grimace of rumination. 'Things that have rarity value

– that you might not see again. As I said, things that speak to you. Things of which there's a sort of … clarity about what they are … a quietness about them, even a stillness,' he replied, searching for words beyond grasp.

Then his eyes lit up, as he thought of an example to illustrate his point, and held it up, in mime. 'I found this tooth, a boar's tooth, mounted in silver with the inscription upon the base "Roasted upon ye Thames Jan 15th 1715/6" – I'm not selling it!' Once we had considered this treasured memento from a frost fair together, in another mime for my delight, Andrew produced a copper pie dish with the words 'Lincoln's Inn 1779' upon it, folding his fingers as if to grip the sides of the invisible dish. Then, returning to the material world, Andrew passed me a tiny delft tea bowl in pale porcelain with Chinese figures on the outside and the softest blackbird-egg blue interior. It was a mid-eighteenth-century English tea bowl and as I cradled it in my palm, where it sat so comfortably, he told me in triumph it was worth a thousand pounds. 'Holding a delicate thing like that in your hand puts you in touch with the past. It's the story that connects us,' he said, intoxicated by the magic of the bowl, and breaking into a broad grin.

I spent much of my childhood being taken around the country antiques shops of Devon and Somerset by my mother and father, and the romance of these places and my parents' delight at their finds remain vividly with me today. I do not know if Andrew's path and mine crossed back then, but I do know that Andrew Coram has soul and his antiques shop is a proper one, of the old school, where authentic treasures are still to be found.

BUYING VEGETABLES
FOR LEILA'S SHOP

Culinary Life, Market Life

IN SPITE of these warm bright days, in the early hours of a Monday night Leila McAlister and I were shivering at the Covent Garden Market, where I had accompanied her on the weekly trip to buy fresh produce for her shop in Arnold Circus. The advance in the weather has delivered such a wealth of seasonal fruit and vegetables into the market that it warmed our spirits to discover some magnificent new arrivals, still fresh from the fields.

But it was no straightforward matter to seek out these prizes, because the market is a labyrinth without signs. You arrive in a dark car park, as if you were on the periphery of a large airport or an industrial estate. Then you enter through any of the myriad doors to find yourself inside a warren of interconnected premises belonging to the different wholesalers, all stacked with produce. And each one of these backs on to the car park and also faces in the other direction on to the narrow market aisles, where the traders display their wares beneath harsh halogens.

Several times, I asked Leila, 'Were we here before?' as she led me on an elaborate journey, weaving and criss-crossing through the market she has come to know intim-

ately over twelve years buying at Covent Garden. In and out of gloomy warehouses, where vast towers of vegetables loomed over us in the half-light, into chilled white rooms where small batches of choice crops awaited, and out to the car park again to probe newly arrived pallets, Leila followed her instinct, checking the consistency of the vegetables, expertly shelling peas in one hand and swallowing them, absentmindedly chewing scraps of asparagus, tasting tarragon, and all done with the pre-occupied expression of one on a quest.

Among the profusion of bland, industrially farmed fruit and vegetables dominating the market, grown to achieve consistency of size, shape, colour and flavour, and be available all year round, Leila is seeking produce from traditional or small growers that may come in limited quantities for just a few weeks when the crop is in season. 'I am looking for things that come from somewhere and taste of something,' as she puts it, with succinct and delicate irony.

Leila's van was the lone small vehicle in a line of large white trucks in the car park, and Leila was the only female customer in a market that is staffed by men, yet Leila herself is not intimidated by this enclave of querulous masculinity. 'They don't make any allowances,' she granted with a weary smile, 'but they know their stuff and they work really hard. And though I am an insignificant customer in terms of quantity, they do respect that I come down myself each week and pick what's good.

'I bought some lovely radishes here last week and they were joking because they were muddy and they said, "We knew you'd buy these,"' Leila revealed to me with a cheeky grin as we approached a counter, before turning to the trader and asking with a complete lack of self-consciousness, 'Got any dirty potatoes?'

Muddy vegetables are at a scarcity because clean ones sell better, when the truth is that mud keeps vegetables fresher longer by protecting them from sunlight and drying out – especially true of root vegetables, which are less likely to turn green and sprout if they are covered in mud. Yet mud is the enemy of clean refrigerators where many shops store their vegetables, and the benign dark earth, which is the source of these plants, is commonly perceived as mere dirt. 'Washed vegetables need more refrigeration but we don't have that,' explained Leila. 'We rely upon the natural cooling of our shop, due to the brilliance of the Victorian design and its venting system.' And she was lucky that night, because we carried away a sack of beautiful muddy Maris Piper potatoes, grown in England, in triumph.

There are half a dozen wholesalers where Leila gets the majority of her stock, but she always takes an eagle-eyed sweep around the market too. 'After years and years, I have come to recognise the growers – "the mark", as they call it at the market. And I write to them if I like what they grow,' she admitted. 'I am always on the lookout for interesting new producers whose crop I can buy through the market.'

Early on Tuesday, Leila drives her new stock back along the river and up to Arnold Circus, where, first thing, you will see the weekly spectacle of the vegetable boxes being made up upon the pavement in Calvert Avenue, ready for distribution with some of the freshest vegetables in London, while the handsome displays which characterise Leila's Shop are renewed with the latest arrivals from the market. Any other shop with Leila's small turnover would purchase their stock indirectly, through a distributor, but Leila McAlister chooses to give up one night every week and search the market personally, applying her experience and critical faculties to get the fruit and vegetables herself, because it is her pleasure and her passion.

BRICK LANE MARKET III

Human Life, Market Life

JOHN CALCUTT has been trading on Brick Lane each Sunday since 1974. 'I'm from Hoxton and I used to come down here when I was a little boy, and the stall next to me sold performing fleas,' he recalled affectionately, casting his eyes up and down the market. 'It was absolutely packed by eight in the morning. They used to ring a bell at one o'clock then, and you had to stop.' Now semi-retired, yet still energetic and limber, John comes from Dagenham to sell rugs here and in Deptford three days a week. 'I still come because I've got a mortgage to pay,' he confided as he began to fold up his wares, turning morose in his weariness. 'I'm just hanging on,' he confessed to me in a whisper. 'I don't even break even, but I don't mind coming, as long as I don't lose too much money.' It was an admission that revealed John's depth of sentiment for Brick Lane. But then John remembered that he is close to paying off his mortgage, the result of thirty-seven years' hard work here in the market, and he brightened visibly. 'Another three months and I'll be free in July!' he declared, triumphant.

LAURA AND MILLY are two skinny art students from London Metropolitan University who have been trading here on Brick Lane for seven weeks, selling books and bric-a-brac from a folding table. 'It's been tough, we're not going to lie, but today's been really good,' revealed Milly, sharing an emotional grin of achievement with Laura. 'This is our food money for the week. We'll go food shopping tonight before we get the bus back to Stratford,' she added in excited anticipation of a feast, revealing how essential the stall is to their survival during their studies.

The pair fell into market life almost by accident. 'We got pissed one night and thought, "We'll give it a go!"' confessed Laura with a blush, making light of the origin of this brave endeavour that has made such a difference to their quality of life, 'and now we're both addicted, because it's too much fun.'

MARGE HEWSON
NURSERY NURSE

Human Life, Past Life

ON ANY SCHOOL MORNING in Spitalfields, you may always rely upon spotting Marge Hewson between eight thirty and nine o'clock, traversing the roads from Greatorex Street to the Chicksand Estate, trudging around in all weathers, ringing doorbells and collecting up her beloved charges until she has acquired a crocodile of as many as twenty small children, whom she ushers safely to Christ Church School in Brick Lane, where she has been Nursery Nurse for forty years.

And as a consequence, she is one of the most popular people you could meet, cherished by generations of local people, for whom Marge's benign presence is an integral part of their childhood landscape. 'As big as they are, they'll still stop me and ask for a hug in the street, even teenagers,' she revealed with a proud blush, as an indicator of the outcome of a life lived at the very centre of her community.

'I must admit I have never got away from here, but I am not unhappy with it,' confided Marge upon quiet consideration, when I dropped by to visit her at the school after four o'clock, once it had emptied of pupils and peace reigned. 'You can't really put into words what it was like,' Marge

said to me, with shrewd reserve and a self-effacing smile, before proceeding to evoke her Brick Lane childhood with lyrical ease.

'I was brought up in Flower and Dean Street, just off Brick Lane – the 'Flowerie', we called it. Just a few small shops and tenements, all pulled down now. You knew everybody and everybody knew you, and nobody had any money. You learned to stand on your own two feet. I think I had a very happy childhood.

'Children don't have freedom now. When I was ten, me and my friend would take a picnic and go to Victoria Park and spend the whole day there. We were often out on the street until ten o'clock at night. There was a policeman on the beat and we used to stand around the lamp post until he came at nine thirty, and he'd say, "It's time you went home." So we'd stay until he came back on his round again later and then we'd all run home to bed.

'We weren't allowed to go up Brick Lane beyond Princelet Street because of the Maltese cafés with prostitutes standing outside. We used to try to bunk into the Mayfair cinema across the road if we could get in

the back door. At the bottom of Osborn Street was a bomb site called the Chimney Debris where we played, and we went to Woolworths to buy bamboos, and make bows and arrows, and played Robin Hood there. There was no TV, so I went to the library every day. I used to go swimming every day too, at the Goulston Street Baths, and I balanced my little brother with his bottle where I could see him in the changing rooms, so I could keep an eye on him while I swam lengths. Then we'd buy stale cakes from the bakery on the corner afterwards.

'Every Saturday we played bagatelle or Newmarket, and we had a jar of pennies and my mother would turn them out, and as a family we'd all sit down together. I'd see all the boys come on leave from National Service on Saturday night to visit their girls. They'd all go up Whitechapel Waste to Paul's Record Shop, where I was too young to go – the boys in their suits and the girls all dressed up. And on Sunday mornings, there was always an escapologist in chains who escaped from a sack on the corner of Wentworth Street. It was lovely to go and watch him.'

Christ Church School is 100 yards from Flower and Dean Street, where Marge grew up, and while her contemporaries have moved out of the neighbourhood, apart from a foray to the Isle of Dogs, Marge has chosen to live within walking distance of her old territory, and she finds it suits her very well. In her time, the East End has been transformed by slum clearance and rebuilding, and the movement of peoples in and out of the neighbourhood. And although she would never claim it, Marge through her emotional presence at the school over four decades has become part of the consistent identity of this place as a magnanimous harbour to newcomers, carrying forward the best of the old into the new East End.

'I began here at the school in 1979, before East Pakistan became Bangladesh. There weren't too many Bengali children here then, but as others left and more arrived it became 100 per cent Bengali. Now I see another change. We have more children of different races, including Colombians and Eastern Europeans, which makes it a truly multicultural school. When the Bangladeshis first came there wasn't much English spoken. They used to turn up at all times of the day and with layers and layers of clothing against the cold.

'At first we had only one big classroom and fifty children with just me and one teacher. A lot didn't speak English and sometimes I would take a child home but the mother wouldn't answer the door because she didn't understand the language, so then I'd have to grab a passer-by to translate. Conditions were hard for Bengalis, with families living in one room in tenements, and we worked as a team to help with their problems, taking them to hospital or the doctor if they didn't speak English.'

I realised Marge Hewson was reluctant to talk about all the work she did, because she chooses discretion when speaking of the past disadvantage of those who are her community today. Instead she wanted to confess how much it means to have this role at the school which has given her such a profound emotional reward and sense of belonging.

'I came here for six months and I stayed forty years, and there are children here now – I knew their parents when they were little. I like this school. I know all the people and I know this area back to front. I've got a lot of affection for the families round here. If I lost my purse, or I needed anything, I could knock on any door and they would help me, I know. I love my life in Brick Lane.'

A NIGHT IN THE BAKERY
AT ST JOHN

AT MIDNIGHT, once the last diners have departed from St John Bread and Wine, the head baker and pastry chef, Justin Piers Gellatly, wheels his gleaming black motorcycle in from Commercial Street and parks it in the middle of the floor. The restaurant that feels so large when it is full of customers seems to diminish once it is empty and all the chairs are stacked up. Now the chefs are gone from the kitchen, and until the clock on Christ Church, Spitalfields, reaches eight o'clock in the morning, the place is the sole preserve of the bakers.

Justin greeted me with a cheery, 'Good morning!' when I arrived shortly after twelve to join the team, as he and Luka Mokliak both set to work to make 400 loaves and have them ready before the chefs reappeared in eight hours. At once, the huge porridge-grey lumps of gelatinous wet shining dough were hauled from the proving cupboard – where they had been sitting since they were made yesterday – and, using scales to ensure a consistency of size, Justin and Luka wasted no time in cutting up the living dough into pieces and shaping them into loaves.

First in the sequence of different loaves comes the sourdough, which takes longest to prove because it is a natural yeast. Once it is shaped, each piece of sourdough is placed into a proving basket made of a single spiral of bamboo that imparts the characteristic design of concentric circles on the dough. It is a furious business to prepare 160 of these, but Justin and Luka make short work of flouring the baskets, shaping and working the dough with swift efficiency, folding it always inwards like the corners of an envelope.

As they filled the baskets, they arranged them on trays and stowed them under the table in racks, then, once the racks were full, the loaves were stacked on counters and spilled out on to the restaurant tables, to allow the yeast to do its work for a few more hours before they go into the oven. After the sourdough, Justin and Luka set to work on the white, the rye and the raisin breads, which have live yeast added to the dough and prove more quickly. Sandwich loaves and baguettes are arranged on linens to prove, with the cloth folded in pleats to prevent the loaves sticking to each other.

By two thirty all the loaves were shaped, and the warm air was thick with a delicious hazy aroma of dough, and by three o'clock the first white loaves were in the oven. The

rhythm of the night changed as the first flurry of activity was complete and Justin shifted his attention to baking, while on the other side of the room Luka made dough ready for tomorrow night.

Using a peel (a long wooden paddle), Justin loaded the loaves into the four shelves of the deck oven. Each of the doughs is ready to go into the oven at a different time, and the readiness can vary according to all kinds of factors, so Justin was constantly pulling, patting and sniffing his loaves to assess the progress of the proving process. Equally, each of the doughs needs a different baking time and different conditions, which requires judgement too. Justin hovered for hours, sweating and preoccupied, alter-

nately checking the loaves in the oven and the dough in the racks – all in order to bring out one rack of loaves when they are baked, at the same time as another batch reaches the moment they are ready to go in. It is a challenging game of weighing all the variables and every night it is different. On this night, the white dough was a little dry, which required slower cooking and gave Justin concern for his loaves waiting to go into the oven.

As he tipped each loaf from the linen on to the peel, Justin shaped it up again gently, then scored the surface with a razor, which allows the crust to open up in the oven and permits the loaf to bloom. Justin used an old-fashioned double-edged razor to do this because he has not found a knife sharp enough to match the resistance of the dough, which is sufficient to blunt two razors each night. 'If you lose one of these everything stops!' he declared, holding up the razor with an absurd grimace. Once the loaves were in the oven, Justin flipped them on to the baking surface with practised ease and, when the shelf was full, he sprayed steam from a diffuser into the oven to create the thicker, more leathery than crisp, crust that is characteristic of his bread.

At five, the butcher arrived with his delivery for the restaurant, placing it in the food store housed in the former secure vault of the building, which was once a bank. During the earlier part of the night the tempo of conversation had been brisk as Justin maintained a vigorous buoyant energy, but now the pace was quieter. Justin was computing all the baking in his mind, while Luka was quietly measuring out flour and salt and water, and conscientiously stowing tomorrow's dough in the prover. Last to go into the oven were the sourdough loaves as dawn came over Commercial Street and, at five thirty, Justin opened the double doors of the restaurant, admitting the cool fresh air to ameliorate the steamy atmosphere of the baking. By the time the milkman arrived with his delivery, the first loaves were ready and Justin was relieved that the white loaves had turned out well. He held up a family loaf in triumph.

Making up the bread orders in trays

among the restaurant tables, Justin ended the night by taking the finished loaves from the oven as they were ready and stacking them up to create a satisfying display, still radiating heat and all discreetly crackling to themselves as they cooled down – an extraordinary sound I had never heard before. 'That's what first drew me to baking!' revealed Justin with a proud grin.

Accepting his gift of a loaf, I carried my beautiful sourdough home as the sun rose, grateful to have enjoyed the company of two fine bakers and witnessed an everyday yet magical routine that has been taking place in these streets each night as long as people have been living in Spitalfields.

PHILIP PITTACK AND MARTIN WHITE

CLOTH MERCHANTS

Human Life

PHILIP PITTACK AND MARTIN WHITE, who describe themselves as clearance cloth merchants, run the last remaining cloth warehouse in Spitalfields. Between them, these two agreeable gentlemen possess more than 120 years of experience in textiles. Philip is the third generation to work in the industry and Martin's mother's family were in the same trade too.

Philip Pittack, the handsome fellow with the scissors, began working for his father at the age of fourteen, pursuing the same trade as his grandfather from premises in Mare Street, Hackney. Together they travelled

around the country, buying up waste textiles from cloth mills and selling it on to be reconstituted and woven into new fabric. It was in effect recycling, before the term was invented. Fifty years ago, he moved into his current business as a clearance cloth merchant, buying surplus from mills when too much was manufactured or when it came out the wrong colour. For the past eighteen years, he has been working in partnership with Martin White, operating out of an old stable block backing on to the railway, just off Brick Lane. When they opened here, there were as many as thirty other cloth warehouses in Spitalfields but today Crescent Trading is the only one.

These two men, Messrs Pittack and White, could be on the stage because they both have such a natural gift for repartee, keeping the funnies coming and flirting outrageously with all the fashion students and young designers who are their primary customers, and who are reduced to helpless giggles by the routines. Ten years ago, Crescent Trading sold wholesale, no order less than 100 pounds was accepted and they would not cut a roll of cloth, but today everyone is welcome. And although Philip and Martin regret the scaling down of the trade, I can see that they enjoy the endless parade of youngsters who come through the door, eyes boggling at the possibilities offered by all this cloth.

Because Crescent Trading deals only in clearance, including clearance stock from their competitors' warehouses elsewhere in London, this has to be the cheapest place to buy fabric – while equally, much of it is excess from mills' special orders, often for companies like Prada and Chanel, which means you can discover cloth of the highest quality that might not be available anywhere else, and much of it is manufactured in this country too. In fact, Crescent Trading is a key part of our local economy, as this is where all the smaller fashion companies and designers starting out come, relying on being able to buy tiny amounts of superfine quality at rock-bottom prices.

I was honoured to be invited into the inner sanctum of the office, a makeshift construction of a room with a wide window looking out on to the warehouse, a cosy homely place with worn carpet tiles, bottles of HP sauce, jars of cashew nuts, tabloid lovelies taped to the wall, a great big map of Britain with pins in it, Philip's son's graduation photo and collecting boxes for Jewish and other charities. This is where I enjoyed a conversation with Martin White, who described himself as the Sorcerer of Fabrics. I hope Philip will forgive me if I say that Martin is unquestionably the more stylish of the pair, obviously taking a great deal of care with his appearance, quiffed grey hair, dark raincoat, monocle dangling and pearl tiepin glinting. Philip introduced his business partner affectionately, saying, 'Rather than sit at home, Mr White prefers to work, utilising his expertise in the textile industry,' which caused Martin to smile regally, raising his eyebrows with pride.

Describing his years in the trade from the pinnacle of his current position, Martin said, 'I started in 1946, when there were still coupons on fabrics and I have seen all the changes since that time. I was dealing in fabrics, my mother's family were always in the business. I started on my own, buying and selling. There used to be a lot of cloth mills in this country then, producing woollens, cottons, silks and synthetics, but now almost all of them have gone. There are no cotton mills any more and just a few woollen mills. A linen mill we dealt with in Ireland sold all their looms to India recently. China will take over the textile industry, because they can copy anything, but they will never be able to match the quality of wool suiting from the mills in Huddersfield and Bradford, which is the best in the world, because of the water. You've heard of "the old mill by the stream"?'

At this point, a female customer arrived and Martin raced out to the warehouse floor, leaving me puzzling over this enigma. So I followed him, to witness the performance, entering mid-dialogue. 'You look like an honest girl,' quipped Philip graciously. 'I was told about these two charming gentlemen,' replied the girl, holding her own creditably. 'My friend told me about this brilliant place,' she added with a broad smile, rolling her eyes to take in the vast array of textiles piled in every corner. Then, before she could say another word, Philip turned to me with a gleeful grin, spreading his arms in extravagant triumph at this spontaneous expression of the evidence of their own fabulousness. 'Hear that – out of the horse's mouth!' Turning back in an instant to the woman with a theatrically subservient gesture, he said, 'No offence intended to the young lady...' The apology was duly ac-

cepted with a quiet nod of appreciation and once the comedy overture was complete, and the participants were now as old friends, trading commenced, rolls of fabrics flew around, were measured and cut into shape with grace.

The young woman sauntered from the warehouse satisfied with her bargains, just turning at the door as she entered the sunlight to give a sentimental wave to the fine gentlemen who had made her afternoon. It was a wave reciprocated in unison by the comedy duo, who turned back to me rubbing their hands in pleasure at the exchange, though I could not tell if it was due to the transaction itself or simply in delight at the social encounter, or both. It was a moment from a classic British sitcom.

I seized the chance to enquire about the specific quality of the water in the north of England that plays such a significant part in the exemplary quality of the wool suiting produced in Huddersfield and Bradford. My query was the cue for an elaborate charade in which Philip and Martin enacted each stage of the process of textile production, from the spinning of the woollen yarn, through the dyeing and the weaving, every aspect of which requires washing. 'Even we don't understand it,' admitted Philip with uncharacteristic diffidence. 'It's like the whisky in Scotland, the water is everything,' he said, taking the opportunity to show me the stack of crates of Springbank malt whisky from the Campbeltown distillery that is his personal supply, stowed in a discreet corner as a tested and reliable method to keep warm in the bone-chilling climate of the old warehouse. 'In summer, people think we have air-conditioning, but it's just the eighteen-inch-thick walls!' declared Philip breezily, always looking on the bright side, even standing swaddled in his duvet coat, as we shivered together in the office that seemed even colder than the rest of the building, if that were possible.

Already the next chapter in the history of Crescent Trading was dawning, because the venerable building that makes such a beautiful cloth warehouse is to become a hotel and Philip and Martin have no choice but to leave in a matter of months. This is in spite of an undertaking by the powers-that-be that the area is zoned for light industrial use. 'Money talks and bullshit walks, if you pardon my French!' said Philip, in desultory summary of the circumstance.

The rise of the neighbourhood has given landlords an appetite to increase revenue from properties, but if as a result we lose crucial businesses (like Crescent Trading and Gardners') that support the unique small enterprises in the East End, then we destroy a community which gives the place part of its distinctive life. Over all the years, these dignified small tradesmen of Spital-fields have been earning a living while providing an essential service to many, and I cannot resist admitting to you that I feel they deserve better.

SPITALFIELDS ANTIQUES MARKET II

HARVEY DERRIELL is a lean and soulful Frenchman, and a connoisseur of tribal art from West Africa, with his prized collection of sculptures, textiles and beads. 'Fourteen years ago, I went to Mali, and I fell in love with the place and the people and I wanted to return. Now I go back four times a year,' revealed Harvey, brimming with delight. I was dismayed to learn that the Golonina bead market is closed, but Harvey reassured me that beads are still to be found. 'In Bamako, they ask, "What do you want? Drugs, gold, diamonds, girls, boys or beads?"' he explained.

JOHN THE HAT has been dealing in silver-plated cutlery and old Sheffield ware since being made redundant from his job as a bank manager in Covent Garden eighteen years ago. 'It's a living,' admitted John with a good-humoured shrug, while polishing his cherished stock of 'shell and line' and 'king's pattern'. Reticent about his motives in choosing this speciality, John was eager to inform me with a proud grin that 'The quality of silver plate from the 1930s is far greater than you find today,' before justifying his status as a sole trader by declaring that, 'A partnership is a leaky ship.' Yet in spite of his irascible posture, I remain convinced of John's irresistibly warm-hearted nature.

ALTHOUGH NANA JAN (pictured here with her loyal assistant Daniel) is selling everything because she has cancer, she continues to live a life that is as far beyond self-pity as you could imagine. 'I never expected to see my grandchildren and now I have great-grandchildren!' she whispered excitedly, before revealing the tattoo of an angel filling her chest – which she had done when a double mastectomy left her unable to look at her body. Sometimes adversity can bring out extraordinary qualities in people and Nana Jan is a bold example to us all.

SARAH AND ROY are a devoted couple from Dagenham. 'I make the money while he's the hard-working one who carries the heavy boxes around,' admitted Sarah mischievously, slipping a protective arm around Roy. On one side of the stall are Sarah's jewellery and clothes, while on the other are Roy's toy soldiers, Action Men and Ladybird books. 'I do feel sad parting with some, because I remember playing with them,' Roy confessed to me – inspiring Sarah to wrap her arms around him, with a fond kiss, declaring, 'Bless him, he loves it!'

THE LOST WORLD
OF THE LAUNDRETTES

WHEN I WENT into the chemist next door and asked the assistant if she knew when this Coin Wash opened, she laughed in my face. The launderette in Hoxton has been closed for years and the Speed Queen was dethroned long ago, I discovered. This enigmatic shutter painted by Ben Eine is now the portal to a lost world that will never open again. Let me explain. I embarked upon a tour of the neighbourhood launderettes in anticipation of savouring the delights on offer, but it proved to be an elusive and contradictory quest.

On the other side of Arnold Circus from the Community Launderette stands the former Boundary Estate Laundry as a reminder of the origins of this culture, when pools, bathhouses and laundries were established in the nineteenth century to improve the living conditions and hygiene of people who lived in the East End. Ironmongers Row Baths still functions as a majestic architectural temple to the benign qualities of water, providing an environment for relaxation, a medium for exercise and the means to get your clothes washed too. This is the last place where you can still take a bath or have a swim, and get your laundry done at the same time. We also visited the York Hall Baths, which have a plate in the entrance announcing 'Baths & Laundry', but while the baths have been spruced up in recent years the laundry has been shut down. Sarah and I peered furtively through the whitewashed window in the Cambridge Heath Road at the ranks of gleaming machines that will never spin again.

Although the Coin Wash in Hoxton is gone, over in Hoxton Street we were relieved to find the Laundry Room open and welcoming, with its cheerful daffodil-yellow livery. Here we were received by Eileen Long, who has been running the place a few years and keeps it spotless. Having lived in Hoxton thirty-six years, Eileen is a proud advocate of the place and is passionate about local history, explaining that she once lived in the flat on the site of Benjamin Pollock's Toy Theatre Shop. Eileen confided that, years ago, when a notorious East End gangster put his hand upon her head and offered protection from those who might abuse her on account of her height, she rejected the offer outright because she has always stood up for herself, winning respect in the neighbourhood that she enjoys today.

On a spring morning, the Laundry Room is a pleasant place to spend a few hours, pass time or read a book and strike up a random conversation with whoever passes through, but I noticed it was open twenty-four hours and when I asked Eileen about night-time she rolled her eyes mysteriously.

As we travelled east, I regret to report we encountered launderettes empty of customers with cracked panes, where a pervasive

melancholy reigned and I could not but wonder how long these will last. Yet on each occasion we were welcomed by generous women who had found it within themselves to preside with kindness. I love launderettes for the spaces they provide where people can be comfortable together even as strangers, enjoying innocent camaraderie and spending time outside the home in a relaxed arena of social possibility.

At the Laundry Room over in Broadway Market, we were delighted to be greeted by Nency, a white-haired woman with gracious old-fashioned manners, who told me she was accustomed to regular visits from photographers. 'They tell me it's classic. I asked my daughter, "What is classic?" and she said, "It's when something cannot be improved upon,"' Nency declared with restrained irony. She showed me her private shrine on the reverse of the storeroom door that commemorates the love of her life, Mustapha, known as Jimmy, who came from Cyprus to steal her heart in 1950. Nency keeps these photographs here as a constant reminder, recording Nency and Mustapha as a happy young couple, Nency and Mustapha and their children, Nency and Mustapha as a senior couple, Mustapha as she last remembered him and Mustapha's grave. All of the joy and heartache of life in five photographs on the back of a laundry door.

Over at Smarty Pants in Bethnal Green Road it was another story. The owner, Mr Patel, with impressive initiative, has lived up to the name of his business by diversifying into dry cleaning, repairs and alterations to create a thriving trade. 'These girls will tell you what kind of service I give them!' he announced with a glint in his eye and his customers within earshot. 'Oh yes, he always offers us a cup of tea if we want it and always does our repairs on time,' confirmed Linda enthusiastically – as she tipped soap powder into her machine – just in case there could be any misunderstanding. Like the community-minded residents of the Boundary Estate, Mr Patel has proved that there is a future for the evolved launderette, but I have hopes that those where Eileen, Nency and all the other fine matriarchs preside will also be with us for many years to come, because they still have devoted customers.

Nevertheless, I have spared you pictures of those that are closed and those that are open but always empty, because it seemed shameful to air the dirty laundry in public and I did not want to write an elegy for launderettes. You must not let me pine for the lost world of the launderettes, because they are the epilogue to a series of social changes taking the East End from the unsanitary conditions that induced outbreaks of cholera, to become a place where today almost everyone has bathrooms and washing machines at home. It will suffice to know there is still one launderette somewhere, in case my washing machine breaks down or I should need the spiritual consolation of human company one quiet morning.

ALAN HUGHES

MASTER BELLFOUNDER

Human Life, Past Life

IF I TELL YOU that my favourite sound in the world is that of bells pealing, you will understand why the Whitechapel Bell Foundry has always been a source of fascination for me. Every time I walk past the ancient walls of the foundry (the oldest manufacturing company in the land – founded in 1570), I wonder about the alchemical mystery of bellfounding taking place inside.

You can imagine my excitement when I went to meet the current master bellfounder, who is the latest in an unbroken line of master bellfounders that stretches back to 1420. Stepping inside, out of the rain in Whitechapel Road, I found myself in the foundry reception, which is lined with old photographs and compelling artefacts, like the wooden template (displayed

William Hughes, master bellfounder from 1945

over the entrance like the jaws of a whale) that was used when Big Ben was manufactured here. Among all the black and white photos, my eye was drawn by some recent colour pictures of a royal visit, with Her Majesty in a vivid shade of plum and Prince Philip looking uncharacteristically animated. I was just thinking that the bell foundry must work a very powerful magic upon its visitors indeed, when a figure emerged from the office and I turned to shake the hand of Alan Hughes, the master bellfounder. Alan's great-grandfather Arthur Hughes bought the business in 1884, which makes Alan a fourth-generation bellfounder.

The sense of awe that filled me as I shook hands with this polite man in a natty blue suit can only be compared to that when I was first taken to meet Father Christmas in a department store grotto. I composed myself as best I could, as Alan led me through a small office where two people worked behind neat desks and a fake cat dozed eternally in front of the stove, to arrive in the boardroom where a long table with a red cloth upon it occupied the centre of an elegantly proportioned Georgian dining room. We drew up chairs and commenced our conversation as the Whitechapel drizzle turned to dusk outside.

I was beguiled by Alan's fine manners and elegant light tone, which kept me wondering whether everything he said was actually tentative, contingent, as if he were simply trying out thoughts to see how I would react. I took this as an indicator of his relaxed assurance. Alan wears his role with the greatest of ease, as only someone born into the fourth generation of an arcane profession can do, and it occured to me that maybe the royal visit had been an occasion for mutual recognition between those born into family businesses.

Alan has worked here for forty-four years and, describing the changes he has seen, he glanced over my shoulder to the window several times, as if each time he glanced upon a different memory of the Whitechapel Road. The East End was a busy place in the 1950s, as Alan first recalled it, not only because of the docks but because of all the factories and the manufacturing that happened here. 'Whichever way it was blowing, you got this lovely smell of beer on the wind – from Truman's or Watney's or Charrington's or Courage or Whitbread,' Alan told me, explaining the locations of the breweries at every point of the compass. In the 1970s and 80s, when the docks and factories had closed, Alan found the place desolate.

He peered from the window and there was no one in the street. 'And then things started getting trendy. Instead of closing they started opening – and now, suddenly, it's OK to be in Whitechapel!' said Alan, clasping his hands thoughtfully on the table and looking around the room with a philosophical grin. 'But this place hasn't changed at all. I always find it vaguely amusing.'

Tentatively, I asked Alan what it meant to him, being part of this long line of bellfounders. Alan searched his mind and then said, 'I don't think about it very often. I would like to meet some of those people – Thomas Mears (master bellfounder from 1787), who would know the place today, and Thomas Lester (master bellfounder from 1738), who had this part built. It would be nice to have a conversation with him. He would recognise most of it.' Then the gentle reverie was gone and Alan returned to the present moment, adding, 'It's a business,' in phlegmatic summation.

'Our business runs counter to the national economy,' he continued. 'If the economy goes down and unemployment rises, we start to get busy. Last year was our busiest in thirty years, an increase of 27 per cent on the previous year. Similarly, the 1920s were very busy.'

I was mystified by this equation, but Alan has a plausible theory. 'Bell projects take a long time, so churches commit to new bells when the economy is strong and then there is no turning back. We are just commencing work on a new peal of bells for St Albans after forty-three years of negotiation. That's an example of the time scale we are working on – at least ten years between order and delivery is normal. My great-grandfather visited the church in Langley in the 1890s and told them the bells needed rehanging in a new frame. They patched them. My grandfather said the same thing in the 1920s. They patched them. My father told them again in the 1950s and I quoted for the job in the 1970s. We completed the order in 1998.'

Alan broke into a huge smile of wonderment at the nature of his world and it made me realise how important the continuity between the generations must be, so I asked him if there was pressure exerted between father and son to keep the foundry going.

'My great-grandfather never expected the business would outlive him. He had three sons and the sale of the business was arranged, but my grandfather refused to sign the contract, so the other brothers left and he took over. My grandfather ensured his sons had good jobs and even my father wasn't convinced the business could succeed, so he studied foundry technology for four years at every foundry in the south – thinking he could work for them – but every single one of those has now closed.' Then Alan looked out of the window again, gazing forward into time. 'As a master bellfounder,

you never retire. We go on until we die. My grandfather, my father and my uncle all died of a heart attack at eighty.'

The implications of Alan's conclusion are sobering for him personally, even though he has many years to go before eighty. 'You're very eloquent,' I said respectfully. 'No, I'm not!' he retorted cheekily. 'You have such interesting things to say,' I replied lamely. 'No, I don't!' he persisted gamely, obstinately raising his eyebrows.

Nevertheless, Alan's life as a bellfounder is remarkable to me and maybe to you too. Seeing his life in comparison to his predecessors, Alan embraces the patterns that prescribe his existence, for better or worse, and his personal mindset is the result of unique circumstances, the outcome of four generations of bellfounding. Even if it is his nature to maintain a stubborn levity,

Alan has my greatest respect for his immodest devotion to bells.

Now, it was time to visit the foundry, so I followed him with rising excitement through old doors, along passages, crossing a courtyard stacked with bells and into the vast workshop where the bells are made. There were huge bells and moulds for bells, bells in progress and bells completed, and piles of metal dust everywhere and pieces of heavy lifting equipment looming over us. This is where the sound of bells pealing originates, I thought. I felt like an astronaut on the moon – it was wondrous yet strange, but this was Alan's home planet. He strolled around the filthy workshop in his neat blue suit, scrutinising progress on the bells, happy among his sublime creations, which will be pealing to delight the ears of generations yet unborn, when we are all gone.

IN THE DEBTORS' PRISON

WALKING INTO a cell from an eighteenth-century prison in Wellclose Square was an especially vivid experience for me because, if I had lived then, I and almost everyone I know would have invariably ended up in here at some point. Although almost nothing is known of the occupants of this cell, they created their own remembrance through the graffiti they left upon the walls during the few years it was in use, between 1740 and 1760, and these humble inscriptions still recall their human presence after all this time.

No one could fail to be touched by the

emotional storm of marks across the walls. There are explicit names and dates carved with dignity and proportion, and there are dozens of crude yet affectionate images, presumably carved by those who could not write. There are also a few texts, which are heartbreaking in their bare language and plain sentiment, such as 'Pray Remember the Poor Deptors'. The spelling of 'deptors' after the model of 'Deptford' is an especially plangent detail.

About six feet wide and ten feet long, with a narrow door in one corner and lined with vertical oak planks, this is one of several cells that once existed beneath the Neptune public house. There is a small window with wide bars, high upon the end wall, corresponding with street level – not enough to offer a view, but just sufficient to indicate if it was daylight. There would have been straw on the floor and some rough furniture, maybe a table and chairs, where the inmates might eat whatever food they could afford to buy from the publican, because this was a privately managed prison run for profit.

Wellclose Square was once a fine square between Cable Street and the Highway, which barely exists any more. St Peter's School, with its gleaming golden ship as a weathervane, is the only building of note today, though early photographs reveal that many distinguished buildings once lined Wellclose Square, including the Danish Embassy, conveniently situated for the docks. When the Neptune was demolished in 1912, two of the cells were acquired by the Museum of London, where I was able to walk into one and meet Alex Werner, the curator responsible for putting it on display. 'We're never going to know who they are!' he said with a cool grin, extending his arms to indicate all the names and pictures that people once carved with so much expenditure of effort, under such grim conditions, to console themselves by making their mark.

It is a room full of sadness, and visitors to the museum came and went but did not linger. In spite of their exclamations of wonder at the general effect of all the graffiti, people did not wish to examine the details too closely. The lighting in the museum approximates to candlelight, highlighting some areas and leaving others in gloom, so I took along a flashlight to examine every detail and pay due reverence to the souls who whiled away long nights and days upon these inscriptions.

In a dark corner near the floor, I found 'All You That on This Cast an Eye, Behold in Prison Here Lie, Bestow You in Charety' painstakingly lettered in well-formed capitals. The final phrase struck a chord with me, because I think he refers to moral charity or compassion. Even today, we equate debt with profligacy and fecklessness, yet my experience is that people commonly borrow money to make up the shortfall for necessary expenses, when there is no alternative. I was brought up to avoid debt, but I had no choice when I was nursing my mother through her terminal illness at home. I borrowed because I could not earn money to cover household expenses when she lived a year longer than the doctors predicted, and then I borrowed more when I could not make the repayments. It was a hollow lonely feeling to fill in the lies upon the second online loan application, just to ensure enough money to last out until she died, when I was able to sell our house and pay it off.

So you will understand why I feel personal sympathy with the debtors who inhabited this cell. Every one will have had a reason and a story. I wish I could speak with Edward Burk, Iohn Knolle, William Thomas, Edward Murphy, Thomas Lynch, Richard Phelps, James Parkinson, Edward Stockley and the unnamed others to discover how they got here. In spite of the melancholy atmosphere, it gave me pleasure to examine their drawings incised upon the walls. Here in this dark smelly cell, the prisoners created totems, both to represent their own identities and to recall the commonplace sights of the exterior world. There are tall ships with all the rigging accurately observed, doves, trees, a Scots thistle, a gun, anchors and all manner of brick buildings. I could distinguish a church with a steeple, several taverns with suspended signs, and terraces stretching along the whole wall, not unlike the old houses in Spitalfields.

I shall carry in my mind these images upon the walls of the cell from Wellclose

Square for a long time, created by those denied the familiar wonders that fill our days. Shut away from life in an underground cell, they carved these intense bare images to evoke the whole world. Now they have gone, and everyone they loved has gone, and their entire world has gone generations ago, and we shall never know who they were, yet because of their graffiti we know that they were human and they lived.

TOM'S VAN

Street Life

TOM THE SAILOR took me to see his van. 'It's packed up,' he explained, adding with philosophical levity, 'Nothing lasts for ever,' as he led me through the busy streets with his dog Matty tugging eagerly at the leash all the way – and stopping occasionally to check bins for interesting stuff – until we arrived back in the safety of the tiny yard behind black corrugated-iron gates, where he parks his van and sleeps in the shack at the rear. 'He's at home,' Tom declared, as he released Matty from his lead, once we were standing together in the quiet to survey the van, which was overflowing with all the gear that Tom sells on Brick Lane each day.

'I got this van for next to nothing, three hundred quid – it's worth four hundred quid for scrap – and it's been a hell of a good van,' admitted Tom, praising the old blue van covered with slogans that is a familiar sight in Spitalfields, as if it were a thoroughbred he was reluctantly putting out to grass. 'I'm clearing it out now,' he confided, raising a

smile of anticipation. 'It's full of what I've picked up, stuff that's been thrown away – it's all worth money, especially if you're a vendor. I'm finding things I didn't know I had ... Old mobile phones in their boxes complete with chargers – big ugly old ones.'

This is how Tom has created a life for himself and Matty, rescuing what others discard and selling it on Brick Lane while sleeping on an old couch in a windowless shed. As Matty climbed into the cabin of the van and curled up where he delights to snooze, Tom swung back a door to show me his own dwelling by the glimmering light of a bicycle lamp – a cell less than ten feet square of bare brick and concrete, piled with books and blackened pans, and with an old sofa partly concealed in an alcove. 'How can you live like this?' I asked, unable to believe that anyone could exist in such frugal conditions. 'What about the cold?'

'It's what I am used to,' announced Tom defiantly, eager to dispel my concern. 'I enjoy the way I am. I don't want to live like other people – it's called survival. I got gas for cooking in bottles. I could have water and electricity, but I don't need it.' Seeing that I was not convinced, Tom expanded his explanation to emphasise that this was his choice. 'I've got my light. It only costs me batteries and I can bring in water. If you've got water you've got rates. If you've got electricity you've got bills. But if you've got a torch, you buy batteries and if you run out of them, then you go without ...' Seeing that I was at a loss for words, Tom assumed a friendly smile and asserted his personal notion of liberty. 'People get thrown out of their homes, and they're making it so hard you haven't got a chance – so the best chance you can have is to have nothing,' he said. When I thought of the stream of brown envelopes that come through my letter box, I could not deny that Tom had a point, but I doubt if I would have the courage to cut loose as he has done.

So, amazed by Tom's stamina and resilience, both physically and emotionally, I turned our conversation back to his van and the question of how he could replace it. 'I've got cash,' he said. 'It's a recession – so they say. There should be lots of vans going cheap because of the parking fines. A friend of mine has a Jaguar and he parked it in a loading bay and they want to charge him thousands in fines or take it from him. There's something wrong when you can take a man's Jaguar from him.' And he shook his head in bemused disappointment.

Then, as he padlocked the yard to leave, unable to resist the magnetic pull drawing him back to Brick Lane, where he spends all his waking hours, Tom added, 'The owner was here. He said, "You're all right, mate. Keep an eye on the place for me."' With subtle grace, Tom had absolved me of any responsibility for him, but more than this I was impressed by the strength of his character and the austerity of his vision of life, which has come to define the nature of his existence, granting him the particular freedom that suits his temperament.

'Be lucky, adieu!' he wished me, as we shook hands outside the beigel shop, arriving back in Brick Lane at the centre of the world.

COLUMBIA ROAD MARKET VI

Human Life, Market Life

DAWN HAD NOT YET BROKEN when I rose in the dark to walk up the road to have a chat with Denis Madden, one of the most spirited traders in the Columbia Road Market. When I arrived at six thirty, he was already set up and bright with anticipation for the day's trading.

'I've been here forty years, since I was seventeen,' he revealed to me with a grimace, rubbing his hand together in sentimental contemplation. 'I met this girl. She was third generation, her family had been trading here since the 1930s. They used to come down from Hoxton on a horse and cart. I was playing football on a semi-professional basis at the time, but her father – he became my father-in-law – put me on the stall and I was a natural. Previous to that, I was somebody who couldn't take to anything. I'd had at least fifteen jobs – disaffected, you might say. But it's very easy for me to stand behind a stall and shout, and meet people. I just took to it.'

Denis had been up since three thirty this morning, driving from Hertfordshire. 'I shall be tired come four thirty this afternoon,' he admitted with a shrug. 'You'll see it in my eyes.' And he gestured to his eyes, enacting a cartoon version of sleepiness. I

admire his stamina, because this pitch in Columbia Road is just a third of his business. Yesterday, Denis was trading, as he does every Saturday, in Saffron Walden, and on Friday in Uppingham in Rutland – and he spends two days each week prepping, back in Hertfordshire. Yet Denis is full of magnanimous humour and energy, unaffected by trading outdoors in all seasons. 'You learn to tolerate the cold. You accept the bad weather in winter just as you accept the good weather in summer. The only real problem comes with the flowers when the water freezes. Some don't like getting frozen and defrosted again,' he explained in characteristically practical terms. After forty years trading here, Denis takes it all in his stride now.

'I've already retired once, packed it up and moved to France, but I found I kept coming back to sort things out,' Denis con-fessed to me, rolling his eyes with an absurd grin of self-parody and spreading his hands as if to say, 'What can I do?' The market is his life and he is not going to give it up any day soon.

MARIANNA KENNEDY

DESIGNER

Human Life

BEHIND THIS ENIGMATIC FAÇADE – lettered 'W&A Jones' – at 3 Fournier Street, directly across from Christ Church, Spital-fields, is the showroom, workshop and home of designer Marianna Kennedy. The lofty spire of Nicholas Hawksmoor's church reflects in the crown glass panes of her shopfront.

For years I have walked past this place and wondered what goes on here, so I was very excited to go inside and meet Marianna

in person. Entering through the door on the right, I found myself in a bare eighteenth-century hallway, where at the old stairwell I was greeted by a woman dressed in ele-gant charcoal tones who spoke with a soft Canadian accent. Marianna invited me up-stairs and I followed in her footsteps until we arrived in her beautifully proportioned panelled living room. As I craned in wonder at the window, looking down on to Fournier Street and raising my eyes to the steeple towering overhead, Marianna busied herself screwing up newspaper with professional aplomb. She was lighting a fire in my hon-our, so we could enjoy a fireside chat.

Observing my curiosity, Marianna of-fered me a tour of the house and then, with a playful levity, she was off again, vanishing from the room like the White Rabbit. I fol-lowed her up more stairs, round and round, with each storey offering a new perspective backwards into all the secret gardens and yards that comprise the spaces between these ancient houses in the vicinity of the church. There are so many of these wonderfully irregular old staircases in Spitalfields, each with its own creaking language and each leading to surprises. At the top of this one, we turned sharply and ascended a final narrow flight, barely two feet wide, to pass through a door and arrive on the roof, where, hidden behind the parapet, Marianna has created an astounding secret garden with a wildflower meadow. The rooftop is on a level with the bell tower of the steeple across the road, and Marianna stood patiently in the meadow with all the mysterious poise of a heroine in a Wilkie Collins novel – while I gazed across the rooftops of Spitalfields, admiring the ramshackle irregularity of the old tiled roofs and chimney pots.

Once we were back by the fireside, Marianna settled into a wing chair illuminated by the morning sunshine and became eloquent in her affection for the architecture of the old houses here. She explained that she first came to stay in Fournier Street twenty-five years ago while a student at the Slade. Marianna and her husband renovated 42 Brushfield Street (the house with the sign 'A. Gold, French Milliners') before taking on the current property in a derelict state, prior to their repairs, ten years ago. Working with the Spitalfields Trust over all this time, Marianna has developed a sympathetic instinct for the decor of these spaces through the subtle use of traditional paint colours for panelling and old floors. 'It is all about lack of ego, restraint and humanity,' she admitted to me. 'You can make some-

thing look so natural, like it has always been there,' she explained, before adding significantly, 'That is a very hard thing to do.' Certainly, Marianna's home confirms this aesthetic, a working house with elegant spaces that serves as the ideal showplace for her furniture designs.

Above the fireplace in her living room is a huge bronze foliate mirror with tinted mercury glass to Marianna's design, here in a corner is a lacquerwork table with cast bronze legs, hanging against the stairwell window is a dazzling collection of colourful transparent resin casts of plasterwork details and in each room there are the lamps

of traditional design, also cast in brightly coloured resin – these are her signature pieces. All these artefacts are unmistakably contemporary and yet, because they are skilfully made by craftsmen using techniques that have been around for centuries, they complement the interior of the old house.

As we made our way down to the shop to say goodbye, I congratulated Marianna on recreating such a beautiful house. 'It still has its magic,' she said with understatement, and, after my experience that day, I can happily confirm her assertion.

LARRY GOLDSTEIN
TOY SELLER AND TAXI DRIVER

Human Life, Market Life, Past Life

LARRY GOLDSTEIN, who sells toys in Petticoat Lane each Sunday, showed me this photograph of his grandfather Joseph Goldstein, born in 1896 in the village of Inyema in Poland. Joseph had two elder brothers and, although there are no photographs of them, they are the true heroes of this story – because at the time of the pogroms against the Jews, these two brothers realised they had enough money for one brother to escape, so they gave it to Joseph.

In 1915, at the age of nineteen, Joseph travelled to Brick Lane via Hamburg to join an uncle who had a business selling lemonade. Yet when he arrived by boat in the Port of London, Joseph was told he must either enlist or return to Poland. Joseph enlisted, occasioning the photograph you see here, and was sent off to fight in the First World War. He never learned what became of his brothers and today the village of Inyema does not even exist.

Although these events happened nearly a century ago, they remain vividly in mind for Larry, Joseph's grandson. 'It is amazing that his brothers put him first, so that he could get out of the country and carry on the name Goldstein, when they were murdered or tortured by the Russians. It's touching when you come to think about it,' Larry confided to me with quiet humility, during his hour's lunch break from driving his taxi. These events have cast a certain tender emotionalism upon subsequent family history, because all are aware that they are the descendants of the brother who survived to begin a new life in Spitalfields.

Having escaped Poland, Joseph was lucky enough to survive the First World War too.

No wonder he got married in April 1918, as the war was coming to its end, to Amelia (known as Milly). Milly Viskin was born in Pedley Street, Spitalfields, in 1894 and her father was a cabinet maker. At first, they lived with her parents in Hare Street (now known as Cheshire Street) and he was able to get a job as a presser in Flower and Dean Street, off Brick Lane.

Joseph and Milly had five children, Sid, Jack, Cecilia, Janet and Dave. And today it is impossible to look at the wedding-day photograph of Jack with his father, taken in 1955, and not appreciate Joseph's intense expression of pride upon this special day in the light of his personal history. To my eyes, the picture of Larry with his grandparents Joseph and Milly, taken at his bar mitzvah in 1970, has a similar quality – it is the visual link between Larry in the present day and the world that Joseph knew in Poland, over a century ago.

Larry fondly recalls visiting Joseph and Milly when he was a child. 'They always made you welcome and they were always

there when you needed them, even though they had no money. They died very close to each other, within a year, because they were so attached.'

Larry told me Jack and his uncle Sid ran a stall with Joseph on Saturdays in Kingsland Waste, selling photographic equipment. It was a precedent that Larry adopted once he got married. 'My wife's dad had a double pitch in Church Street, off the Edgware Road, so he said we could have one, selling wooden boxes and china fig-urines. Then, in 1972, we had some friends in Petticoat Lane who said we could sublet a pitch, and we changed our commodity over to teddy bears, because the stall was licensed for toys. I had a friend who imported teddy bears and he said, "I'll give you a couple to try out," and it took off from there.'

Nearly forty years later, Larry is still selling teddy bears on Petticoat Lane. His joyous display of brightly coloured children's toys is a landmark, and he is one of

the very last Jewish traders today in what was once a Jewish neighbourhood. 'Coach parties used to be dropped off at the Aldgate end of Petticoat Lane and Christmas clubs came to spend all their money,' he told me, describing the heyday of the market. 'You had to get an affidavit from the rabbi to trade in those days. Before the repeal of the Sunday trading laws, Petticoat Lane and Wembley were the only licensed Sunday markets, but now it's only just worth my while.'

Larry is a hard-working, self-respecting individual, driving the taxi to make ends meet, as well as trading in the market. Once he had found a parking place in Spitalfields, Larry had less than an hour to tell me his story and drink a cup of tea before he had to get back on the road. Yet in spite of the challenges he faces today, Joseph's story sets everything in perspective for Larry Goldstein, who cherishes his childhood memory of his grandfather. 'He was a very kind-hearted man. Although he spoke very little English, he always liked to bet on the favourites at the dogs, so my dad used to place the bets for him at the betting shop. His children and his grandchildren were his life. He was so grateful to be alive after what he had been through.'

AT JAMES INCE AND SONS
UMBRELLA MAKERS

Human Life, Past Life

THE FACTORY of James Ince and Sons, the oldest-established umbrella makers in the country, is one of the few places in London where you will not hear complaints about the rainy weather, because, while our moist climate is such a disappointment to the population in general, it has happily sustained generations of Inces for over two centuries now. If you walked down Whites Row in Spitalfields in 1824, you would have found William Ince making umbrellas, and six generations later, I was able to visit Richard Ince, still making umbrellas in the

East End. Yet although the date of origin of the company is conservatively set at 1805, there was one William Inch, a tailor listed in Spitalfields in 1793, who may have been father to William Ince of Whites Row – which makes it credible to surmise that Inces have been making umbrellas since they first became popular at the end of the eighteenth century.

You might assume that the weight of so much history bears down heavily upon Richard Ince, but it is like water off a duck's back to him, because he is simply too busy manufacturing umbrellas. Richard's father and grandfather were managers with a large staff of employees, but Richard is one of only four at James Ince and Sons today, and he works alongside his colleagues as a member of the team, cutting and stitching, personally supervising all the orders. Watching them at work this week provided a glimpse of what William Ince's workshop might have been like in Spitalfields in 1824, because although synthetics and steel have replaced silk and whalebone, and all stitching is done by machine now, the essential design and manufacturing process of umbrellas remains the same.

Between these two workshops of William Ince in 1824 and Richard Ince in 2011 exists a majestic history, which might be best described as one of gracious expansion and then sudden contraction, in the manner of an umbrella itself. It was the necessity of silk that made Spitalfields the natural home for James Ince and Sons. The company prospered there during the expansion of London through the nineteenth century

and the increase in colonial trade, especially to India and Burma. In 1837 they moved into larger premises in Brushfield Street and, by 1857, filled a building on Bishopsgate too. In the twentieth century, workers at the factory in Spitalfields took cover in the basement during air raids and then emerged to resume making military umbrellas for soldiers in the trenches during the First World War and canvas covers for guns during the Second World War. Luckily, the factory itself narrowly survived a flying bomb, permitting the company to enjoy post-war success, diversifying into angling umbrellas, golfing umbrellas, sun umbrellas, promotional umbrellas and even a ceremonial umbrella for a Nigerian chief. But in the 1980s a change in tax law, meaning that umbrella makers could no longer be classed as self-employed, challenged the viability of the company, causing James Ince and Sons to shed most of the staff and move to smaller premises in Hackney.

This is some of the history that Richard Ince does not think about very much, while deeply engaged through every working hour with the elegant contrivance of making umbrellas. In the twenty-first century, James Ince and Sons fashion the umbrellas for Rubeus Hagrid and Mary Poppins, surely the most famous brollies on the planet. A fact which permits Richard a small yet justly deserved smile of satisfaction, as the proper outcome of more than 200 years of umbrella making by seven generations of his family. His smile in its quiet intensity reveals his passion for his calling. 'My father didn't want to do it,' he admitted with a grin of regret, 'but I left school at seventeen and I felt my way in. I used to spend my Saturdays in Spitalfields, kicking cabbages around as footballs, and when we had the big tax problem, it taught me that I had to get involved.' This was how Richard oversaw the transformation of his company to become the lean operation it is today. 'We are the only people who are prepared to look at making weird umbrellas, when they want strange ones for film and theatre,' he confessed with yet another quiet smile, as if this indication of his expertise were merely an admission of amiable gullibility.

On the ground floor of his factory in Vyner Street is a long block where Richard unfurls the rolls of fabric and cuts the umbrella panels using a wooden pattern and a sharp knife. Then he carries the armful of pieces upstairs to Rita Smith, the irresistibly charming machinist with vivid green eyes that match her uniform, who sits perched by the window, eager to sew the panels together, deploying a deceptively casual expertise honed over sixty years at her machine. Seventy-six-year-old Rita has

sewn umbrella covers for three generations of Inces – Richard, Wilfred and Geoffrey, Richard's father, whose picture she glances at occasionally for reassurance, high upon the wall in the workroom. 'I never wanted to try anything else. My aunt Eva got me the job when I was fifteen and I worked beside her at first. If I got it wrong, she said, "Do it again or I'll knock you off your chair!"' confided Rita to me mischievously, enacting the role of Aunt Eva with fearsome conviction. 'I started in Spitalfields in 1950 as a machinist,' she continued brightly. 'Upstairs there used to be a cutter for ladies' and gentlemen's umbrellas and one for garden umbrellas, and below four machinists who did garden umbrellas and three who did ladies' and gents' and golf umbrellas, as well as six "tippers", who sewed the covers on by

hand.' All the time Rita spoke, she worked, almost automatically, sewing the triangular panels of slippery fabric in pairs, combining them into fours and then adding a thin, perfectly even seam all round the circumference, once she had made a complete cover of eight pieces.

As soon as the covers are sewn, Job Forster takes them and does the 'tipping', which consists of fixing the 'points' (which attach the cover to the ends of the ribs), sewing the cover to the frame and adding the tie which is used to furl the umbrella when it is not in use. Job was making some huge umbrellas for the Berkeley, used by the hotel's doormen to shepherd guests through the rain, and I watched as he clamped the bare metal frame to the bench, revolving it as he stitched the cover to each rib in turn, to complete the umbrella. Then came the moment when Job opened it up to scrutinise his handiwork. With a satisfying 'thunk', the black cover expanded like a giant bat stretching its wings taut and I was spellbound by the drama of the moment – because now I understood what it takes to make one. I was seeing an umbrella for the first time, thanks to James Ince and Sons (Umbrella Makers) Ltd.

GARY ARBER'S COLLECTION

Past Life

I RETURNED to Gary Arber's printing shop in the Roman Road to collect the correspondence cards he had printed for me at the old printing works and toy shop opened by his grandfather W. F. Arber in 1897 and of which he is the last custodian.

Gary is an extraordinarily talented man, not just an ex flying ace but also a skilled technician who has maintained the printing presses for the last half-century and done all the typography in the printing works too, including drawing illustrations for print jobs. This is in addition to doing all his own plumbing and wiring here and at home, always undertaking car repairs himself, and leaving time over to be an expert wildlife photographer and RSPB conservation warden at weekends. It is refreshing to meet a man with so many varied accomplishments and it gives Gary a certain confidence. He demonstrates an appealing modesty too when, for example, he shows you the sash window he is in the process of renovating. As you are probably aware, a sash window is a complex piece of joinery, but Gary had already disassembled one, replaced the rotten timber and reinstalled it, when he showed me the next one he was going to tackle.

Once upon a time, six printers worked here in the printing shop, alongside compositors, trimmers, shop assistants and managers, but now there is just Gary knocking around on four floors of the works doing a little printing, playing patience on his computer and repairing the sash windows when he feels like it. Alone, like Prospero on his island, surrounded by his secret kingdom, Gary does as he pleases – when not interrupted by a string of admiring young visitors who come to wonder and in the hope that Gary will tell more of his beguiling tales. I count myself among this group of devotees who appreciate Gary Arber for his dignified flippant philosophising as a palliative to the earnest literalism of modern life.

As anyone who has visited the shop will know, the strings above the counter once suspended a fine display of boxed toys. This was more than a generation ago and Gary has carried on working here without ever tidying up. Our culture is puritanical when it comes to order and organisation. We are taught to believe there is innate moral value in tidiness, but it is an entirely spurious notion. I have often wondered what it would be like if you never changed anything, never threw anything away and never cleared up. Gary's printing works conscientiously illustrates the result of such an independent-spirited approach. Almost everything from the last century of business remains and the textures of human activity are vivid. You

might assume that the past is gone, vanished like the wind, but in Gary's world time is manifest in the layers and layers of things used by all those who were once here. Gary accepts that his existence is contingent too, confiding to me that, in spite of multiple leaks, he will not be shelling out for the new roof that is required because he would rather leave that for the next owner who comes along – a sentiment that is touching in its unsentimental realism.

In the meantime, Gary is the custodian who alone knows the stories, who alone knows how everything works, who can pick up anything and tell you what it is and why it is there. For example, Gary pointed out the Alto Lagonda printing press, one of six in the basement, the machine that printed the handbills for the Suffragettes. It is ac-

companied by a Wharfedale, a Heidelberg, a Supermatic, a Golding Jobber and a Mercedes Glockner, all from the early twentieth century except the Supermatic. Gary described that machine as 'new', because it was manufactured in the 1950s. Only the Heidelberg is in use at present. This is the one that printed my cards, and when Gary set it in motion for me, it whirred into life with all the easy grace of a vast sea beast twirling in deep water.

Gary's grandparents, Walter and Emily, lived on the floors above the shop, but once they died Gary's father, also Walter, turned their first-floor living room into a compositor's room (the 'comp room', as Gary terms it) and the rest of the living space became storage for the print works. The golden 1930s wallpaper and chocolate colour scheme make an attractive background to the tall cabinets of trays of type and compositors' desks set on either side of a compositor's stone. A Health and Safety inspector, with a bureaucratic mania worthy of Peter Sellers, once insisted that the walls must be whitewashed because people have to work in white rooms, apparently. However, Gary stood his ground like a true Englishman and the 30s wallpaper remains today in all its shabby glory.

Most of the type here is worn out with use and we walked upon a layer of thousands of tiny pieces of dusty grey metal type spilled on to the floor of the comp room, undulating like the lunar surface and crunching beneath our feet. Gary delighted to snatch a case of type from the cabinet and show me the V and J compartments in the bottom right corner – apart from the rest of the letters because they were added to the alphabet later, after the design of printers' cases had been standardised, centuries ago. This case was all capital letters. 'This is the upper case,' announced Gary gleefully, before putting it back and pulling out the one beneath with a flourish, 'and this is the lower case!' In an instant, I understood the origin of the terminology I have used all my life to distinguish what in school were referred to as 'the big letters and the small letters'. I shall never forget that, as long as I live. Neither shall I ever forget my visits to this unique printing shop and now, every time I use my handsome correspondence cards (that he printed for me so kindly at the price

they were thirty years ago) I will always think affectionately of Gary there in the eternal magic kingdom that is W. F. Arber & Co. Ltd.

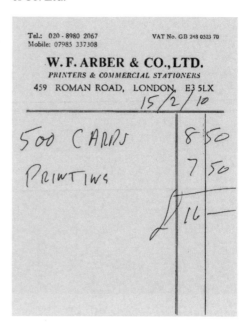

ROB RYAN

PAPERCUT ARTIST

Human Life

IN A QUIET STREET off the Old Bethnal Green Road, there is a large wooden door. If you go through a smaller door within this large one, you enter a passage, under an arch, that leads to a courtyard where there is another door. Go through this door, climb up a staircase and you will find the secret den of Rob Ryan, the papercut artist. With his luxuriant curls and thick beard, working here in this old loft, intent upon his cre-

ations, Rob Ryan might appear as a romantic nineteenth-century figure – like 'The Tailor of Gloucester' – if it were not for the hoodie and Ray-Bans that bring him bang up to date.

'I am not a connoisseur of papercutting,' Rob declares in self-deprecating style, when I ask him about the origins of his work, as we cosy up on a couch upholstered in denim jeans. Years ago, before the seismic shift in cultural hierarchies that happened at the end of the last century, Rob was a painter who included words in his paintings and got a lot of flak for it. 'Cheating' was the particular crime levelled at him at the Royal College of Art, where Rob was studying printmaking.

Rob produces a scruffy old paperback of Tyrolean papercuts – if there was a eureka moment, it was the discovery of this book. Making papercuts, he explains, was a natural extension of the screenprint stencils that he was already cutting and the symmetrical nature of these papercuts did not allow for the inclusion of words. So papercutting was the 'cure' for the 'malaise' of sticking words in his pictures.

Rob's story is a startling reminder of how the hegemony of the art world has changed now, but it does not begin to account for the extraordinary flair that he brings to everything he touches. This is work of immense appeal that celebrates life and the complex emotions that colour our daily experience.

Obviously, the 'cure' was completely ineffectual, because his work is full of words that provide an important dynamic to the images. 'I love the work of William Blake, and those English twentieth-century graphic artists like Eric Ravilious, Edward Bawden, Eric Fraser,' Rob explains, and his work is an honourable inheritor of this lively tradition.

There is an emotional fullness and energy to all of Rob's work that speaks of an artist who has found his perfect medium. Quickly, he saw the limitations of entirely symmetrical papercuts and that is when the words came back in again. Getting passionate, he gestures theatrically and, in delight, declares of papercutting, 'There is no cheating! There is no right! There is no wrong!'

Things start to get exciting now, as he offers me an apple and moves over to his work table to commence a papercut. His energy changes and a serene Rob Ryan emerges as he opens a notebook and begins purposefully to copy a sketch in pencil on to a sheet of paper on a light box. Then he transfers the paper to a green cutting board

and begins to cut it out with a scalpel in swift, confident strokes. There is a different, more intense, atmosphere in the room now, everything focused on the quick movement of the blade between Rob's nimble fingers, and I reach over to capture the moment with my camera. Then it has passed, Rob inscribes the papercut and kindly presents it to me as a souvenir.

It is an image of a mother and child playing together. As I examine the treasured scrap, when I get back to my desk, I am conscious of the sinuous subtle lines of the delicate cut that give these figures life and movement, capturing an ephemeral moment of intimate affection between parent and child.

In a papercut, all the elements have to be connected – human figures have to hold hands or touch – and as a result of this technical requirement, this sense of connection has become a defining element in Rob Ryan's work, as both technique and subject matter. The breathtaking skill on display brings an audience to these works, but it is the language that gives depth in the exposure of ambivalent or raw emotion, and this emotionalism, whether light or dark, creates an exciting counterpoint to the control required to make them.

Years ago, Rob had a studio at the Bishopsgate end of the Spitalfields Market, until it was demolished. He regularly used to eat a huge roast lunch at the Market Café in Fournier Street before it shut at eleven in the morning, to set him up for a day's work. Now he has become one of the most popular artists, in our neighbourhood and far beyond too, and I like to think that in his use of familiar domestic images, he captures something of the essence of the life of this place as it is lived now.

THE RETURN OF PAMELA FREEDMAN

Human Life, Night Life, Past Life

PAMELA HARRIS was a West End girl, born in 1923 in the Bricklayers' Arms in Berwick Street, Soho – the pub managed by her parents, Hetty and Albert Harris, just around the corner from the Blue Posts, run by her grandfather. This was the only world Pamela knew, until one fateful day when the treasurer of the pub's Christmas club absconded with all the savings and her father did the honourable thing, paying back the money to his customers out of his own pocket. It was a noble action that changed his family's lives for ever.

As a consequence, Hetty and Albert lost the Bricklayers' Arms and in 1935, when Pamela was thirteen, they started a whole new life in the East End, managing the Princess Alice in Commercial Street. 'When my mother saw it, she said, "Never in a million years! I can't live in a place like that." The state of it was disgusting,' revealed Pamela, when I met her at the Princess Alice on her first return visit since the 1960s, gazing wistfully around at the location that was once central to her life, rendered barely recognisable by alterations now. 'The brewery sent the builders in and when they opened up the old counter, the rats ran everywhere. When my mother saw the seamen's lodging house on the top that was rotten and neglected, she was frightened she might fall through the ceiling. The first

thing the brewery did was demolish the top floors,' she told me with gleeful satisfaction, explaining the curiously stunted architecture of the building today.

Although it was inauspicious circumstances that brought them to the East End, Hetty and Albert created a vibrant life at the Princess Alice, with a large crowd of friendly regulars. But a far greater challenge was to come when the Second World War brought bombing, setting the East End ablaze, as Pamela recounted to me. 'We had one night when the buzz bombs started. Daddy and I saw a buzz bomb catch 300 people coming out of work from Old Street. They all died.

A lot of our customers were killed. We made dugouts in the cellar and we slept down there. We lay there listening to the clicking of the tram lines as the bombs hit. We kept coming up to see if anything was left standing. One night I came up from the cellar and everything was on fire. We told the firemen to take the beer and use it to put out the flames. We had no glass in the windows of the pub and the brewers said, "Stay open." We had no power and the brewers said, "Get candles and stay open." On the night the war ended, we sold out and we went up to the West End to celebrate.'

In the midst of this chaos, Pamela got

married to Alf Freedman, who lived across the street. 'We grew up together and we were the same age. He was in the RAF for five years as a meteorological officer in North Africa, while I was a fire warden for three years. He came back from abroad and we decided to get married. Both families knew a lot of people and God forbid anyone should be ignored. It was the first big wedding after the war. Sandys Row Synagogue was too small, so we had it at the New West End Synagogue, St Petersburgh Place, Bayswater, and 400 people came to the dinner. I was twenty-four when I got married and left the Princess Alice for good. All the draymen turned up early in the morning outside in the street to see me off. After I got married, I lived in a nice flat in Kensington, but my husband was still away in the service. We were married nearly sixty years. We had a very good life. We worked hard and we went all over the world.'

Destiny took her back to the West End, her place of origin, and the foray into the East End became a single episode in her long life, but I think Pamela's experiences here endowed her with a fearless quality and an unsentimental appreciation of the value of existence that have remained with her. On the day in 1964 that her father, Alf, died at seven in the morning, the brewery expected her mother to open the Princess Alice, and although Hetty technically had a year's grace as a widow, Pamela and her brother gave notice to the brewery at once. They departed the East End with their mother in a taxi and never looked back, until last week, when Pamela returned to the Princess Alice at the invitation of her grandson Jeremy Freedman, who works at Sandys Row Synagogue. Although, wisely, Pamela did ensure they kept the contents of the cellar from the Princess Alice when they left, which she and her family are still drinking to this day, including bottles of whisky now worth over 500 pounds each. But it was farewell to the East End, as Pamela herself said to me plainly, 'We had no cause to come this way.'

Pamela Freedman is a person of extraordinary vitality, a charismatic diminutive woman with bright confident eyes, a shrewd yet upbeat generous manner and a shrill energetic way of talking, constantly punctuating her speech with phrases like, 'You tell people things, they wouldn't believe you!', 'So many stories, am I boring you?' and, her favourite exclamation, 'Unbelievable!' This last word serves as her personal leitmotif when called upon to consider the events of her life. Yet she was as delighted and curious to meet Rebecca Lees and Nick Waring – the young couple who are the current landlady and landlord of the Princess Alice – as they were astounded to meet her.

Recalling her own time behind the bar, Pamela outlined her personal method of dealing with troublesome customers. 'My secret weapon was a siphon of soda behind the counter. I could let go as well as anybody, because I didn't care, even though I was the governor's daughter,' she declared.

Describing Hetty and Albert's style as landlords, she said, 'Everything had to be regimented. If you put a bottle the wrong way round, God help you ...' A comment which drew a strong reaction from Rebecca, who dug her partner Nick in the ribs. 'Just like me!' she exclaimed. Sizing them up with the benefit of a lifetime's experience, Pamela revealed her approval of the current management. 'You're what I call "of the old school", but it's bloody hard work, isn't it?' she confided, as they all exchanged a look of mutual recognition

THIS BELL WILL RING WHEN WE KISS GOODNIGHT

MR PUSSY IN SUMMER

Animal Life

THOSE OF YOU who are luxuriating in the warmth of summer, spare a thought for my cat, Mr Pussy, who has a fur coat surgically attached and spends his languorous days stretched out upon the floor in a heat-induced stupor. As the sun reaches its zenith, his activity declines and he seeks the deep shadow, the cooling breeze and the bare wooden floor to stretch out and fall into a deep trance that can transport him far away to the loss of his physical being. Mr Pussy's refined nature is such that even these testing conditions provide an opportunity for him to show grace, transcending dreamy resignation to explore an area of meditation of which he is the supreme proponent.

In the early morning and late afternoon, you will see him on the first-floor window-sill here in Spitalfields, taking advantage of the draught of air through the house. With his aristocratic attitude, Mr Pussy seeks amusement in watching the passers-by from his high vantage point on the street frontage and enjoys lapping water from his dish on the kitchen windowsill at the back of the house, where in the evenings he also likes to look down upon the foxes gambolling in the yard.

Whereas in winter it is Mr Pussy's custom to curl up in a ball to exclude draughts, in these balmy days he prefers to stretch out to maximise the air flow around his body. There is a familiar sequence to his actions, as particular as stages in yoga. Finding a sympathetic location with the advantage of cross-currents and shade from direct light, at first Mr Pussy will sit to consider the suitability of the circumstance, before rolling on to his side and releasing the muscles in his limbs, revealing that he is irrevocably set upon the path of total relaxation.

Delighting in the sensuous moment, Mr Pussy stretches out to his maximum length of over three feet, curling his spine and splaying his legs at angles, creating an impression of the frozen moment of a leap, just like those wooden horses on fairground rides. Extending every muscle and toe, his glinting claws unsheathe and his eyes widen gleaming gold, until the stretch reaches its full extent and subsides in the manner of a wave upon the ocean, as Mr Pussy slackens his limbs to lie peacefully with heavy lids descending.

In this position that resembles a carcass on the floor, Mr Pussy can undertake his

journey into dreams, apparent by his twitching eyelids and limbs as he runs through the dark forest of his feline unconscious, where prey are to be found in abundance. Vulnerable as an infant, sometimes Mr Pussy cries to himself in his dream, an internal murmur of indeterminate emotion, evoking a mysterious fantasy that I can never be party to. It is somewhere beyond thought or language. I can only wonder if his Arcadia is like that in Paolo Uccello's *The Hunt in the Forest* or whether Mr Pussy's dreamscape resembles the water meadows of the River Exe, the location of his youthful safaris.

There is another stage, beyond dreams, signalled when Mr Pussy rolls on to his back with his front paws distended like a child in the womb, almost in prayer. His back legs splayed to either side, his head tilts back, his jaw loosens and his mouth opens a little, just sufficient to release his shallow breath – and Mr Pussy is gone. Silent and inanimate, he looks like a baby and yet very old at the same time. The heat relaxes Mr Pussy's connection to the world and he falls, he lets himself go far away on a spiritual odyssey. It is somewhere deep and somewhere cool and he is out of his body, released from the fur coat at last.

Startled upon awakening from his trance, like a deep-sea diver ascending too quickly, Mr Pussy squints at me as he recovers recognition, giving his brains a good shake, now the heat of the day has subsided. Lolloping down the stairs, still loose-limbed, he strolls out of the house into the garden and takes a dust bath under a tree, spending the next hour washing it out and thereby cleansing the sticky perspiration from his fur.

Regrettably, the climatic conditions that subdue Mr Pussy by day also enliven him by night. At first light, when the dawn chorus commences, he stands on the floor at my bedside, scratches a little and calls to me. I waken to discover two golden eyes filling my field of vision. I roll over at my peril, because this will provoke Mr Pussy to walk to the end of the bed and scratch my toes sticking out under the sheet, causing me to wake again with a cry of pain. Having no choice but to rise, accepting his forceful invitation to appreciate the manifold joys of an early summer morning in Spitalfields, it is not an entirely unwelcome obligation.

AT THE GRAPES IN LIMEHOUSE

Night Life, Past Life

OF A SUMMER'S EVENING it has become my habit to take an occasional stroll from Spitalfields down to Limehouse, to enjoy a few drinks at the Grapes. Out of all the historic riverside pubs, this tiny place, dating from 1585, has best retained its personality and charm, still resembling the Six Jolly Fellowship Porters in *Our Mutual Friend*, for which it is believed Charles Dickens took the Grapes as his model in 1865.

In its whole construction it had not a straight floor and hardly a straight line, but it had outlasted and clearly would yet outlast, many a better trimmed building, many a sprucer public house. Externally, it was a narrow lop-sided wooden jumble of corpulent windows heaped one upon the other as you might heap as many toppling oranges, with a crazy wooden verandah impending over the water, but seemed to have got into the condition of a faint-hearted diver who has paused so long on the brink that he will never go in at all ...

Coming down Narrow Street, parallel to the Thames, you arrive at a handsome eighteenth-century terrace and walk straight off the pavement into the bar of the Grapes,

leaving the sunshine behind to discover that the building is just one room wide – no more than fifteen feet across. In the cool gloom you find yourself in a bare-boarded barroom full of attractively mismatched furniture and look beyond to the source of glimmering light, which is the river. Stepping through into the cosy back bar, no larger than a small parlour, you realise this is the entire extent of the ground floor.

With an appealing surfeit of old brown matchboarding and lined with picture frames containing a whole archive of prints, photographs and paintings that tell the story of this venerable pub and outline its connection to the work of Dickens, this is one of the most charismatic spaces I know.

Through the double doors, you find yourself upon the veranda and the full expanse of the water is quite overwhelming to behold at this bend in the river, where it twists towards Greenwich shimmering in the distance. In fact, this is the frontage of the pub because, until recently, most customers would have come directly from the river. James McNeill Whistler's lithograph of 1859 shows a gangplank laid across from this balcony on to a barge. If you are searching for the riverside atmosphere that once existed here, come one misty autumn evening, enjoy a drink while watching the lights of passing boats gleaming through the raindrops upon the panes, and relish your proximity to the grim murky depths from the safety and warmth of the parlour.

Dickens described the landlady of the Six Jolly Fellowship Porters thus.

Miss Potterson, sole proprietor and manager ... reigned supreme on her throne, the bar, and a man must have drunk himself mad drunk indeed if he thought he could contest the point with her. Being known on her own authority as Miss Abbey Potterson ...

It was my pleasure to ascend the narrow staircase to the dining room overlooking

the river, where Dickens once sat. Here I enjoyed the honour of taking afternoon tea with the current sole proprietor and manager, the gracious Miss Barbara Haigh, who like her fictional predecessor also reigns supreme. As we sipped our tea, sitting close by the curved windows overlooking the water, it was as if we were in the stateroom of a great ship and the passing vessels, which interrupted our conversation – including a magnificent brown-sailed Thames sailing barge – were there for our sole amusement, displaying themselves simply for Barbara's inspection.

The redoubtable Barbara, who has been landlady here for the past sixteen years, is a proud ex-Bunny Girl from the London Playboy Club in Park Lane, as well as a keen enthusiast for the works of Dickens and a passionate custodian of the history of the

Grapes. With so many exciting avenues to pursue, we barely knew where to commence our conversation. As she spoke fondly of her twelve years at the Playboy Club, working her way up to become top bunny (appointed room director at the club), it became apparent that Barbara still retains the physical confidence and poise from these years. I was stunned when she produced images of herself cavorting with David Frost, describing the camaraderie between the bunny girls and recalling when the club shut for ever in 1982. 'We'd all become close friends, and we still have our reunions here each September, but when the club closed, I thought, "I'll offer myself to a brewery and ask, 'What do you want to do with me?'"' Barbara's Playboy years certainly taught her how to couch a proposition.

Working at first in partnership, Barbara quickly realised she could run a pub better by herself and, after a spell at the Brown Bear in Leman Street, she was offered the Grapes. But she was not at all enthusiastic at first. 'I came down here to take a look at the end of February. It was freezing cold and windy. Quite desolate. I thought, "I'm not coming here to the back of beyond." All I heard was the creak of the sign blowing in the wind. But I came back for dinner and I fell in love with the place. When I first came here I used to sit in the bar after it was closed. Now I feel I was destined to be here,' explained Barbara, dismissing her former scepticism and casting her grey eyes with a tender smile of proprietary satisfaction around the narrow dining room, where she has created a reputation for serving fish

delivered fresh daily from nearby Billingsgate Market.

'I haven't changed it at all,' continued Barbara, her eyes glittering with defiance and affection, 'but not a week went by during the first twelve years without a stand-up row, to preserve it as it is and stop the brewery's unwanted interference. I altered nothing but the atmosphere. I have warmed it up by loving the place. I've had three lots of staff in the last sixteen years, terrific teams that ran like clockwork. Then in 2006 I was offered the choice of redundancy or buying the lease, so now it is mine, until the three-hundred-year lease expires in 2042. Then we'll see what happens, because after all this time no one knows who owns the freehold.'

Over these years, Barbara has lived in the tiny flat with river views perched precariously up on the top, and connected to the pub by a fine 1720s staircase. Her precious spare time has been spent researching the history and collecting the pictures that line the walls, becoming fascinated with Emily Judge, the model for Abbey Potterson, the landlady in *Our Mutual Friend*. With some remarkable detective work, Barbara has uncovered a portrait of Emily in an oil painting by the Victorian seascape artist Charles Napier Hemy, entitled *Limehouse Barge Builders*, which shows her bringing a basket of victuals to the group of men working on the shore, and wearing a stunning red cape. It cannot be an accident that it is the same hue as the leather jacket Barbara wears in her photograph here.

We shall all be waiting to see if the mysterious freeholder appears in 2042, but in the meantime I will continue popping down to the the Grapes in the hope of stumbling upon a Bunny Girls' reunion.

MARK PETTY

TRENDSETTER

Human Life, Street Life

THIS IS WHAT I CONSIDER A CLASSIC Mark Petty outfit. It has the high-waisted flares, wide lapels and tie – all in a vibrant colour scheme – and Mark wears it with the audacious flair that we have come to expect from him. Anyone who frequents Brick Lane on a regular basis will be familiar with Mark and his boldly coloured leather suits, because he has honoured us by adopting these streets as his stage, or rather his catwalk, upon which he performs his theatrics of fashion.

Mark and his clothing have become part of the fabric of our neighbourhood, and it always lifts my spirits to spot him among a crowd of unremarkably dressed people, bringing a splash of eye-catching colour to elevate the scene. It is a joy that is compounded when I see him later in an entirely different outfit – an event which can occur several times in the same day, increasing the delight and admiration of the many residents who hold Mark in esteem as our self-styled ambassador for colour.

Among all the snazzy dressers of Shoreditch, what makes Mark special is that he designs his own clothes, not merely to look fashionable but as an unmediated expression of himself. More than anyone else I can

think of, Mark uses clothing to express who he is. He shows how he feels – revealing his inner self openly – and in the process his liberationist example has become an inspiration to us all.

'The reason I started was because in the 70s I was too young to wear the fashions, and by the time I was old enough flared trousers had gone,' explained Mark as we sat in his pink living room in a quiet corner of Bethnal Green. 'So I went round to Mr Singh at Batty Fashions in the Bethnal Green Road to see if he could make me

some. I have no training in fashion, yet I cut my own cardboard patterns, though it wasn't easy at first doing flares.

'I tried going out in Bethnal Green and the reaction was very hostile – from children who threw bottles at me – but I thought, "I'll persevere because fashion is too drab and life should be full of colour." I'm not the kind of person that gives in. So I went to Ridley Road Market in my lilac 70s outfit and on the whole the reaction was good. I find each area is different. You can't ascertain in advance whether you'll get mugged or chased. The older people here say, "You're a rebel," and I get requests to wear particular outfits. My most popular request is for pink.

'I'll never forget the gang of Scottish football supporters I met at a bus stop in Shoreditch High Street. They said, "It takes a lot of nerve to wear what you're wearing," and asked to be photographed with me. Hopefully something good will come of it and people will realise that life isn't all beige and black, and you need to express yourself. It needs a kick up the backside. When I went to Tottenham, where they all wear baseball caps, tracksuits and have designer dogs, they said, "You're ruining our culture!" In Croydon, when they realised I was from east London, they said, "We don't get a lot of people from the North here."

'I moved to London from Essex sixteen years ago. I was born in Oxford but my mother decided to marry and live in Essex. I had a problem in Essex at school because I had a West Country accent. They said, "You're a foreigner so we don't like you!" My mother's been there thirty years now and they still say to her, "You'll never be one of us." I was forced out of Braintree. It was all over the newspaper headlines. Once you come through that you can come through anything. I used to lie on the floor of my flat with my three cats in the dark and pretend to be out. This went on for months, until they came round at night with flaming torches and smashed all the windows.

'Moving to London, I found people in pubs and clubs very cold, and I settled in London in Tottenham on the Broadwater Estate, which had a fearsome reputation. I thought, "I'm here on my own," so I got Rose, an English bull terrier, but it was quite terrifying even walking to the park with the dog. As they said to me in Islington when they saw my outfit, "There's not a lot of people that's got the courage."

'I must know everyone in Bethnal Green now. They say, "You're quite a celebrity round here," but I never thought of it that way. I just did what I had to do. We had a lot of builders round here last year, so I used to try my designs out on them to see what they thought. Unfortunately they've gone now. I used to get a lot of offers but none have been taken up. I went to Walthamstow Market recently and the girls were holding their boyfriends' hands because they were looking at me rather than their girls. If only people could experiment more and show their bodies. Even women here dress like men. The worse thing they ever did was invent the remote control. No one gets any exercise any more.

'I've noticed in Romford and Ilford that guys are starting to wear pink. You'd expect it to be the little skinny ones but it's the big butch guys. A woman said to me in Bethnal Green Tesco, "You're corrupting our men! It's dirty and perverted." I said, "That's pathetic." Her twenty-four-year-old son wants to dress like me apparently and I get the blame. If people don't express themselves they're always repressed, but you only have one life and you have to live it as you think fit. The kids still abuse me and the police are useless, so I have to take care of myself. You have to stand up to them. They say they don't like how I look, and I tell them, "If you don't like it you can put up with it," because I've been through so much that I'm not going to be persecuted any more.'

It was a painful journey Mark travelled to realise the truth of himself and square up to the violence, hatred and ignorance he confronted as a consequence of his emotional honesty. Yet in the face of this resistance he has found moral courage. I was humbled to recognise Mark's strength of character as he told his stories filled with magnanimous humour and sympathy for his tormentors.

Nowadays, the clothing he adopted as a declaration of fearless independence has become Mark's life and, as we talked, he produced outfit after outfit to show me, each more extravagant than the one before. Simultaneously his armour and his joy, Mark takes great delight in his multi-coloured wardrobe, which incarnates the transformation act he has pulled off to emerge as the peacock of Brick Lane.

COLUMBIA ROAD MARKET VII

Plant Life, Market Life

THERE WAS A PARTY in my garden last night but, rather than face the debris, I got out of bed at dawn, headed out the door and walked up the road to the market instead, passing St Anne's, the Brazilian church, where I could hear the young Brazilians, who had been up all night partying, still singing for joy.

I bought a tray of sixteen assorted cornflowers, sufficient to fill two pots to stand on an exposed sunny wall and give me a display of flowers in soft blues and delicious strawberry pinks for the rest of summer.

Almost nothing speaks of high summer in England as vividly as the cornflowers that I think of scattered among wild poppies in meadows of golden corn. I remember them from the 'Cottage Garden Mixtures' of seeds that I used to buy for my childhood garden. This domesticated variety comes under the charming name of Bachelor's Button and I love the subtle complexity of the snowflake patterns adopted by the flowers, each one presenting a different intricate delight, perfectly counterpointed by the grey-green foliage.

AT STEPHEN WALTERS & SONS LTD
SILKWEAVERS

Human Life, Past Life

WHEN JULIUS WALTERS of Stephen Walters & Sons says, 'I am just a weaver,' it is an unselfconscious masterpiece of understatement, because he is a ninth-generation weaver – the custodian of the venerable family business founded by his ancestor Joseph Walters in Spitalfields in 1720 and moved to Suffolk by his great-great-great-great-grandfather Stephen Walters in the nineteenth century, where today they continue to weave exemplary silk for the most discerning clients internationally, building upon the expertise and knowledge that have been accumulated over all this time. This is the company that wove the silk for the Queen's coronation robes and for Princess Diana's wedding dress.

Michael Hill of Drakes Ties in Clerkenwell takes the train from Liverpool Street several times a year to visit the mill and place his orders for silks that are woven there exclusively for Drakes each season, so I leapt at the opportunity to travel up with him and see for myself what has become of one of Spitalfields' eighteenth-century silk weavers.

Thomas Gainsborough's portrait of Joseph Walters was there to greet us when we arrived at the long, finely proportioned

brick silk mill overlooking the green water meadows at the edge of Sudbury, where his ninth-generation descendant Julius came down the stairs to shake my hand. Blushing to deny any awareness of the family resemblance, which his secretary was at pains to emphasise, he chose instead to point out to me the willows that had been felled recently – as a couple are each year – for the manufacture of cricket bats.

We convened around a long wooden counter in a first-floor room where the luxuriously coloured strike-offs – as the samples are called – were laid out for Michael Hill to see, glowing in the soft East Anglian light, now that Michael was here to make his final choice from the different options upon the

table. There is such exquisite intricacy in these cloths that have tiny delicate patterns woven into their very construction, drawing the daylight and delighting the eye with their sensuous tones. Yet lifting my gaze, I could not prevent my attention straying to the pigeon holes that lined the room, each one stacked with patterned silks of every hue and design. A curious silence prevailed here, yet somewhere close by there was a centre of loud industry.

'It comes from everything,' Michael replied with a bemused smile, when I asked what informed his choices. 'It comes from when I used to drive around with my father, who was a tie maker, memories of what his generation were wearing, and generally only from other designers in terms of doing something different.'

'Everything we do comes from *somewhere*,' interposed Julius Walters, speaking cryptically, as he swung open a door and the unmistakably appealing smell of old leather bindings met my nostrils. There were hundreds of volumes of silk samples from the last two centuries stacked up in there, comprising thousands upon thousands of unique jewel-like swatches, still fresh and bright as the day they were made. Some of these books, often painstakingly annotated with technical details in italic script, comprised the life's work of a weaver and all now bear witness to the true colours of our predecessors' clothing. A vast memory bank woven in cloth, all available to be reworked for the present day and brought back to new life.

Spellbound by this perspective in time, I awoke to the clamour of the mill as we descended a staircase, passing through two glass doors and collecting ear plugs, before entering the huge workshop filled with looms clattering where new silk cloths were flying into existence. Here I stood watching the lush flourishes of acanthus brocades and tiny complex patterns for ties appear in magical perfection as if they had always existed, yet created by the simple principle of selecting how the weft crosses each thread of the warp, whether above or below.

With the bravura of a showman and the relish of an enthusiast, Julius led us on through more and more chambers and passages, into a silk store with countless

coloured spools immaculately sorted and named – crocus and rose and mud – into a vaporous dye plant where bobbins of white thread came out strawberry after immersion in bubbling vats of colour, into a steaming plant where rollers soften the cloth to any consistency, into the checking office where every inch is checked by eye and finally into the despatch office where the precious silken goods are wrapped in brown paper and weighed upon fine red scales.

There are so many variables in silk weaving, so many different skills and so much that could go wrong, yet all have become managed into a harmonious process by Stephen Walters & Sons over nine generations. In his time, Julius has introduced computers to track every specification of tens of thousands of orders a year – one

every five minutes – created by so many short runs, and new technology has provided a purifier which uses diamonds to cleanse dye from the water that eventually returns to the water meadow, renewing the watercourse that brought his ancestors from Spitalfields to Suffolk 150 years ago.

'All my school holidays and spare time were spent at the mill – but then I went away, and came back again,' confided Julius quietly as we made our farewells. 'With eight generations behind you, it changes the way you approach your life. It's not about this year, it's about managing the company from one generation to the next, so you deal with your employees and your customers differently.'

Now you know what it means when Julius Walters says, 'I am just a weaver.'

RON GOLDSTEIN

CAMBRIDGE AND BETHNAL GREEN BOYS' CLUB

Human Life, Past Life

IF – LIKE RON – YOU WERE YOUR parents' tenth child, growing up in a tiny terraced house with a clothing factory on the top floor in Boreham Street, Brick Lane, and sharing a room with your three elder brothers, then you might also be impatient to join the boys' club round the corner in Chance Street and have somewhere to let off steam and have fun. Even though strictly you had to be eleven, Ron was able to join the Cambridge and Bethnal Green Boys' Club in 1933, when he was only ten,

because his older brother Mossy was a club captain and pulled a few strings.

At this moment a whole new world opened up to Ron. For the price of a half-penny a week subscription, each night he would be in the front of the throng of boys waiting impatiently in Chance Street for the seven o'clock opening of the club, hungry for fulfilment of the evening's promise. Squeezing past the office where membership cards were checked, he went first to the canteen in the hope of wolfing a tasty saveloy, while others were already getting stuck into a quick game of table tennis, before the photography class started at seven thirty. This was the primary focus of the evening for Ron – because he was the proud owner of a Box Brownie that he bought for two shillings from Woolworths. Harry Tichener, who ran the classes, was a West End photographer who inspired his East End pupils by teaching them how to use and develop colour film before most people had even seen a colour photograph – encouraging a lifelong enthusiasm for photography in Ron. At eight thirty sharp the photography class was over, and it was time for Ron and the others to enjoy a brisk run down Bishopsgate to the Bank of England and back again without stopping, followed by a refreshing shower at nine thirty, then a prayer in the gymnasium before going straight home to bed in Boreham Street.

And so at ten years old, life acquired a totally new momentum for Ron. It was so special to him that even today, more than seventy years later, he remains close friends with many of the boys he met then and they are still enjoying regular happy reunions, celebrating the lifelong friendships that were forged at the club.

Opened in 1924 by altruistic undergraduates as a Jewish boys' club, the Cambridge and Bethnal Green Boys' Club had an ethical intent from the beginning, adopting the motto, '*Serva corpus, cole mentem, animam cura*' – keep fit, cultivate your mind, think of your soul. These lofty ambitions were reflected in the lively range of activities on offer, including boxing, art, photography, gym, travel talks with lantern slides, amateur dramatics and play reading, harmonica classes, health lectures, first aid lessons, hobbies, science lectures, swimming, shoe repair, philately, essay writing and debating.

In retrospect, Ron fondly appreciates the raising of expectations that the club encouraged. 'Half of the boys would have ended up as the next generation of gangsters and criminals if it had not been for the club. It was our first time to mix with people who never had to work from an early age and our first chance to consider the ethical side of life. We were a bunch of young tearaways. The club managers from Cambridge had a very upper-class way of

talking and we used to take the mickey, but it was different at the weekend camps. Everyone dressed the same and we all mucked in together.'

Harry Tichener's photographs speak eloquently of the joy engendered by the club and of the easy affectionate atmosphere, creating a warm playful environment in which the boys were able to feel free and enjoy the respect of their peers. Each weekend there were rambles when the boys took their cameras and enjoyed afternoon hikes within striking distance of London, stopping off at pubs to quench their thirst with half pints of shandy. During summer weekends there were camps, when everyone travelled down to the country together, set up their tents, cooked meals and enjoyed outdoor pursuits, returning to the East End weary and sunburnt on Sunday night. Once a year, this was extended to a week's summer camp at a more exotic location, such as Frome or Banbury or Wimborne. Ron only attended two summer camps, but he also recalls with delight the year he was disappointed, when he was unable to go due to a strained heart muscle that confined him to the Royal London Hospital. To his everlasting delight, a basket of fruit from Fortnum & Mason arrived from one of the club's wealthy patrons and no one in the hospital had ever seen such a generous gift to a teenage boy.

When the twin Lotinga brothers, George and Rowland, took over in 1936, they removed the Jewish prerequisite of membership of the club, opening it to everyone, as a radical and egalitarian response to the rise of anti-Semitism, manifested by Oswald Mosley and the fascists in the East End. In this context, the playful club photographs take on another quality, because there is something noble in the existence of a social space devoted to nurturing human sympathy, created while others are setting out to breed hatred. The boys were not unaware of the value of their freedom either, as evidenced by the seventeen-year-old lad that Ron remembers, who told his mother he was going on a weekend camp with the Cambridge and Bethnal Green Boys' Club but ran away to fight in the Spanish Civil War instead.

At thirteen years old, in 1936, Ron started in Fleet Street as a runner for the Associated Press Picture Agency, which required working evenings and limited his opportunities to go to the club. But he remained a member until war broke out in 1939, attending the camp at Greatstone, near Hythe, at the age of sixteen, during that famously beautiful last summer before hostilities were declared.

When war commenced, Ron's father moved the family out of London to Hove and before long Ron, and many other members of the club, found themselves enlisted. Some achieved heroism in the service and many died, while others came to prominence in post-war civilian life, yet although the Cambridge and Bethnal Green Boys' Club finally closed in 1990, there are still enough members around to remind us of this honourable endeavour, which set out to encourage the best in people despite the tyranny of circumstance.

AT LIVERPOOL STREET STATION

Night Life, Past Life

WHEN I WAS CALLOW AND NEW to London, I once arrived back on a train into Liverpool Street Station after the last tube had gone and spent the night there waiting for the first tube next morning. With little money and unaware of the existence of night buses, I passed the long hours possessed by alternating fears of being abducted by a stranger and being arrested by the police. Liverpool Street was quite a different place then, dark and sooty and diabolical – before it was rebuilt in 1990 to become the expansive glasshouse that we all know today – and I had such an intensely terrifying and exciting night then that I can remember it fondly now.

Old Liverpool Street Station was both a labyrinth and the beast in the labyrinth too. There were so many tunnels twisting and turning that you felt you were entering the entrails of a monster, and when you emerged on to the concourse it was as if you had arrived, like Jonah or Pinocchio, at the enormous ribbed belly.

I was travelling back from spending Saturday night in Cromer and stopped off at Norwich to explore, visiting the castle and studying its collection of watercolours by John Sell Cotman. It was only on the slow stopping train between Norwich and London on Sunday evening that I realised my mistake and sat anxiously checking my wristwatch at each station, hoping that I would make it back in time. When the train pulled in to Liverpool Street, I ran down the platform to the tube entrance, only to discover the gates shut, closed early on Sunday night.

I was in my summer clothes, and although it had been warm that day, the night was cold and I was ill-equipped for it. If there was a waiting room, in my shameful fear I was too intimidated to enter. Instead, I sat shivering on a bench in my thin white clothes, clutching my bag, wide-eyed and timid as a mouse – alone in the centre of the empty dark station and with a wide berth of vacant space around me, so that I could, at least, see any potential threat approaching.

Dividing the station in two were huge ramps where postal lorries rattled up and down all night at great speed, driving right on to the platforms to deliver sacks of mail to the waiting trains. In spite of the overarching vaulted roof, there was no sense of a single space, as there is today, but rather a chaotic railway station criss-crossed by footbridges extending beyond the corner of visibility, with black arches receding infinitely in the manner of Piranesi.

The night passed without any threat, although when the dawn came I felt as relieved as if I had experienced a spiritual ordeal, comparable to a night in a haunted house in the scary films that I loved so much at that time. It was my own vulnerability as an out-of-towner versus the terror of the unknowable Babylonian city, yet – if I had known then what I know now – I could simply have walked down to the Spitalfields Fruit and Vegetable Market and passed the night in one of the cafés there, safe in the nocturnal cocoon of market life.

Feeling guilty, and eager to preserve the secret of my foolish vigil, I took the first tube to the office in west London where I worked then and changed my clothes in a toilet cubicle, arriving at my desk hours before anyone else.

Only the vaulted roof and the Great Eastern Hotel were kept in the dramatic transformation that created the modern station and now the dark cathedral where I spent the night is gone. Yet a magnetism constantly draws me back to Liverpool Street, not simply to walk through, but to spend time wondering at the epic drama of life in this vast terminus where a flooding current of humanity courses through twice a day – one of the great spectacles of our extraordinary metropolis.

Shortly after my night on the station experience, I got a job at the Bishopsgate Institute in Spitalfields and Liverpool Street became familiar, accessed through the tunnels that extended beyond the station under the road, delivering me directly to my workplace. I noticed the other day that the entrance to the tunnel remains on the Spitalfields side of Bishopsgate, though bricked up now. And I wondered sentimentally, almost longingly, if I could get into it, would I emerge into the old Liverpool Street Station and visit the haunted memory of my own past?

NIKI CLEOVOULOU

DRESS DESIGNER

Human Life, Past Life

NIKI HAS ALWAYS BEEN A perfectionist, since she first learned sewing and pattern cutting in Cyprus before coming to London at the age of thirteen in 1959. 'I could never pass any faults. I don't care about the money, I don't care about the time, I don't care about the trouble, so long as I can do something good for the customer, then I can be happy,' she declared with a grin of satisfaction, speaking of her work today as a designer and maker of haute couture gowns for special occasions – in plain words, a traditional dressmaker.

'I couldn't go to school because of the war in Famagusta,' revealed Niki regretfully, giving the reason for her journey across Europe in her early teens, leaving the village of Stylloi to live with her brothers in Neasden, who were students at that time. 'Within three days they took me to the factory in the West End where my older sisters worked. I was a machinist, making skirts for ladies' suits,' she told me. And so Niki's working life in London commenced. Her photograph serves to illustrate this moment, revealing Niki as a poised young woman, full of life and anticipation at the possibilities of existence.

In those days, Niki's godfather, Sophocles, came regularly to the Spitalfields

Market to buy fruit and vegetables, and he always got his hair cut by a young bachelor, Kyriacos Cleovoulou, at the salon in Puma Court. It was a chance meeting that was to decide the course of Niki's life, because their respective families decided to put Niki and Kyriacos together. 'They came over to see my family in Neasden. It was very difficult for us to go outside or even be alone,' admitted Niki, rolling her eyes with a blush and a shrug. 'It was arranged, we got engaged within two or three weeks and married three months later.

'We came to live here in Spitalfields in 1970, but the building had to be fixed up because it was in a poor state and we did the salon first. I remember the men with barrows of fruit and vegetables running around shouting at four in the morning, and people going to cafés for breakfast early. You could do your shopping at dawn. It was very friendly, like a family. My husband used to go and buy boxes of fruit. He knew everyone and they knew him, because they all came here for haircuts! He used to open very early in those days.

'A year after we were married, we went to Cyprus together for two months and when we came back he stopped cutting hair and worked with me in the factory, where I taught him how to sew trousers. But then the factory burned down, so my husband went back to hairdressing. "Hairdressers always have money in their pocket," he used to say, because he never had to wait until payday as other professions did. He set up a sink and all he needed was a comb and scissors to earn money.'

Although Niki had great affection for the sociable life and community that she encountered living in proximity to the market, she was less enthusiastic about the living conditions in the tiny rooms above the salon in Puma Court, where she brought up her two young sons George and Panayiotis, while still doing sewing from home. 'It was very difficult. There was no bathroom, so my husband fixed one up in the hallway and we had a kitchen at the back,' she confided,

thankful that within five years they were able to buy a house in Palmers Green and Kyriacos could commute on the train to Liverpool Street each day.

Throughout all these years, Niki earned money through her sewing and yet, as she confessed to me, she was secretly frustrated because she never got to design dresses, as she had always wished. 'I was doing my dress designs but only for the people that knew me. I thought, "If only, if only everyone knew what I could do, I could make a dress for the Queen" – I had so much confidence in myself and my gift.' Niki never gave up her ambition and, even though she was qualified in pattern cutting in Cyprus, she also took a City & Guilds Diploma that qualified her in this country too. Then, just ten years ago, working in partnership with her daughter Stavroulla (widely known as Renée) she created Nicolerenée, making bespoke wedding dresses and gowns for special occasions, working from the old family premises in Puma Court.

My conversation with Niki took place over a cup of tea in a quiet corner of Cleo's Barber Shop, the salon where her husband, Kyriacos, began cutting hair in 1962 – where her godfather, Sophocles, came for a haircut in 1969 and discovered that Kyriacos the barber was an eligible bachelor. It is a location charged with powerfully emotional resonance for Niki and now, five years after Kyriacos's death, their three children, Panayiotis, George and Stavroulla, have reopened the barber shop, continuing the tradition for a second generation. We walked through to Niki's premises next door, once derelict, now a showroom full of elegant silken gowns arrayed upon rails, all examples of her talent and expertise. Here Niki took out a favourite pink dress, full of proud memories, that she made for herself and wore frequently in the 1960s, still in immaculate condition today.

This is a story that shows how external events can affect a life, sending Niki from Cyprus to London and from Neasden to Spitalfields, while equally illustrating the power of resolute self-belief to overcome obstacles. As Niki confirmed when she held up the dress in triumph, cast her eyes around the rails of dresses filling the tiny shop and said with a smile, 'In the end all my wishes have come true, because I have the shop here today with my daughter, and I am a very happy person, especially when I can talk about my work!'

BRICK LANE MARKET IV

Market Life

HENRY WILLIAM LEE began selling bicycles from a stall in Sclater Street each Sunday in the 1880s, a trade carried on by his son Henry George Lee and – 130 years later – his grandson Richard Lee still continues to do good business there today. A remarkable feat in the apparently transient world of the street market, making Richard the stallholder with the longest continuous business in Brick Lane, by far.

'My dad was born into it in 1913, died at eighty-six, and he was here till the end,' recalls Richard. 'I first came down here when I was five, and I was thirteen when I started working on the stall.' With a vital spirit, thick ginger hair and a constant expression of eagerness, Richard is commonly to be seen in front of his stall in Sclater Street with his oily hands wrapped around his body and tucked into his armpits, rocking back and forth on the balls of his feet, in readiness for the next customer.

'People know me,' he declares. 'I was selling to them when they were kids and now I'm selling to their kids. I don't tuck anybody up. I sell quality stuff and I sell it cheap.' Even as he spoke, cyclists of all ages were arriving – children included – pulling up and balancing on their bikes to ask, 'How much for coloured tyres?', 'Any back wheels?' and 'How much are your D-locks?' And Richard has an answer for everyone off the top of his head, reaching back into the organised chaos of his stall, where everything is miraculously no further than arm's length, to produce straight handlebars or

brake calipers or anything else that might be required cycle-wise.

It was no surprise to learn that his son Ray is a magician, because there is an aura of the conjuror about Richard's performance – producing the unexpected with an ease that belies his expertise. 'I'm due to retire but I can't afford to retire,' he says. 'I do a sixteen-hour day. It's not easy getting up at four and then when you go home, there's all the bookwork.' Yet I was unconvinced by Richard's complaint, because it gives him such visible pleasure to be in the spot where his father and grandfather were before him – even in a street that has changed beyond all recognition – and I hope we shall see him there for many years to come, because this is the longest-running show on Brick Lane.

ROBSON CEZAR
KING OF THE BOTTLE TOPS

Human Life

IF YOU ARE a regular in the pubs around Spitalfields, you may have noticed a man come in to collect bottle tops from behind the bar and then leave again with a broad smile, clutching a fat plastic bag of them with as much delight as if he were carrying off a fortune in gold coins. This enigmatic individual with the passion for hoarding bottle

tops is Brazilian artist and Spitalfields resident Robson Cezar, and he needs to collect thousands because he makes breathtakingly intricate pictures with them.

Each day, Robson cycles from Spitalfields down to his studio at Tower Bridge, where he stores his vast trove – the king of bottle tops in his counting house – spending hours sorting them lovingly into colours and designs as the raw material for his very particular art – an art which transforms these ill-considered objects into works of delicacy and finesse, contrived with sly humour, and playing upon their subtle abstract qualities of colour and contrast.

It all started a couple of years ago, when Robson asked Sandra Esqulant at the Golden Heart in Commercial Street to collect her bottle tops for him. For months she gathered them conscientiously and it gave Robson the perfect excuse to drop in regularly. He started with small pictures but quickly they grew larger and more elaborate. As a consequence, Robson often sets out now to visit several bars each night to collect the harvest of bottle tops he needs, which is obligingly – if incidentally – created by the thirsty boozers of our neighbourhood.

And in return for getting their bottle tops,

Robson makes pictures for the pubs. At first he made a golden heart in bottle tops as a personal gift for Sandra, but when the Bell in Middlesex Street offered him the opportunity to cover the exterior of the pub with bottle tops, he seized the opportunity to do something more ambitious. Using over 6,000 and subtly referencing the colours of the red brick and the green ceramic tiles, Robson has contrived a means to unify the exterior of the building and render it afresh as a landmark with his witty texts. And since they were installed, people smile and stop in Middlesex Street to take photographs when they come across Robson's bottle-top panels on the Bell. With such eye-catching street appeal, his work is a natural complement to the alphabet Ben Eine painted on all the shutters along this street.

At the Carpenter's Arms in Cheshire Street, landlords Eric and Nigel have been obligingly collecting bottle tops for a while. Robson made a picture for them too. Hung up on the roof beam in the bar, this is in a different vein from his works at the Golden Heart and the Bell – creating a stir among the regulars, who are puzzling over the choice of phrase, SCREAM PARTNERS, for the Carpenter's Arms. Go round to take a look yourself and if you cannot work it out at once, then a couple of drinks will increase your powers of lateral thinking.

Robson Cezar came to Spitalfields in the footsteps of fellow Brazilian artist Hélio Oiticica, who, along with Caetano Veloso, was one of the many Brazilian cultural exiles in London in the 1960s. Oiticica staged an exhibition at the Whitechapel Gallery in

Hélio Oiticica, Spitalfields 1969

Robson Cezar, Spitalfields 2009

1967, introducing the new cultural movement of Tropicalia to Europe by recreating
a favela in the gallery.

Now Robson is creating his own Tropicalia here in the twenty-first century, re-
inventing this poverty aesthetic with a pop
exuberance that reflects the cosmopol-
itanism of his own life experience – which
began in a favela in Brazil and took him from
South to North America and eventually to
Europe, where he found his home in the East
End of London.

Combining the sensibility of a fine artist
with the painstaking technique of a folk
artist, Robson's bottle-top pictures are egalitarian in nature yet sophisticated in intent.
They look like signs but they are not signs,
or rather they are pictures pretending to
be signs. The lush shimmering beauty of
Robson Cezar's work enchants us with all
the bottle tops that litter our streets unregarded, and reminds us of all the other
pitiful wonders of human ingenuity that we
forget to notice.

ON THE ROUNDS WITH THE
SPITALFIELDS MILKMAN

Human Life, Street Life

DAWN HAS BROKEN OVER THE East End and there goes Kevin, the agile milkman, sprinting down the street with a pint of milk in hand. With enviable stamina, Kevin Read gets up at two thirty each morning, six days a week, and delivers milk in a round that stretches from the Olympic Park in the east to Hoxton Square in the west, doing the whole thing at a run.

The East End is a smaller, more peaceful place in the morning, before all the people get up, and I was inspired to see it through Kevin's eyes when I joined him on his round at four thirty. As we careered around in the early sunshine, travelling effortlessly from one place to another down empty streets that are Kevin's sole preserve for the first three hours of daylight at this time of year, landmarks appeared closer together and the busy roads that divide the territory were quiet. Kevin's East End is another land, known only to early birds.

'I never look at it as a job. It's my life,' admitted Kevin, still enthusiastic after thirty years on the rounds. 'Born in Harlow. Educated in Harlow. Top of the class at school. Bunked off at fourteen. Failed all my exams. Moved to London at fifteen. Started as a rounds boy at the Co-op Dairy, just at week-

ends until I got a proper job. Left school at sixteen. Junior Depot Assistant at Co-op, swept yard, parked milk floats and made coffee for the manager. Don't know what happened to the proper job!' said Kevin with a shrug. It was the prologue to the story of Kevin's illustrious career, which began in Arnold Circus, delivering milk to the Boundary Estate in 1982, where he ran up and down every staircase, making a long

list of calls for each block. Today Kevin still carries his vocabulary of Bengali words that he picked up then.

In the intervening years, an earthquake happened. The Co-op Dairy was bought by Express Dairies, then Kevin worked for Unigate until that was sold to Dairy Crest, next working for Express Dairies until that was also sold to Dairy Crest, and finally working for Hobbs Cross Farm Dairy until they went out of business. Quite a bumpy ride, yet Kevin persevered through these changes, which included a dire spell in the suburbs of Chingford. 'They complain if you put the milk on the wrong side of the doorstep there!' he revealed with caustic good humour, outlining a shamelessly biased comparison between the suburbs and the inner city streets that were his first love.

While we drove around in the gathering dawn, Kevin told me his life story – in between leaping from the cabin and sprinting off, across the road, through security doors, up and down stairs, along balconies, in and out of cafés, schools, offices, universities and churches. No delivery is too small and he will consider any location. Yet it is no small challenge to work out the most efficient route each day, taking into account traffic and orders that vary daily. Kevin has two fat round books that describe all the calls he must do, yet he barely opens them. He has it all in his head, 200 domestic calls (on a system of alternating days), plus 130 offices, shops and cafés. 'A good milkman knows how to work his round,' stated Kevin with the quiet authority of a seasoned professional.

Setting a fierce pace, always quick, never hurried, he was continually thinking on his feet. With practised dexterity, Kevin can carry six glass bottles effortlessly in his bare hands, with the necks clutched between each of his fingers. He makes it all look easy, because he is an artist. The wide chassis of Kevin's diesel milk float permits him to cross speed bumps with one wheel on either side – avoiding chinking milk crates – if he lines up the float precisely, and during our seven hours together on the round, he did it right every time.

Yet, before he embraced his occupation, Kevin rejected it. When the industry hit a bump, he tried to find that 'proper job' which haunted him, working in a kitchen and then a bakery for three years. But one day he saw a milk float drive by the bakery and he knew his destiny was to be in the cabin. Taking a declining round on the Cattle Road Estate, he built it up to 100 calls, and then another and another, until he had five rounds with four milkmen working alongside him. A failed marriage and divorce meant he had to sell these rounds to Parker Dairies. But then in 1999 the dairy offered him his old territory back – the East End. 'I realised the only time I was happy was when I was working for myself,' confided Kevin with glee. 'It was my favourite round, my favourite area, my favourite pay scheme, commission only – next to my first round, Arnold Circus! The best of everything came together for me.'

But, returning to the East End, Kevin discovered his customers had become further apart. Where once Kevin went door to door, now he may have only one or two calls in a street, and consequently the round is wider. Between three thirty and eleven thirty each morning, Kevin spirals around the East End, delivering first to houses with gardens and secure locations to leave milk, then returning later to deliver milk to exposed doorsteps, thereby minimising the risk of theft, before finally doing the rounds of offices as they open for business. During the day Kevin turns evangelical, canvassing door to door, searching for new customers, because many people no longer realise there is a milkman who can deliver.

Kevin is a milkman with a mission to rebuild the lost milk rounds of the East End, and he has become a local celebrity in the process, renowned for his boundless energy and easy charm. Now happily settled with his new partner, whom he met on the round, he thinks he is delivering milk, but I think he is pursuing life.

RODNEY ARCHER

AESTHETE

Human Life

RODNEY ARCHER kindly took me to lunch at E. Pellicci yesterday, but first I went round to his eighteenth-century house in Fournier Street to admire his cherished fireplace that once belonged to Oscar Wilde. One day in 1970, Rodney was visiting an old friend who lived in Tite Street, next to Wilde's house, and saw the builders were doing renovations, so he seized the opportunity to walk through the door of the house that had once been the great writer's dwelling. The fireplace had been torn out of the wall in Wilde's living room as part of a modernisation of the property and the workmen were about to carry it away, so Rodney offered to buy it on the spot. For ten pounds he acquired a literary relic of the highest order, the fine pilastered fireplace with tall overmantel, which today has become a shrine to Wilde and the centrepiece of Rodney's first-floor living room. You can see Spy's famous caricature of Wilde up on the chimney piece, but the gem of Rodney's Wilde collection is a copy of Lord Alfred Douglas's poems with pencil annotations by Douglas himself. Encountering these artefacts – which already possess such a potent poetry of their own, amplified by their proximity to each other – is especially enchanting in this environment.

Rodney lives in his old house, allowing the patina of age to remain, enhanced by his sensational collection of pictures, carpets, furniture, books, china and God-knows-

Rodney made his home in London's most magical street in 1980. It came about after his mother fell down a well at the Roundhouse and broke her hip while attending a performance of *The Homosexual (or The Difficulty of Sexpressing Yourself)* by Copi, in which Rodney was starring. It was the culmination of Rodney's distinguished career of just eight years as an actor, which included playing the Player Queen in *Hamlet* at the Bristol Old Vic in a production with Richard Pasco in the title role and featuring Patrick Stewart as Horatio.

After she broke her hip, Rodney's mother told him that her doctor insisted she live with her son, much to Rodney's surprise. Gamely, Rodney agreed, on the condition they find somewhere large enough to live their own lives with some degree of independence, and rang up his friends Riccardo and Eric, who lived in Fournier Street, asking them to keep their eyes open for any house that went on sale. Within three months, a house came up. It was the only one they looked at and Rodney has lived there happily ever since. Thirty years ago, Spitalfields was not the desirable location it is today. 'My mother thought I was joking when I told her where I wanted to live,' declared Rodney, raising his eyebrows. 'Now it would nice if there were more people living here who were not millionaires. I visit people in houses today where there are ghosts of people I used to know and the new people don't know who they were. It's sad.'

Rodney's roots are in east London. He was born in Gidea Park, but once his father (a flying officer in the RAF) was killed in

what, accumulated over all the years he has lived there, transforming it into a three-dimensional map of his vigorous mind and imagination, crammed with images, stories and all manner of cultured enthusiasms. No single item is of great monetary value in itself, yet everything is charismatic. In Rodney's house, anyone would feel at home the minute they walked in the door, because everything has arrived in its natural place but nothing feels arranged. It is a relaxing place, with reflected light everywhere, and although there is so much to look at and so many stories to know, it is peaceful and benign, like Rodney himself. Rodney's style could never be replicated by anyone else, unless you became Rodney and you could live through those years again.

action over Malta in 1943, his mother took Rodney and his sister away to Toronto when they were tiny children and brought them up there on her own. Rodney came back to London in 1962 with the rich Canadian accent (which sounds almost Scottish to me) that he retains to this day, in spite of the actor's voice training he received at LAMDA which has imparted such a mellifluous tone to his speech. After his brief years treading the boards, Rodney became a drama teacher at the City Lit and ran the Operating Theatre Company, staging his own play *The Harlot's Curse* (co-authored with Powell Jones) in the Princelet Street Synagogue with great success.

'When I retired, I decided to do whatever I wanted to do,' announced Rodney with a twinkly smile, at this point in his life story. 'Now I am having a wonderful third act. Writing about that time, my mother, the cats and me ...' he said, introducing the long-awaited trilogy of autobiographical fiction that he is currently working on. The first volume will cover his first eight years in Spitalfields, concluding with the death of his mother in 1988, the second volume will conclude with the death of his friend Dennis Severs in 1999 and the third with the death of Eric Elstob. (Elstob was a banker who loved architecture and left a fortune for the refurbishment of Christ Church, Spitalfields.) 'There is something about the nature of Spitalfields, that fact becomes fiction. As you become involved with the lives of people here, it gets you telling stories,' explained Rodney.

Now it was time for lunch and, as we walked hungrily up Brick Lane towards Bethnal Green in the summer sunshine, the postman saluted Rodney and, on cue, the owner of the pie and mash shop leaned out of the doorway to give him a cheery wave too. Then, as if to mark the occasion as auspicious, we saw the first shiny new train run along the recently completed East London Line, gliding across the newly constructed bridge, glinting in the sunlight as it passed over our heads and sliding away across Allen Gardens towards Whitechapel. This is the elegant world of Rodney Archer, I thought.

Turning the corner into Bethnal Green Road, I asked Rodney about the origin of his passion for Wilde and when he revealed that he once played Algernon in *The Importance of Being Earnest* at school, his intense grey-blue eyes shone with excitement. It made perfect sense, because I felt as if I was meeting a senior version of Algernon who retained all the wit, charm and sagacity of his earlier years, now having 'a wonderful third act' in an apocryphal lost manuscript by Oscar Wilde, recently discovered among all the glorious clutter in a beautiful old house in Fournier Street, Spitalfields.

SYD'S COFFEE STALL

SHOREDITCH HIGH STREET

Culinary Life, Past Life, Street Life

THIS IS Sydney Edward Tothill pictured in 1920, proprietor of the coffee stall that still operates, open for business five days a week at the corner of Calvert Avenue and Shoreditch High Street, where this photo survives, screwed to the counter of the East End landmark that carries his name. 'Ev'ry-body knows Syd's. Git a bus dahn Shoreditch Church and you can't miss it. Sticks aht like a sixpence in a sweep's ear,' reported the *Evening Telegraph* in 1959.

The story began in the trenches of the First World War, when Syd was gassed. On his return to civilian life in 1919, Syd used his invalidity pension to pay 117 pounds for the construction of a top-quality mahogany tea stall with fine etched glass and gleaming brass fittings. And the rest is history, because it was of such sturdy manufacture that it remains in service over ninety years later.

Jane Tothill, Syd's granddaughter, who upholds the proud family tradition today, told me that Syd's Coffee Stall was the first to have mains electricity, when in 1922 it was hooked up to the adjoining lamp post. Even though the lamp post in question has been supplanted by a modern replacement, it still stands beside the stall to provide the power supply. Similarly, as the century progressed, mains water replaced the old churn that once stood at the rear of the stall and mains gas replaced the brazier of coals. In the 1960s, when Calvert Avenue was resurfaced, Syd's stall could not be moved on account of his mains connections and so kerbstones were placed around it instead. As a consequence, if you look underneath the stall today, the cobbles are still there.

Throughout the nineteenth century, there was a widespread culture of coffee stalls in London, but, in spite of the name – which was considered a classy description for a barrow serving refreshments – they mostly sold tea and cocoa, and in Syd's case 'Bovex', the 'poor man's Bovril'. The most popular snack was saveloy, a sausage supplied by Wilson's, the German butchers in Hoxton, as promoted by the widespread exhortation to have 'A Sav and a Slice at Syd's'. Even the Duke of Windsor, when Prince of Wales, stopped by for a cup of tea from Syd's while on nocturnal escapades in the East End.

With his wife May, Syd ran an empire of seven coffee stalls and two cafés in Rivington Street and Worship Street. The apogee of this early period in the history of Syd's Coffee Stall arrived when it featured in a silent film, *Ebb Tide*, shot in 1931, starring the glamorous Chili Bouchier and praised for its realistic portrayal of life in east London. The stall was transported to Elstree for the filming, the only time it has ever moved from its site. While Chili acted up a storm in the foreground, as a fallen woman in tormented emotion upon the floor, Syd was seen in the background discharging his cameo as the proprietor of an East End coffee stall with impressive authenticity.

In spite of Syd's success, Jane revealed that her grandfather was 'a bit of a drinker and gambler' who gambled away both his cafés and all his stalls, except the one at the corner of Calvert Avenue. When Syd Junior, Jane's father, was born, finances were rocky and he recalled moving from a big house in Palmers Green to a room over a laundry the very next week. May carried Syd Junior while she was serving at the stall and it was preordained that he would continue the family business, which he joined in 1935.

In the Second World War, Syd's Coffee Stall served the ambulance and fire services during the London Blitz. Syd and May never closed, they simply ran to take shelter in the vaults of Barclays Bank next door whenever the air-raid warning sounded. When a flying bomb detonated in Calvert Avenue, Syd's stall might have been destroyed if a couple of buses had not been parked beside it, fortuitously sheltering the stall from the explosion. In the blast, poor May was injured by shrapnel and Syd suffered a mental breakdown, leaving their young daughter, Peggy, struggling to keep the stall open.

The resultant crisis at Syd's Coffee Stall was of such magnitude that the Mayor of Shoreditch and other leading dignitaries appealed to the War Office to have Syd Junior brought home from a secret mission he was undertaking for the RAF in the Middle East in order to run the stall for the ARP wardens. It was a remarkable moment that revealed the essential nature of the service provided by Syd's Coffee Stall to the war effort on the home front in east London, and I can only admire the mayor's clear-sighted sense of priority in using his authority to demand Syd's return because he was required to serve tea in Shoreditch. As he wrote to May in January 1945, 'I do sincerely hope that you are recovering from your injuries and that your son will remain with you for a long time.'

Syd Junior was determined to show he was more responsible than his father and,

after the war, he bravely expanded the business. Along with this wife, Iris, he started catering for weddings and events, adopting the name Hillary Caterers as a patriotic tribute to Sir Edmund Hillary, who scaled Everest at the time of the coronation of Elizabeth II. No doubt you will agree that as a caterer for weddings, Hillary Caterers sounds preferable to Syd's Coffee Stall. In fact, Syd Junior's ambition led him to become the youngest-ever president of the Hotel and Caterers' Federation and the only caterer ever to cater on the steps of St Paul's Cathedral, topping it off by becoming a Freeman of the City of London.

Jane Tothill began working at the stall in 1987 with her brothers Stephen and Edward, and the redoubtable Clarrie, who came for a week 'to see if she liked it' and stayed thirty-two years. Jane manages the stall today with the loyal assistance of Francis, who has been serving behind the counter these last fifteen years. Nowadays the challenges are parking restrictions, which make it problematic for customers to stop, hit and run drivers who frequently cause damage, which requires costly repair to the mahogany structure, and graffiti artists, whose tags have to be constantly erased from the venerable stall. Yet after ninety years and three generations of Tothills, during which Syd's Coffee Stall has survived against the odds to serve the working people of Shoreditch without interruption, it has become a symbol of the enduring spirit of the populace here.

Syd's Coffee Stall is a piece of our social history that does not draw attention to itself, yet deserves to be celebrated. Syd Senior might not have survived the trenches, or he might have gambled away this stall as he did the others, or the bomb might have fallen differently in 1944. Any number of permutations of fate could have led to Syd's Coffee Stall not being here today. Yet by a miracle of fortune, and thanks to the hard work of the Tothill family, we can enjoy London's oldest coffee stall here in our neighbourhood. We must cherish it now, because the story of Syd's Coffee Stall teaches us that there is a point at which serving a humble cup of tea transcends catering and approaches heroism.

BILL CROME
WINDOW CLEANER

Human Life, Spiritual Life

BILL CROME IS A VENERABLE window cleaner with thirty years' experience in the trade, who makes a speciality out of cleaning the windows of the old houses in the East End. You might assume cleaning windows is a relatively mundane occupation and that, apart from the risk of falling off a ladder, the job is otherwise without hazard – yet Bill's recent experiences have proved quite the contrary, because he has supernatural encounters in the course of his work that would make your hair stand on end.

'It wasn't a career choice,' admitted Bill with phlegmatic good humour. 'When I left school, a man who had a window-cleaning business lived across the road from me, so I asked his son for a job and I've been stuck in it ever since. I have at least sixty regulars, shops and houses, and quite a few are here in Spitalfields. I like the freedom, the

meeting of people and the fact that I haven't got a boss on my back.' In spite of growing competition from contractors who offer cleaning, security and window cleaning as a package to large offices, Bill has maintained his business manfully, even in the face of the recession, but now he faces a challenge of another nature entirely. Although, before I elaborate, let me emphasise that Bill Crome is one of the sanest, most down-to-earth men you could hope to meet.

'I've heard there is a window cleaner in Spitalfields who sees ghosts,' I said, to broach the delicate subject as respectfully as I could. 'That's me,' he confessed without hesitation, colouring a little and lowering his voice. 'I've seen quite a few. Five years ago, at the Society for the Preservation of Ancient Buildings in Spital Square, I saw a sailor on the second floor. I was outside cleaning the window and this sailor passed in front of me. He was pulling his coat on. He put his arms in the sleeves, moving as he did so, and then walked through the wall. He looked like the sailor on the Player's Navy Cut cigarette packet, from around 1900 I would guess, in his full uniform.

'And then I saw a twelve-year-old girl on the stair. She was bent down, peering at me through the staircase. I was about to clean the window and I could feel someone watching me. Then, as I turned, she was on the next floor looking down at me. She had on a grey dress with a white pinafore over the top. And she had a blank stare.

'I did some research. I went to a spiritualist church in Wandsworth and one of the spiritualists said to me, "You've got a friend who's a sailor, haven't you?" They told me how to deal with it. When we investigated we found it was to do with the old paintings at the Society for the Preservation of Ancient Buildings. Among the collection were portraits of a sailor and of a girl. Once I was walking up to the top floor and I looked at the picture of the girl and she had a smiling face – but when I went back to collect my squeegee, I looked again and she had a frown. It sounds really stupid, doesn't it? I found a leaflet in the house explaining about the history of the paintings and how the family that gave them were dying off. The paintings are off the wall now, yet they had a nice feeling about them, of sweetness and calm.'

Bill confirmed that since the paintings were taken down, he has seen no more ghosts while cleaning windows in Spital Square and the episode is concluded, though the implications of these sinister events have been life-changing, as he explained when he told me of his next encounter with the otherworldly.

'I was cleaning the windows of a house in Sheerness, and I looked into the glass and I saw the reflection of an old man right behind me. I could see his full person, a six-foot four-inch man, standing behind me in a collarless shirt. But when I turned round there was no one there.

'I went down to the basement, cleaning the windows, and I felt like someone was climbing on my back. Then I started heaving. I was frozen to the spot. All I kept thinking was, "I've got to finish this window," but as soon as I came out of the basement I felt very

238

scared. Speaking to a lady down the road, she told me that in this same house, in the same window, a builder got thrown off his ladder in the past year and there was no explanation for it. I won't go back and do that house again, I can tell you.'

As Bill confided his stories, he spoke deliberately, taking his time and maintaining eye contact as he chose his words carefully. I could see that the mere act of telling drew emotions, as Bill re-experienced the intensity of these uncanny events while struggling to maintain equanimity. My assumption was that although Bill's experience at the Society for the Preservation of Ancient Buildings might be attributed to a localised phenomenon, what happened in Sheerness suggests that Bill himself is the catalyst for these sightings.

'I feel that I have opened myself up to it because I've been to the spiritualist church a few times,' he revealed to me. 'I do expect to see more ghosts because I work in a lot of old properties, especially round Spitalfields.

I don't dread it but I don't look forward to it either. It has also made me feel like I do want to become a spiritualist, and every time I go along, they say, "Are you a member of the church?" But I don't know. I don't know what can of worms I've opened up.'

Bill's testimony was touching in its frankness – neither bragging nor dramatising. Instead he was thinking out loud, puzzling over these mysterious events in search of understanding.

As we walked together among the streets of ancient dwellings in the shadow of the old church in Spitalfields, where many of the residents are his customers, I naturally asked Bill Crome if he had seen any ghosts in these houses. At once he turned reticent, stopping in his tracks and insisting that he maintain discretion. 'I don't tell my customers if I see ghosts in their houses,' he informed me absolutely, looking me in the eye. 'They don't need to know and I don't want to go scaremongering.'

SPITALFIELDS ANTIQUES MARKET III

LOTTIE MUIR AND AMANDA BLUGLASS met through Soulmates seeking romance and discovered instead a shared passion for 'Thames treasures and coastal coterie'. 'I am a mudlarker and a letterpress fanatic,' explained Lottie, 'so I collect Roman glass and medieval pottery, which wash up against my flat in Rotherhithe, and I arrange my discoveries in type cases.' Lottie's finds are complemented by things selected by Amanda, who is a sculptor. 'All are chosen for shape or some kind of sculptural beauty,' she added with calm authority, in contrast to Lottie's giddy excitement on this first day of their new venture.

THE DISTINGUISHED MR SINGH is modelling a dress sword which belonged to the Lieutenant General to the Tower of London between 1880 and 1890, a fine example that was once presented to Lord Chelmsford. 'I must differentiate myself from the general public and I do it by an emphasis on quality,' explained Mr Singh and, casting my eyes upon his impressive selection of antique silver cutlery, I found no reason to disagree. If you see Mr Singh, impeccably dressed English gentleman and dealer in militaria and classy bric-a-brac, either here in Spitalfields or at St James, Piccadilly, be sure to pay your respects and wish him 'Good day'.

MATTHEW MCFARLANE is a freethinking one-man band who enjoys the community here as much as the selling. 'I can leave my stall unattended and no one will touch it,' he vouched confidently. Matthew contends that his stall merely offers him a day off from his work as a set builder and designer of shop windows, but I could see he possesses a good eye – and the rescued chairs he has reinvented testify to an ingenious sensibility. 'There is something hauntingly beautiful about dishevelled furniture, left to waste, yet with so much more to give,' he added, revealing his true soulful self.

THE GRACIOUS SONOE SUGAWARA is proudly holding an exquisite nineteenth-century girl's silk undergarment. Sonoe originally sold vintage English clothes from a stall in a Tokyo department store and now sells kimonos in London too, moving back and forth two or three times a year with a full suitcase in both directions. 'My boyfriend's great-grandparents were dealers before the war, collecting nineteenth- and early-twentieth-century kimonos,' revealed Sonoe with a significant nod, accounting for the origins of her stock of ravishingly beautiful fine antique kimonos.

JOAN ROSE AT
GARDNERS' MARKET SUNDRIESMEN

BETWEEN THE AGES OF twelve and four-teen years old, Joan Rose regularly visited Gardners' Market Sundriesmen (established 1870) in Commercial Street to collect orders of paper bags from Bertie Gardner for her grandfather Alfred Raymond, proprietor of Raymond's greengrocers (founded 1900) in Calvert Avenue, next to Arnold Circus, where Leila's Shop is today. Joan, now eighty-four, has not been back to Gardners' since she was evacuated from London at fourteen years old, so I took her along to meet Bertie's grandson, Paul Gardner, who runs the shop today – a fourth-generation paper bag seller

and the owner of Spitalfields' oldest family business.

Paul never met his grandfather Bertie, but Joan remembers him clearly, always wearing his brown dustcoat. 'He didn't talk down to you. Even though I was twelve years old, he'd say, "Can I help you?"' recalled Joan, appreciative of the respect that Bertie, whom she knew as Mr Gardner, paid to her as a young woman over seventy years ago. Once I made the introductions, Joan and Paul began their conversation by discussing bags. 'Would you mind going over to Gardners', we're short of two-pound bags?' Joan announced gleefully, quoting a commonplace line of her grandfather's, to outline the premise of her visits to Commercial Street so long ago. 'I think we had bags printed here,' queried Joan, as Paul indicated a dusty old brown paper carrier with images of fruit printed upon it as an example, while he and Joan exchanged a nod of joyful recognition. 'They were much wider in those days, weren't they?' she commented to Paul, who directed her to the contemporary equivalent hanging on the opposite wall, which is taller. And he grinned, revealing that a certain professional rapport had been cemented between them.

Surrounded on all sides by packets of paper bags, Joan sat herself down upon a stack, gazing around her with a child's delight at this spectacle from her youth, as Paul served a stream of customers coming in for bags. Joan was fascinated by the familiar brass scales with a large scoop that stands on Paul's counter, and the old weights with iron loop handles that sit upon shelves behind the counter. 'When a bomb landed on Calvert Avenue, a four-teen-pound weight like that blew off the shelf and hit my grandfather in the head and nearly killed him,' she informed me, widening her eyes in amazement at the wonder of his survival.

Once the flurry of customers had departed, Paul produced two of his ancient account books with entries for 'Raymond' to show Joan. One was from the 1890s, when Paul's great-grandfather James serviced the scales for a Mr Raymond in Quaker Street. 'One of my grandfather's brothers, I think,' explained Joan. 'They were all coster-mongers.' The other entry was for a Mr Raymond in Dalston Lane in 1920, who was slow to clear his account. The page was annotated with the phrases, 'Reminder sent', then 'Stiff letter', before payment was eventually received by cheque in 1923. Joan was dubious about this entry, because her grandfather never wrote cheques, he always gave her an envelope of cash to pay for the bags, which may account for the lack of surviving paperwork. With regret, she dismissed this unreliable character from Dalston Lane as another of her grand-father's brothers.

Joan recounted to Paul how Bertie Gardner occasionally walked into her grandfather's shop to make deliveries in person, with the cursory, 'Alf, here's your bags!' – a cue for Alfred to search through the wooden block of wood with scoops in it where he kept his change. Hearing this story was the cue for Paul, the grandson, to bring out the block of wood with scoops out of it that has served four generations of his family to store coins. The merest sight of it was a delight for Joan. 'But he never kept notes in it!' she retorted, wagging her finger in amused qualification, a comment that was itself another cue for Paul. This time, with a mischievous smile, he brought out an old Oxo tin and then a Fuller's cake

tin that he uses to keep his bank notes in today, causing Joan to clasp her hands in rapture.

Then, with a natural sense of theatre, Joan opened her handbag and produced a photograph of Raymond's greengrocers taken in the 1930s and, sure enough, there were the bunches of brown paper bags that came from Gardners'. As more customers arrived in Paul's shop, they also became party to this impromptu display, sharing expressions of wonder at these images, and amazed to meet a returned customer in the shop from more than seventy years ago. For a moment the haste of the day was stilled.

Joan and Paul parted with a kiss, intimate acquaintances now through an unlikely bond, and, as we walked up Commercial Street together, Joan confided to me with a smile, 'His grandfather had a longer face, but he does look just like him.'

BLACKIE

THE LAST SPITALFIELDS MARKET CAT

Animal Life, Market Life, Past Life

HERE YOU SEE BLACKIE, the last Spitalfields market cat, taking a nap in the premises of Williams Watercress at 11 Gun Street. Presiding over Blackie – as she sleeps peacefully among the watercress boxes before the electric fire with her dishes of food and water to hand – is Jim, the nightman who oversaw the premises from six each evening until two next morning, on behalf of Len Williams, the proprietor.

This photograph with a nineteenth-century barrow wheel in the background and a 1950s electric heater in the foreground, could have been taken almost any time in the second half of the twentieth century. Only the date on the 'Car Girls Calendar' betrays it as 1990, the penultimate year of the Spitalfields Fruit and Vegetable Market, before it moved further east to Stratford.

In spite of Jim the nightman's fond expression, Blackie was no pet, she was a working animal who earned her keep killing rats. Underneath the market were vaults to store fresh produce, which had to be sold within three days – formalised as first-, second- and third-day prices – with each day's price struck at two in the morning. But the traders often forgot about the

fruit and vegetables down in the basement and it hung around more than three days, and with the spillage on the road which local residents and the homeless came to scavenge, it caused the entire market to become a magnet for vermin, running through the streets and into the labyrinth beneath the buildings.

It must have been paradise for a cat that loved to hunt, like Blackie. With her jet-black fur, so black she was like a dark hole in the world running round on legs, vanishing into the shadow and appearing from nowhere to pounce upon a rat and take its life with her needle-sharp claws, Blackie was a lethally efficient killer. Not a submissive creature that could be easily stroked and petted, as domestic cats are, Blackie was a proud beast that walked on her own, learned the secret of survival on the streets and won independent status, affection and respect through her achievements in vermin control.

'They were all very pleased with Blackie for her great skill in catching rats. She was the last great market cat,' confirmed Jim Howett, who first met Blackie when he moved into a workshop above the watercress seller in 1988. 'The other traders would queue up for kittens from Blackie's sister's litters, because they were so good at rat-catching. Blackie brought half-dead rats back to teach them how to do it. Such was Blackie's expertise, it was said she could spot a poisoned rat at 100 feet. The porters used to marvel that when they said, "Blackie, there's a rat," Blackie would focus and if the

rat showed any weakness, or wobbled, or walked uncertainly, she would turn her back and return to the fire – because the rat was ill, and most likely poisoned. And after all, Blackie was the last cat standing,' continued Jim, recounting tales of this noble creature who has become a legend in Spitalfields today. 'The story was often told of the kitten trained by Blackie, taken by a restaurant and hotel in the country. One day it brought a half-dead rat into the middle of a Rotary Club function seeking approval, as it had learned in Spitalfields, and the guests ran screaming.'

The day the Fruit and Vegetable Market left in 1991, Blackie adjusted, no longer crossing the road to the empty market building. Instead she concentrated on maintaining the block of buildings on Brushfield Street as her territory by patrolling the rooftops. By now she was an old cat and eventually could only control the three corner buildings, and one day Charles Gledhill, a book binder who lived with his wife, Marianna Kennedy, at 42 Brushfield Street, noticed a shadow fly past his window. It was Blackie he saw, and she had fallen from the gutter and broken a leg on the pavement below. 'We all liked Blackie, and we took care of her after the market left,' explained Jim, with a regretful smile, 'so we took her to the vet, who was amazed. He said, "What are you doing with this old feral cat?", because Blackie had a fierce temper. She was always hissing and growling.

'But Blackie recovered, and on good days she would cross the road and sun herself on pallets, although on other days she did not move from the fire. She became very thin and we put her in the window of A. Gold to enjoy the sun. One day Blackie was stolen from there. We heard a woman had been seen carrying her towards Liverpool Street in a box, but we couldn't find her, so we put up signs explaining that Blackie was so thin because she was a very old cat. Two weeks later, Blackie was returned in a fierce mood by the lady who had taken her. She apologised and ran away. Blackie had a sojourn in Milton Keynes! We guessed the woman was horrified with this feral creature that growled and scratched and hissed and

arched its back. After that, Blackie got stiffer and stiffer, and one day she stood in the centre of the floor and we knew she wasn't going to move again. She died of a stroke that night. The market porters told me Blackie was twenty when she died, as old as any cat could be.'

Everyone knows the tale of Dick Whittington, the first Lord Mayor of London, whose cat was instrumental to his success. This story reminds us that for centuries a feline presence was essential to all homes and premises in London. It was a serious business to keep the rats and mice at bay, killing vermin that ate supplies and brought plague. Over its three centuries of operation, there were innumerable generations of cats bred for their ratting abilities at the Spitalfields Market, but it all ended with Blackie. Like *Tess of the D'Urbervilles* or *The Last of the Mohicans*, the tale of Blackie, the last great Spitalfields market cat, contains the story of all that came before. Cats were the first animals to be domesticated, long before dogs, and so our connection with felines is the oldest human relationship with an animal, based up the exchange of food and shelter in return for vermin control.

Even though Blackie – who came to incarnate the spirit of the ancient market itself – died in 1995, four years after the traders left, her progeny live on as domestic pets in the East End and there are plenty of similar short-haired black cats with golden eyes around Spitalfields today. I spotted one that lives in the aptly named Puma Court recently, and, of course, there is Madge who resides in Folgate Street at Dennis Severs' House, and Mr Pussy, whose origins lie in Mile End but who has shown extraordinary prowess as a hunter in Devon, catching rabbits and even moorhens, which surely makes him a worthy descendant of Blackie.

ISABELLE BARKER'S HAT

Past Life

EVEN THOUGH I took this photograph of the hat in question, when I examined the image later it became ambiguous to my eyes. If I did not know it was a hat, I might mistake it for a black cabbage, a truffle, or an exotic dried fruit, or maybe even a sinister medical specimen of a brain preserved in a hospital museum.

Did you notice this hat when you visited the Smoking Room at Dennis Severs' House in Folgate Street? You will be forgiven if you did not, because there is so much detail everywhere in this extraordinary house, and by candlelight the hat's faded velvet tones merge into the surroundings. It feels entirely natural to find this hat in the same room as the painting of the gambling scene from William Hogarth's *The Rake's Progress*, because it is almost identical to the hat Hogarth wore in his famous self-portrait, of the style commonly worn by men when they were not bewigged.

Yet, as with so much in this house of paradoxes, the hat is not what it appears to be upon first glance. If it caught your eye at all – because it is so at home in its chosen spot that the gloom contrives to conjure virtual invisibility for this austere piece of headgear – if it caught your eye, would you give it a second glance?

It was Fay Cattini who brought me to Dennis Severs' House in the search for Isabelle Barker's hat. Fay and her husband, Jim, befriended the redoubtable Miss Barker, an elderly spinster, in the last years of her life until her death in 2008 at the age of ninety-eight. To this day, Fay keeps a copy of Isabelle's grandparents' marriage certificate, dated 14 June 1853. Daniel Barker was a milkman who lived with his wife, Ann, in Fieldgate Street, Whitechapel, and the next generation of the family ran Barker's Dairy in Shepherd Street (now Toynbee Street), Spitalfields. Isabelle grew up there as one of three sisters before she moved to her flat in Barnet House, round the corner in Bell Lane, where she lived out her years – her whole life encompassing a century within a quarter-mile at the heart of Spitalfields.

'I was born in Tenter Ground (now the site of the 1930s Holland Estate), known as the Dutch Tenter because there were so many Jews of Dutch origin living there. My family were Christians but we always got on so well with the Jews – wonderful people, they were. We had a dairy. The cows came in by train from Essex to Liverpool Street and we kept them while they were in milk. Then they went to the butchers. The children would buy a cake at Ostwind's the baker around the corner and then come and buy milk from us,' wrote Isabelle in the Friends of Christ Church, Spitalfields, magazine in 1996, when she was a mere eighty-seven years old.

Fay Cattini first became aware of Isabelle when in her teens she joined the church choir, which was enhanced by Isabelle's sweet soprano voice. Isabelle played the piano for church meetings and tried to teach Fay to play too, using an old-fashioned technique that required balancing matchboxes on your hand to keep them in the right place. 'I grew up with Isabelle,' admitted Fay. 'I think Isabelle was one of the respectable poor whose life revolved around home and church. She had very thin ankles because she loved to walk. In her youth she joined the Campaigners (a church youth movement) and one of the things they did was to march up to the West End and back. She enjoyed walking, and she and her best friend, Gladys Smith, would get the bus and walk around Oxford Street and down to the Embankment. Even when she was old, I never had to walk slowly with her.'

Years later, Fay and Jim Cattini shared the task of walking Isabelle over to the Market Café in Fournier Street for lunch six days a week. In those days the café was the social focus of Spitalfields, as Fay told me. 'Isabelle was quite deaf, so she liked to talk rather than listen. At the Market Café, where she ate lunch every day, Isabelle met Dennis Severs – Dennis, Gilbert and George, and Rodney Archer were all very sweet to her. I don't think she cooked or was very domestic, but walking to the Market Café every day – good food and good company – then walking back again to her small flat on the second floor of Barnet House, that's what kept her going.'

In fact, Fay remembered that Isabelle gave her hat to her friend Dennis Severs, who called her his 'Queen Mother' in fond acknowledgement of her innate dignity and threw an elaborate eightieth birthday party for her at his house in 1989. But although nothing ever gets thrown away at 18 Folgate Street, when we asked curator David Milne about Isabelle Barker's hat, he knew of no woman's hat fitting the description – which was clear in Fay's mind because Isabelle took great pride in her appearance and never went out without a hat, handbag and gloves.

'Although she was an East End person,' explained Fay affectionately, 'she always looked very smart, quite refined, and she spoke correctly, definitely not a Cockney. She had a pension from her job at the Post Office as a telephonist supervisor, but everything in her flat was shabby because she wouldn't spend any money. As long as she had what she needed, that was sufficient for her. She respected men more than women and refused to be served by a female cashier at the bank. Her philosophy of life was that you didn't dwell on anything. When Dennis died of Aids she wouldn't talk about it and when her best friend, Gladys, had dementia she didn't want to visit her. It was an old-fashioned way of dealing with things, but I think anyone who lives to ninety-eight is impressive. You had to soldier on, that was her attitude. She was a Victorian.'

When Fay produced a photo of Isabelle with Dennis Severs at her eightieth birthday party, David realised at once which hat once belonged to Isabelle Barker. Even though it looks spectacularly undistinguished in this picture, David saw the hat in the background of the photo on the stand in the corner of the Smoking Room – which explains why the photo was taken in this room that was otherwise an exclusively male enclave.

At once, David removed the hat from the stand in the Smoking Room, where it had

sat all these years, and confirmed that, although it is the perfect doppelgänger of an eighteenth-century man's hat, inside it has a telltale label from a mid-twentieth-century producer of ladies' hats. It was Isabelle Barker's hat! The masquerade of Isabelle Barker's hat fooled everyone for more than twenty years and, while we were triumphant to have discovered Isabelle's hat and uncovered the visual pun that it manifests so successfully, we were also delighted to have stumbled upon an unlikely yet enduring memorial to a remarkable woman of Spitalfields.

TONY PURSER

FLOWER SELLER OF FENCHURCH STREET

Human Life, Plant Life, Street Life

ALTHOUGH THE MAN in the foreground is unaware, this photograph records a historic moment in the City of London – Tony Purser's last day selling flowers from his stall in the vicinity of Fenchurch Street Station after fifty-two years of business. I took the opportunity to walk over from Spitalfields and sit with Tony to keep him company for a few hours on his last afternoon. A dignified popular figure with a ready smile, Tony told me he remembers the very

first day of business. He was driving around in a van with his father, Alfie, in 1959, looking for a place to sell flowers, and they drew up outside Fenchurch Street Station, parked the van and decided to start trading at once. 'It was quite a success, but I wasn't that interested,' said Tony, bemused at his former self. 'I was just a kid. I was cold and wanted to go home.' Tony never dreamed that he would still be there over half a century later, yet his father's instinct was a good one, because the passing trade ensured that for fifty years Tony earned a living selling fruit and flowers in the heart of the City.

Without a licence in the early years, Tony and Alfie were regularly arrested, their stock was confiscated, they were fined three shillings and spent the night in the cells at the Bishopsgate Police Station – an event that recurred until they were granted a licence in 1963. 'My father started in the 1940s and my grandfather was in the business before him, so he thought you didn't need a licence, but if you're licensed you don't get any trouble from the police,' explained Tony ruefully. 'He was a fruiterer just after the war, one of seven brothers and sisters, who all worked for him at one time or another. He was still working when he was eighty-four – a good old boy, he was – but I want to enjoy a bit of life before I die,' Tony admitted with a smile of eager anticipation at the thought of no longer getting up every morning at half past three, working until seven at night and spending all day on the street exposed to the weather.

In 1998, when Fenchurch Street Station was rebuilt and rents increased, Tony moved over to a new location nearby at the foot of the neat little medieval tower of All Hallows Staining in Mark Lane. He enjoyed another ten years of profitable trading there, but in these last two years Tony has made no money at all, though he has continued undaunted, going to the flower market at dawn, setting up stall each day and selling flowers to a dwindling number of loyal customers while living off his savings.

Tony decided to retire, recognising that the market for the street flower seller has been taken by supermarkets and companies supplying corporate displays where once a secretary would have simply bought a bunch of carnations for reception. 'Business is so bad, I've barely paid the rent,' he announced to me with a grimace and a shrug of grudging acceptance. 'Otherwise I'd have handed it down to one of the boys, my son, my two grandsons or two great-grandsons.'

Nevertheless, the news of Tony's retirement brought an unexpected series of affectionate responses from his last loyal customers, as he recounted to me proudly. 'I served one guy yesterday who has been buying from me for thirty-two years. A retired chap who came in specially to bring me a bottle of champagne and wish me well. A little girl I've seen here for four years, I know she's got no money – not that there's many of them round here, but they're the best kind of people – she brought me a bottle of malt whisky. And a lady I haven't known very long, she brought me a card. It's those you don't expect that do it. You see these people for years and you don't know their lives. I don't suppose many of them know my name, but some people are just very nice.

'One guy, he gave me five pounds for a banana!' continued Tony with crazed amusement, now that he had detached himself emotionally, uplifted by these gestures of appreciation. In confirmation of Tony's situation, there were more people asking for directions than customers on that last afternoon and our conversation was constantly interrupted by enquiries for directions to the intriguingly named Seething Lane. 'I get plenty of enquiries. If I had a pound for every one I should be a rich man,' commented Tony, rolling his eyes ironically. Yet Tony always gave directions as if it were the first time he had been asked, which struck me as remarkable largesse after fifty-two years. Tony's heroic composure was both in line with the strength of character that has got him through the last half-century trading on the street and indicative of his sense of relief at letting go of the responsibility too. 'I'm not angry, because the trade has been good to us; we've done very well. We used to take the whole of August off, though I've not had a holiday in twelve years. I'm sad because it's been my life, but the trade is over,' he confessed to me in a quiet moment.

Once the flower buckets were empty, Tony began giving away bags of fruit to surprised customers who had only asked for an apple or a banana. He gave me a bag of oranges to take back to Spitalfields. Then Mark, a droll Liverpudlian, stopped by to pick up the weekly bunch of flowers for his wife. He shook hands with Tony, brandishing the lilies for his wife. 'That's the last she'll see for a while,' he quipped. It was the end of an era at Fenchurch Street Station.

BEN EINE

STREET ARTIST

Human Life, Street Life

BEN EINE, the street artist famous for painting letters of the alphabet on shops in Shoreditch, told me that he had never been able to persuade more than three shop-keepers in a row to let him do his paintings on their shutters – until Jessica Tibbles, the enterprising curator of the Electric Blue Gallery in Middlesex Street, persuaded twenty-six to grant permission for Ben to paint a whole alphabet.

This grand endeavour, painting 'a' to 'z' sequentially on shutters along the entire length of the street, is a community initiative in which the traders of Petticoat Lane

have come together to welcome an artist bringing vibrant colour to these grey streets at the border of the City. On one side of Middlesex Street are the dilapidated nineteenth-century shops of Tower Hamlets, which exist in sharp contrast to the modernist block belonging to the City of London on the other side. Yet Ben Eine's alphabet, which now adorns both sides of Middlesex Street proposes a sympathetic conversation. His letters, deriving from nineteenth-century woodblock display types, draw the eye to appreciate the details and proportion of the brick terraces, while the bright colour palette that he employs enlivens the geometric concrete edifice opposite. Even though the architectural language may be in discord, Ben's happy paintings humanise the environment, utilising a vocabulary that everyone can relate to, thereby unifying the streetscape.

While he was working on his magnum opus in Petticoat Lane, I joined him as he painted his way from 'n' to 'r'. His Shoreditch alphabet has become inextricable from the identity of its location, and the popularity of these works have led Ben to paint them in Paris, New York, Los Angeles, Osaka, Tokyo and Budapest. Ben admitted to me that he has now painted more than 200 letters of the alphabet on shutters, and waved his dirty finger in the air playfully, proudly displaying the thickened skin upon the tip of his forefinger, where he presses the nozzle on the can, formed as his hand grew accustomed to spray-painting over the years.

Ben grew up in south London, but he has affectionate memories of when his mother brought him to Petticoat Lane to buy him his first grown-up leather jacket at eleven years old. Today he is excited to be back and bringing his vision to play upon this famous street. It is the very first time Ben has painted lower-case letters, a new departure that reflects the significance of this commission, and he showed me an outline of the complete alphabet he drew that he carries in his bag for reference, though I never saw him look at it.

Each time he sets out, Ben puts enough spray paint for three letters in his bag, but does not decide in advance upon the colour combinations, both to avoid repeating preferred schemes and to invite a wild element into the composition.

Ben works fast – each letter takes less than an hour – commencing by sketching the body of the letter, establishing the horizontal and vertical lines, then adding the background but leaving space for the outline of the letter. Although in the first instance Ben has only bought spray cans in colours he likes, he says the first two colours for each letter can almost be chosen at random. The most important decisions are the colour for the surround and the colour of the horizontal stripes within the body of the letter, the latter being the crucial element to the success of each painting as a composition.

I was wary of talking to Ben and interrupting his furious pace, but he read my thoughts, turning from the shutter with his can in hand and declaring generously with a cock-eyed grin, 'You can ask me questions while I work. I can paint and talk at the same time.' Although he is a married man with three children, Ben retains the charisma of an artful urchin, with his pants falling down, his glasses always at a squint and his habit of rocking on the balls of his feet, as if he might run off any time.

There is a magic moment when he takes a can and gives it a shake while standing in front of a new shutter, taking in the potential with a single gaze. The intense shaking of the can manifests the accumulating thoughts in Ben's mind. It is a rush of mental energy that culminates in the first lines he paints, defining the entire image, and drawn with such confidence, as if he were tracing an invisible image that was already there – which it is, in his mind's eye.

'I hate doing "o"s!' admitted Ben, rolling his eyes with good-natured irony, as he traced out a huge full moon in pale blue. 'You spend all your time painting circles.' The blue barely registered on the steel shutter, but when Ben added the violet background, it jumped into relief. The colours spoke to each other. Then the drama ramped up a level, as he approached the shutter with a new can to commence the outline. In an instant, the pale blue popped when he added the red, causing the entire painting to sing. Finally, he added yellow horizontal stripes and the composition unified in a moment of exhilaration for Ben. He had reconciled all the elements into a harmonious whole, and raised a paint-stained hand in triumph.

All of Ben's painting is a performance, and there was a constant crowd of passers-by, shopkeepers, residents, and a few stray tourists, all rapt by the spontaneous drama of Ben at work. A Nigerian lady came out of her shop, selling African batik fabrics, to admire Ben's 'q', which matched the tones of her colourful outfit. 'Nice one!' she cried in delight. Then a senior gentleman, walking slowly with a zimmer frame, emerged from Petticoat Square and halted to gather his strength and take in Ben's dazzling 'o'. 'It's looking good,' he exclaimed, filled with sudden animation as he cast his eyes up and down the street in pleasure to see the whole alphabet.

Although there is an immense history in Petticoat Lane, ever since the Jewish people left half a century ago there has also been a sense of absence in these streets. The residents and traders there have shown a sense of vision and community in supporting Ben Eine to create this glorious gallery of joyful, quirky paintings celebrating life and the city. I hope this unlikely alphabet will bring more people to appreciate this neglected corner of east London. Go and take a look for yourself.

NORMAN PHELPS

MODEL BOAT CLUB PRESIDENT

Human Life, Past Life

THIS IS NORMAN PHELPS, President of the Victoria Model Steam Boat Club, proudly displaying his ratchet lubricator that he made recently – just the latest example of an enthusiasm that began in 1935 when, at the age of five years, he fell into the boating lake in Victoria Park. It might have been a tragedy but instead it was the beginning of a lifetime's involvement with model boats, and seventy-five years later, you can still find him at the lakeside on Sundays, giving the benefit of his experience to the junior members of the club.

Norman was understandably wary of speaking to me, because the last time he gave an interview in 1951, he got taken for a ride by the *News Chronicle*. Although Norman spoke at length about the venerable club, all that got published was a souped-up account of how he courted his wife at the lake over the model boats. Seizing the opportunity to set the record straight, Norman generously sat down with me next to the boating lake and spoke with ease.

'I was always known, not by my father's name of Phelps, but as Watson – because my mother was famous as "Dolly Watson" on account of running the sweet shop in

Rockmead Road, where I grew up. I stayed in London all through the Blitz and I saw the city burning and I saw this park blown apart, and our house was destroyed by a rocket in early 1945. Because of the bombing, everyone knew everyone else. I saw neighbours dead on the pavement and I heard people crying out from beneath the wreckage of buildings where we could never dig them out. I saw the Home Guard practising with wooden rifles because we didn't have real ones. It was crazy!

'Funnily enough, I married a girl from Sewardston Road, on the other side of the park. I met her dancing at the Hackney Town Hall and because we were keen dancers and won prizes, we decided we would race model boats and see if we could win. We joined separately, but we did our courting through the club, and she won a lot of prizes and ruffled a few feathers. She's been running boats her whole life and she still is at seventy-eight.

'We got married in 1956, had our reception in the clubhouse and I was made secretary of the club at the same time. They gave us a presentation box of cutlery as a wedding present that we have today. In the early days, I supported my wife because she had such an enormous predilection to compete. She's won so many prizes, we've got boxes full. If we turned up to compete, other people would say, "Let's give up now!" It was the art of straight-running. I did the designing and she did the maintenance and cleaning. My wife was the talent. I tended to stay in the background and be the club secretary and that was enough.

'To be a great straight-runner you have to know a lot about the water and the wind, and the boat itself has to be considered too. The greatest talents in the world have competed here. So many people have gone now but I saw all the greatest exponents, like Stan Pillinger of Southampton, John Benson of Blackheath, Peter Lambert of St Albans, Jim King of Welwyn and Edgar Westbury, editor of *Model Engineer*. In this club we were lucky. We had pawnbrokers, jewellers, butchers, several tug skippers from the Thames – many of our members were skilled people. They didn't have any money, so they built boats out of cocoa tins and orange boxes, producing some of the finest straight-running hulls in the club.'

Norman recognises that the flourishing of the boat club was in direct correlation with the heyday of skilled trades. He speaks passionately of the deference that existed between the members who all brought their different areas of experience and abilities to the boat club, and the culture of mutual respect that went with it, based never upon economic status but always upon skill. Tanned and lined from endless summers on the lake, still with thick white hair and a scrawny energetic physique, he looks like a character drawn by Mervyn Peake. Possessing an eloquent tongue and a raucous laugh, Norman is engaging company too, with tender stories to tell of former members, especially his friend Bill – 'even though he was a south London boy, we managed to see eye to eye'.

'So many have pegged out. I can't get my head round it. I suppose I'm next for the

have people ringing up because they can't even put kits together today,' Norman declared in breathless amazement, before lowering his voice further and raising his brows to confide, 'None of our members can give out their home addresses, because the boats have become too valuable and they don't want to get turned over.

'Who needs a computer?' asked Norman in derision. 'I have a problem with the lubrication of my boat engine to solve.' But in spite of his disaffection, the contemporary world is affecting the boat club in ways that are not entirely disadvantageous, and even skills nurtured through computer games have their place here. 'We have lowered the age limit for membership from twelve to ten, because nowadays ten-year-olds are better with the radio controls than we are,' declared Norman, revealing a progressive spirit.

chop,' he continued with a droll grimace, crossing his arms protectively. Yet Norman remains fiercely proud of the culture of the boat club and their marvellous vessels, honed to perfection over so many years. 'This is still the home of straight-racing. We have the greatest talents here,' he said, indicating a pale young man in waders enjoying a quiet sandwich, who blushed readily as I was authoritatively informed that he was the grandson of 'a great talent'. 'These skills are rare now. I spoke to the editor of *Model World* recently and he told me they

I can understand Norman's ambivalence when he has lived through such big times, during which the Victoria Model Steam Boat Club sailed on as a beacon of civility across troubled water. Its survival today, as one of only two in existence (along with Blackheath), makes it all the more important as a reminder of the best of that other world, before the computer, when just a few people sat behind desks and most possessed a skilled trade that enabled them to earn their living and achieve self-respect too.

RETURN TO W. F. ARBER & CO. LTD
PRINTING WORKS

Past Life

THERE HAVE BEEN changes at W. F. Arber & Co. Ltd (the printing works opened by Gary Arber's grandfather in 1897 in the Roman Road) since I was last here. At that time, Gary was repairing the sash windows on the upper floors, replacing rotten timber and reassembling the frames with superlative skill. This spring, he was the recipient of a small grant from the Olympic fund for the refurbishment of his shopfront, which had not seen a lick of new paint since 1965.

The contractors were responsible for the fresh coat of green, but Gary climbed up a ladder and repainted the elegant lettering himself with a fine brush, delicately tracing the outline of the letters from the originals, just visible through the new paint. This was exactly what he did once before, in 1965, tracing the lettering from its first incarnation in 1947, when the frontage was spruced up to repair damage sustained during the war.

No doubt the Olympic Committee can sleep peacefully in their beds now, confident that the reputation of our nation will not be brought down by shabby paintwork on the front of W. F. Arber's shop, glimpsed by international athletes making their way along the Roman Road to compete in the Olympics at Stratford in 2012. Equally, Gary is happy with his nifty new paint job, and so all parties are pleased with this textbook example of the fulfilment of the ambitious rhetoric of regeneration in east London which the Olympics promise.

If you look closely, you will see that the glass bricks in the pavement have been concreted over. When Gary found they were cracking and there was a risk of some passer-by falling eight feet down into the subterranean printing works, he obtained quotes from builders to repair them. Unwilling to pay the price of over 5,000 pounds suggested, with typical initiative Gary did the work himself. He set up a concrete mixer in the basement, filled the void beneath the glass bricks with rubble, constructed a new wall between the building and the street, and carried all the materials down the narrow wooden cellar stairs in a bucket, alone. Gary's accomplishments fill me with awe, for his enterprising nature, repertoire of skills and undaunted resilience.

'I shouldn't be alive,' said Gary with a wry melancholic smile, referring not to his advanced years but to a close encounter with a doodlebug, while walking down the road on his way to school during the war. 'The engine cut, which means it was about to explode, and I could see it was coming straight for me, but then the wind caught it and blew it to one side. We lost all the glass in the explosion! Another day, my friend David Strudwick and I were eyeballed by the pilots of two Focke-Wulf Fw 190s. We saw them looking down at us but they didn't fire. David joined the air force at the same time I did. He flew Nimrods and died many years later, while making a home run during a cricket match in Devon.'

Such thoughts of mortality were a sombre counterpoint to the benign season of the year, which led Gary to recall the happy day his father and grandfather walked out of the printing works at dawn one summer's morning and, in their enthusiasm for walking, did not stop until they got to Brighton, where they caught the train home, having walked sixty miles in approximately twelve hours.

In those days, Gary's uncles Len and Albert worked alongside Gary's father and grandfather here in the print shop, when it was a going concern, with six printing presses operating at once. Albert was an auxiliary reserve fireman who was killed in the London Blitz and never lived to see his baby daughter born. Gary told me how Albert worked as a printer by day and as a fireman every night, until he was buried hastily in the City of London in an eight-person grave. 'I don't know when he slept,' added Gary contemplatively. There was no trace of the grave when Gary went back to look for it, but now Albert is commemor-ated by a plaque at the corner of Athelstane Grove and St Stephen's Road.

Whenever I have the privilege of speaking with Gary, his conversation always spirals off in fascinating tangents that colour my experience of contemporary life, proposing a broad new perspective upon the petty obsessions of the day. My sense of proportion is restored. This is why I find it such a consolation to come here, and it makes me understand why Gary never wants to retire. Each of Gary's resonant tales serves to explain why this shop is special, as the location of so much family and professional life, connected intimately to the great events of history, all of which remain present for Gary in this charmed location.

Now that Gary is a sole operator, with only one press functional, he is scaling back the printing operations. And I joined him as he was taking down the printing samples from the wall, where they have been for over half a century, since somebody pasted them on to some cheap paper as a tempor-ary measure. It was the scrutiny of these printing specimens that occasioned the reminiscences outlined above. Although these few samples comprise the only arch-ive of Arber's printing works, yet even these modest scraps of paper have stories to tell, of businesses long gone, because Gary re-members many of the proprietors vividly as his erstwhile customers.

I was fascinated by the letters ADV, indicating the Bethnal Green exchange, which prefix the telephone numbers on many of these papers. Gary explained that this was created when smart people who lived in the big houses in Bow Road objected to having BET for Bethnal Green, which they thought was rather lower class, on their notepaper. There were letters to *The Times* and a standoff with the Post Office, until the local schoolmaster worked out that dialling BET was the same as dialling ADV – which might be taken to stand for 'advance', indicating an optimistic belief in progress, which everyone could embrace. So just like Gary's Olympic paint job, all parties were satisfied and looked to the future with hope.

DANNY TABI

FURRIER

Human Life, Past Life

AT SIX IN THE MORNING Brick Lane was empty of people, but Danny Tabi, the last furrier in Spitalfields, was already at work when I arrived at Gale Furs. In 1963, when Danny started, hundreds of people were employed in the fur trade and the streets were thronged with workers from all the different garment industries making their way to work at six, but now there is just Danny. Others who merely import furs call themselves furriers, but Danny is the only one still working here at an occupation that must surely rate as one of the oldest known to mankind. I sat alone with Danny in the empty workshop at Gale Furs as the sun rose over Whitechapel and he told me his story.

'I was walking down Fournier Street, looking for a job one day, and above the Market Café was a furrier. He interviewed me and said could I start on Monday. So I got a job starting the next week. Then, as I

came out of there and walked back towards Brick Lane along Fournier Street, when I got to Gale Furs at No. 8, I asked if they had any vacancies. The proprietor, Solly Shamroth, said yes and I could start the following day. So I went there rather than the other place and this was how my association started with Gale Furs. If I had turned left rather than right that day in Fournier Street, my life would have been different.

'I started at the firm, working with a guy called Max Ross, as a nailer. That's a person that used to shape the furs by stretching them when they were wet. I picked up the nails off the floor and dampened the skins for him, then I used to go downstairs and pick up the needles from between the cracks in the floorboards with a magnet – nothing was wasted. In those days when you started in a firm like that you did everything – swept floors, did errands and got the cheese rolls too. Also on Friday my job was to clean three cars!

'I could tell you a million stories of the street and the customers, and all the characters. Everyone had their special way of doing things. Morrie Klass, who taught me how to cut, he turned up for work in detachable collars, immaculately turned out, dapper like a City gent. He read the *Guardian* and *The Times* and spoke perfect Queen's English. Maxie Ross, the nailer, he was a chain smoker, always with a cigarette or a cigar. He used to leave a pint of milk on

the windowsill until it had congealed for a week and drank it sour because he loved it that way. He picked up nails and pieces of string and made use of it. He couldn't walk past something he could use. One time, he had to go to a funeral but he had no proper black tie, so he wore a bow tie! Maxie was a champion ballroom dancer, and he and Morrie won competitions in the ballrooms. That's where Maxie met his wife, and his son used to play drums for Joe Loss. That was how I got to go to West End clubs, because he got complimentary tickets and passed them on to me as a young lad of sixteen and seventeen.

'Along the way I learned all my skills and, as the factory started dwindling in workers, I found myself taking the places of the people who had left. People just retired, but no one came in to the trade. Instead they were encouraged to go into office work. When you couldn't replace them, you had to do certain things yourself. I found myself doing more cutting, making and sewing too. I learned my trade during the 60s and 70s, then I started using my skills in the late 70s and 80s. During the 60s, when there were eighteen people working in the furrier's, it was a beautiful thing – turning out coats, collars, cuffs, stoles and hats, you name it we made it. It wasn't just the work, it was the atmosphere.

'Every single time you make a garment it's different, because fur is a living thing. You work from scratch, one skin at a time, every time – when you match up pieces, the fur has to be the same length. It's definitely an art. You can't explain what you did from arriving in the morning to going home at night. I've enjoyed my work over the years. I made a white collar from fake fur for Princess Diana. I've worked for lords and ladies. Katie Price is wearing one of my coats at present, and Kate Moss and Jemima Khan both have pieces of my work. They go to the West End stores to buy stuff but we make them here.

'I was born at 136 Brick Lane in the attic in a one-room flat. My mother lived there with me and my brother, Ray. We weren't brought up in luxury. At one point we lived in a hostel in Cable Street, because housing wasn't available to mixed-race families. I've worked since I left school. I never claimed benefits and I can count on my two hands the days off. I must be one of the longest-serving people in Brick Lane – I've always worked here.

'I love walking down Brick Lane at five thirty in the morning. I can hear echoes from the past of when I walked down there suited and booted. I get emotional. People have moved away, but I have always been drawn to the area. This used to be the dregs here, but there's nothing wrong with Brick Lane. I'm pleased to see lots of young people come now. I pop out to get something and there's crowds of young people. It's incredible.'

Danny worked for Gale Furs for thirty years before he took it over, and now he is the proprietor and sole employee. Leaving the factory premises at 8 Fournier Street in 1994 (it has become a private house now), today Danny works from a small nondescript second-floor space in Whitechapel.

The magnet Danny used to pick up pins when he started work at Gale Furs in 1963

On one side are the rails of coats and other pieces that have come in for renovation and repair, with prime garments displayed upon stands as superlative examples of the furrier's art, and on the opposite side is the work table, pierced with infinite lines of little holes created when Danny transfers the pattern to the skins. Everywhere, scraps of fur are piled and paper patterns hang in sheaves from the wall.

I was fascinated to watch Danny work at his cutting table, displaying natural dexterity, confidence and love of what he does, using the tools that have always been with the company, many of which are 100 years old or more, but still serviceable and in fact perfectly suited to the job. I felt privileged to be there in this sanctum and to understand that Danny extended his trust and welcome to me.

'It's going to die a death,' he declared without any regret, explaining that the Chinese are now the whole world's furriers, as he took me through the various tools of his trade, demonstrating the purpose and telling the story of each one. A new world opened to me as Danny outlined the processes and techniques that meet in the creation of garments of fur. We kept eye contact, like teacher and pupil, as he took me through what it takes to make a fur coat, which might require seven weeks' work. Picking up the tools, he mimed how he used them, specifying each of the distinctive requirements of the job and sometimes at a loss for words when there were none to describe the methods of working with fur, and I had simply to follow his expert demonstration.

Today, Danny does all the different jobs and possesses all the skills of the eighteen staff that once worked for Gale Furs. He is widely respected for his talent and forty-seven years of experience at the high end of an exclusive luxury trade. No one is learning from Danny and, irrespective of your feelings about the origin of fur, there is an undeniable poignancy about the culture of the furrier, which is an intricate, refined expression of a certain vein of human ingenuity, with its own language, history and tools, and of which Danny is now the last exponent in a place where once so many people pursued this ancient trade.

Market Life

'NEED BROUGHT ME HERE,' Kevin Stocker revealed to me with a phlegmatic grin on a slow Sunday in Sclater Street. 'Most of the regional markets are dying out, so you've got to go where you can find the customers. And I like the hustle and bustle here. It's a very sociable place.' Of expansive temperament, Kevin is a skilled man who has done many jobs in his varied career – 'I trained as a plumber and hated every minute of it' – but now he sells bric-a-brac at boot fairs and antiques markets to earn a living. 'I've been doing it fifteen years,' he calculated. I joined Kevin for a chat with him and neighbouring stallholder Christine. 'I call her "Lucky" because every day she bought off me I had a lucky day,' he informed me, catching her eye.

'We're all here by default, because it's what we know,' said Christine with a chuckle. 'For me it's all about the people – it's the social aspect as well as earning enough to pay the odd bill.' A woman who has travelled the world, Christine worked her way up from trading at car boot sales to international antiques fairs, until she started a theatre group exploring the subject of mental health inspired by her own experience of mental illness. Two years ago, she quit the theatre and resumed her role in the all-consuming drama of the market. 'I live in Dagenham and I own a Skoda,' she explained, puffing on her cigarette excitedly. 'When I first got started again, I used to come on the bus with all my things and it almost killed me!' A popular character in the Sclater Street Market, Christine is renowned for her raucous humour and splendid cornrows.

BLACKBERRY SEASON
IN THE EAST END

Culinary Life, Plant Life

IT IS BLACKBERRY SEASON. In Spital-fields, I always feel a pang to be reminded of the seasonal delights that I am missing here in the midst of the city. When I was a child, I thought the chief virtue of growing up was the opportunity to reach blackber-ries that grew higher in the hedgerow. I spent so many seasons trailing behind my parents on blackberry-picking expeditions down deep lanes and along the banks of the River Exe, carrying baskets and plastic bags – and armed with umbrellas or walking sticks to pull down elusive branches from above.

It was an exciting yet risky endeavour, if you were to avoid getting scratched by thorns or stung by nettles, but we were prepared to endure these petty hazards for the sake of blackberry jam to enjoy in the winter months ahead.

As a consequence, even today I feel that a summer without picking blackberries is incomplete and so, in order to exercise my ability to reach those higher branches, I set out to find some blackberries in the East End. I took a bus to Bow and got off at the church, walking through the streets until I came to Three Mills Island. Just fifty yards along the towpath of the River Lee, I found blackberries growing in profusion, cascading from the old walls of abandoned factories, and set to work picking them, pulling down those top branches that are especially heavy with fruit. Within minutes, a mother and her two children who had been similarly occupied came past clutching their bags of blackberries and, without a second thought, we exchanged greetings. It was the natural camaraderie of purple-fingered blackberry pickers.

At the end of August the variety of autumn berries was already diverse, scarlet rosehips, shiny black elderberries, delicately segmented pink spindleberries, red hawthorn berries, purple sloes and even golden greengages. I lost sense of time, absorbed in picking blackberries, making my slow progress along the hedge. The quiet river was covered in green pondweed where moorhens made aimless trails, and I stood to watch the lonely heron in contemplation, until it gave flight when a District Line train rattled over the bridge towards central London. I followed the towpath north, aware that I was walking a narrow passage of green between the new housing developments of Hackney Wick on one bank of the river and the Olympic site on the other. High winds sent clouds racing across the sky and the sunshine I had been granted for my blackberrying expedition was short-lived, turning to rain before I reached Bethnal Green.

In Spitalfields, I tipped my modest haul of blackberries into an old bowl – gleaming berries that come for free and incarnate all the poetry of late summer in England. I was satisfied that the annual ritual had been observed. It was the joyful culmination of summer. My passion for blackberry picking is sated for another year and tonight there will be blackberry crumble. Within weeks, the flies will get to the bushes and blackberries can no longer be picked. Each year presents this momentary opportunity, once they become ripe and before they are ruined – weather permitting. You are given one chance to pick blackberries before summer is over. For someone like myself, ever eager to seize the ephemeral pleasures of existence, it is a chance that cannot be missed.

CHARLIE BURNS
KING OF BACON STREET

Human Life, Past Life, Street Life

YOU MAY NOT HAVE SEEN Charlie Burns, the oldest man on Brick Lane, but I can guarantee that he has seen you. Seven days a week, Charlie, who is ninety-six years old, sits in the passenger seat of a car in Bacon Street for half of each day, watching people come and go in Brick Lane. The windscreen is a frame through which Charlie observes the world with undying fascination and it offers a deep perspective upon time and memory, in which the past and present mingle to create a compelling vision that is his alone.

For a couple of hours, I sat in the front seat beside Charlie, following the line of his gaze and, with the benefit of a few explanations, I was able to share some fleeting glimpses of his world. The car, which belongs to Charlie's daughter Carol, is always parked a few yards into Bacon Street, outside the family business, C. E. Burns & Sons, where they deal in second-hand furniture and paper goods. Carol runs this from a garden shed constructed inside the warehouse and lined with a rich collage of family photographs, while Charlie presides upon the passage of custom from the kerbside.

Many passers-by do not even notice the man in the anonymous car who sits impassive like Old Father Time, taking it all in. Yet to those who live and work in these streets, Charlie is a figure who commands the utmost respect and, as I sat with him, our conversation was constantly punctuated by a stream of affectionate greetings from those who pay due reverence to the king of Bacon Street, the man who has been there since 1915.

The major landmark in Charlie's field of vision is a new white building on the section of Bacon Street across the other side of

Brick Lane. But Charlie does not see what stands there today, he sees the building that stood there before, where he grew up with his brothers, Alfie, Harry and Teddy, and his sister, Marie – and where the whole family worked together in the waste-paper merchants' business started by Charlie's grandfather John in 1864.

'We lived on this street all our life. We were City people. We all grew up here. We were making our way. We were paper merchants. We all went round collecting in the City of London and we sold it to Limehouse Paper Mills. There was no living in it. Prices were zero. Eventually we went broke, but we still carried on because it was what we

did. Then, in 1934, prices picked up. We were moving forward, up and up and up. We carried on through the war. We never stopped. This was my life. We used to own most of the houses in this street. They were worth nothing then. They couldn't give them away.'

Once the business grew profitable, the family became involved in boxing, the sport that was the defining passion of the Burns brothers, who enjoyed a long-standing involvement with the Repton Boxing Club in Cheshire Street, where Tony Burns, Charlie's nephew, is chief coach today.

'Somehow or other, we got into boxing and then we were running the Bethnal

Green Men's Club and then we took a floor in a pub. We were unstoppable. We used to box the Racing Men's Club. We used to box at Epsom with all the top jockeys. We made the Repton Boxing Club. I was president for twenty years and I took them to the top of the world. When we joined there was only one boy in the club. (He still comes over and sees me.) We built them up, my brothers, myself and friends. They all done a little bit of boxing.

'We had some wonderful boxers come here. They were all poor people in them days. They were only too glad to get into something. We used to take all the kids with nothing and get them boxing. They played some strokes but they never did anything bad. Everything we done was for charity. We were young people and we were business people and we had money to burn.

'All of the notorious people used to come to our shows at the York Hall. We had the Kray brothers and Judy Garland and Liberace. I remember the first time I met Tom Mix, the famous cowboy from the silent films. We met all the top people, because this was the place to be. I had a private audience with the Pope and he gave me a gold medal because of all the work we did for charity.'

You would think that the present day might seem disappointing by contrast with memories like these, but Charlie sits placidly in the front seat of the parked car every day, fascinated by the minutiae of the contemporary world and at home at the centre of Bacon Street.

'This place, years ago, was one of the toughest places there was, but one of the best places to be,' he announced, and I could not tell if Charlie was talking to himself, or to me, or the windscreen, until he charged me with the rhetorical question, 'Where else can you go these days?' I was stumped to give Charlie a credible reply. Instead, I peered through the windscreen at the empty street, considering everything he had said, as if in expectation that Charlie's enraptured version of Bacon Street might become available to me too.

Charlie reminded me again, 'We were paper merchants. We were moving forward,' as he did several times during our conversation, recalling an emotional mantra that had become indelibly printed on his mind. It was an incontestable truth. We were King Lear and his fool sitting in a car beside Brick Lane. Becoming aware of my lone reverie, Charlie turned to reassure me. 'I'll get some of the boys round for a chat and we'll go into it in depth,' he promised, with quiet largesse, his eyes glistening and thinking back over all he had told me. 'This is just a little bit for starters.'

THE DOOR TO
SHAKESPEARE'S LONDON

Literary Life, Past Life, Street Life

I HAVE BEEN WONDERING if there is anything left in the neighbourhood from Shakespeare's time, when his plays were performed here at the Theatre and the Curtain Theatre in Curtain Road at the end of the sixteenth century. The Norman church of St Leonard's, Shoreditch, that Shakespeare knew was demolished in the early eighteenth century, but I heard a story that a door from the church had been preserved, a door that Shakespeare could have walked through.

When I spoke to the Reverend Paul Turp, he confirmed that the new church had re-used much of the material from the earlier building and that the paving of the portico included twelfth-century stone. In fact, he believes that the current building was constructed using the floor of the Norman church as its foundation, and the tombs of the Shakespearian actors are buried down below, just waiting to be rediscovered. My enquiry became the premise for an exploration, and when I met the Rev. Turp on the steps of the church, he handed over a flashlight, a single gesture that filled me with immense anticipation.

Standing there on the porch in the afternoon sunlight, the Rev. Turp began by con-juring a picture of the moment the Roman army arrived on the other side of the road to secure a source of fresh water. This was the wellspring of the River Walbrook at the junction of Shoreditch High Street and Old Street. From a camp here at the crossroads, the Roman army controlled England and Wales. The road west led to Bath, the road north led to York, the road east to Colchester and the road south to Chichester. When I heard this I realised that Old Street truly is an old street.

The Anglo-Saxon word *suer*, meaning stream, gave the neighbourhood its name 'Shoreditch', and it was this stream that undermined the old church, leading to its demolition. Even after the building of George Dance the Elder's church in 1740, there were problems with flooding and the ground level was built up to counter this. Only the top three steps out of the ten at the front of the church are visible now, the rest are underground. Similarly, the lower crypt was filled to stabilise the structure, which is very frustrating for the Rev. Turp, because he believes that the floor of the lower crypt is the floor of the Norman church, where the tombs of the Shakespearian actors are. This is the floor that William Shakespeare walked upon whenever he came for services, the weddings of his fellow actors or when his brother Edmund's son was buried here in 1607.

As I stood in the depths of the crypt with the Rev. Turp, beneath a dusty brick vault, peering down to the mysterious lower vault that has been filled in, the physical space came to manifest the distance between us and Shakespeare's world. The Rev. Turp wants to excavate through the layers of rubble and human remains to reach it. 'If I can find a stone with the name Burbage on it then I shall be satisfied,' he confessed, referring to the joiner James Burbage, who built the first theatre in Shoreditch, and his son Richard, who was the first actor to play Romeo, Hamlet and Richard III.

We were standing in the underworld of the imagination, it was packed with the dead, though just a fraction of the more than 76,000 buried at this site. We peered deep into small family vaults on each side, where piles of coffins had collapsed upon each other, broken open over time, creating a mishmash of bones. Many coffins were discovered to have been filled with bricks, indicating that the undertakers had sold off the bodies before burial – though fortunately the families of the dead never knew. We gazed through a large central vault where, beneath a surface that resembled dunes, countless layers of coffins were stacked up yet broken in upon each other to create a morass of unknown depth. Under the porch, on a level with corners of lead coffins sticking out from the surface, we were literally walking upon the dead. The Rev.

Turp told me tests were done to check whether the remains of those who died of smallpox still presented any risk of infection today, and I was reassured to learn that although the virus was present, it was inert.

In the crypt, I was confronted with the great number of dead that exist, filling the space between us and Shakespeare's world, when I had just hoped to walk through a door and be transported there. So I asked the Rev. Turp about the surviving door from the earlier church and, leading me back from the depths, he took me to the Clerk's House, facing Shoreditch High Street, which has the door in question built into it. Maybe it was the experience of the crypt, but as I walked through the churchyard, wiping the sinister dust off my hands and relieved to be out in the air, I thought of lines from *Romeo and Juliet* (first performed at the Curtain Theatre). Mortally injured,

Mercutio says of his wound, "'tis not so deep as a well, nor so wide as a church-door; but 'tis enough, 'twill serve. Ask for me tomorrow, and you shall find me a grave man.'

Once I saw the old door, I was disappointed at first, though I tried to hide it from the Rev. Turp. The door was tall and narrow, with panels that appeared eighteenth or nineteenth century in style, not the wide medieval church door I had envisaged. The Rev. Turp explained it was from a side entrance, but I began to wonder. Not only were there two layers of railings between me and the door – which was locked – but even if I were able to walk through it, could I accept that this door was around in Shakespeare's time? Then something unexpected happened, by chance the resident of the Clerk's House arrived home at that moment and, without thinking twice, I leaned through the railings to ask if I could see the reverse of the door. He said, 'Yes. Come in.' So, leaving the Rev. Turp standing, I ran out of the churchyard gate and into the gate of the Clerk's House – and through the door.

At once, I could see from the back of the door that it was ancient, with primitive iron hinges, and acceptably medieval in its robust contruction. Then my host showed me old panelling, also incorporated into the building, at the top of the stairs, of proportion and construction that were of the Renaissance or earlier. Now I was persuaded of the history of the door and, as I stood to take my picture, looking out from behind the portal to Shakespeare's London, a black cat ran down the stairs and out of the door, turning to look back at me, as if in confirmation of my good luck at this discovery.

MAVIS BULLWINKLE

SECRETARY

Human Life, Past Life

THIS IS THE FIRST PHOTO of the remarkable Mavis Bullwinkle, seen here attending a Christmas party in 1932 at the Drill Hall in Buxton Street hosted by the Rev. Holdstock of All Saints' Church, Spitalfields – Mavis can easily be distinguished to the left of the happy crowd, because she is a baby in her mother Gwendoline's arms. In this picture, you see her at the centre of life in Spitalfields and even though this hall does not exist any more and the church it was attached to was demolished in 1951, and everyone else in this photo has gone now too, I am happy to report that Mavis is still alive and kicking, to carry the story of this world and continue her existence at the centre of things in the neighbourhood.

Mavis's grandfather Richard Pugh was a lay preacher who came to Spitalfields with his wife and family from North Wales in

1898. Here he held Bible classes at All Saints and spoke at open-air meetings and, in the absence of social workers, counselled men from the Truman Brewery on their family problems. His mother paid for him to return alone to Wales to see her for two weeks' annual holiday from the East End each year. But Mavis's grandmother Frances never had a holiday. She said, 'Why should people take notice of you when you talk of living the Christian life, when you have an easier time than they do?' Then, in 1905, Richard died unexpectedly of pneumonia and Frances was left almost bereft in Spitalfields. She had to leave the church house and take care of her seven children alone. She received a modest pension from the Scripture Readers' Union until her youngest son, Albert, was fourteen, the Truman Brewery gave her a small grant twice a year and she took work scrubbing floors. The family moved into Albert Family Dwellings, a large nineteenth-century block in Deal Street, where subsequently Mavis grew up, living there until it was demolished in 1975, when they were rehoused in a new block in Hanbury Street.

When I visited Mavis in Hanbury Street, less than 100 yards away from the site of Albert Family Dwellings and she described her grandmother, who died when she was six, an extraordinary perspective became apparent, connecting our world with that of Spitalfields more than a century ago. 'I remember her shape and her North Wales accent, a lilt,' Mavis told me, conjuring the image in her mind's eye. 'She would always call my father Alfred, when everyone else called him Alf. She was short of stature and she worked hard.'

Mavis's testimony of life in the East End is one of proud working-class families who strove to lead decent lives in spite of limited circumstances. 'People like to think that they were all drunks who dropped their "h"s, and they were dirty,' she said, eager to dispel this misconception. 'Years ago, people were poor but they were completely clean. You can wash without a bathroom, but it takes a lot of work. My father used to put the water on to boil and pour it into the bath. And in the Family Dwellings, it was very well maintained, low rents, strict rules and a uniformed superintendent. When my mother was small and people had large families, if the superintendent saw children playing after eight o'clock, he'd say, "Go to bed!" and you had to do it. I often think of it now when I see children playing outside at eleven at night. Then everyone used to know each other and help one another. If you were going away on holiday, you'd tell everyone and they'd wave you goodbye.'

Mavis's story of her family's existence in Albert Family Dwellings spans the original flat where her grandmother lived with her two maiden aunts, and then Mavis's parents' flat that she grew up in. Mavis took care of her mother and the two aunts, who lived to be eighty-six, ninety and ninety-five respectively, even after they all moved out – seventy years after they first moved in as an act of expediency. But by then the nature of the place had changed and it was condemned as part of a slum-clearance programme. 'It suddenly went downhill in the

late 50s, when the housing association sold it,' admitted Mavis with a regretful smile, looking from her living-room window across the rooftops of Spitalfields, to the space where Albert Family Dwellings formerly stood, a space that holds so much of her family history. If Mavis had married, she would have left Spitalfields, but instead she stayed to care for the elderly members of her family and worked for forty years as a secretary in the social work department at the Royal London Hospital, where she was born in 1932. A woman of dauntless temperament, even now retired, she returns one day a week on a voluntary basis to do typing for the friends of the hospital and on another day each week she does reading with a reception class at Christ Church School in Brick Lane, where she is a governor.

In Mavis's personal landscape, Spitalfields' neighbouring territory, the City of London, holds an enduring fascination as a symbolic counterpoint to these streets where she makes her home. 'I love the City because I went to school there at the Sir John Cass School,' she confided with pleasure, 'and my father worked as a clerk in the City, at the Royal London Oil Company, for fifty-one years. To go from Tower Hamlets to the City, crossing Middlesex Street, was like crossing the River Jordan to the Promised Land. Everyone in Stepney used to dream of living in the City. Before the war, all kinds of people lived in the City, caretakers and such, not just rich people like now.' And then Mavis ran into another room to bring a framed certificate to show me and held it up with a gleaming playful smile of triumph. It read, 'Mavis Gwendoline Bullwinkle, Citizen of the City of London'.

Mavis Gwendoline Bullwinkle, citizen of Spitalfields, is a woman who makes no apology to call herself a secretary, because she is inspired by the best of that proud nineteenth-century spirit which carried a compassionate egalitarian sense of moral purpose.

AT THE BOYS' CLUB
ANNIVERSARY DINNER

Night Life, Past Life

I HAD THE PLEASURE OF attending the Cambridge and Bethnal Green Boys' Club eighty-sixth anniversary dinner at the invitation of my new friend, club member Ron Goldstein. Entering the bar, I was immediately in the thick of a loud, exuberant party of a hundred old boys in dark suits and club ties – the majority were octogenarians – all laughing and greeting each other flamboyantly in unselfconscious joy.

The rare spectacle of so many happy people together in one room stopped me in my tracks. These were boys of modest origins who grew up on the Boundary Estate and in the surrounding streets of Bethnal Green and for whom the boys' club (founded in 1924) offered a place of refuge where they could participate in cultural, educational and physical activities that served to raise their expectations of life. And many of the bonds of friendship formed there a lifetime ago exist to this day, as these lively reunions testify.

Aubrey Silkoff, the boy who wrote his name on the wall in Navarre Street, Arnold Circus, on 19 April 1950, came to greet me. Like me, he was a newcomer attending his first reunion, but already he was swept along by the emotion of the occasion. 'I've just met people I haven't seen for fifty years!' he declared with breathless excitement, introducing three childhood friends, Alan Kane, David Goldsmith and Melvyn

Burton, who also wrote their names on the wall in 1950 when they used to play together. 'We were happy in those days,' announced Alan, turning sentimental and speaking on behalf of his pals. 'Do you know why? Because we hadn't got a pot to piss in!' he continued, answering his own question, guffawing and breaking into a huge smile, while the others exchanged fond satirical glances. Reunited, the excited dynamic of their childhood friendship took over and, as I cast my eyes around the room, I realised that while all these men lived as husbands, fathers and grandfathers in daily life, tonight they were free to be boys.

Once everyone was gathered, Maxie Lea, MBE, the diminutive and playful club secretary, invited us to walk through into the dining room, where Ron and I took our seats at large round tables. Then Monty Meth, MBE, the bright-eyed club chairman, welcomed everyone, reading out apologies for absence, saluting an old boy who had flown in from Dallas for the night and remembering those who had died since last year. Each name was received with cheers, applause and cheerful hammering on the tables, with the greatest affectionate response reserved for those who were here last year and all previous years, but who would never be seen again.

After a chicken dinner followed by chocolate gateau, Tony and Irving Hiller stood up to sing, providing the opportunity for everyone to express the sentiment that had been building up all evening. The gentleman next to me confided that he had been friends with Tony – a talented songwriter

who won the Eurovision Song Contest in 1976 – since they both met in kindergarten at the age of four, eighty years ago. All shyness was overcome now, bonds of friendship had been reaffirmed and it was time to play – beginning with the club song, which provided the catalyst to release any lingering inhibitions.

So, as members of the best club of all
We're shouting Cambridge
With a C-A-M-B-R-I-D-G-E
Whizz bang, Whizz bang, Whizz bang rah
Who in the hell do you think we are?
C-A-M-B-R-I-D-G-E!

It was the cue for everyone to wave their hands, link arms, or stand and gyrate, as distant memories of years ago came back to life. Although very little alcohol was drunk, everyone was high on emotion. A sense of mortality intensified the delight for some, and in the midst of the skylarking and high jinks a few tears of joy were discreetly wiped away.

Few of these men live in the East End any more, although many grew up here before the Blitz, in a world we perceive today through black and white photographs of terraces with children playing in the street. Quite literally, some of these men were those children in the photos. Yet in their hearts they all still live in the East End, as incarnated by the spirit of emotional generosity, decency and respect that was encouraged by the boys' club and which forms the basis of their common understanding. It is not the East End today, but it is an East End that has a vibrant existence between members of this generation whenever they come together. My experience of the Cambridge and Bethnal Green Boys' Club reunion dinner was a living vision of the very best of this lost world.

Through my many conversations, I learned that while they have achieved professional careers and some have been honoured for distinguished service in the forces, none was ashamed of his origins. All were eager to come and show their gratitude to the boys' club that had provided such a life-changing experience – because, as the years go by, they recognise the familiar sense of belonging together more than they can belong to the increasingly unfamiliar geographical space of the East End.

I shook hands with Aubrey Silkoff at the end of our first reunion dinner, as we both contemplated the spectacle of multiple farewells that filled the room. 'Everyone turned out well, didn't they?' he said, nodding his head in approval as the quiet realisation came to him. I think he will be back next year.

PRINCE OF ENGLAND
UNDERGROUND DANCER

Human Life, Night Life

AS SKINNY AS A COAT HANGER and as lithe as an eel, this is underground dancer Nikolas Snode – widely known among the cognoscenti by his sobriquet Prince of England – who kindly introduced me to his eclectic and glitzy circle of friends for a thrilling Saturday night out at On the Rocks in Shoreditch, where he is one of the shining stars of the current renaissance in vogueing. 'You'll see craziness!' he promised.

Arriving at one in the morning, it was as if I had walked into a magical dream. I drifted in elated disorientation in half-light through the billowing coloured smoke and lasers, encountering all manner of ethereal creatures, until I discovered the catwalk, where colourful spirits strutted and tottered with endearing whimsical idiosyncrasy as they assumed the fashion-model poses that are the constituents of vogueing. Yet the atmosphere cleared in an instant when Prince appeared in disco pants and a hoodie, demonstrating the hair-raising ability of a young John Travolta to draw attention on the dance floor. With a spring coiled up inside him, the core of his being was manifest and everyone watched rapt as he uncurled his spindly limbs with heart-stopping control.

'I am an old-way voguer. It's all about exteriors and it's fierce. It's a mixture of military and martial arts and hieroglyphics. It's all about lines,' he declared to me with a thin crooked smile of jollity afterwards, still coming down from his performance yet raising his narrow eyebrows as his eyes shone in eagerness to proclaim the credentials which connect him to the origin of his chosen form of expression.

'My mentor is Archie Burnett of the legendary House of Ninja, who was taught by Willi Ninja – known as the godfather of vogueing. They have a community in New York, like a faith house, where black and Hispanic kids who are thrown out of their homes can go to stay and learn dance. But since I am in the UK, I skype them twice a week,' he revealed. Inspired by this direct connection to the House of Ninja and so thin he looks like a drawing of himself, Nikolas has constructed a life devoted to excellence in vogueing.

Undoubtedly, vogueing has unlocked something extraordinary in Nikolas, and I was delighted to be welcomed by his affectionate community of cartoon princesses of indeterminate gender and pop urchins in outsize singlets, who meet to party together in the early hours, and enjoy being playful in the free expression of their imaginative selves. They are the admiring courtiers and he is their Prince, with the redoubtable Scottee as the court jester in a lacy body suit, in this glamorous secret night kingdom in the Kingsland Road. 'You've got to be given your name, you can't choose it,' Nikolas explained to me cheerfully. 'My friend Supple, the Dance Scientist, said to me, "You should be Prince of

England because there is no one more English than you in the underground scene," and now everyone knows me as Prince. It's cool, because I never pitched it and I quite like it.'

Then, with an excited gleam of absurd humour, Nikolas, the evangelist of vogue, regaled me with the legend that vogueing began when the New York prisons banned pornographic magazines and inmates had to make do with copies of *Vogue* instead. Frustrated by this, they began re-enacting the models' poses and staging pose-off contests, which became dance battles. Refined by drag queens in the ballrooms of Harlem, the style eventually reached mainstream exposure in the 1980s – though 'Madonna's song is not even a vogue song, you can't easily vogue to it!' Nikolas qualified authoritatively.

Even at twenty-two, Nikolas is already a seasoned professional. He was in *Les Misérables* for ten months in the West End when he was twelve and spent his tender years as a working child performer, before emerging as a major talent on the underground dance scene. And with plenty of willing students, Nikolas teaches vogueing and its counter-

part, waacking – a style that draws its vocabulary of movement from silent films. 'Most people lack self-confidence and everybody likes to walk like a model, so vogueing can help increase confidence,' he informed me persuasively, preaching the gospel of vogue. 'Although vogueing came out of the drag scene in the first place, the culture of vogue became so bitchy in the 90s that it put women off, but I am trying to encourage them back – because the idea is to feel good about yourself, not to put others down.'

Fascinated by the possibility that dance can liberate people, I was touched by the delight I saw around me that night among those who take such joy in exploring ambiguous identity. Yet equally, I was aware that there was also an element of masquerading. 'I'm a straight guy who does it,' admitted Nikolas shyly, without wishing to sound apologetic, 'although many people would probably assume that I am gay – but I do it because I like the power of it. My mentor, Archie, was the first straight person to join a vogueing house. He has a good phrase, he says, "You don't have to be Chinese to enjoy Chinese food!"'

WITH THE PIGEON FLYERS
OF BETHNAL GREEN

Animal Life, Human Life

WITH THE PIGEON-RACING SEASON drawing to a close, I joined Albert Stratton, pigeon flyer, and his pal Keith Plastow on a Saturday afternoon in Bethnal Green to await the return of the young birds – born this spring – given an outing each year as the penultimate race of the season. Even though these fledglings only pecked their way out of the egg in March, many have already spent months in training, building up their stamina with practice flights of twenty-five miles from Harlow three times a week. This Saturday, Albert had eleven young birds among 800 competitors, flying 112 miles and 107 yards, from Newark in Nottinghamshire to Bethnal Green.

As soon as I got the call to say 'The birds are up!' I raced over from Spitalfields to Albert's house, arriving at three thirty. Then we all sat together in nervous anticipation in the garden for half an hour, gazing anxiously at the sky while he amused us with a constant stream of droll banter and, in time-honoured fashion, his wife, Tracey, reclined on the couch in the living room, relaying us the results in the Tottenham game. 'It's a heartbreaking sport, pigeon racing,' confessed Albert, turning melancholy, his eyes fixed firmly on the occluded sky. 'It's like supporting Tottenham Hotspur – if only you got out as much as you put in.'

Albert reminded me that pigeons fly at

fifty miles per hour with no wind, but can reach speeds of eighty miles an hour with a gale behind them. Saturday's wind was from the south-west. 'Not helpful! It slows them down and pushes them out to the east, which gives the easterly flyers an advantage,' he declared, exchanging a grimace with Keith. 'Let's hope it's not like last week. We were twenty minutes behind the rest.' Albert hoped the first of his birds – liberated at one thirty in Nottinghamshire – would arrive home shortly after half past three but, when four o'clock approached, he shook his head in disappointment as we all checked our watches. 'Give me my hat,' Albert asked Keith, exasperated and clutching at straws now, 'or they won't recognise me.'

Positioning himself next to the pigeon shed, Albert waited with a cup of nuts ready for the first arrival, while Keith occupied the back door of the house, puffing on a cigarette to relieve the tension as he peered into the unyielding sky. Then two pigeons appeared, a blue cock and red pied bird. They circled, but instead of flying down to the pigeon shed, landed on the roof of the flats in the next street, looking down at us curiously. Albert and Keith were beside themselves simultaneously with excitement and frustration.

'Three hours flying and then five minutes walking up and down!' quipped Albert through gritted teeth, as he shook the peanuts in his cup to encourage his birds to land. At once they flew down, increasing the tension further by alighting on the gutter over our heads. With intense self-control, Albert shook his cup of nuts again, calling tenderly, 'Come on, come on,' and after a short pause both birds landed on the wooden platform attached to the pigeon shed. Yet even now the tension did not abate, because we had to wait again, in speechless excitement, for the birds to enter the shed through the 'trap'.

Then Keith ran over, dropping his cigarette as he swiftly pulled the ring off the first bird once it entered the 'trap' and put it triumphantly into the special clock that records the arrival times. These clocks were all synchronised earlier in the day, and we would only discover who had won when the members gathered at Albert's house later and the club president unlocked the clocks with the only key. Meanwhile a falcon circled overhead and Albert grew concerned for his other pigeons. 'Poor little birds,' he said, turning emotional with relief now that a couple had arrived, asking, 'Where's the other nine?'

'We ain't seen anyone else's birds,' Keith reminded Albert hopefully, as he continued putting the rings in the clock and keeping a running total of the times when more pigeons arrived, while Albert became sardonic in defeat, announcing, 'The winner will be here soon. Whoever's won it will knock at the door.' Hopes of victory abandoned, Albert's sole concern was the safe return of his beloved pigeons, and, over the next hour, as they appeared in ones and twos, like weary children returning from an afternoon's ramble, he was particular to make sure they had slaked their thirst. Sympathetically observing them stretching their tired wings, Albert commented, 'He's had enough,' as a favoured bird dropped down from the sky and sought refuge in the pigeon shed.

'It takes over your life,' Albert revealed to me, caught in the emotion of the moment and speaking frankly of his lifelong passion for pigeon flying. 'It's worse than golf. I've not been separated from my pigeons for a night, when I could help it,' he confided, referring to a recent spell in hospital. 'They go on holiday without me,' he continued, referring to his family, as he consoled himself with the parental delights of his chosen sport. 'It's not just the racing, it's the breeding. It's very satisfying when you put a couple of birds together and they have healthy young ones.'

We were interrupted by a knock on the door, and four excited members of the Kingsland District Homing Society entered carrying their clocks. At the stroke of six thirty they all stopped their clocks, which they lined up on the floor for John Hamilton, president and clock setter, to unlock them with his key and tabulate the figures that would give a winner.

Tracey served tea and these minutes of waiting gave the opportunity for bravado and banter as the members, who are all old friends as well as arch competitors, faced each other out making conversation. First up was a discussion about how many young pigeons had gone missing. Les Hicks (last week's winner as well as this week's favourite) declared nine out of nineteen lost, with alacrity. Next up was a discussion about those ignorant fools who denigrate pigeons as flying rats, and, in the ensuing discourse to counter this prejudice, I learned that the Queen is patron of the Royal Pigeon Flying Society and that pigeons have saved thousands of lives in war. Finally the members compared the size of their first ever pay packets, the lowest being three pounds and highest twelve pounds and ten shillings but I failed to ascertain who was the winner in this subtly competitive debate.

After writing out the figures and scrutinising the printouts from the clocks, John Hamilton had a winner – but Albert Stratton, club secretary, was dubious and insisted on checking the figures with his calculator before the result could be disclosed. Yet after the average velocities of each of the birds had been calculated again, Albert confirmed the president's result unambiguously, although he chose to add that the victor had emerged only one decimal point ahead. Tracey came in to stand beside her husband to give him moral support as John Hamilton announced the official result. The winners were Mr and Mrs Albert Stratton. It was an unexpected climax to an emotional afternoon.

MICK PEDROLI

DENNIS SEVERS' HOUSE

Human Life, Past Life

THE FACE AT THE WINDOW is Mick Pedroli, house manager at Dennis Severs' House in Folgate Street. In January 1995, when Dennis Severs invited Mick to leave his home town of Amsterdam and come to work here, Mick had never been to the East End of London. But he took a leap of faith and arrived on 3 March to commence his new job and new life in London, and he has been here ever since.

'I slept in the Dickens room at first,' Mick recalled wryly, referring to a primitively furnished garret in the attic, 'but then the roof started leaking, so I moved into the Lekeux room next to it and then that started leaking too. I worked preparing the house during the day and, as it was open to the public every evening, I either had to go out or help Dennis. It was a lonely place to be away from home, living in a dark cold old house – but it was all-consuming too.'

After just a week, Dennis departed for New York, leaving Mick to host the tours and bring order to the management of the house. 'I improvised, because I had no idea what to say when visitors asked questions,' Mick confessed to me with the gallant self-deprecatory irony that is his forte, as we sat in the cool of the Victorian parlour surrounded by overstuffed upholstery and a surfeit of bric-a-brac, all enfolded by wallpaper crowded with oppressive roses.

Clearly, Mick's improvisatory abilities are immense, because he stayed the course, playing the role of peacemaker to the mercurial Dennis Severs in his last years and then steering the house forward after Dennis's death from Aids in 1999 to the present day, with more visitors through the door each year than ever before. Where once the cultural establishment dismissed Dennis Severs' House for details of historical inaccuracy, now the tide has changed and it is appreciated for the quality of imagination at play.

This was Dennis Severs' genius, and today Mick, with his colleague David Milne, upholds the endeavour, filling the house every day with spontaneous details, flowers, food and freshly rumpled bed sheets – as if the Jarvises, the family of eighteenth-century residents that Dennis Severs invented, had just left a moment ago. So convincing is the evocation that Dennis once fell into a row with a guest who claimed to be descended from the imaginary family in question. It was a spat that met its conclusion when Dennis threw the woman out into Folgate Street and Mick had to apologise and give her her money back.

The house is an innately dramatic space and, if you ask him, Mick has a lexicon of tales that he refers to as 'the soap opera', rolling his eyes at all the theatrics he has witnessed over the years. 'The first time I had a row with Dennis, I went upstairs to bed and locked my door with a chair because I was scared he might come after me in the night,' admitted Mick – raising his eyebrows – in testament to the force of Severs' personality, which remains capable of inspiring such loyalty, even in his absence. 'They were the best of times. We used to sing together and dance around the house as we were preparing for the visitors,' explained Mick with a weary smile, reeling off a list of Dennis Severs' favourite disco hits, and searching around with his eyes to trace the images that linger in the shadows of these quiet rooms, which still harbour the presence of their creator.

Once Dennis became sick, Mick found himself in a role that demanded greater involvement than he ever expected. 'It was a very difficult time when Dennis changed from being a vibrant person to a fragile ill man over six months. When he discovered his cancer was terminal, he lay down in the bedroom and I held his hand and cried. "I so envy you your tears," he said. He was very pragmatic and accepted it. When he was in hospital for extended periods, I had to come in six or seven times a day to empty the buckets collecting the leaks. It was a really dark picture, Dennis's body eaten away by cancer and the old house leaking.

'I was with him when he passed away. He died on 27 December and on 3 January we were open to the public. Then he lay here in state in the dining room, in a coffin lined with red velvet and decorated with black ribbons, for friends to come and say goodbye before he was taken to Christ Church on 6 January. Two hundred people gathered in the street outside as the bells tolled a death knell and we all walked behind the hearse drawn by four black horses.'

The unspoken irony is that in setting out to evoke the life of the past, Dennis Severs created the magnificent scene upon which the drama of his own death would be played out. Today in Dennis Severs' House, the living and the dead coexist equally within the eternal present that the house proposes. Through tending the reality of the Jarvises, Mick and his fellow curators have become a parallel family of those who worked alongside Dennis. Even though the story of Dennis and his circle may be less apparent to the visitor than the fictional Jarvises which the rooms are set up to describe, theirs is a story that deepens an appreciation of the house as an emotional space for the contemplation of the ephemeral nature of existence.

'The kitchen is my favourite place,' revealed Mick, eyes gleaming with delight. 'I think it is the most unpretentious room, soulful and warm, quiet and safe. It doubled as my sitting room when I lived here. On my first New Year's Eve, we had a big party. Dennis had his A-list friends upstairs in the drawing room while I had my party downstairs. We had our music and all these people were dancing in the kitchen. It was surreal.' Mick's choice of room reflects his own egalitarian nature, as the ex-proprietor of a coffee bar in Amsterdam,

and fifteen years later, Mick's perseverance appears to have carried him through the experience that threatened to overtake his life. 'Of course, there is a deep emotional involvement here for me,' he conceded with equanimity, before adding, 'but it is a job. I have working hours now and I have a life. If I meet people who ask what I do, I say I do admin.' Let me admit I was not entirely persuaded.

Once you open up a dream space, as Dennis Severs did, it can take on a life of its own, drawing everyone into its vortex. He may be dead and lying in his grave, but his imaginative world still flourishes in Folgate Street, just waiting to enchant the unwary visitor. When you arrive and Mick Pedroli greets you at the door with a polite invitation to hold silence, he is inducting you as a participant in the drama that Dennis Severs set in motion. There is only one thing to do, take a deep breath and step over the threshold.

Market Life

PATRICIA GREEN told me that her father, Ronald, began selling menswear from this pitch when he obtained a licence in 1956 – although the family were in Sclater Street long before that, when it was an animal market.

'Originally his father used to be down here selling birds,' explained Patricia, 'and my father used to sell birdseed as a boy. He stayed until he was seventy-six, and was down here until a few weeks before he died.' Leaving school at fourteen, Ronald worked in a pawnbrokers and then a department store, before opening his own shop, selling menswear in Upton Park and on Sclater Street each Sunday. 'I started coming down here to the market with him when I was five years old,' admitted Patricia fondly, casting her eyes along the street to see the invisible crowds of long ago. 'There were so many people you couldn't walk through it, you just got carried along with the crowd. You never used to see any women. It was a men's market – maybe one in fifty was a woman.

'I don't go to bed on Saturday night,' she explained to me with a grin. 'I just sit on the bed and maybe have forty winks, before I get up at ten past one to make the sandwiches and flask of tea. I get here around three o'clock and by the time I have set up and unloaded all the stuff it's a quarter to five, then at six o'clock I go and have a little chat with my friends.' It is a routine that few would choose, yet even though she is retired Patricia is keen to come every week. 'I have regular customers and I know a lot of people who've been here for years – but every now and again someone disappears,' she confessed in a diplomatic whisper.

At the next stall is Patricia's brother Robert Green, who helps out his friend Simon Lynch selling household goods. 'I've been here since 1977, when I left school and started working alongside my father,' he declared proudly. 'In forty years, I have only missed five Sundays – that was when I broke my leg and had to take five weeks off.'

When Robert reached fifty, he and his sister sold their father's shop. 'We used to work seven days,' he said. 'Since I left school, my entire life had been the business and I wanted to have more time, but to tell you the truth I don't have any more time than I had before.' He shook his head in good-humoured perplexity. 'After all these years, I still try to serve someone enthusiastically,' he informed me, raising a hand as a point of honour, 'even if they are only buying a bottle of washing-up liquid, and though I don't need the money, I treat them with as much respect as if they were buying 100 pounds' worth of stock years ago.'

With the ease of one who is at home in the world, Robert has an innate sense of decency and delight in what he does. 'I hope to make money – but it doesn't really matter, because I've always done it, so I'd feel out of place if I didn't do it. I am used to being down here at three in the morning in the freezing cold every week,' he said, declaring both his own nature and his affection for the market. 'It's a combination of things – tradition, culture and a lot of history. This is a very old market here.'

I stood at Robert's side as eager customers paid for their purchases and he continued talking over his shoulder animatedly. 'It's tradition because years ago everything else used to shut and this was the only place open on a Sunday,' he told me. 'It's culture because there's a lot of people on the other pitches who, even if we are not exactly friends, they always come and tell me what they are doing. And it's history because some of the customers I remember when they were young and now they are in their seventies and eighties. We've all grown old together. There's a lot more to it than just coming down here to sell a few things.'

AT THE BUNNY GIRLS' REUNION

Night Life, Sex Life

ONE SUNDAY NIGHT at the end of summer I attended the most glamorous party of my life. It was a Bunny Girls' and *Playboy* models' reunion hosted by ex-Bunny Barbara Haigh, esteemed landlady of the Grapes in Limehouse. Never have I encountered more voluptuous charismatic ladies per square metre than were crammed joyfully together in the tiny barrooms of this historic riverside pub that night. I was thrilled to join this exuberant sisterhood of more than a hundred garrulous alpha females for a knees-up. Squeezing my way through the curvy bodies – fine specimens of their sex who have all got what it takes to succeed in life – I arrived on the river frontage, where waves were crashing theatrically over the veranda as if, in re-enactment of Botticelli's *Venus*, each of these goddesses had just emerged triumphant from the Thames spray to delight the souls of mere mortals like myself.

The first Aphrodite to catch my eye was cheeky Bunny Sandie, the seventh Bunny to join the newly opened Playboy Club in Park Lane in 1966, who is more formally known these days as Lady Sandra Bates. Within seconds of our introduction, Sandie gleefully revealed she had bedded Sean Connery, Frank Sinatra, Warren Beatty and Telly Savalas, emphasising that her most important conquest was Sir Charles Clore, owner of Selfridges and Mappin & Webb. 'I was living in a house in Mayfair at the time, but the owner put it up for sale and wanted to throw me out, so I told Charles and he bought it for me!' she declared with a glittering smile, rolling her chestnut eyes, batting her eyelashes and clutching her hands in girlish pleasure. 'You should see my art collection!' she proposed recklessly, now that her husband Sir Charles is no more, as we shared a glass of wine on the

veranda and the setting sun lit up the clouds, turning the river livid pink.

It was a remarkable overture to an unforgettable evening, because these girls know how to party. Bunnies had flown in from all over the world – Las Vegas, the Bahamas, Egypt and as far away as Australia and Tasmania to celebrate the glory days of the British Playboy Club, which ran from 1966 until 1980. As Marilyn Cole (the first full-frontal nude in the history of *Playboy* in 1972) put it so elegantly in her speech of welcome, 'When people ask, "Where did you go to school?" I say, "Fuck that, I went to the University of Playboy! You learn much more about life."' An astute comment that drew roars of approval from the assembled Bunnies.

Marilyn, resplendent in a quilted leather miniskirt and thigh-length high-heeled boots, ushered me over to meet her famously reclusive husband, Victor Lownes, who opened the London Playboy Club. Formerly in charge of all Playboy's gaming operations, Victor Lownes is a bon viveur who was once Britain's highest-paid executive, counted Francis Bacon and Roman Polanski as friends and reputedly had five girls a day, sometimes two at once. He looked at me benignly from under a mop of white hair across the chasm of our different experiences of life. 'Do you miss it?' I enquired tentatively, and Victor rolled his twinkly eyes in good-humoured irony. 'What do you think? I am eighty-two years old!' he replied with dignified restraint.

There was a giddy atmosphere in the Grapes that night and so I chose to embrace

'What is a playboy? It is someone who is getting more sex than you are.'

the spirit of the occasion and mingle with as many Bunnies as possible. 'I was a young girl from a very strict religious background in Birmingham who ran away from home,' admitted Bobbie, one of first black Bunnies, who worked at the Playboy Club from 1975 to 1980. 'I was shopping one day and I went along to "a cattle drive" and out of fifty girls was one of a handful accepted to be a Bunny. I had four wonderful years that totally changed my life. It was a terrific experience. I have run my own business for the past twenty years and the things I learned at Playboy set me on the road to be able to do that.'

'There was only one rule, "Don't touch the Bunnies!"' explained Bunny Erica, raising a finger of authority. 'Membership of the Playboy Club came with a key, which members handed in when they arrived and collected when they left. If somebody went too far the management took away their key. So the men always behaved respectfully. You were never forced to do anything. It's made to seem cheap now – but we wore two pairs of tights, our costumes were fitted and stiffened with whalebone, we even put toilet rolls down the front as padding – it was an illusion. We were supposed to share tips, but I put mine down my costume and when I took it off all the banknotes would fall out. The money was fabulous. Playboy gave us the most amazing part of our lives. It gave us freedom. It gave us a love of humanity. It enlightened us.'

'I was the very first UK Bunny to be hired in 1966,' declared Bunny Alexis, still glowing with pride over forty years later. 'I was a dancer at the Talk of the Town in Leicester Square on twelve pounds a week, but at Playboy I earned 200 pounds. I was already married with a child and on the strength of my two years as a Bunny I was able to buy our first house in Wood Green. It was the hardest work, eight hours a day on five-inch heels with just one half-hour break. But it was good fun and we met all the most amazing people – 1966 was a very good year!'

People often ask what happened to the 1960s, yet here the evidence was all around me. It was a buzz to be in a room full of such self-confident women who knew who they were and were supremely comfortable with it too, women with their wits about them, who counted brains among other natural assets when it came to interactions with the opposite sex, women who knew how to make the best of the situation they found themselves in at the Playboy Club – unashamedly constructed as an arena of male fantasy yet, paradoxically, as all these women testify thirty years on, it provided opportunities for them to take control of their lives.

Undoubtedly there were those who, as Bunny Serena put it succinctly, 'screwed their way to the top', but equally there were many who, as Bunny Lara confirmed, found it 'an empowering experience. They sent us on management training courses, and I learned how to handle people and manage staff – all of which has come in useful ever since in everything I have done.' She now runs a young offenders' programme, training staff in conflict management. Many women I spoke with occupy senior management roles in the gaming and entertainment industry today – including one who manages a chain of casinos – in jobs that would have been closed to them previously.

Above all, these were women who were full of life. They had seen so much life and had so many stories to tell that it was wonderful simply to be among them, confirming Bunny Lara's fond verdict on her experience working at the Playboy Club: 'The camaraderie was phenomenal.'

CLIVE MURPHY
ORAL HISTORIAN

Human Life, Literary Life

ABOVE A CURRY HOUSE IN Brick Lane lives Clive Murphy, like a wise owl snug in the nest he has constructed of books and lined with pictures, photographs, postcards and cuttings over the thirty-six years that he has occupied his tiny flat. Originally from Dublin, Clive has not a shred of an Irish accent. Instead he revels in a well-educated vocabulary, a spectacular gift for rhetoric and a dry taste for savouring life's ironies. He possesses a certain delicious

arcane tone that you would recognise if you have heard his fellow countryman Francis Bacon talking. In fact, Clive is a raconteur of the highest order and I was a willing audience, happy merely to sit at his feet and chuckle appreciatively at his colourful and sometimes raucous observations.

I was especially thrilled to meet Clive because he is a writer after my own heart who has made it his business to seek out people and record their stories. At first in Pimlico and then here in Spitalfields through the 60s and 70s, Clive worked as a 'modern Mayhew, publishing the lives of ordinary people who had lived through the extraordinary upheavals and social changes of the first three-quarters of the century before they left the stage'. He led me to a bookshelf in his front room and showed me a line of nine books of oral history that he edited, entitled *Ordinary Lives*, as well as his three novels and six volumes of ribald verse. I was astonished to be confronted with the achievements of this self-effacing man living here in two rooms in such beautiful extravagant chaos.

Naturally, I was immediately curious about Clive's books of oral history. Each volume is an autobiography of one person, recorded and edited by Clive, 'ordinary' people whose lives were revealed in the telling to be compelling and extraordinary. They are *A Funny Old Quist*, memoirs of a gamekeeper, *Oiky*, memoirs of a pigman, *The Good Deeds of a Good Woman*, memoirs of an East End hostel dweller, *A Stranger in Gloucester*, memoirs of an Austrian refugee, *Endsleigh*, memoirs of a river keeper, *At the Dog in Dulwich*, memoirs of a struggling poet, *Four Acres and a Donkey*, memoirs of a lavatory attendant, *Love, Dears!*, memoirs of a chorus girl, and *Born to Sing*, memoirs of a Jewish East End mantle presser. The variety of subjects was intriguing and bizarre, and Clive outlined his personal vision of creating a social panorama, 'to begin with the humblest lavatory attendant and then work my way up in the world until I got to Princess Margaret'.

Much to Clive's frustration, the project foundered when he got to the middle classes, and he coloured visibly as he explained, 'I found the middle classes had an image of themselves they wanted to project and they asked to correct what they had said afterwards, or *they told downright lies*, whereas the common people didn't have an image of themselves and they had a natural gift for language.' I was keen to understand the origin of Clive's curiosity, and learn how and why he came to edit all these books. And when he told me the story, I discovered the reasons were part of what brought Clive to England in the first place.

'I lived a sheltered life in Dublin in a suburb and qualified as a solicitor before I came to England in 1958. My mother wanted me to be solicitor to Trinity College, where her father was Vice-Provost, but I had been on two holidays to London and I'd fallen in love with the bright lights. I wanted to see a wider variety of people. So as soon as I qualified I left Dublin, where I had been offered a job as a solicitor at four pounds and ten shillings a week, and came to London, where I got a job at once as a liftman at a Lyon's Corner House for eight pounds a week and I have lived here ever since.

'I was staying in Pimlico and there was a retired lavatory attendant and his wife who lived down below, and they invited me for supper. He had such a natural gift for language and a quaint way of expressing himself, so I said, "Let's do a book!" and that was *Four Acres and a Donkey*. Then I was living in another house and by complete chance there was another retired lavatory attendant, a woman who had once been a chorus girl, so I did another book with her, too, that was *Love, Dears!*

'At that time there was an organisation called Space which let out abandoned schools and warehouses to artists. In 1973 I answered their letter in *The Times* and they found me this empty building. It was the Old St Patrick's School in Buxton Street. I lived in the former headmaster's study and that's where I recorded my first East End book. I had nothing but a tea chest, a camp bed and a hurricane lamp. There was no electricity but there was running cold water. Meths drinkers used to sit on the doorstep night and day, and at night they would hammer on the door, trying to get in.

I was a bit frightened because I had never met meths drinkers before and I was all alone, but gradually three artists came to live in the school with me.

'Then I had to leave the schoolhouse because I was flooded out and, after a stint on Quaker Street, I saw an ad in Harry's Confectioners and moved here to Brick Lane in 1974. The building was owned by a Jewish lady who let the rooms to me and a professor from Rochester University who only came to use his place in vacations, so it was wonderfully quiet. There was a cloth warehouse on the ground floor then which is now the Aladin Restaurant. Every shopfront was a different trade. We had an ironmonger, an electrician and a wine merchant with a sign that said "Purveyors to the diplomatic service". The wine merchant also had a concoction she sold exclusively to the meths drinkers but that wasn't advertised.

'I thought when I came here to Spitalfields I was going to be solely a writer. I had taught at a primary school in Islington, but very soon I became a teacher of children with special needs here. Occasionally, I used to go in the middle of the night to buy food from a night stall outside Christ Church, Spitalfields, called the Silver Gloves. I had no money hardly and I used to live off the fruit and veg thrown out by the market on to Brushfield Street. But I found it exciting to be here because I found lots of people to interview. I had already written two novels and I was busy recording Alexander Hartog and Beatrice Ali, and I was happy to be learning

about them, because I did lead a very restrictive life before I came to England.'

It interested me that Clive now writes poetry, because there is an unsentimental appreciation of the poetry of the human condition that runs through all his work. He chose his subjects because he saw the poetry in them when no one else did and the books, recording the unexpected eloquence of these 'ordinary' people telling their stories, bear witness to his compassionate insight.

As a writer in the early days of writing pen portraits, I was curious to ask Clive what he had learned from all his interviews with such a variety of people. 'The gamekeeper said to me, "You mean you don't know how to skin a mole?"' Clive recalled with relish, evoking the gamekeeper in question vividly, before returning to his own voice to explain himself. 'I am amazed that we are all stuck in our little worlds – he really thought everyone would know that.'

Clive gave me copies of his two East End books and, as we sliced open a box, I was delighted to discover 'new' copies of books from 1975, beautifully printed in letterpress with fresh unfaded covers and some with a vinyl record inside to allow the reader to hear the voice of the protagonist. I could not wait to go home to read them and listen. Now I will never be able to walk down Brick Lane again without thinking of Clive Murphy, living there above the Aladin Restaurant, as a beacon of inspiration to me while I am running around Spitalfields pursuing my own interviews.

AT THE PEARLY KINGS AND QUEENS' HARVEST FESTIVAL

THE PEARLY KINGS AND QUEENS came together from every borough of London and gathered in the square outside the Guildhall in the City of London for a lively celebration to mark the changing of the seasons. There was maypole dancing and morris dancing, there was a pipe band and a marching band, there were mayors and dignitaries in red robes and gold chains, there were people from Rochester in Dick-

ensian costume, there were donkeys with carts and veteran cars, and there was even an old hobby horse leaping around – yet all these idiosyncratic elements successfully blended to create an event with its own distinctive poetry. In fact, the participants outnumbered the audience and a curiously small-town atmosphere prevailed, allowing the proud Pearlies to mingle with their fans and enjoy an afternoon of high-spirited chit-chat and getting their pictures snapped.

I delighted in the variety of designs that the Pearlies had contrived for their outfits, and on this bright Sunday afternoon in early autumn they made a fine spectacle, sparkling in the last rays of September sunshine. My host was the admirable Doreen Golding, Pearly Queen of the Old Kent Road and Bow Bells, who spent the whole year organising the event. And I was especially impressed with her persuasive abilities, cajoling all the mayors into a spot of maypole dancing, because it was a heartening sight to see a team of these dignified senior gentlemen in their regalia prancing around like eleven-year-olds and enjoying it quite unselfconsciously too.

In the mêlée, I had the pleasure of encountering George Major, the Pearly King

of Peckham (crowned in 1958), and his grandson Daniel, the Pearly Prince, sporting an exceptionally pearly hat that is a century old. George is an irrepressibly flamboyant character who took the opportunity of his celebrity to steal cheeky kisses from ladies in the crowd, causing more than a few shrieks and blushes. As the oldest surviving member of one of the only three surviving original Pearly families, he enjoys the swaggering distinction of being the senior Pearly in London, taking it as licence to behave like a mischievous schoolboy.

Nearby I met Matthew (Daniel's father) – a Pearly by marriage not birth, he revealed apologetically – who confessed he sewed the 6,000 buttons on George's jacket while watching *Match of the Day*.

Fortunately, 'The Lambeth Walk' had been enacted round the Guildhall Yard and all the photo opportunities were exhausted before the gentle rain set in. And by then it was time to form a parade to process down the road to St Mary-le-Bow for the annual harvest festival. A distinguished man in a red tail coat with an umbrella led the procession through the drizzle, followed by a pipe band setting an auspicious tone for the spectacle of the Pearlies en masse, some in veteran cars and others leading donkeys pulling carts with their offerings for the harvest festival. St Mary-le-Bow is a church of special significance for Pearlies because it is the home of the famous Bow Bells that called Dick Whittington back to London from Highgate Hill, and you need to be born within earshot of these to call yourself a true Cockney.

The black and white chequerboard marble floor of the church was the perfect complement to the pearly suits, now that they were massed together to delirious effect. Everyone was happy to huddle in the warmth and dry out, and there were so many people crammed together in the church in such an array of colourful and bizarre costumes of diverse styles that, as one of the few people not in some form of fancy dress, I felt I was the odd one out. But we were as one, singing 'All Things Bright and Beautiful' together. Prayers were said, speeches were given and the priest re-

minded us of the Pearlies' origins among the costermongers in the poverty of nineteenth-century London. We stood in reverent silence for the sake of history and then a Pearly cap was passed around in aid of the Whitechapel Mission.

Coming out of the church, there was a chill in the air. The day that began with summery sunshine was closing with autumnal rain. Pearlies scattered down Cheapside and through the empty City streets for another year, back to their respective corners of London. Satisfied that they had celebrated summer's harvest, the Pearlies were going home to light fires, cook hot dinners and turn their minds towards the wintry delights of the coming season, including sewing yet more pearl buttons on their suits during *Match of the Day*.

THE CAT LADY OF SPITALFIELDS

Animal Life, Past Life, Street Life

I WENT ROUND to enjoy a cup of tea and a shot of rum with Rodney Archer in his cosy basement kitchen in Fournier Street, eager to learn more about the Cat Lady of Spitalfields photographed by Phil Maxwell in the 1980s. She was an enigmatic presence who made it her business to befriend all the felines in Spitalfields and although

she shunned human society, Rodney used to know her.

'Joan went all around the neighbourhood feeding the cats regularly and she had names for them. And you'd see her crouching, looking through the corrugated-iron surrounding Truman's Brewery, waiting for the cats to come, and then they suddenly all

appeared. I think once I saw her there and I asked her what she was doing, and she said, "I'm waiting for the cats to appear."

"'My darlings,' she really did call them, "My darlings," and it was wonderful in a way that she had this love of cats and spent her life encouraging them and feeding them and keeping them alive. I could never quite work it out, but she had a bag, like one of those shopping trolleys, full of cat food. Now, either she'd taken the tops off the tins or something, since I noticed – because she had a kind of witch-like aspect – that although she put her hands right into the tin to feed them and then just threw it down, I never saw any cat food on her hands. It was like something out of *Grimm's Fairy Tales*.

'Over the years, I would chat to her, but she was someone that you had to have some time for, because once she began she went on and on. She lived down off Brick Lane and she had her own flat, and I don't know if it was a council flat, but eventually she was moved to south London. I think she was not an easy neighbour and, perhaps she was surrounded by immigrants, she certainly didn't like anyone from any other place but England.

'So, I'd chat with her when she'd come up from south London on the 40 bus – I think that stops at Aldgate. Every day she would come back, even though she had moved on, and she would make her way round the neighbourhood. She wore these snow boots. I remember once commenting on her new boots, and they were a gift from her sister.

The Cat Lady was strange – she spent all her money on the cats – she was like a character out of Dickens. She was almost a street person, except she had a place to live. And she did get benefits and she wasn't an alcoholic or anything. She was very doughty. She had a bit of a moustache.

'She was the kind of woman who, a hundred years ago, people would have been fearful of in a way. There was something awesome about her, because she had her own aura and she was there to feed the cats, and the cats were much more important to her than people. And I'd talk about my cat to her, and I think once she stopped by my door and I opened it, and my cat sat looking at her and she would ask me about him. I don't know if she had any cats at home. I don't know how old she was exactly. She must have been in her sixties or seventies, I suppose.

'She had this mantra which was "Cats are better than rats." At that time, the market was still operating and you had all the fruit and vegetables, and the rats would come out to feed. You might see a rat running along the kerb. A lot of people said they were looking forward to the market closing because the area would be cleaner and neater, but I regretted that it left and there weren't cabbages everywhere.

'I think I first saw the Cat Lady on the corner of Fournier Street and Brick Lane. She had great physical endurance, but I think she must have been exhausted by her journey every day, because she would often stop and she'd stop for quite a long time, and she'd just be there looking around. I suppose she might have been looking for the cats. That's why you could pass her and catch up with her and ask her how she was doing.

'So one day I just spoke to her. Maybe I'd seen her around and I said, "Are you feeding the cats?" And she told me, and I said I had a cat and so we talked about cats and the wisdom of cats and all that kind of thing. And afterwards I'd see her quite often, but I couldn't always stop because sometimes it was difficult to know how to reply if she was saying something you disagreed with.

'It's a strange thing – when I think again about the Cat Lady, I wonder, "My God, did I make this up?" but I wouldn't have made up that she died. And I do remember going to her funeral because I was one of the only mourners there.

'I can't remember how I discovered that the Cat Lady had died. Somehow, someone who knew her must have told me. The funeral was out at the East London Crematorium. Her sister was there from the north of England. She seemed to be a kind of middle-class woman who'd married and had a family and was quite respectable in a way that Joan wasn't. I don't know if the Cat Lady had any other family. I don't think she had any close relatives at all – she didn't talk much about her past life – but she was the great mother of all the cats.'

IN SPITALFIELDS IN AUTUMN

Plant Life, Spiritual Life

THE RAIN IS FALLING ON Spitalfields, upon the church and the market, and on the streets, yards and gardens. Dripping off the roofs and splashing on to the pavements, filling the gutters and coursing down the pipes, it overflows the culverts and drains to restore the flow of the Black Ditch, the notorious lost river of Spitalfields that once flowed from here to Limehouse Dock. This was the watercourse that trans-

mitted the cholera in 1832. An open sewer piped off in the nineteenth century, the Black Ditch has been co-opted into the drainage system today, but it is still running unknown beneath our feet in Spitalfields – the underground river with the bad reputation.

The shades of autumn encourage such dark thoughts, especially when the clouds hang over the City and the Indian summer has unravelled to leave us with incessant rain, bringing the first leaves down. In Spitalfields, curry touts shiver in the chill and office smokers gather in doorways, peering at the downpour. The balance of the season has shifted and sunny days have become exceptions, to be appreciated as the last vestiges of the long summer.

On such a day recently, I could not resist collecting some conkers that were lying neglected on the grass in the sunshine. And when I got home I photographed them in that same autumn sunlight to capture their perfect lustre. Ever since I came to live in the city, it has always amazed me to see conkers scattered and ignored. I cannot understand why city children do not pick them up, when even as an adult I cannot resist the temptation to fill a bag. In Devon, we raced from the school gates and down the lane to be the first to collect the fresh specimens. Their glistening beauty declared their value even if, like gold, their use was limited. I did not bore holes in them with a meat skewer and string them, to fight with them as others did, because it meant spoiling their glossy perfection. Instead I filled a leather suitcase under my bed with conkers and felt secure in my wealth, until one day I opened the case to discover they had all dried out, shrivelled up and gone mouldy.

Let me admit, I feel the sense of darkness accumulating now and regret the tender loss of summer, just as I revel in the fruit of the season and the excuse to retreat to bed with a hot-water bottle that autumn provides. I lie under my quilt and I feel protected like a child, though I know I am not a child. I cannot resist dark thoughts. I have a sense of dread at the winter to come and the nights closing in. Yet in the city, there is the drama of the new season escalating towards Christmas and coloured lights gleaming in wet streets. As the nights draw in, people put on the light earlier at home, creating my favourite spectacle of city life, that of the lit room viewed from the street. Every chamber becomes a lantern or a theatre to the lonely stranger on the gloomy street, glimpsing the commonplace ritual of domestic life. Even a mundane

scene touches my heart when I hesitate to gaze upon it in passing, like an anonymous ghost in the shadow.

Here in Spitalfields, I have no opportunity to walk through beech woods to admire the copper leaves – instead I must do it in memory. I shall not search birch woods for chanterelles this year either, but I will seek them out to admire in the market, even if I do not buy any. Instead I shall get a box of cooking apples and look forward to eating baked apples by the fire. I have been busy cutting up broken pallets and scrap timber from the streets, and I already have a respectable woodpile stacked up. I am looking forward to lighting the fire. I am looking forward to Halloween. I am looking forward to Bonfire Night. I am looking forward to Christmas. The summer is over but there is so much to look forward to.

ALL CHANGE AT CRESCENT TRADING

Human Life

FOR THE PAST EIGHTEEN YEARS Philip Pittack and Martin White have traded from a charismatic old stable block in Quaker Street, but since the landlord has acquired planning permission to convert the building into a hotel, they are moving to an industrial unit across the road. These are momentous days for Crescent Trading, so I went along to show moral support.

I gasped to see the old warehouse, once packed to the rafters, now cleared of cloth, and discovered Martin there, a dignified figure, ruminating like Hamlet in an empty theatre. Meanwhile Philip hauled a trolley piled with bolts of cloth across the street outside, pink in the face with exertion and yet full of cheery resolve to make it to the new premises, where they have taken out

a five-year lease. 'He's seventy-nine and I am sixty-seven,' confessed Philip as he ran up a ladder with a roll of fabric over his shoulder, demonstrating the careless abandon of a thirteen-year-old. 'When the lease

Already customers are crossing the road, and they seem to like the new arrangement, where everything can be seen at a glance. Crescent Trading is a treasure trove for small designers and design students, who can buy cut lengths they could not get anywhere else, discovering rare high-quality fabrics at a fraction of the cost they would pay at a mill. Even as Philip and I were talking, Mr Amecci, a designer in a snazzy deep blue serge trench coat with fur collar, fedora and 40s moustache interposed. 'Don't write this up,' he begged me with winsome irony, 'because I don't want everyone to know! What I like about this place is that I can get things I wouldn't get elsewhere, like mohair, mohair mixes and chinchilla at discount prices.' Then Matsuri, another cool-cat designer, entered in a Guy Fawkes hat with waist-length locks straggling out beneath, and eager for blazer-striped fabric. Regretfully, Philip had to send him back across the road to the old warehouse for it.

finishes he will be eighty-four and I will be seventy-two.' At just 2,000 square feet, the new warehouse, constructed of breeze-blocks with a metal shuttered door, is half the size of the old one, so Philip has invested in a racking system, which means he can stack the cloth higher but is obliged to climb more ladders.

Not many men at his time of life would take on this challenge, yet with heroic enthusiasm Philip has embraced the whole process of hauling every one of all the thousands of rolls of cloth across the road manually and installing them in the racks, then taking them down and rearranging them to achieve a satisfactory order. As Martin declared later, deliberately and without overstatement, 'Philip's done a job which is a mighty one and it is quite incredible how it's been done.'

Philip was simultaneously excited by the custom and frustrated by the circumstance. 'We've come to the point of no return, where we are running back and forth across the road!' he admitted to me, rolling his eyes and waving his hands in self-dramatizing resignation. Yet within a month, the move will be complete and so I persuaded Philip to take me on a sentimental tour, visiting the first-floor storage space that once had a lift shaft big enough to bring shire horses up to be stabled. We passed a huge reptilian conveyor belt for bringing rolls of cloth upstairs – broken ten years ago, it will never run again – and we entered the vast empty warehouse, breathtaking in its lyrical state of dereliction, and possessing an atmosphere that no industrial unit can ever match.

These are emotional times at Crescent Trading. 'I'm petrified,' admitted Philip when we were in private, revealing the nature of the passion that has driven him to manhandle every roll of cloth across the road. 'We were happy. We had our feet under a table for eighteen years. Now we eke out a living and times are very difficult. We have to work because all our money is sitting on the floor. This street used to be all small businesses, a trouser maker, three printers, a quilter and a dressmaker. I am angry that the council zoned this street as small businesses and now it's going to be just a hotel and a housing block.' And then, concerned that he might have lowered my spirits with this outburst, he put his hand into a box and slipped a bottle of whisky into my bag as I walked out of the door.

My sympathies are with Philip Pittack and Martin White for many reasons, not just because of the whisky, or because they carry the history of the textile industry in Spitalfields with them, but most importantly because they are two of the most soulful and witty gentlemen you could ever hope to meet. They are heroes, wielding scissors and tape measures. Legends in the rag trade, they know as much as anyone could ever know about cloth and they love meeting all the young fashion students who come seeking inspiration. Whenever you visit Crescent Trading you will discover joy, because they sell it by the yard.

Thanks to sheer willpower, canny ingenuity and a superhuman expenditure of physical energy on Philip Pittack's part, Crescent Trading is still here. Everything has changed, yet nothing has changed.

MYRA LOVE

RAROTONGAN PRINCESS

Human Life, Past Life

'MY MOTHER was the Queen of Rarotonga, so I am a princess,' admitted Myra Love, with a gentle ambivalent grin, when I pressed her. Yet her ancestry on her father's side is equally impressive. She is a Maori of the Te Atiawa tribe of Petone, and her ancestors include two eighteenth-century Scots from Selkirk – an explorer and a whaler – who married Maori princesses, Robert Park (brother of Mungo Park) and John Agar Love. 'I always say my legs are Scottish,' Myra added with a smirk, claim-

magnificence and widening her eyes in skittish delight. 'Most of Wellington belongs to us now and we got the railway station back last month.'

In this moment, I was afforded a glimpse of the woman who was born to be Queen of Rarotonga, because even though she does not choose to enact her public role, Myra's abiding concern is the stewardship of the land on behalf of her people and her driving force is her desire to leave it in a better state. In another age, Myra might have led her tribe in battle, but today she fights at the High Court instead. 'We are a warlike people,' Myra informed me proudly, accompanying the declaration with a winning smile. She knows that the success of her endeavour will define her legacy when she is long gone and, in this sense, her concerns are parallel to those of medieval English royalty, seeking to unify the realm for generations to come.

'When I was a child, there was a feeling that we were second-class citizens,' continued Myra with a shrug. 'If I was put down for being a Maori, my grandmother would say, "Remember they're walking on our land," and she owned quite a lot of land. My father was going to change how land was owned in our part of the country, but he went to war and got killed instead. He was a leader of men. I was only five when he left. He went to Sandhurst and was the first Maori to command a battalion in the Second World War, but Maori leaders always fight alongside their men, and he was shot.

'I was the youngest of three siblings so I didn't count for very much until they died,

ing the European thread in her lineage with some pride.

Today Myra's residence is a one-bedroom flat in Bethnal Green – as far away as it is possible to be from her ancestral land – yet she still feels her responsibilities to her people, revealing a sense of duty when she speaks of the politics of land. 'I never learned Maori because my grandmother said, "English is the language of power, and you have to be fluent in English and get the land back" – and we have. We formed corporations and we're able to reclaim it today because the leases are coming up after 100 years. There's loads of land that we gave away for beads and blankets, and we're getting it back,' Myra told me, swelling with and then I became very important, because now I own a lot of land. I'm getting some of the land in New Zealand and some of the land in Rarotonga. And my siblings' descendants are fighting me for it and I am defending it in the High Court. I'm partitioning it out because I don't want it for myself and I don't want them to sell it, and I intend to stay as healthy as possible because they all want me to die.'

Stepping into Myra's warm flat, painted in primary colours and crowded with paintings, plants, photographs, legal books, jewellery and musical equipment, I entered the court of a woman of culture. Not in the least highfalutin, she balances her serious intent with emotional generosity, which made it an honour to sit beside her as she opened her photo album. And Myra made it clear that she became the author of her own destiny when she made the break at twenty-

one and ran away – like Audrey Hepburn in *Roman Holiday* – to find a new life in the wider world.

'Once my grandmother died, the family disintegrated and I was moved out of the family house, so I decided to leave. Every Christmas we met together, but when she was gone there was a fight for the land, so because my family were all angry, I chose to go to America and become a jazz singer.

'I sold a piece of my land to my uncle for 300 pounds and bought a P&O ticket to San Francisco. You think everywhere's going to be like New Zealand, so it was a bit of a shock when I got off the boat, because I was a bit of a hokey girl. But it was exciting and, going through the Golden Gate Bridge, I thought, "My dreams are coming true." And some girls on the boat told me they knew Oscar Peterson, and they took me to the Black Hawk Club and there was Oscar Peterson. But I thought, "I'm going to New York," so I got on a train. It was 1958 and I had 100 pounds left. I was an innocent abroad. In New York, I stayed on Bleecker Street, just around the corner from Marlon Brando.

'It was such a joy to visit places you'd only read about in books. At school I learned Wordsworth's "Upon Westminster Bridge" and when I came to London I had to go there at dawn. By then, I had only about twenty-five pounds left, but money went a long way in those days.'

Myra told me it takes thirty years to learn to be a jazz singer, and she also filled those thirty years with getting married, having three children and getting an Open University degree. 'I got divorced because he wouldn't let me go on singing,' she confided, spreading her hands philosophically. 'When we broke up, I did a teacher training course and my first job was in the East End. I've always worked in underprivileged areas, and I've sent more kids to university than I've had hot dinners. These kids, they know a little about a lot, and they've got the ability to latch on to something. They're more than people who don't live in the area know, because their struggle has been long. I've always believed that knowledge is power and that's what I've tried to teach these kids.'

Recognising their situation equated with that of her own people, Myra discovered a sense of camaraderie with the people of the East End, which drew her to adopt the place as her home from home. And so it was that Myra Love, the heroic Rarotongan princess – devoted to fighting for the rights of her tribe – became a popular figure in the East End today, renowned for singing jazz at the Palm Tree in Bethnal Green. 'I get my kicks from meetings with old East Enders,' she confessed enthusiastically. 'They're a tough breed. These people are just like me – they're Maoris!'

COLUMBIA ROAD MARKET VIII

Human Life, Market Life

THERE WAS A MISTY HAZE OVER THE City and the distant sound of gulls as I left home early to speak with the redoubtable Josephine Ferguson, who can boast half a century of trading at Columbia Road. When I arrived she was nursing an injured foot that had been run over by a trolley, but as soon as I introduced myself she dismissed it as nothing, her glittering grey eyes lifting to meet mine. 'I've been here since I was twenty-two and now I'm seventy-two,' she declared with a gracious smile, framed by her long straight red hair emerging from a knitted cloche hat.

Josephine's first husband was Herbert Burridge, one of the family that above all others has defined the nature of this market for generations. And although he is no longer alive, Josephine is supported today on her stall by her two energetic daughters, Denise and Daphne, who hovered protectively as we spoke, and by her son, Stephen Burridge, who has a stall at the other end of the market. Additionally, Josephine's grandson, who is in floristry, supplies the handsome gourds which are in season now.

Personally, Josephine specialises in cacti and succulents, as well as a range of ferns, bulbs and cyclamen. 'Mostly it's a thing that men don't sell, because you need to lay out a lot of money for a small profit. You've got a lot of your money tied up in them and if it's severely cold you could lose them,' she explained cautiously, casting a maternal glance of affection over all her bizarrely shaped, spiky yet tender cacti nestling in their trays.

Although in retirement, Josephine still gets up at five to come here from Enfield every Sunday and in the week she helps out her son with his business. 'It doesn't seem to have changed much,' she said, glancing around and reflecting on her fifty years

trading in Columbia Road. 'My husband used to say that years ago they had to run with baskets on their heads to get a pitch. Somebody blew a whistle and they ran. Lady Burdett-Coutts set it up and she tried to get a railway here to help the traders.'

'I like it, we all like it,' admitted Josephine, confirming her statement with a smile and contemplating the chaotic scene that surrounded her with equanimity. 'It gets you out and it's an adrenalin rush. Even if you don't make a lot you've achieved something and it gets you by for another week. The only thing I don't like is the rain.' And then, as if Josephine had tempted the gods, with a wry grin Denise reached out her hand to the gentle raindrops that had begun to fall from the low cloud which hung over the East End this morning.

Mother and daughter exchanged a momentary glance of recognition, before setting to work eagerly, preparing the stall for yet another Sunday's trading, confident in their shared belief that the rain would pass over.

THE SECRETS OF CHRIST CHURCH,
SPITALFIELDS

Past Life, Spiritual Life

THERE IS SUCH A pleasing geometry to the architecture of Nicholas Hawksmoor's Christ Church, Spitalfields, completed in 1729, that when you glance upon the order of the façade you might assume that the internal structure is equally legible – but in fact it is a labyrinth inside. Like a theatre, the building presents a harmonious picture from the centre of the stalls, yet possesses innumerable unseen passages and rooms backstage.

When I joined the bell-ringers in the tower last New Year, I noticed a narrow staircase spiralling up further into the thickness of the stone spire, beyond the one I had climbed to the bell-ringers' loft. Since then I have harboured a curiosity to ascend those steps, and so I returned to climb that mysterious staircase to discover what is at the top. As you ascend the worn stone steps within the thickness of the wall, the walls get blacker and the stairs get narrower and the ceiling gets lower. By the time you reach the top, you are stooping as you climb and the giddiness of walking in circles permits the illusion that, as much as you are ascending into the sky, you might equally be descending into the earth. There is a sense that you are beyond the compass of your experience, entering indeterminate space.

No one has much cause to come up here and, when we reached the door at the top of the stairs, Iesah Littledale, the head verger, was unsure of his keys. As I recovered my breath from the climb, while Iesah tried each key in turn upon the ring until he was successful, I listened to the dignified tick coming from the other side of the door. When Iesah opened the door, I discovered it was the sound of the lonely clock that has measured out time in Spitalfields since 1836 from the square room with an octagonal roof beneath the pinnacle of the spire. In this room lit only by diffuse daylight from the four clock faces, the renovations that have brightened up the rest of the church do not register. Once we were inside, Iesah opened the glazed case containing the gleaming brass wheels of the mechanism turning with inscrutable purpose within their green-painted steel cage, driving another mechanism in a box up above that rotates the axles, turning the hands upon each of the clock faces. Not a place for human occupation, it was a room dedicated to time and, as intervention is required only rarely here, we left the clock to run its course in splendid indifference.

By contrast, a walk along the ridge of the roof of Christ Church, Spitalfields, presented a chaotic and exhilarating symphony of sensations, buffeted by gusts of wind beneath a fast-moving sky that delivered changing effects of light every moment. It was like walking in the sky. On the one hand, Fashion Street and on the other Fournier Street, where the roofs of the eighteenth-century houses topped off with weavers' lofts created an extravagant roofscape of old tiles and chimney pots at odd angles. Liberated by the experience, I waved across the chasm to residents of Fournier Street in their rooftop gardens opposite, like one waving to people from a train.

Returning to the body of the church, we explored a suite of hidden vestry rooms behind the altar, magnificently proportioned apartments to encourage lofty thoughts, with views into the well-kept rectory garden. From here, we descended into the crypt to enter the cavernous spaces that until recent years were stacked with human

remains. Today these are empty lime-washed spaces with little to recall the thousands who were once laid to rest here until it was packed full and closed for burial in 1812 by the Rev. William Stond, MA, as confirmed by a finely lettered stone plaque.

Passing through the building, up staircases, through passages and in each of the different spaces from top to bottom, there were so many of these plaques of different designs in wood and stone, recording those buried here, those who were priests, vergers, benefactors, builders, and those who rang the bells. In parallel with these formal memorials, I noticed marks in hidden corners, modest handwritten initials, dates and scrawls, many too worn or indistinct to decipher. Everywhere I walked, so many people had been there before me,

and the crypt and vaults were where they ended up.

My visit started at the top and I descended until I came to the small private vaults constructed in two storeys beneath the porch, where my journey ended, as it did in a larger sense for the original occupants. These delicate brick vaults, barely three feet high and arranged in a criss-cross design, were the private vaults of those who sought consolation in keeping the family together even after death. I crawled into the maze of tunnels – all cleaned out now – and ran my hand upon the vault just above my head. This was the grave where no daylight or sunshine entered, and it was not a place to linger on a bright afternoon.

Christ Church gave me a journey through many emotions, and it fascinates me that this architecture can produce so many diverse spaces within one building and that these spaces can each reflect such varied aspects of the human experience, all within a classical structure that delights the senses through the harmonious unity of its form.

AN AFTERNOON WITH ROA

Animal Life, Street Life

I GOT A MESSAGE to say that Roa – the street artist responsible for the squirrel in Redchurch Street and the crane on Brick Lane – was painting a wall at the back of the foundry in Old Street, so I raced over, only to discover an empty car park with a lone security guard sitting in a car. I expected him to ask me to leave, but when I enquired about Roa, he told me with some excitement that the artist was expected at any moment.

In fact, Roa had started painting the day before, as evidenced by a pile of finely drawn creatures – a rat, a fox, a weasel and a heron – adorning the raw end of a build-ing where an adjoining structure had been removed. Just as I was admiring this, a skinny pink-faced young man in a woollen hat came round the corner carrying the front end of a steel ladder, with a portly builder in a blue football shirt bringing up the rear. They put the ladder down in front of the wall and shook hands, then the builder left.

The lanky young man stepped forward to greet me, all smiles and offering a paint-splattered hand – and I was immediately struck by an intensity in his pale blue eyes as vivid as any of the scrawny febrile creatures which have become his trademark.

surface just as the cave artists placed their drawings to fit the contours of the rock face.

Contemplating the animals, all with their eyes shut, I wondered if they were dead or sleeping, a crucial distinction in the meaning of the picture. 'Often my paintings have been the last thing that happens to a building before it is destroyed,' said Roa. 'That has happened so many times. In some of those places you feel like life stopped at a certain moment.' I asked him whether his animals were sleeping or dead. 'I don't know,' he said with a shrug, before casting a thoughtful eye over his work. 'I like to think they are sleeping.'

We were shivering in the east wind that blows along Old Street, so I went to fetch hot drinks and slices of apple pie, and upon my return I was amazed to see a party of 100 students with cameras emerging from the car park, all beaming contentedly. 'They were on a graffiti tour,' explained Roa affably when I handed him his double espresso, 'so I invited them in to take a look.'

As the afternoon wore on, Roa reached even higher up the wall, sketching the outline of a heron above the squirrel with the end of a roller on a long telescopic pole, stretching out with it and twirling it down to dip it into the paint pot before swinging it back up again to slap it on to the wall far above his head, all with the comedic grace of a young Buster Keaton. Roa's custom is to outline his figures with black and then fill them in with solid white before adding the shading and hatching, using a spray can, that bring dynamic life to his animals. These finished works possess such finesse

Yet in spite of being full of life, there was a gentleness about him too, and although I was immediately concerned that he needed to start painting, he was happy to stand and chat while puffing amiably upon a rolled-up cigarette. Then, 'All right, action!' he exclaimed, as he turned on his heel, climbed the ladder and began sketching out the hind quarters of an animal about twenty feet up on the wall.

As he worked, Roa maintained a pattern of drawing, moving the ladder along and stepping back to see the bigger picture. Yet he had no sketch, the composition was in his mind's eye and the nature of the picture was conceived to reflect the qualities of this particular wall, which had a ridge halfway up where he was drawing a second pile of creatures – arranging the shapes upon the it is as if the designs simply sit upon the surface of the wall, entirely belying the effort to mediate the irregular surface beneath.

A grasp of dramatic potential in his works is one of the qualities that makes Roa such a superlative street artist. Naturally, there is a tension in the existence of these wild creatures in the city, a tension amplified by their monstrous scale, but, beyond this, Roa knows how to place them. You walk up Hanbury Street and the three-storey crane appears around the corner. You walk down Redchurch Street and the ten-foot squirrel leaps out from Club Row. Here in Old Street, the effect is more subtle, since the painting is in a car park, but the tip of it is visible from the street, which will draw people in to confront the whole thing. Most excitingly, commuters sitting on the top deck of the bus will have a jolt this morning to see this huge pile of sleeping animals, manifesting the somnolent state they might wish to return to, in preference to work, if they had the choice.

For the last five years, Roa has been painting his animals on walls all over the world in response to a chain of invitations. He has spent only a few months in his home town of Ghent in the last year, and now has come to regard wherever he is engaged in the familiar act of painting as his home. Roa makes a living but not a fortune, doing the projects he likes rather than those that pay. Mostly, he gets no monetary reward for his work at all and commonly, as at Old Street, pays for the paint out of his own pocket too.

'Even when the conditions are difficult, I really enjoy this,' Roa admitted to me, his eyes gleaming, as we stood alone in the empty car park in the dusk, clutching hot drinks to keep warm. And after all this investment of care and energy, he is happy to walk away and leave his inspirational work out in the street, subject to fate. 'That's what I like about painting outside,' Roa explained to me. 'It's not something harassing you every day at home.' In a few days, Roa will be gone again, like a migratory bird, leaving us the benefits of his life-affirming talent.

TONY JACK

TRUMAN'S BREWERY CHAUFFEUR

Human Life, Past Life

'I WAS BORN IN Balmoral Castle and I grew up in Windsor Castle,' Tony Jack told me proudly, without bragging. 'They were both pubs in Canning Town.' It was a suitably felicitous beginning for an East End hero who was barely out of his teens before he joined the RAF and sent this picture home inscribed, 'To Mother, Myself in a rear cockpit of a Harvard with the sun in my eyes. Love Tony'. Yet destiny had even greater things in store for Tony. He was appointed to secret government work in

Princes Risborough, where his sharp young eyes qualified him as an expert in photographic interpretation of aerial surveys, snooping on Jerry. If Tony spotted activity behind enemy lines, the information was relayed to our spies in the field, who went to make a reconnaissance.

From there, young Tony was transferred to work in the Cabinet War Rooms deep beneath Whitehall, where he barely saw daylight for weeks on end, taking solace in rooms lit with ultraviolet to induce the sensation of sunlight. Tony was involved in developing photographs of the Blitz and making maps, but at the culmination of hostilities he was brought the document that ended the war, to photograph it and make fifty copies. With his outstanding eye for detail, Tony noticed that the date had been altered in ink from 7 May to 8 May 1945 and, with the innocent audacity of youth, Tony tentatively asked Winston Churchill if he would prefer this aberration photographically removed. 'The Americans wanted the war to end on one date and the Russians wanted it to end on another,' growled the great man to the impertinent young whippersnapper in triumph, 'but I got my way, May the 8th!' And thus the correction duly remained in place upon the historic document.

When Tony told me these stories as we sat together drinking tea in Dino's Café in Spitalfields, I did wonder how he could possibly follow these astounding life experiences when the war ended, but the answer was simple. Tony got a job as a chauffeur driving a Rolls-Royce for the Truman Brewery in Brick Lane.

'There were seven of us and we were nicknamed the Black Crows on account of our black uniforms. We used to kick off the day by picking up the directors from railway stations and driving them to the brewery. During the day we used to drive them to and fro visiting pubs and there also was a certain private aspect, which we kept quiet about, taking their wives shopping. Most of the other chauffeurs had once driven delivery trucks for the brewery. They couldn't tell you the names of the streets but they knew where all the pubs were, that's how they navigated around London!

'You couldn't wish to work in a better environment than a brewery,' admitted Tony in rhapsodic tones, as he opened a worn plastic bag to show us his cherished cap badge and buttons. And then, caught in the emotion of the moment and experiencing a great flood of memories, Tony launched into a spontaneous eulogy about the brewery, which gained an elegiac lustre in the description.

He told me the name of the head brewer was Gun Boat Smith. He told me the brewery had two black London taxis for visiting pubs incognito, registration numbers

HYL55353 and 4. He told me there were two chefs in the canteen – one named Harry was a woodcarver who carved fancy work for churches and the other was a glass engraver who could put a painting into a glass and copy it on to the surface. He told me that John Henry Buxton (descendant of Thomas Buxton, one of the founders of the brewery) asked, 'What regiment were you in?' and, when Tony revealed he was in the RAF, declared, 'Well, never mind!' He told

me that a man called Cyclops was responsible for the 'finings' which filtered the beer, as well as repairing the bottling girls' clogs and distributing pints of beer to the delivery men in the mornings. He told me that the phone number of John Henry Buxton's country home was Ware 2, a source of endless amusement when you asked the operator to connect you. He told me that the brewery staff manned the roof with buckets of water when the great Bishopsgate Goods Yard fire of 1964 sent burning cinders drifting into the sky. He told me that the brewery had its own customs officer because beer was taxed as it was brewed in those days. He told me that there was always a cooper on call night and day to make repairs, in case a barrel of beer split in a pub. He told me that the dray horses sometimes got out at night and wandered around, which terrified him because they were magnificent creatures. He told me that there was a priest who worked in the electrical shop who would marry employees. He told me that there was a man who was solely responsible for all the uniform badges and buttons, who was the TGWU representative and also Mayor of Bethnal Green. He told me that there was a rifle range below Brick Lane which still exists and the cleaners refused to go there alone because there were so many rats. He told me that the dray horses were all sent to a retirement home in Long Melford. He told me that the brewery organised sports days and beanos on alternate summers. He told me that the sports days were held at Higham Park, Chingford, where they brought in circus acts to entertain the children. He told me that the beanos were at Margate. He told me that they hired two trains from Liverpool Street to get them there, and a paddle steamer to take them on a trip over to Folkestone and back for a sit-down dinner at Dreamland. He told me that there was always plenty of beer on the train coming back. He told me that they were wonderful days out. He told me that Truman's were unique in the sense that you had no need to go outside.

One day Tony was candidly given advance notice by the chairman, while driving him in the Rolls-Royce, that the brewery was being sold to Grand Metropolitan and chauffeurs would no longer be required. So Tony switched to working as a security guard for many years. 'I know every inch of the brewery,' he assured me authoritatively. Then, in 1969, Tony became a cab driver, which he continued to do until 2007. 'I retired just before I was eighty. I was happy because I was driving around and it was all I wanted to do in life,' he confided to me with a lightness of tone, revealing endearing modesty and impressive stamina.

All the astonishing details of Tony Jack's vibrant description of life at the brewery were whirling in my mind as we crossed Commercial Street and walked down Brushfield Street together in the autumn sunlight, before shaking hands in Bishopsgate. And then he hopped on a bus to Clerkenwell, where he lives, quite the most sprightly octogenarian I have met. It must be something in the beer.

AT SHAKESPEARE'S FIRST THEATRE

Literary Life, Past Life

OVER IN SHOREDITCH, just a few minutes' walk from where I sit writing in Spitalfields, is the site of a seventeenth-century playhouse called the Theatre built by James Burbage in 1576, where William Shakespeare's career as a dramatist began. In this, the first custom-built public theatre, Shakespeare played as an actor and his first plays were performed, notably *Romeo and Juliet* and an early version of *Hamlet*.

Stepping through a blank door in the wooden hoarding in New Inn Yard, I walked along a raised pathway to look down upon the archaeological dig and see where the earth has been painstakingly scraped back to reveal the foundations of the ancient playhouse. Senior archaeologist Heather Knight of the Museum of London indicated the section of curved stonework which comprised part of the inner wall of the theatre and next to it a section of the paving of the passage where, more than 400 years ago, the audience walked through into the body of the theatre, once they had paid their penny admission. Beyond this paving, a beaten-earth floor has been uncovered, sloping gently down in the direction of the stage. This is where the audience stood to watch Shakespeare's early plays for the first time.

For any writer, Shakespeare is a name that has a resonance above all others, and once Heather Knight explained what I was seeing, it took a while for the true meaning to sink in. My head was full of the cacophony of the dusty sunlit street and the discordance of heavy traffic and, superficially, the site itself was like any other archaeological dig I have visited. But then the words of Hamlet came to me, 'To die, to sleep. To sleep, perchance to dream. Ay, there's the rub. For in that sleep of death what dreams may come, when we have shuffled off this mortal coil, must give us pause ...' And my stomach began to churn, because I knew I was standing on the other side of Shakespeare's unfathomable dream. It was as if I could feel the tremor of the London earthquake of 1580 coursing through my body. The monstrous city grew diaphanous and the street sounds faded away.

We know no more of what happens in the sleep of death than Shakespeare did. Yet we can say we do know the literal substance of the dreams evoked by these lines from *Hamlet* – the things that were to come in the space where Hamlet's words were spoken by James Burbage's son Richard, who was the first to play the role.

We know that after a disagreement in 1598 the Theatre was covertly demolished by the theatre company while the freeholder, Giles Allen, was away for Christmas and the materials used to construct the Globe in Southwark the following spring. We know that a factory was built on the site in the seventeenth century, then a house in the eighteenth century and a warehouse in the nineteenth century, until it became a lumber yard in the twentieth century, before archaeologists came along with sonar devices in the twenty-first century to ascertain the position of the theatre – although the workers in the lumber yard and all the local people always knew the yard was on top of 'Shakespeare's theatre'.

But it was never Shakespeare's theatre in his day. It is unlikely that the audience here were aware of any particular significance in the event, when they heard his words, because he was an unknown quantity then. Plays were performed just once from cue scripts without any rehearsal or expectation of posterity. Each actor had a roll of paper with their character's lines, plus their cue lines – so they knew when to speak. The implications of this were twofold. Firstly, the actors had to listen attentively to each other so they did not miss their cues. Secondly, beyond a broad knowledge of the story the actors might not know exactly what was going to happen in a scene. It placed the actor in the present tense of the dramatic moment, discovering it for the first time and knowing no more than their character did. The actor playing Romeo might take the poison without knowing that Juliet was going to wake up.

Shakespeare's plays were conceived to play upon the spontaneous poetry of the elusive instant that, for both actors and audience, occurred uniquely. The embrace of this ephemeral moment is innate to the form of Shakespeare's plays and it is their subject too – the fleeting brilliance of life. These works were delights that, as transient as butterflies on summer days, existed without expectation of longevity. The beautiful paradox is that, in recognition of their superlative quality, Shakespeare's colleagues collated and printed them, so that his words could travel onwards through time and space to become the phenomenon we know today. And this modest piece of earth in Shoreditch is where it all began.

Releasing me from my idle speculation upon the dust, Heather Knight held up a new discovery. It was an earthenware ale beaker that she found recently, with a lustrous green glaze, which fitted the hand perfectly – a drinking vessel that Shakespeare would recognise, of the style that would be used in the tavern scenes at the Boar's Head in *Henry IV Part One*, first performed at the Theatre. Heather has never found a complete beaker before and because it was discovered at the Theatre and is contemporary with Shakespeare, it is a magic artefact. It is something from Shakespeare's world that he could have seen or touched. Although we can never know, we are permitted to dream.

THE COBBLERS OF SPITALFIELDS

Human Life, Street Life

'WHEN I LEFT SCHOOL AT SIXTEEN, I told the careers officer I didn't want an office job, I wanted to do something creative, so he set up appointments for me with a shoe repairer and a watch repairer,' Gary Parsons, the proprietor of Shoe Key in the Liverpool Street Arcade, told me. 'The interview with the shoe repairer was on a Friday and I started work on the Monday, so I never went to the other interview,' he explained with the alacrity of one who now describes himself not as a shoe repairer but 'the shoe repairer'.

Shoe repairmen have long been my heroes, the last craftsmen on the high street – where you can still walk into a workshop, inhale the intoxicating fragrance of glue and watch them work their magic on your worn-out shoes. Even better than new shoes, there is something endearing about old shoes beautifully repaired. And so, in the heartfelt belief that – although it is commonplace – the modest art of shoe repair should not be underestimated, I set out on a sentimental pilgrimage to pay homage to some of my favourite East End cobblers.

When the crash happened in the City, news crews descended upon Gary at Shoe Key in Liverpool Street to learn the true state of affairs from the authority. They wanted to know if City gents were getting more repairs rather than buying new shoes, or if the crisis was so deep that they could not even afford to mend the holes in their soles. Yet Gary dismissed such scaremongering, taking the global banking crisis in his stride. 'There was a slump in the winter of 2008, but since July 2009 business has been steady,' he informed me with a phlegmatic understatement that his City clients would appreciate.

Seventeen years ago, Gary built this narrow bar at the entrance to the Liverpool Street Arcade, where he and his colleague Mike Holding work fifty-four hours a week, mending shoes with all the flamboyant theatrics of cocktail waiters. They felt the blast of the Aldgate bomb here in 2005 and each winter they suffer the snow landing upon their backs, so three weeks ago they hung up a new tarpaulin to afford themselves some shelter from the future whims of fortune.

Round the corner from Shoe Key, I visited Dave Williams, a gentleman with time for everyone, comfortable in his enclosed booth in Liverpool Street, directly opposite the station. Dave told me he was the third generation in his trade. 'My grandfather Henry Alexander and my father, Norman, were both saddlers and harness makers. My father, he's a Freeman of the City of London now. They were from an Irish immigrant family in Stepney. In those days, if people had trouble with their boots they took them along to the harness maker and gradually the trade in repairs took over.

'My training was at my father's knee. I left school at sixteen and I have been doing this twenty-seven years. I think this trade is pretty much recession-proof. It's always been a good trade and I do very well thank you.' In contrast to Gary at Shoe Key, Dave was full of self-deprecatory humour. Passing bags of shoes over to a couple of girls, 'That's two satisfied customers this year!' he declared to me with a cheeky smirk, the ceaseless repartee of a man who is sole trader and star turn in his own personal shoe repair theatre.

Over in Camomile Street, at the base of the tall Heron Tower, Kiri and George, the energetic double act at Michael's Shoe Care, enjoy the privilege of having a door to their neat little shop, where everything is arranged with exquisite precision. The additional service at Michael's Shoe Care is the engraving of trophies, cups, plaques and statuettes, which – as George explained to me enthusiastically – are in big demand now that corporate life has become increasingly about hitting targets and setting employees in competition against each other. George, who has been here twenty years, leaned across with eyes gleaming in anticipation and confided his hopes to me. 'A lot of places closed down round here recently and thousands of people were moved out, but the new build opposite will be complete next year, with a lot of new office space to rent. It's just a question of waiting and more people will come to us.' I glanced up at the gleaming tower above, and thought of all the engraved trophies that are going to be required to reward all the corporate striving upon its forty-seven floors. Yet in spite of the pathos of this bizarre appropriation of sports day trophies, I was happy in the knowledge that Kiri and George will be secure in their jobs for years to come.

Up at Well Heeled in Bethnal Green, Ken Hines – a veteran of forty-seven years of shoe repair – had a different angle which he delighted to outline. 'I was going to be a blacksmith but there was no work in it, so I did shoe repair instead. I like doing it. I've always enjoyed doing it. My father was a docker and my family were all butchers in Wapping. My brother still has the butchers down the street. When I started here twenty-seven years ago, there were four shoe repairers in Bethnal Green, but now I am the only one. We don't want to modernise. We don't want to go modern, because we're not a heel bar. We're going back to the beginning of the nineteenth century. There's a lot of people bringing vintage shoes and we can take them apart and put them back together again. There's nothing we can't do to a pair of shoes here.'

Ken invited me into his workshop, crowded with magnificent well-oiled old machines, prized hand tools and shelves

piled with dusty bags of shoes that no one has collected. 'This stitching machine is over a hundred years old. We use it more than ever,' he said, placing a hand affectionately on the trusty device. 'Soles should always be stitched on. You buy a pair of shoes and the soles aren't stitched on, they're no good,' he declared, pulling huge sheets of leather from a shelf to demonstrate that every sole is cut by hand here. While Ken stands for the traditions of the trade, training up an apprentice at the old shop in Bethnal Green, his enterprising son Paul has opened more branches of Well Heeled in shopping centres. But such ambition is of little interest to Ken. 'There's a lot of knowledge you pick up, being around older men,' he informed me, getting lost in reminiscence as he lifted his cherished shoe repair hammer. 'This was given to me by an old boy thirty-five years ago. It was over eighty years old then and I still use it every day.'

My final destination was Shoe Care at the top of Mare Street in Hackney where John Veitch, a magnanimous Scotsman, welcomed me. 'I done it since I left school,' he revealed proudly, speaking as he worked, hammering resolutely upon a sole. 'I saw one of the boys doing it and I thought, "That's the thing for me!" and I'm still happy in it twenty-four years later. It's the challenge I like. It's something different every day. Stiletto heels are our bread and butter. The cracks in the pavements have been good for us. And the recession has been helping too. We get a lot more quality shoes in for repair, when in the past people would just throw them away.'

At the end of my pilgrimage I had worn out plenty of shoe leather, yet it had been worth it to encounter all these celebrated cobblers, and be party to some of the unique insights into human life and society which shoe repair brings. It is a profession that affords opportunity for contemplation as

well as the engaged observation of humanity, which may explain why each cobbler I met was both a poet and a showman to a different degree. I admired them all for their independence of spirit and ingenious talent, devoted to the mundane yet essential task of putting us back on our feet when we come unstuck and our soles wear thin.

LENNY HAMILTON
JEWEL THIEF

Criminal Life, Human Life, Past Life

MID-AFTERNOON ON A weekday is a good time for a discreet liaison at the Carpenter's Arms in Cheshire Street (the pub that used to belong to the Krays), especially if you are meeting a jewel thief. Lenny was initially averse to the location. 'What do you want to go to that filthy old place for?' he complained, until I reassured him they had cleaned it up nicely, though when he told me the story of his personal experience of the Kray twins I came to understand why he might harbour an aversion.

'I used to go round to their house in Vallance Road on and off for three years, until Ronnie burned me with the pokers, and his mother and Charlie had a go with him over it,' said Lenny with a pleasant smile, introducing his testimony, before taking a slug of his double Courvoisier and lemonade. It was a story that started well enough before it all went so horribly wrong.

'I was just six weeks out of the army, doing my National Service (I used to box for the army), when I went back to work in Billingsgate Fish Market at the age of twenty-six. Georgie Cornell looked after me – he was the hardest man I ever saw on the cobbles, but he had a heart of gold as well. He gave me five pounds to buy my mother some flowers and said, "Make sure you give her the fucking change!" He was a nice fellow. He used to line up all the tramps at the market and give them each half a crown and make sure they got a mug of tea and two slices of dripping toast. Then with the change, he'd say, "Now go down and buy yourselves a pint."

'Leaving work, I was walking down Maidment Street, and on the corner I saw this big fellow wrestling with these two little fellows. So I went to help them, they got away and I got arrested, because the guy I was wrestling with was a police officer. When I got taken down to Arbour Square Police Station, he said to me, "Do you know what you've done? Them two young fellows was the Krays and now they've got away. They're on the run from the army." I apologised and they let me go.

'Later, when the Krays got control of a snooker hall, the Regal, I was playing snooker there and they came in and this fellow put his hand on my shoulder and said, "You don't know who I am, do you? I am Reggie Kray – and this is my brother Ronnie." I thought I was seeing double, you couldn't tell them apart. They took me across the road to a pub called the Wentworth to buy me a drink because I did them a favour. They liked me at first. That's how I came to be going round their house for nearly three years.

'One day, I was down the Regency Club working for Harry Abrahams. He had his own "firm" and Albert Donahue was part of it. One of the Krays' "firm", Pat Connolly, was there and he was drinking with a young couple. Then some fellows arrived from south London and sent us all a drink over. I ordered one for myself and the young fellow, but I didn't know what the girl was drinking, so I asked her, "What do you want, love?"

'The fellow that was with her went to cut me with a razor! Pat Connolly said, "You don't do that to Lenny." So the fellow asked to have a talk with me in the toilet and I thought he wanted to say sorry. As I went into the toilet, walking in front of him,

someone said, "Watch your back!" and he went to cut me down the back with his cut-throat razor. I dived down to the cubicle door, and ducked and dived, as he came at me with the razor. Then I got up and smashed him in the face and I didn't realise that I broke his nose. I also didn't realise he was Buller Ward's son, Bonner – and Buller was friends with the Krays.

'My pal Andy Paul was living with me at the time, because his wife had thrown him out, and he worked with the Krays as a doorman. Once he came home at one in the morning when I was in bed and said, "Ronnie wants you on the phone at Esmeralda's bar. You'd better phone him up because you know what he's like. He'll come round and smash the place up." So I got a cab all the way to Knightsbridge to Esmeralda's in Wilton Place, and asked the cab driver to wait.

'I went in and walked upstairs. All the gambling tables were closed down and there were seven or eight people standing on either side. They told me to go in the kitchen and when I opened the door Ronnie Kray was standing opposite. He said, "Nothing to worry about, Lenny." He had a big armchair next to the cooker and he invited me to sit down, asking, "What's going on, Lenny? You caused a bit of trouble in the Regency. We get protection money from them." I sat down.

'He said, "All right, you can go now." I stood up again and, as I turned to leave, I was wondering what was going on, when he said, "Get hold of him." Two geezers grabbed hold of me and then I saw it. I thought they were pokers but they were steels that are used to sharpen knives. Ronnie had them on the gas and they were white-hot. They had wooden handles and the first one Ronnie picked up he dropped because it was so hot, so he went and got an oven glove. Then he picked one up and came over to me, to frighten me, I imagined. He singed my black curly hair. I pissed myself. I was terrified. Next he started setting fire to my suit that I only had made two weeks before.

'He went back and got another hot poker, dabbed it on my cheeks and held it across my eyebrows and burned my eyebrows off. I'm half-blind in this eye because of it. Then he went back and got another poker and, as he came back, he said, "Now I'm going to burn your eyes out," and he really meant it. As he came towards me, Limehouse Willy called out from the crowd, "No, Ron, don't do that!" (A nice fellow he was.) Ronnie switched, he turned and walked away.

'They let me go and I hurried out, and the cab driver was still waiting outside. When he saw the state of me, he wanted to take me to Scotland Yard, but I said, "No, mate, don't do that, just take me home." Then, as we were driving along, he said, "I think there's a car following us," and it was one of the Krays' cars. They were following to see where I was going, so I went round to my friend Harry Abrahams' house. When he came home with his friend Albert Donahue, he said, "There's only one person who would do that." So he and Albert went round the twins' home with guns next morning, and the twins told him they did it because I got too flash – too big for my boots.

'About two days later, my protector from Billingsgate, Georgie Cornell, came round and gave Harry Abrahams' wife 200 pounds with instructions to take care of me. "Look after Lenny, take the expenses out of that." A day later, a big surprise, Charlie Kray came round and gave her 100 pounds and said, "Don't let my brothers know." Finally, Dr Blaskar, the Krays' doctor, came round – he liked to drink and gamble – and he treated me, gave me stuff for the burns.

'But then in 1967, when the police were after the Krays, I was in Wandsworth Prison and they got a message smuggled in to me. I was in a single cell and when I returned from the doctor one day there was an envelope on the table (it's in the Black Museum at Scotland Yard now). The note read, "If the Old Bill comes round, keep your mouth shut or we are going to shoot your kids." My children were six and seven years old and living with their mother in Poplar. I'm not a grass but I couldn't risk my kids being shot, so I went to see the governor and gave him the letter. Within two hours, the police were round. They said, "Look, Lenny, if you help us, we'll help you. We'll give your children twenty-four-hour police protection," which they did. They moved me to East-church Prison on the Isle of Sheppey and then to Bow Street to give evidence against Ronnie Kray. On my evidence, he got committed to the Old Bailey.'

We were all alone in the empty barroom and, when Lenny told the part about the poker, he fixed me eye to eye and, extending a single finger, pushed his fingertip into my face. I was speechless. It was extraordinary to hear a first-hand account of the reality of characters that have become mythical. It is easier to accept the East End's history of violence as mere fiction, even when you know the truth. Ironically, Lenny's volatile experiences have fused his emotional story into a powerful narrative with its own literary structure.

Lenny has no patience with those who romanticise the Krays as working-class heroes. 'They were scum. The lowest of the low. You never robbed or hurt your own people, that was the old East End code. The Krays controlled people through fear. They hurt so many people. I've been in a bar when they were there and people would arrive, order a drink, then go out to the toilet and walk straight out the back door to escape.'

Today, after plastic surgery, and many years on the straight and narrow since doing

time, Lenny is a different man – though, even walking with a stick, he retains a powerful physical presence as a legacy of his boxing years. Yet, behind this assured façade, I sensed something else, an intensity in his eyes, his 'snake eyes' he calls them, that indicates a spirit forged in a dark world of violence.

Lenny doesn't pretend to be a saint. 'I'm not proud of what I done,' he admitted openly, speaking of his days blowing safes and thieving jewels. 'I used to have a friend in Hatton Garden who bought all the gear off me and gave me good deal. I took him a 680,000-pound job one day and, after he'd melted down the gold and recut the diamonds, I got 100,000 pounds. He asked me to push my finger through a card and then he made me this,' revealed Lenny with relish, displaying the dazzling ring upon his finger with its single glittering diamond. Always keen to emphasise that he only stole from those with insurance, Lenny even managed to make it sound like he was doing a favour for people sometimes. 'There was a man whose business was going under. He came to me and said, "There's nothing in the safe but if you blow it up, I can claim there was." I felt sorry for him so I blew the safe while he was away for the weekend. Then he took the insurance payment and moved to Brighton.'

Lenny could have talked all day, but after three double Courvoisiers and lemonade, I called a taxi to take him on to a pub in the Roman Road where his pals were waiting to continue the long afternoon of storytelling. When I enquired about some recent scars on his head, he explained that he had been beaten up on the street by muggers, but he shrugged it off lightly. You have to credit Lenny for his resilience, he still possesses undaunted enthusiasm and appetite for life.

Standing up to leave, Lenny caught sight for the first time of the painting of Ronnie and Reggie Kray that hangs on the barroom wall in the Carpenter's Arms and brandished his stick in a flash of emotion. For a moment, I was expecting the sound of broken glass, but Lenny quickly relented, turning away with a grin and a wave to me, because the taxi was waiting outside and he had better things to do.

A DRESS OF SPITALFIELDS SILK

Past Life

IN 1752, WHEN ANN FANSHAWE was twenty-eight years old, her father, Crisp Gascoyne, was appointed Lord Mayor of London. Since Margaret, her mother, had died back in 1740, it fell to Ann to assume the role of Lady Mayoress and this spectacular dress of Spitalfields silk, which was purchased by the Museum of London from one of her descendants in 1983, is believed to have been made to be worn just once, upon the great occasion.

Born in 1724, Ann was the eldest daughter of Crisp Gascoyne of Bifrons House in Barking, marrying Thomas Fanshawe of Parsloes Manor in Dagenham at the age of twenty-one. In 1752, when she stepped out as Lady Mayoress, Ann had three children – John, six years old, Susanna, five years old, and Ann, four years old. Ten years later, Ann died at the birth of her fourth child, Mary, in 1762. Parsloes Manor no longer exists but *The History of the Fanshawe Family* by H. C. Fanshawe, published in 1927, records this couplet engraved upon one of the windows there by Ann and Thomas.

> *Time 'scapes our hand like water from*
> *a sieve,*
> *We come to die ere we come to live.*

Becoming Lord Mayor of London was an auspicious moment for Ann's father (who had been Master of the Brewers' Company in 1746) and he saw his eldest daughter step out in a silk dress that was emblematic of his success. The design contains images of hops and barley interwoven with flowers spilling from silver cornucopia, alternating with anchors and merchants' packs in silver, all upon a background of white silk

threaded with silver. It was a dress designed to be seen by candlelight and the effect of all this silver thread upon white silk, in a dress trimmed with silver lace, upon his eldest daughter adorned with diamonds, was the physical embodiment of Gascoyne's momentous achievement. To crown it all, H. C. Fanshawe describes a lost portrait of Ann, 'which shows her to have been strikingly handsome'.

The *Covent Garden Journal* of 3 November 1752 reported,

The Appearance at Guildhall, on Thursday last, was very noble, particularly that of the Ladies, many of whom were extremely brilliant ... The Ball about ten o'Clock was opened by Mrs. Fanshaw (as Lady Mayoress, who made a most splendid Figure) ...

The Huguenot weavers were renowned for both their technical finesse and their elegance of design. Such was the skilful incorporation of the expensive silver and coloured threads in the cloth for Ann Fanshawe's dress that they were only used where they were visible, with very little wasted upon the reverse. According to the American critic Andrea Feeser, the dye used for the blue flowers was rare indigo from South Carolina, where Ann's brother-in-law Charles Fanshawe was stationed as a Rear-Admiral and had access to the indigo dye.

When Natalie Rothenstein, the authoritative scholar of Spitalfields silk, wrote to the curator at the Museum of London in July 1983 about the dress, she authenticated the fabric, but also could not resist declaring her distaste for the design.

334

I am sure that the dress is Spitalfields and indeed the floral style is just right for the date 1752–3. I am sure too, that the design is unique – created for one rich lady. The bales and anchors ought to refer to a merchant, while the ears of corn and horn of plenty reveal the prosperity he brought to the city as well as his family's execrable taste.

Commonly, silks were woven in lengths of cloth sufficient for several dresses, but in this instance the design was likely to have been made solely for this garment. A customer bought a design from a mercer and six months was the lead time for the weaving of the silk cloth, which could have been made up into a dress in little more than a week. Natalie Rothenstein describes the chain of transactions thus.

Silk was generally imported by a silk merchant. It was then sold through a broker to a silkman who, in turn, supplied the master weaver with the qualities and quantities required. Either the silkman or the master weaver had it thrown and dyed. The master weaver would normally obtain an order from a mercer and instruct his foreman. The latter, based at the master weaver's warehouse, would measure out the warp for the journeyman, who returned it when completed.

When the culmination of this process arrived and the great day came, Ann had to get dressed. No underwear was worn, just a shift of fine linen, probably with some lace at the neck, then silk stockings and garters to hold them up. Next came her stays of whalebone, that we should call a corset, and then her hooped petticoat, also with whalebone and cross-ties to maintain the oval shape of the dress and not allow it to become circular. At last, Ann could put on her dress, which came in three pieces, first the skirt, then the stomacher, followed by the bodice. There were no hooks or buttons to hold it all together, so pins would be used and a few discreet stitches where necessary. Lace sleeve ruffles were added and a lappet upon her head. Finally, diamonds upon the stomacher and around Ann's neck, plus shoes and a fan, completed the outfit.

Now Ann was ready for her appearance, except her dress was two metres wide and she could not walk through a door without turning sideways. Getting in and out of a carriage must have been a performance too. Ann was fully aware that her dress was not designed for sitting down, but fortunately she did not expect to sit.

What can we surmise about Ann's experience in this dress? I was surprised at the workmanlike manufacture of the garment, which was sewn together quickly and presented no finish upon the inside. The quality and expense of the materials were what counted, the tailoring of the dress was not of consequence. Almost like a stage costume, it was a dress to create an effect.

Maybe Ann was the apple of her father's eye and she was proud to become his angel, incarnating the supremacy of their family in the City of London, or maybe she felt she was tricked out like a tinsel fairy in a ridiculous dress with symbols of brewing woven into the fabric, tolerating it all for the sake of her dad. No doubt her husband, Thomas Fanshawe, was present at the occasion, but maybe her children stayed behind at Parsloes Manor and did not see their mother wearing the famous dress. Did Crisp Gascoyne, her father, get sentimental on the night, shedding a tear for his wife, and wishing that she had lived to see the day?

We shall never know the truth of these speculations, but everyone wants to have their moment of glory – looking their best at a significant occasion in life – and I should like to think that, on the one day she wore it, this dress delivered that moment for Ann Fanshawe.

PHIL MAXWELL AND SANDRA ESQULANT

PHOTOGRAPHER AND MUSE

Human Life

'ONE DAY, about fifteen years ago, Sandra took a hula hoop and started hula-hooping on the traffic island in the middle of Commercial Street, and, without even thinking about it, I took a picture of her,' recalled Phil Maxwell, outlining the spontaneous origin of his photographic relationship with Sandra Esqulant, landlady of the Golden Heart. No one has taken more photographs in Spitalfields than Phil, the pre-eminent street photographer of the East End, and so it was inevitable that he would turn his camera upon Sandra, whose playful nature is a gift to photography.

Once the pub for the Truman Brewery, the Golden Heart was kept by Sandra and her husband, Dennis, until he died, leaving her to continue alone. Sandra has risen to the challenge heroically and today, in Spitalfields, she is among the few who con-

nect us to that earlier time, when the life of the brewery and the Fruit and Vegetable Market dominated, and the Golden Heart opened at dawn to serve the porters. As a consequence, she is one who commands such affection among residents of the surrounding streets that the question, 'How's Sandra?' is exchanged as a kind of greeting, and the answer is taken as indicative of the state of things in general in this particular corner of London.

'I'd be completely broke and she'd always lend me twenty quid,' admitted Phil with an uncharacteristic blush. 'After the hula hoop, she let me take pictures of her any time. I was photographing her once when she was dancing in the bar and one of the customers told me to stop, and Sandra said,

"Phil can take pictures of me any time, he's my photographer."'

We were sitting in Phil's studio in Greatorex Street, in anticipation of the arrival of the great lady for a photo session, and just as Phil began glancing discreetly at his watch, Sandra made her entrance – worthy of a heroine in a musical comedy – bearing cakes and coffees and an abundance of goodwill, and exclaiming, 'Oh, Phil, I love you!'

As we consumed our Danish pastries, Phil took the opportunity to focus his lens upon Sandra, while reminding her of the hula hoop incident, a cue for further hilarity. 'As you know, I like making people happy, even though I've been a bit down myself recently,' she confided to me, placing a hand upon my wrist. 'I used to wind people up by saying I could do it for two days non-stop. My biggest thrill was doing it at two or three in the morning,' she continued, filling with glee at the mere thought of nocturnal hula-hooping on a traffic island. 'The police would come round and they'd say, "Don't worry. That's just Sandra."'

'So when shall we do your portrait?' queried Phil, interposing the question as if it were something far off, but catching Sandra's attention and causing her to sit up quickly, in the manner of a schoolgirl when a teacher enters.

Phil sat behind his camera, which was on the tripod, and Sandra sat facing him, expectant and eager.

I sat to one side, observing both photographer and subject, fascinated by Sandra's impassive mode of readiness, with chin lifted just as she raises her countenance at the bar to greet a customer. Over all this time it has become the gaze that she raises to meet life.

Phil shifted his attention between the view through the lens and looking over the camera to meet Sandra's eyes. In the silence of the intimate moment, emotions coursed through Sandra's features like currents in water, and as she looked towards the lens it was if she were looking through it, deeper and deeper.

'She's not a person who tries to hide anything when the camera is in front of her,' commented Phil afterwards, once Sandra had departed, leaving a space in the room, a vacuum where her presence had been. 'There's never a moment when she isn't the centre of attention, but she doesn't demand your attention – you just can't help looking at her,' he said.

GATHERING WINTER FUEL IN SPITALFIELDS

Street Life

IN COMMON WITH everyone else these days, I am feeling the pinch, so last winter, when my boiler broke, I gave up on it and relied upon fires instead. There is plenty of scrap timber lying around the streets of Spitalfields in the form of abandoned broken pallets. Also, the constant renovations provide an endless supply of firewood waiting to be salvaged from kerbside skips.

Now it is time to start lighting fires and gathering fuel again. Last winter, friends would keep a lookout on my behalf and sometimes in the morning I found pallets kindly placed outside my house in the night.

My neighbour lends me his power saw and I lay the pallets down on the pavement and cut them up. After months of practice, I have learned to do this expertly with the minimum number of saw cuts. Like a master butcher slicing through the ribs of a prize bull, I make four cuts with my saw along the whole length of the pallet, traversing the slats, and then flip it over to cut through the base supports. I make short work of these pallets and in no time at all I am sweeping the sawdust from the pavement and stacking up a satisfyingly neat woodpile. A couple of pallets provide only a few evenings' worth of heat, so this is a constant task for me during the winter months.

To keep warm in the depths of last winter, I lay in front of the fire on my sofa under a large sheepskin blanket, with a hot-water bottle cradled underneath and Mr Pussy on top of me too. The first thing I did last Christmas Day was to go out into the frost and cut up pallets. The truth is I grew up in a house with no heating, my family regularly wore overcoats indoors and I remember visiting my grandmother in Chard one Christmas to discover her in her fur coat and hat, mixing ingredients in a bowl on the kitchen table. My other grandmother was confined to a tuberculosis clinic in Bovey Tracey during the 1920s, where they believed that fresh air was curative, to the extreme that she once wrote in a letter of waking in her bed to find a blanket of snow upon the covers. The snow had blown in during the night from Dartmoor through the open door and windows. It is no wonder she died a year later, aged twenty-three.

My own discomfort rates as nothing beside this, but I did find it hard to wake to see my own breath in the bedroom and then heating water in pans before going into the cold bathroom for a wash, as I did all last winter. Now my boiler is repaired but I will still be collecting firewood because, in spite of the work and dirt entailed, I love fires – and I would rather gather wood in the streets than pay any more than I can avoid to the power companies, currently profiteering off our human need to be warm.

When I came to live in an old house in Spitalfields, I certainly did not anticipate it might mean living in historic conditions too!

SPITALFIELDS ANTIQUES MARKET IV

JO AND RICHARD WATERHOUSE are proud father and daughter. It is Jo's stall, but 'He's my encourager,' she explained, turning round to show the patch on her sweater that her father had darned expertly for her. Jo began trading a few years ago in Totnes, where she supported herself through Dartington Hall by a stall in the Butterwalk Market. I was particularly attracted by Jo's stock of unused vintage bicycle bells at just three pounds each. Father and daughter had driven up for the day from Arlesey in Bedfordshire, 'well known for its cement works, mental hospital and artificial limb factory', apparently.

PAUL THE URBAN SHEPHERD said, 'I work with serious clothing but make it fun. My stock is countrywear, not made in the city but worn in the city,' said Paul, introducing the trend for men's clothing from the provinces, appropriated by fashionable gallants here in London and worn with an urban attitude. Fondly drawing my attention to the quality on display, he explained, 'It's very well made – designed to last a lifetime – and, if it doesn't fit exactly, it can easily be tailored to the new owner.' A style ambassador, Paul intuitively understands the necessary balance of levity and sobriety in menswear.

SHAHID AND GILLANI ARJUMAND are dealers of repute. Shahid trades in Victorian and Georgian silver, cutlery, coins and fountain pens, while Gillani sells jewellery. 'I used to work for an insurance company and she was in retail, but we both left to go full-time in 2000. And we have brought up three children on this. They have been to university, married and bought homes,' revealed Shahid, gesturing to all the piles of broken fountain pens, knives and forks, brooches and rings, while exchanging a glance with Gillani at the remarkable success of their joint endeavour.

STUART IS A proud silver-haired gentleman who grew up in Exmouth Market. 'My father was a market trader and I used to do Hoxton Market when I was five. I've been here all my life and I paid cheap rent, but all of a sudden you've got to earn 400 or 500 pounds a week to live here. I'm homeless now. I'd rather sleep in my van than pay 200 pounds rent a week,' he confided to me, buzzing with defiant energy. 'I like to come with a new pitch each week. I was brought up with markets. I've done other things and come back. I've got the Gypsy blood in me,' declared Stuart, an aristocrat among traders who drives around all week, discovering new things to sell in Spitalfields.

THE OLDEST CEREMONY
IN THE WORLD

Night Life, Past Life

EACH NIGHT A LONE FIGURE in a long red coat walks down Water Lane, the narrow cobbled street enclosed between the mighty inner and outer walls of the Tower of London. Sometimes only his lamp can be seen through the thick river mist that engulfs him when it rises up from the Thames and pours over the wall to fill Water Lane, but he is indifferent to meteorological conditions because he is resolute in his grave task.

He is the Gentleman Porter and it is his responsibility to lock up the Tower, a duty fulfilled every single night since 1280, when the Byward Tower that houses the guardroom was built. And over seven centuries of repetition without remiss – day after day, down through the ages, through the Plague, the Fire and the Blitz – this time-hallowed ritual has acquired its own cherished protocol and tradition, becoming known as the Ceremony of the Keys. It is the oldest, longest-running ceremony in the world, and it continues today and it will continue when we are gone.

John Keohane, the current Gentleman Porter (a role also known since 1485 as the Yeoman Porter, and since 1914 by the title of Chief Yeoman Warder), invited me over

to the Tower to watch the ceremony and granted me the rare privilege of taking pictures of a run-through for an event that, at the request of the Sovereign, has never been photographed.

'Welcome to my little house by the river,' declared John cheerily in greeting. 'That's what the Tower is, it's my home.' There was a sharp breeze down by the Thames that night, and I was grateful to be led by John into the cosy octagonal vaulted guardroom in the Byward Tower, which has been manned night and day since 1280 and has the ancient graffiti ('Roger Tireel 1622', among others), the microwave and the video collection to prove it.

Here, John's old friend Idwal Bellis, a

ing at the fireplace and they pointed at him,' he revealed, gesturing to the spot in question. 'He never spent another night in here again.'

At 9.53 p.m., it was time for John to light the huge old brass lantern, take up his bunch of keys and venture out into the glimmering dusk, mindful of the precise timing of the seven-minute ceremony that must finish on the exact stroke of ten. The only time this did not happen, he informed me, was 29 December 1940, when a bomb fell within fifty feet and blew the warders off their feet. They picked themselves up, completed the ceremony and wrote a letter of apology to the King for being three minutes late – and he graciously replied to say he fully understood because of the enemy action taking place overhead.

genial Welshman, was preparing to spend a long night on duty. 'People try to break into the Tower of London all the time,' he confided with an absurd smile, explaining, 'They climb into the moat and we contact the police to take them away. Occasionally, the Bloody Tower alarm goes off and no one knows why, and sometimes foxes set off alarms too.' Like John, Idwal joined the Yeoman Warders in 1991 after a long army career, and in the last twenty years he has seen it all, except one thing. 'My predecessor, Cedric Ramshall, was here one night and the room filled with frost. He saw two men in doublets with long clay pipes stand-

Leaving the guardhouse, John walked alone with his lantern down Water Street to the entrance to the Bloody Tower, where he picked up an escort of Tower of London guards uniformed in red with bearskins on their heads, who returned down Water Lane with him to the gates. 'At the Middle Tower, I meet Mr Bellis and together we lock, close and secure the gates, while the soldiers offer us protection,' he explained to me with uncomplicated purpose. This prudent addition to the ritual was made in 1381 when an elderly Gentleman Porter was beaten up and left for dead by protesters against Richard II's poll tax.

My heart leapt in my chest when, as the black doors closed upon the modern City with a thunderous bang, centuries ebbed away and I found myself suddenly isolated

'Halt! Who comes there?'

in the medieval world, in the sole company of soldiers in scarlet uniforms in a pool of lamplight in the ancient gatehouse – just as I might have done any time in the past 700 years. Once the huge doors were shut and barred, while a pair of guards stood on either side and a shorter one held up the lamp as John turned the key in the lock with a satisfying clunk, the escort re-formed and marched swiftly together back down Water Lane into the gathering darkness, with John Keohane at the head, leaving Idwal Bellis to return to his cosy guardroom.

Keeping discreetly to the shadows, I followed down Water Lane, creeping along beneath the vast stone walls towering over me. It was at this moment that a sentry stepped from the shadows – in the dramatic coup of the evening – challenging those approaching out of the dusk, crying, 'Halt! Who comes there?' With barely concealed affront, John stopped his escort, announcing, 'The keys!' And in a bizarre moment, centuries of repetition was rendered into the present tense, happening for the first time – as those involved embraced the irresistible drama of the instant and the loaded gun pointed at them.

'Whose keys?' persisted the sentry – turning either dim-witted or insubordinate. 'Queen Elizabeth's keys,' announced John, citing the Sovereign, who is his direct em-

ployer. 'Pass Queen Elizabeth's keys, for all is well!' responded the sentry, a stooge stepping back into the shadow.

And then John, accompanied by his escort, marched triumphantly up into the precinct of the Tower, where he met a contingent of guardsmen, waiting sentinel at the head of the stone steps. They presented arms and the clock started to chime, permitting eleven seconds before the stroke of ten. In a moment of brief exultation, spontaneous even after twenty years, John took two paces forward, raising his Tudor bonnet and declaiming, 'God preserve Queen Elizabeth!' Finally, a bugler played the last post and the clock struck ten as he made his

way up the steps to report to the Constable that the Tower was locked for the night.

The guard marched away to their barracks and I stood alone beneath the vast white tower, luminous with floodlight, and cast my eyes around Tower Green, which was my sole preserve in that moment. Then John returned, descending the staircase, and we walked down to the Bloody Tower, where the young princes were murdered and where Walter Raleigh was imprisoned for thirteen years. And before John Keohane and I shook hands and said our good nights, we lingered there for a moment in silent awe at the horror and the beauty of the place.

THE TRANNIES OF BETHNAL GREEN

HESSEL STREET is named in remembrance of Phoebe Hessel (1713–1821) known as the 'Amazon of Stepney', who dressed as a man to enlist in the army to be with her lover – an honourable example which demonstrates that trannies are an integral part of the culture and history of the East End. And I am proud to report that this venerable tradition still flourishes today, reaching its exuberant zenith each year at London's Next Top Tranny Contest, held at the Bethnal Green Working Men's Social Club.

It was my privilege to sit at the head of the catwalk, surrounded by a raucous and appreciative crowd, to witness these glamorous extravagant flowers at close quarters as they competed furiously in this year's nail-biting contest finale. Yet before proceedings commenced, Russella – our long-legged pole-dancing hostess in pink glitter – confessed her motives with a refreshing lack of false modesty, redefining the terms of the contest unambiguously.

'Why would I want to give the title of London's Top Tranny to someone less talented and less good-looking than myself? That's why I am the host tonight, because the winner will be London's Next Top Tranny – after me. They will be London's Next Top Tranny when I die. In other words, over my dead body,' she declared, fluttering her spidery eyelashes as she twisted her sparkly lips into an insouciant smile and tossed her blonde locks with self-conscious grace.

Once the unassailable Russella had asserted her alpha-tranny status, it was time to bring on the contestants – Miss Cairo, Fancy Chance, Stephanie, Polly Sexual, Jean Benett and Strawberry Pickles – and what a gorgeous display of unapologetically ambiguous gender they presented – to delight the most jaded eye and uplift the weariest spirit. Six brave souls who had cast aside conventional notions of dignity in the quest for greatness. Lacking breasts, possessing male body hair (and in one case having a beard), none of these contestants aspired literally to be taken for women. Instead they had adopted female trappings to aid them in exaggerated variations upon the performance of femininity. And, as if to emphasise the point, Russella even staged an uproarious cookery demonstration, making pancakes on stage.

Running through the evening was a compelling dramatic tension between the trannies' performances, which invite our suspension of disbelief, and their clunky pantomime outfits, which simultaneously remind us of their wearers' inauthentic gender. These fearless trannies incarnate a persuasive poetry. It is a question of how far are you prepared to go to humiliate yourself for the sake of becoming fabulous.

And these trannies held nothing back, embracing challenges to retain their dignity while walking in wildly mismatched ill-fitting shoes, displaying extreme emotions while blasted by a wind machine, drinking copious amounts of cider, and eating live worms, raw meat and dog food. Stephanie, a shy senior tranny in a bridal gown, won affection early on for tottering in ill-matched heels displaying swollen ankles and varicose veins, and then, as if to dispel the audience's pity, won a round of applause for eating a whole can of dog food.

It all came down to two contenders – Strawberry Pickles, distinguished by her relentless cheerfulness, and Fancy Chance, who accomplished that rare stage feat of being mean and charming at the same time. She was the dark horse of the contest, wearing trousers and exuding masculinity. I wrongly assumed Fancy was a man performing as a manly woman. Only part-way through the contest did I realise that Fancy Chance was the only entrant going in the opposite direction, from woman to man. She had taken me in from the start. So it was only just that she won, and friends were surprised next day when I said I had been to a tranny contest and a woman won – though I have no doubt Phoebe Hessel would have approved of the result.

There is a strange nobility in the trannies' condition, emerging from the shadowlands of gender into the limelight, so proud and flamboyant, craving attention like children, and seeking affection and respect for their fabulousness. We love them for their excess, their devotion to sentimental songs and inability to lip-sync, their make-up that smears, their wigs that come off and their trashy costumes that come apart. We cherish their magnificent failures. We love them for their audacity. They are delicate creatures of the night-time and we do not want to know where they go in the day-time, because there is an elusive magic to these vibrant personalities unlocked by cross-dressing.

COLUMBIA ROAD MARKET IX

Human Life, Market Life

THE FULL MOON was still reflecting in the puddles from the previous night's down-pour as I walked up to Columbia Road before dawn to speak with young Albert Dean, at his double pitch selling cut flowers at the western end of the market. With his knitted hat pulled down over his ears, hopping from foot to foot and rubbing his hands together enthusiastically in the cold, this wiry young man with sharp eyes in-formed me proudly that, although he has only been working here full-time for about five years, the stall has been in his family for four generations.

Albert Dean is the fourth Albert Dean since his great-grandfather to run the pitch on this site – as long as the market has been here – which means that at any time during the last century you could have come and bought flowers from an Albert Dean at this street corner. The current Albert Dean has been working on the stall regularly since he was seven and, now that his father is in semi-retirement, his energy motors the business into the future. 'I don't see why not. I'd like to think so!' he declared with an eager grin, when I asked if he expects to be here his whole life. 'It's in the blood. I don't know anything different,' he announced, with a hint at the absurdity of his rare horti-cultural pedigree.

Rising at three in the morning, Albert drives down to Columbia Road with a lorry full of flowers each Sunday, setting up at five thirty and returning home again with an empty lorry. Taking Monday off, Albert works for the wholesale side of the business based at Golfside in Cheshunt the rest of the week. Flower orders are sent off on Tuesday, for the coming weekend at Columbia Road and all the wholesale customers, while Wednesday is Albert's second day off in his curiously syncopated routine. Then on Thursday, Friday and Saturday he is sending out deliveries to restaurants, corporate clients and freelance florists, as well as preparing for Sunday, including supplying other stalls in Columbia Road. 'We're about as cheap as you can get,' he assured me with a toothy grin.

And thus the business has rolled on through four generations. Albert already has a daughter of sixteen months, Taylor May, but if a boy comes along there is no question but that he will become Albert Dean V. Albert is measured in his hopes that his children can continue the business. 'I'd like to think so, though it's getting a lot harder with the supermarkets getting better at selling flowers,' he confided cautiously. Yet Albert has the optimistic temperament acquired over four generations that results

in an energetic focus upon the business in hand, telling me that he actually prefers the cold to the heat. 'It's an incentive to keep moving!' he declared brightly, fidgeting in anticipation of all the day's activities to come. 'And it's harder to keep the flowers looking good in the heat.'

With Halloween approaching, Albert has Chinese lanterns (*Physalis*) on sale alongside a fine variety of decorative foliage. 'That's what all the restaurants are ordering this week!' he confirmed, with all the inborn swagger and breezy confidence befitting the fourth-generation Albert Dean, standing on the street corner that is his birthright.

RICHARD AND COSMO WISE

RAG DEALERS

Human Life

THIS IS COSMO, sitting in the trouser store at the warehouse where he works with his father, Richard Wise, tending to the most beautiful collection of second-hand clothes I have ever seen. Father and son live together in the space where they also work together – day in, day out – pursuing their joint passion for extravagantly worn-out clothing. 'We tidied up before you came!' claimed Cosmo, giving an unconvincing and entirely unnecessary apology for the

glorious mayhem of their living space. Yet although it looked like a hurricane had just passed through, there was such an atmosphere of calm that I could happily have curled up among all the old rags and gone to sleep, which is more or less what Richard and Cosmo do each night.

The rags Richard and Cosmo seek are of significant age, from before the Second World War, peasant and working clothes sourced mostly from France and Japan, as Richard explained to me, riffling through rails to select choice examples. 'We are looking for discolouration and holes. When a garment is just about to fall apart, that's when it is at its best. I once had this old pair of women's underpants that were more patches than anything else!' he announced delightedly, holding up the most breathtakingly faded old brown coat I ever saw, informing me with the critical authority of an expert, 'The old patching is better than the new patching.' Cosmo then produced a humble pair of old socks that had been intricately repaired more times than you could count, which we all admired in reverent silence for a moment, until he asked wistfully, 'Where will all the darned socks be in fifty years' time?'

As father and son showed me one cherished example after another of their shabby old jackets, dresses, trousers and jumpers, moth-eaten, repeatedly patched, stitched and darned, and in fabric softened with use, each piece possessing a unique luxurious richness of texture and stories that can never be fathomed, I began to understand how intoxicating this ragged aesthetic could be.

'At a certain age, you realise that what you do is who you are,' said Richard, recalling his life working in finance. 'I think the office is the most evil invention of the twentieth century, worse even than a factory,' his caustic verdict on that world today, revealing a strong independent streak. The current venture began at a time of re-evaluation, while Richard was selling off the clothes of his deceased relatives in Portobello Road Market, after he had abandoned his earlier career. 'I started to enjoy what I was doing, I got better at it and my eye improved. Although it was when we started to go to France that we really developed,' he admitted, referring to the time when Cosmo gave up working as a chef and joined him. Both love the thrill of the chase, getting excited and completing each other's sentences, describing the rapture of their quest, rooting around in French provincial markets, even persuading a shepherd living on a mountain above Lourdes to part with his ancestors' wardrobe – and all in the hope of discovering some rare arcane patched-up and worn-out specimen to delight their sophisticated customers in Spitalfields and Portobello markets.

'For the first time in my life, I can like the face I am putting on,' admitted Richard with a quiet grin of reflection, 'because in this line of business you can be yourself. You are your own master and your time is your own. We buy what we like, not what we think we can sell. So you are risking yourself, showing your own taste, and you're trying to convince people to share your passion.' Cosmo is even more down to earth in his perspective on what they do. 'A market is the oldest form of commerce, buying in one place, selling at another, and living off the difference – and selling old rags is keeping things going, so you're not doing any damage.'

It is no longer the rule for families to be in business together, so I was touched to see Richard and Cosmo, both dressed head to toe in their wares and delighting in their working partnership, like some latter-day Steptoe and Son pursuing their singular line of business in solidarity. I am fascinated by their radical vision and appealingly contrary opinions, giving value to what many find worthless and respecting the culture that lies behind these garments, of people who did not consider their clothes

disposable. And it all came through the love of rags. As Cosmo put it plainly, peering out from under his mop of curly hair and widening his dark eyes, 'The reason we are doing this is because it's a nice way to make a living and our souls are intact.'

A ROOM TO LET IN OLD ALDGATE

Past Life, Street Life

I WOULD DEARLY LOVE TO rent the room that is to let in this old building in Aldgate, photographed by Henry Dixon for the Society for Photographing Relics of Old London. Too bad it was demolished in 1882. Instead I must satisfy myself with an imaginary stroll through the streets of that lost city, with these tantalising glimpses of vanished buildings commissioned by the society as my points of reference. Founded by a group of friends who wanted to save the Oxford Arms, threatened with demolition in 1875, the Society for Photographing Relics of Old London touched a popular chord with the pictures they published of age-old buildings that seem to incarnate the very soul of the ancient city. London never looked so old as in these atmospheric images of buildings forgotten generations ago.

Yet the melancholy romance of these ramshackle shabby edifices is irresistible to me. I want to linger in the shadows of these labyrinthine structures, I need to scrutinise their shop windows, I long to idle in these gloomy streets – because the truth is, these photographs illustrate an imaginary old London that I should like to inhabit, at least in my dreams. Even to a nineteenth-century eye, these curious photographs would have proposed a heightened reality, because the people are absent. Although the long exposures sometimes captured the few that stood still, working people are mostly present only as shadows or fleeting transparent figures. The transient nature of the human element in these pictures emphasises the solidity of the buildings, which, ironically, were portrayed because they were about to disappear too. Thus Henry Dixon's photographs, preserved in the Bishopsgate Institute, are veritable sonnets upon the nature of ephemerality – the people are disappearing from the pictures and the buildings are vanishing from the world; only the photographs themselves, printed in the permanent carbon process, survive as evidence of these poignant visions now.

The absence of people in this lost city allows us to enter these pictures by proxy,

A ROOM TO LET IN OLD ALDGATE

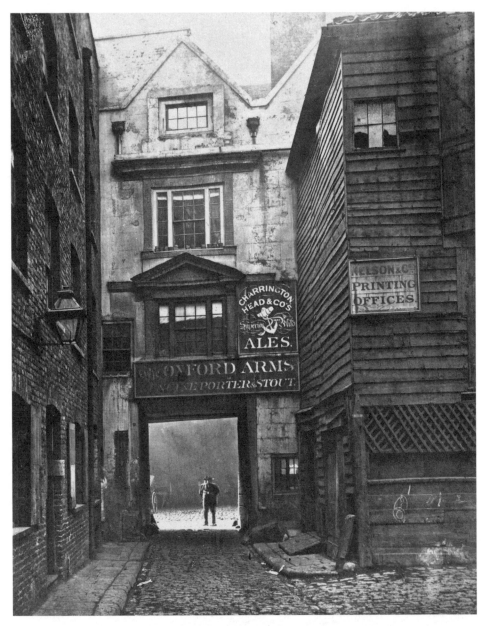

The Oxford Arms

SPITALFIELDS LIFE

Old house in the Palace Yard, Lambeth

and the sharp detail draws us closer to these streets of extravagant tottering old piles with cavernous dour interiors. We know our way around, not simply because the geography remains constant but because Charles Dickens is our guide. This is the London that he knew and which he romanced in his novels, populated by his own versions of the people that he met in its streets. The very buildings in these photographs appear to have personality, presenting dirty faces smirched with soot, pierced with dark eyes and gawping at the street.

How much I should delight to lock the creaky old door, leaving my rented room in Aldgate, so conveniently placed above the business premises of John Robbins, the practical optician, and take a stroll across this magical city, where the dusk gathers eternally. Let us go together now, on this cloudy November day, through the streets of old London. We shall set out from my room in Aldgate over to Smithfield and Clerkenwell, then walk down to cross the Thames, explore the inns of Southwark and discover where our footsteps lead ...

In Cloth Fair

St Mary Overy's Dock

At the corner of Milton Street

Old shambles in Aldgate

A ROOM TO LET IN OLD ALDGATE

361

Paul Pindar's House in Bishopsgate

TERRY O'LEARY

JOKER

Human Life

'FOR TWO YEARS, I cared for my brother – who was diagnosed with HIV in 1987 – in his council flat, but after he died I couldn't stay there because my relationship with him as his sister wasn't recognised by the council, and that's how I became homeless,' said Terry, speaking plainly, yet without self-pity, as we sat on either side of a table in Dino's Café, Spitalfields. And there, in a single sentence, you have the explanation of how one woman, in spite of her intelligence and skill, fell through the surface of the world and found herself living in a hostel with 128 other homeless people.

Terry is a shrewd woman with an innate dignity, and a lightness of manner too. She manages to be both vividly present in the moment and also detached – considering and assessing – though quick to smile at the ironies of life. She wears utilitarian clothing which reveals little of the wearer and sometimes seems a tentative presence, but when you meet her sympathetic dark eyes, she reveals her strength and her capacity for joy.

No one could deny it was an act of moral courage, when Terry gave up her career as a chef to care for her brother at a time when little support or medication was available to those with Aids, moving in with him and

devoting herself fully to his care. Yet in spite of the cruel outcome of her sacrifice, Terry discovered the resourcefulness to create a new existence, which allows her to draw upon these experiences in a creative way, through her work as a performer with Cardboard Citizens, the homeless people's theatre company based in Spitalfields.

'I took what I could with me, the rest I left behind. I took photographs and personal things. You fill your car with your TV, records, books and all the rest of it – but then you find it can be quite liberating because you realise all that stuff is not important,' admitted Terry with a wry smile, recounting a lesson born out of necessity. In the Mare Street hostel in Hackney, Terry stayed in her tiny room to avoid the culture of alcohol and drug-taking that prevailed, but instead she found herself at the mercy of the absurdly doctrinaire bureaucracy. 'I remember the staff coming round and saying, "You have to remove one of the two chairs in your room because you're only allowed to have one,"' Terry recalled. 'You find you're living in a universe where you can get evicted for having two chairs in your room,' she added.

A few months after she came to the hostel, Cardboard Citizens visited to perform and stage workshops, permitting Terry to participate and make some friends – but most importantly granting her a new role in life. 'I was hooked,' confided Terry. 'What I liked about it was the opportunity to talk about our own experiences and how we can make a change. And the best part of it was when the audience became involved and got on stage.' Now that she works for them, Terry describes the aim of the company as being to 'give voice to the homeless and show the situations homeless people face'. They perform in shelters and hostels, creating vital performances that invite audiences of the homeless to participate, addressing in drama the pertinent questions and challenges they face in life – all in pursuit of the possibility of change.

Terry's role is central to the company, as mediator, bringing the audience to the play, and raising questions that articulate the discussion manifest in the drama. She carries it off with grace, becoming the moral centre of the performance. And it is a natural role for Terry, one she refers to as 'Joker' – somebody who will always challenge – anchoring the evening with her sense of levity and quick intelligence, without ever admitting that she understands more than her audience. Though, knowing Terry's story, I found it especially poignant to observe Terry's measured equanimity, even when the drama dealt with issues of grief and dislocation that are familiar territory for her personally.

'You don't have to accept things as they are. You can fight back,' declared Terry, her dark eyes glinting as she spoke from first-hand experience, when I asked how her

understanding of life had been altered by becoming homeless. 'Why is it that the economic underclass are being hammered for the mess that we're in?' she asked in furious indignation. 'I think what's opened my eyes is that there's so much kindness and support coming from people who have got very little. I can't deal with the big picture. I tend to narrow it down to the people in the room and just keep chipping away at small changes. And I'm going to do this for the rest of my life.' There is an unsentimental fire in Terry's rhetoric, denoting someone who has been granted a hard-won clarity of vision, and at the Code Street hostel, where I saw the performance, I was touched to see her exchanging greetings with long-term homeless people she has known over the eight years she has worked with Cardboard Citizens.

As we left Dino's Café and walked up the steps of Christ Church, Spitalfields, she cast her eyes around in wonder at the everyday spectacle of people walking to and fro, and confessed to me, 'I teach up at the Central School of Speech and Drama now and it's quite amazing to think ten years ago I was sitting in a hostel, wondering what's going to happen next and what's my future going to be? Am I going to be like that woman down the hall, drunk off her head, or on crack?'

Terry still thinks about her brother. 'His eyesight started to go and he set fire to the bed,' she told me, explaining why it became imperative to move in with him. 'He was a stubborn guy but he had to concede that he needed help. He was developing dementia and his eyesight was fading.' It was his unexpected illness and death that triggered the big changes in her existence, but today Terry O'Leary lives in a flat of her own again and finds herself at the centre of a whole new life.

A SPITALFIELDS WEAVER'S STOOL

I FOUND THIS in Brick Lane yesterday, disregarded on the pavement outside a leather shop that was being refitted. I walked past and stopped in my path and turned back. I could not believe my eyes. I knew what it was but I never expected to see it there. Nearby stood a couple of workmen who were stripping out the shop and I asked the men if they had cleared out the stool and if I could buy it. Withholding my excitement, I offered five pounds and after a little negotiation my cash was accepted. Maybe they put the stool on the pavement hoping someone would simply take it away and I was a fool to pay – but this question was of

no consequence to me because I had found a Spitalfields weaver's stool. In spite of its bare utilitarian construction, knowing the meaning of this item as an illustration of the history of this place makes it an object of fascination to me.

I knew it was a weaver's stool because Danny Tabi, the last furrier in Spitalfields, has one that he found in the Gale Furs factory in Fournier Street when he began working there in the 1960s. When I visited him early one morning last summer, he proudly pulled the weaver's stool out from under his sewing-machine bench and placed it on his worktable, explaining what it was and pointing out the standardised aspects of the design.

These stools date from an era when it was cheaper to knock together something by hand than get it mass-produced. Essentially constructed from three pieces of one plank, with a couple of cross-pieces and sides to the seat added, this was something a carpenter could make in ten minutes. The 'V' cut into each of the side supports created an approximation to four legs, making it stable upon irregular floors such as are found in the old houses that were appropriated as factories here.

Originally used by weavers at looms, these stools, Danny explained, became standard for machinists in the clothing industry in Spitalfields. The close similarities between the stool I found and Danny's suggest that the design was honed over time to arrive at a standard stool. The splayed angle of the legs and depth of the 'V' are consistent, and the sides of the seat have their ends cut away on both stools. A little higher than a chair, it is tall enough for my thighs to be parallel with the ground when I sit upon it.

Although, in most illustrations I have found, the weaver stands or sits upon a cross-piece attached to the loom, I am aware that there were different looms for different purposes. Maybe when Danny described this as a weaver's stool, he referred to it as a common design used in the weaving indus-try. I cannot know the story of this stool, it can only exist as a general reminder of those who worked with their hands here for centuries in the textile industry. For an object of such cheap manufacture, it has fulfilled its purpose well, outliving those who made it to become a relic of an industry that has all but vanished from these streets.

I like this sad old stool for its functional austerity and evidence of wear. Common-place objects that are used by many people in the course of daily life always speak to me more than rare precious artefacts. I cannot tell if this stool is fifty or 100 years old, but I do know it has seen a lot of use and thereby carries the story of countless thousands of hours expended upon the weaving and sewing of cloth here – where I shall keep it – in Spitalfields.

THE CURRY CHEFS OF BRICK LANE

Culinary Life, Human Life

WITH THE BLIZZARD WHIRLING DOWN Brick Lane, it was the ideal moment for a hot curry to warm the spirits and so, dodging the mischievous curry touts' snow-ball bouts between rival restaurants, I set out to make the acquaintance of some of Brick Lane's most celebrated curry chefs. I was granted admission to the small kitchens tucked away at the back or in the basement of the curry houses, where head chefs mar-shal whole teams of underchefs in a highly formalised hierarchy of responsibility.

It was a relief to step from the cold street into the heat of the kitchens, where I dis-covered our excited subjects glistening with perspiration, all engaged in the midst of the collective drama that results in curry. These were men who – for the most part –

Zulen Ahmed, head chef at Saffron

Head chef Shaiz Uddin with his colleague,
Monul Uddin, tandoori chef at Masala

had worked their way up over many years from humble kitchen porters to enjoy their heroic leading roles, granting them the right to swagger in front of the lens.

I encountered the charismatic Zulen Ahmed standing over his clay-lined tandoori oven beneath the Saffron restaurant, where he has been head chef for ten years now. Trained by the renowned curry chef, Ashik Miah, Zulen served eight years as a porter before progressing to run his own kitchen, now supervising a team consisting of two chefs who do the spicing and make the sauces, a tandoori chef, two cooks who cook rice and poppadums, a second chef who prepares side dishes and a porter who does the washing up. 'The head chef listens to everybody,' he explained deferentially, with his staff standing around within earshot, and thereby revealing himself to be a natural leader.

Across the road at Masala, I met head chef, Shaiz Uddin, whose mother is a chef in Bangladesh. She taught him to cook when

he was ten years old. Shaiz told me he worked in her kitchen as curry chef for seven years, before he came to London ten years ago to bring the authentic style to Brick Lane, where today he is renowned for contriving new dishes for his eager customers.

It was quickly apparent that there is a daily routine common to all the curry kitchens of Brick Lane. At eleven each morning, the chefs come in and work until three to prepare the sauces and half-cook the meat for the evening. At three they take a break until six, while the underchefs, who arrive at three, prepare the vegetables and salad. Then at six, when the chefs return, the rice is cooked and – now the kitchen is full – everyone works as a team until midnight, when it is time to throw out the leftovers and make the orders for the next day. This is the pattern that rules the lives of all involved.

'I like to be busy,' Nurul Alam, head chef at Preem & Prithi, informed me blithely – he regularly cooks 300 curries a night.

Monzur Hussain, head chef at Shampan

Dayem Ahmed, kitchen porter and aspiring chef at Shampan

Over at the Shampan, Monzur Hussain emerged from the kitchen with his brow covered in perspiration to brag about his meteoric rise, commencing as a kitchen porter in 1997, becoming a chef in 2000 and winning Best Chef in the Brick Lane Curry Festival in 2005. Monzur sets an example that is an inspiration to Dayem Ahmed, a porter who has been there just six months, already daydreaming of achieving Best Curry Chef in 2018.

Finally, at the Aladin I met Brick Lane's most senior curry chef, the distinguished Rana Miah, who started work in 1980 as a kitchen porter when he arrived from Bangladesh, graduating to chef in 1988. 'At that time we served only Bengalis, but by 1995 the customers were all Europeans,' he recalled, describing his tenure as chef at one of Brick Lane's oldest curry houses, which opened in 1985 and is second only to the Clifton in age. Rana explained that he runs his kitchen upon the system of 'Handy Cooking', based on the use of large stock

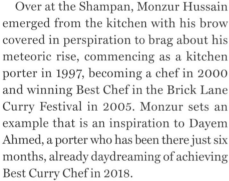

Rana Miah, flanked by Kholilun Rahman and Mizanur Khan at Aladin

pots to cook the food. 'That's the way it's done in Bangladesh,' he confirmed. 'This is a traditional restaurant.' As the longest-serving curry chef, Rana is frequently consulted by the other chefs on Brick Lane and remains passionate about his vocation, arriving before everyone each day and leaving after everyone else too.

I never asked the curry chefs to cross their arms, but they all assumed this stance, independently and without prompting – even Dayem, the kitchen porter, yet to commence his training as a chef, knew what to do. It is a posture that suggests professionalism, dignity and self-respect, yet it also indicates a certain reticence, a reserved nature that prefers to let the culinary creations speak for themselves. So I ask you to spare a thought for these proud curry chefs. Like those engineers slaving below deck on the great steam ships of old, they are the unseen and unsung heroes of Brick Lane's curry mile.

ALL CHANGE AT
15 & 17 FOURNIER STREET

Human Life, Past Life

OVER THE LAST YEAR, I have enjoyed dropping in regularly to 15 and 17 Fournier Street to visit Jim Howett and observe the progress of the mighty works that have been undertaken there by the Spitalfields Historic Buildings Trust to reinstate these two gracious houses, built by joiner William Taylor in 1726, which were carved up to become a mission house for the conversion of Jews to Christianity in 1878.

Jim and I always end up chatting in the attic room of No. 15, which is lined with leaded casements offering mind-boggling views of Nicholas Hawksmoor's Christ Church, Spitalfields, opposite, and where, over our heads, old notches in the beams reveal where the looms for silk weaving were once attached. Since the endeavour was nearing completion, Jim was able to savour the moment up there in his light-filled eyrie above the rooftops, and look back upon a remarkable job achieved in

partnership with Tim Whittaker, Director of the Spitalfields Trust.

'This is the last structural Georgian reconstruction that is going to happen in Spitalfields,' admitted Jim, with a tinge of disappointment in his voice, because although these houses have posed an extraordinary exercise in deduction, it has been one that he has relished. With evangelical fervour, Christ's Mission to the Jews tore the staircase out of the corner house, took out the walls on the ground floor to create a gospel hall and punched doorways between the two buildings to make them one – while subsequent factory usage and then a carve-up into flats in the 1980s ravaged the buildings still further. 'This reconstruction sets it back with a footprint as it was intended,' explained Jim, casting his eyes around the empty rooms in pleasure at the freshly sanded floors, new panelling, windows, shutters and doors, all connected by the tour de force of the project – the new staircase winding up through four storeys, constructed in the eighteenth-century method and to the design of William Taylor.

Entering the house this week was a rare engagement with time travel, to visit a newly constructed eighteenth-century interior where the sawdust was still fresh and history waiting to happen. But when I first came here last spring, Jim took me down into the cellar, where excavations revealed remains of the dwelling that had previously existed upon this site. Beneath the cellar floor was the ground level of a seventeenth-century courtyard with a stone culvert that discharged water towards Lolesworth Field, gone centuries ago. Among the debris beneath the floor, Jim found quantities of charcoal, confirming his belief that the land from here to Bethnal Green was back-filled with rubble from the Fire of London, raising the ground level by as much as two metres and burying a seventeenth-century path below the cellar floor of an eighteenth-century house. Ascending from the gaping muddy chasm of the cellar, the house was in disorder, doorways were being bricked up and holes cut in the floor. It was a composite of discordant spaces connected by eccentric arrangements that required you to walk into No. 17 to reach the top floors of No. 15 and go downstairs in No. 15 to reach the cellar of No. 17 – where the long-suffering residents endured living beneath a daily accumulating layer of builder's dust.

Yet I discovered an exhilarating transformation when I came back months later as the staircase was being fitted in No. 15, spiralling up through the centre of the structure and restoring its spine. Unlike modern stairs, in which the treads are supported on either side, the staircases of the eighteenth century were built one step on top of the next, supported by a central ascending beam – much more sturdy, as well as accommodating to the irregularities of an old building. When Jim first showed me his cherished staircase, it was not all there – you walked up and up, and then it ran out ... But when I next returned, I was greeted with the triumphant news that the stairs had reached the roof and miraculously met the marks in the joists on the top floor where the original staircase had sat.

The sculptural quality of this fine staircase, adorned with barley-sugar twists, brings the building alive with dynamic energy. It takes you on a journey through differently proportioned spaces, all neatly panelled and flooded with light, to arrive at the lantern at the top. The layout of the rooms has been recreated and while there is a scrupulous attention to detail in all the work, idiosyncrasy is restrained – throwing emphasis upon the graceful flow of architectural space. Most importantly, the institutionalisation and its subsequent chaos are gone, humanity has been restored in the recovery of the sympathetic yet relatively modest domestic spaces which comprise this unusual corner house.

'I think we got the best out of all these people. There's never been an argument, because everyone's worked to their strengths,' confided Jim quietly, almost speaking to himself in admitting his responsibility to his team. And realising that his own time to inhabit these houses, which have been his consuming passion for the past year, is now at an end, he added, 'I'll miss it.' Jim and I left the weavers' attic glowing with sunlight and walked down through the empty panelled rooms, where the finishing touches were being made before everyone left.

Now the residents of No. 17 can finally hoover up the dust and the household spirits of No. 15 can experience a moment of peace, renewed and waiting, until the next wave of inhabitants arrive and time can begin all over again.

THIS BELL WILL RING WHEN THERE IS FOG ON THE RIVER

ALBERT HAFIZE

FISH MERCHANT

Culinary Life, Human Life, Night Life

IT WAS THE COLDEST NIGHT of the year so far when I arrived in Billingsgate Fish Market at half past five in the morning to meet Albert Hafize, yet he bounced up to greet me warmly outside Mick's Eel Supply, his spirits undiminished by the Siberian temperatures.

For the past thirty-five years, Albert has been coming here six nights a week, between four and seven each morning, per-

sonally selecting the highest-quality fish for his business, Cleopatra Seafoods, based in a small red-brick building in Whitby Street, between Redchurch Sreet and the Bethnal Green Road, where the fish are trimmed, gutted, filleted, cured or smoked, according to his customers' requirements.

In Billingsgate, the doors were wide open and the cold night air circulated freely throughout the building, which suited

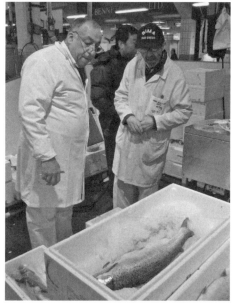

everyone very well, because the sub-zero temperatures provided ideal conditions for all the fish – snug in their blankets of ice and lying head to toe in the thousands of white boxes that filled the market – even if the traders were turning blue. No larger than the average supermarket, the central hall has the feel of an intimate marketplace where you walk among narrow aisles between stalls crammed with all the wonders of the deep, laid out before your eyes and gleaming in the halogen glare, wet and shining in all the vibrant tones of the ocean. As I gawped at the variety of Neptune's kingdom, the large, the small, the colourful and the exotic, with scales, tentacles or claws, I quickly realised that my gaze was returned by myriad fish eyes looking back at me, and some still alive.

Yet this was Albert's familiar constituency and I had to run to keep up with him as he ducked and dived between the stalls, seeking the items upon the list on his red clipboard. Hyper-alert, with acute focus, his eyes never stopped moving, scrutinising the options and checking the prices with the traders, negotiating and collecting the receipts as the porters swept the orders away to his van waiting in the car park. Negotiating the swarm of porters in their long white aprons coming and going with trolleys, we walked outside in the dark beneath the shadow of the Canary Wharf Tower to check the night's haul, comprising a tall pile of boxes on the tarmac, some with fish neatly packed, others with live lobsters crawling around inside and an enigmatic box with an enormous fish tail protruding from one end. Eager to get back to Shoreditch, Albert started loading them into the van in the half-light and I lifted the boxes, passing them to him while he stacked them inside.

While Albert sought the last few items on his list, he arranged for me to have a cup of tea in the café with Sheldon Davis, fish porter and chairman of the union. 'A year or so ago, we were told the badges wouldn't be renewed,' he explained regretfully, holding up the red and white enamelled plate that is his licence to work, issued by the City of London in a system established in 1878. Many porters are third or fourth generation in the trade and I spoke to one whose grandfather started here after being discharged from the army, gassed in the trenches of the First World War. The badge system, which will get wiped out next year, allowed the porters to negotiate with the traders' association and establish working rights. It was a touching encounter, to sit across the table in the corner of the steam-filled café and learn the story from this dignified man, who has been labouring here thirty years, carrying fish from three in the morning, Tuesday to Saturday, and taking home no more than 450 pounds a week. 'You can only fight on and fight on, but the City of London hold all the resources,' he said.

As we drove back along Commercial Road in the dawn, Albert told me that he relied upon the porters to keep an eye on his stock while the van was unsupervised in the car park and was dubious of the logic of removing the established system. But once we arrived in Whitby Street, there was no time

*Sheldon Davis, Chairman of
the Billingsgate Porters' Union*

to speak as he unloaded the fish, passing the heavy boxes from the back of the van to his handful of staff, who had been there all night making preparations. There was not a moment to waste as the boxes were thrown open and all the orders for hotels and restaurants were put together in haste to get them out on the road and up to the West End.

In a tiled room leading off the loading bay, with unceasing motion, Albert was unpacking boxes on a steel bench, lifting fish and scrabbling in the ice with his bare hands to appraise his stock critically and select the choice specimens to deliver to his customers. Next door, in a small white room, two men stood at a stone bench where water ran continuously over the work surface, gutting, trimming and skinning fish, with the tireless persistence of machines, working through the chill of the night.

Once the orders had gone out, I joined Albert upstairs in his office, where he gave a sigh of relief as he removed his lifting belt, now that the physical activity was over for another day and he could devote himself to paperwork. 'The morning is the worst, because all the customers want their orders early. It's very hard work,' he confided to me with a weary shrug, 'but you have to enjoy it or else you wouldn't get up at two in the morning each day. It's fun at the market where you see people every day and everyone knows you and you do business together. The days go quickly.'

Albert's origins are in Egypt and his brother Tony first came to London from Cairo in the employ of an international seafood company, before starting up on his own under the Wheler Street arches in 1968. Twenty-five years ago, when they had the current premises built, the area was all small industrial premises, but now they are the exception – a fish smokery in the midst of the frippery of bars, galleries and boutiques.

'You need to know fish. Once you know fish, you know the origin and quality by experience,' declared Albert, speaking plainly of the knowledge that he employs to make the thousand decisions of each night, selecting, buying and making up orders – thinking in motion, assessing all the options and making the informed choices that earn him his 10 to 15 per cent. It made me wonder if so much exposure to fish had engendered an aversion to seafood, but the truth is quite the contrary, as Albert Hafize confessed to me open-heartedly and with a generous smile, 'I love fish. I eat fish!'

A DEAD MAN IN CLERKENWELL

THIS IS THE FACE OF the dead man in Clerkenwell. He does not look perturbed by the change in the weather. Once winters wore him out, but now he rests beneath the streets of the modern city he will never see, oblivious both to the weather and the wonders of our age, entirely oblivious to everything, in fact.

Let me admit, although some might consider it poor company, I consider death to be my friend – because without mortality

our time upon this earth would be worthless. So I do not fear death, but rather I hope I shall have enough life first. My fear is that death might come too soon or unexpectedly in some pernicious form. In this respect, I envy my father, who always took a nap on the sofa each Sunday after gardening and one day at the age of seventy-nine – when he had completed trimming the privet hedge – never woke up again.

It was many years ago that I first made the acquaintance of the dead man in Clerkenwell, when I had an office in the Close where I used to go each day and write. I was fascinated to discover a twelfth-century crypt in the heart of London, the oldest remnant of the medieval priory of the Knights of St John that once stood in Clerkenwell, until it was destroyed by Henry VIII, and it was this *memento mori*, a sixteenth-century stone figure of an emaciated corpse, which embodied the spirit of the place for me.

Thanks to the Museum of the Order of St John, I went back to look up my old friend after all these years. They lent me a key and, leaving the bright November sunshine behind me, I let myself into the crypt, switching on the lights and walking to the furthest underground recess of the building, where the dead man was waiting. I walked up to the tomb where he lay and cast my eyes upon him, recumbent with his shroud gathered across his groin to protect a modesty no longer required. He did not remonstrate with me for letting twenty years go by. He did not even look surprised. He did not appear to recognise me at all. Yet he looked different than before, because I had changed, and it was the transformative events of the intervening years that had awakened my curiosity to return.

There is a veracity in this sculpture which I could not recognise upon my previous visit, when – in my innocence – I had never seen a dead person. Standing over the figure this time, as if at a bedside, I observed the distended limbs, the sunken eyes and the tilt of the head that are distinctive to the dead. When my mother lost all her faculties, I continued to feed her until she could no longer even swallow liquid, becoming as emaciated as the stone figure before me. It was at dusk on 31 December that I came into her room and discovered her inanimate, recognising that through some inexplicable prescience the life had gone from her at the ending of the year. I understood the literal meaning of 'remains', because everything distinctive of the living person had departed to leave mere skin and bone. And I know now that the sculptor who made this effigy had seen that too, because his observation of the dead is apparent in his work, even if the bizarre number of ribs in his figure bears no relation to human anatomy.

There is a polished area on the brow, upon which I instinctively placed my hand, where my predecessors over the past five centuries had worn it smooth. This gesture, which you make as if to check his temperature, is an unconscious blessing in recognition of the communality we share with the dead who have gone before us and whose ranks we shall all join eventually. The paradox of this sculpture is that because it is a man-made artefact it has emotional presence, whereas the actual dead have only absence. It is the tender details – the hair carefully pulled back behind the ears, and the protective arms with their workmanlike repairs – that endear me to this soulful relic.

Time has not been kind to this figure, which originally lay upon the elaborate tomb of Sir William Weston inside the old church of St James, Clerkenwell, until the edifice was demolished and the current church was built in the eighteenth century, when the effigy was consigned to this crypt like an old pram slung in the cellar. Today a modern façade reveals no hint of what lies below ground. Sir William Weston, the last prior, died in April 1540 on the day that

Henry VIII issued the instruction to dissolve the order, and the nature of his death was unrecorded. Thus my friend the dead man is loss incarnate – the damaged relic of the tomb of the last prior of the monastery destroyed 500 years ago – yet he still has his human dignity and he speaks to me.

Walking back from Clerkenwell, through the teeming city to Spitalfields on this bright afternoon in late autumn, I recognised a similar instinct as I did after my mother's death. I cooked myself a meal because I craved the familiar task and the event of the day renewed my desire to live more life.

STANLEY RONDEAU AT THE V&A

Past Life

STANLEY RONDEAU told me that his Huguenot ancestor John Rondeau was a silk weaver who prospered in Spitalfields, becoming Sexton at Christ Church and commissioning designs in the 1740s from the most famous of silk designers, Anna Maria Garthwaite, who lived almost next door to him in Wilkes Street, in the house on the corner with Princelet Street.

Since Anna Maria Garthwaite's designs were exceptionally prized both for their aesthetic appeal and their functional elegance as patterns for silk weaving, hundreds of her original paintings have survived to this day. So Stanley and I went along to the Victoria and Albert Museum in Kensington to take a look at those done for John Rondeau 270 years ago. We negotiated our way through the labyrinths of the vast museum, which was teeming with schoolchildren, with a growing sense of an-

ticipation, because although Stanley has seen one of the designs reproduced in a book, he has never cast eyes upon the originals.

On the fourth floor, we entered a sanctuary of peace and quiet where curator Moira Thunder awaited us in a lofty room with a long table and large flat blue boxes containing the treasured designs that were the object of our quest. Moira – chic in contrasting tones of plum and navy blue, and with a pair of fuchsia lenses which hinted at a bohemian side – welcomed us with scholarly grace, and duly opened up a box to reveal the first of Anna Maria Garthwaite's designs. Drawn in the wide margin at the top of a large sheet containing an elaborate floral number, this design was the epitome of restraint, with a repeated motif that resembled a bugle flower in subdued tones of purplish brown, labelled 'Mr Rondeau, Feb. 5 1741/2', and intended

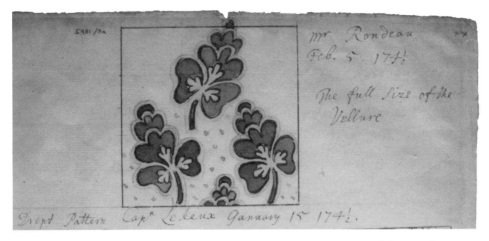

as a pattern to be woven into the body of a velour used for men's suiting.

Stanley, instinctively drawn towards his own name, leaned forward to touch the piece of paper – which caused Moira's eyes to pop, though fortunately for all concerned the priceless design was protected by a layer of transparent conservator's plastic. Once smiles of apology had been exchanged over this faux pas, Stanley enjoyed a quiet moment of contemplation, gazing with his deep-set chestnut eyes from beneath his bushy white eyebrows upon the same piece of paper that his ancestor saw. I think Stanley would have preferred it if 'Mr Rondeau' had been written beside the elaborate floral number, because he asked Moira whether the other design for John Rondeau in the collection was more colourful, but, with an unexpectedly winsome smile, Moira refused to be drawn.

Yet while Stanley's curiosity was understandably focused upon those designs attributed to his ancestor, I was enraptured by the myriad pages of designs by Anna Maria Garthwaite, whose house I walk past every day. Kept from the daylight, the colours in these sketches remain as fresh as the day she painted them in Spitalfields three centuries ago. The accurate observation of both cultivated and wild flowers in these works suggests they were painted from specimens, which permits me to surmise that she had access to a garden, and picked her wild flowers in the fields beyond Brick Lane. I especially admired the sparseness of these sprigged designs, drawing the eye to the lustrous quality of the silk, and Moira, who worked as assistant to Natalie Rothenstein – the ultimate authority on Spitalfields silk – pointed out that weavers rarely deviated from Garthwaite's designs because they were conceived with such thorough understanding of the process.

And then Moira opened the next box, to reveal the second design by Anna Maria Garthwaite for John Rondeau, which Stanley had never seen before. Larger and more complex than the previous, although monochromatic, this was a pattern of pansy or violet flowers divided by scalloped borders into a repeated design of lozenges. Again drawn in the margin, at the top of a piece of paper above a multicoloured design, this has the name 'Mr Rondeau' written in faint pencil beside it. It was a design for a damask, either for men's suiting or a woman's dress, which Moira suggested would be appropriate to be worn at the time of half-mourning – a degree of formalised grief that is unfamiliar to us, yet would have been the custom in a world where women bore many more babies in the knowledge that only a few would survive beyond childhood.

Moira took the unveiling of this second design as her opportunity to outline the speciality of master silk weaver John Rondeau, who appears to have built his fortune, and his company of fifty-seven employees, upon the production of cheaper silks for men, unlike his Spitalfields contemporary Captain Lekeux – for whom Anna Maria Garthwaite also designed – who specialised in the most expensive silks for women. In response to Moira's erudition, Stanley began to talk about his ancestor and the events of the 1740s in Spitalfields with a familiarity and grasp of detail that made it sound as if he were talking about a recent decade. And as he spoke, with the unique wealth of knowledge that he has gathered over a lifetime of research, I could see Moira becoming

drawn into Stanley's extraordinary testimony, revealing new information about this highly specialised milieu of textile production which is her particular interest. It was a true meeting of minds, and I stood by to observe the accumulation of mutual interest, as with growing delight Moira and Stanley exchanged anecdotes about their shared passion.

Recently, Stanley visited the Natural History Museum to hold the bones of his ancestor John Rondeau, which were removed there from Christ Church for study, and by seeing the designs at the Victoria and Albert Museum that once passed before John's eyes in Spitalfields, he had completed his quest. But there was a surprise in store, when Moira revealed that there were other textile designs from the nineteenth century commissioned by another Mr Rondeau, who might be a descendant – but due to a forthcoming refit of the department Stanley would have to wait a year to see them.

'It was a big day,' Stanley admitted to me afterwards, his eyes shining with emotion, as he began to absorb the reality of what he had seen. 'I'll wait a year, and then I'm going to come back,' he added with a grin of determination. It was a cliffhanger, because who knows what extravagant designs of high-flown Victoriana Mr Rondeau of the nineteenth century might have commissioned, in contrast to the understatement of his eighteenth-century predecessor?

COLUMBIA ROAD MARKET X

Human Life, Market Life

THERE WAS AN EVEN GREATER than usual bustle of activity at Columbia Road when the big trucks backed up in the darkness, and traders ran to and fro to unload hundreds of Christmas trees that had arrived from Scandinavia to grace the parlours of the East End. It was an extraordinary spectacle to come round the corner and discover the street transformed into a pine forest, with so many trees lined up in such depth as to create a magic landscape, as if – like Narnia – you could walk into a thicket and come out in another world.

At the western end of Columbia Road, I came across the tree sellers A. E. Harnett and Sons of Stock in Ingatestone, Essex, who have imported an entire forest of lus-

trous sweet-smelling pines of all sizes. Shane Harnett, a fourth- generation nurseryman, told me his family have been selling trees here on this spot in Columbia Road for over a century each Christmas. While Shane and his colleagues busied themselves marshalling their stock in preparation for a furious day's trading, his wife, Yvonne, graciously spared me a few moments for a chat, clutching a cup of hot soup and a sandwich, as we stood together, surrounded by trees in a temporary forest grove.

Throughout the year, Harnett's nursery maintains a double pitch and a casual pitch on Columbia Road, selling plants of all kinds, but for four weeks in December the entire family turns out to lend a hand with the mighty endeavour of the Christmas trees. 'Shane and the family run the nursery and I stay at home,' confided Yvonne with a smile from beneath her fur-lined hat, but that did not stop her from getting up at twenty past two this morning to be here, lending her husband a helping hand, as she has done each Christmas for the past seven years. A woman of spirit, she appeared quite unconcerned by the sub-zero temperatures. 'It's all right,' she reassured me. 'We do it every year, so we know what it's going to be like.'

HOW RAYMOND'S SHOP
BECAME LEILA'S SHOP

Past Life, Street Life

THE TOP PHOTOGRAPH of 15 Calvert Avenue is believed to have been taken one Sunday in 1900, around the time Edward, Prince of Wales and Princess Alexandra came to open the Boundary Estate, and I snapped the lower photograph more than a century later. One day, Joan Rose visited Leila's Café next door at 17 Calvert Avenue and brought out the old photograph (which she always carries in her purse) to show Leila McAlister, explaining that the little boy standing in the doorway was her father. A copy now hangs proudly in Leila's Shop, and served as the inspiration for our escapade when a class from Virginia Road School in Arnold Circus turned out to assist and we stopped the traffic to take the new picture.

Joan (née Raymond) told me that her father, Alfred, was born in 1896 and must have been four or five years old in the picture. The woman beside him in the doorway is Phoebe Raymond, his mother, Joan's grandmother, and the man on the left is his father, Joan's grandfather Albert Alfred Raymond (known as Alf), the first proprietor of the newly built shop. They all lived in the flat up above and you can just see their songbird in the cage, a cock linnet.

Phoebe has her smart apron with frills and everyone is wearing their Sunday best – remarkably for the time, everyone has good-quality boots. Observe the sacks with SPITALFIELDS printed on them, indicating produce from the fruit and vegetable market half a mile away, and the porters' baskets, which Leila still uses today. You can see the awning has been taken up to permit enough light for the photograph and then it has rained. We had the same problem with the weather, but were blessed with a few hours between a sleet shower and a blizzard to snatch our picture.

Joan Rose told me she believes her family are of Huguenot origin and the original surname was Raymond de Foir, which means the people you see in the old photograph are probably descended from the Huguenot immigrants who came here in the seventeenth century. What touched me most was to learn from Joan that her father (pictured here eternally six years old in his Sunday best, on the threshold of his father's shop) went off to fight in the First World War and, aged twenty-two, was there at the Battle of the Somme, when so many died, but returned to run the shop in Calvert Avenue, carrying on his father's business in the same

premises until his death in 1966. Joan grew up here and attended both Virginia Road School and Rochelle School on either side of Arnold Circus. Although she now lives in west London, she remains involved with her old neighbourhood today as Honorary Patron of the Friends of Arnold Circus.

Leila McAlister and Robert Bradshaw, manager of Leila's Shop (pictured on the left of the new photograph in the same spot as his predecessor a century ago), kindly organised our picture, in which the school pupils participated with such enthusiasm. Leila and Robert handed out chocolate brownies and tangerines on the pavement after the photograph was taken and a spontaneous Christmas party ensued, demonstrating that the exuberant energy of children remains a constant across the span of history defined by these two pictures.

THE BARBERS OF SPITALFIELDS

Human Life, Street Life

SPITALFIELDS IS FULL OF BARBERS, though you might not realise it at first because there are only a couple on Brick Lane (where, coincidentally, Sweeney Todd was born at No. 85 in 1756). But a foray into the sidestreets reveals more, and a stroll over towards Bethnal Green or down to Whitechapel will discover others nestling in alleys and appropriating unexpected spaces. Thankfully, most barbers remain resolute as small personal enterprises that speak of the diverse personalities of their owners and the culture of their clientele. I am fascinated by these rare places where men are constantly going to be shaved and trimmed and where, almost uniquely, it is acceptable for men to allow themselves to be vulnerable in a public place, as they

submit themselves to the barbers for intimate grooming rituals. Above all, these are masculine spaces, designed for the comfort of men, run by men for men and where women rarely venture. They are utilitarian in appearance, by contrast with the decoration of women's salons, yet I surmise that men are the more frequent visitors to their barbers.

It seems paradoxical that barbers have such large windows (although obviously good light is required for shaving with a cut-throat razor), when the activity inside is of such a private nature, possibly accounting for the predominance of barbers in sidestreets. On the day I set out to visit some barbers, I could not see into many because the windows were steamed up, creating a visible manifestation on the exterior of the emotional intensity within, and I had reason to question my own enthusiasm as I set out through the sleet on an especially grey afternoon. However, on each occasion as I stepped from the cold street into the warm humidity of the salon, I was met graciously by the barbers and their clients, who even consented to be photographed in their moment of exposure, as long as a certain distance was maintained.

As I observed the men facing up to the lens, I realised that there was an element of display involved, an element of masculine pride, even an element of vanity. Now I knew why barbers have huge windows, the expanse of glass creates a theatre where customers become protagonists in a drama enacted for the audience on the street. My assumption was confirmed when I arrived at a salon where the window was entirely free of condensation and the barber was shaving a handsome young man in the seat next to the window on to a busy street, as if to advertise the prowess of his masculine clientele, implying that any passer-by could join this rank of heroes simply by coming in for a trim.

Starting in Brick Lane, I wove my way through the sidestreets on my bizarre pilgrimage, drifting down through Whitechapel and further south as far as Commercial Road in the unrelenting damp. I visited big salons and tiny salons, full salons and empty salons, sleek new salons and crummy old parlours. And every one secured a different place in my heart, because each possessed a different poetry, a poetry that celebrates human life and hopes, containing the mundane need to be tidy alongside the aspiration to be your best. The humble barber's shop is an oasis of peace and reflection, where cares are shorn away to allow a fresh start. This is where men go to get renewed.

I was told to seek out Charlie, a legendary barber in Stepney, and eventually I found him exactly where I was told he would be, except that his name was Michael, but I was still delighted to encounter this genial Turkish barber, who without a doubt was the afternoon's star turn. To the uninitiated, Michael Gent's Hair Stylists at 345 Commercial Road is the most unremarkable barber's shop you could imagine, but this modest salon has been in operation for over a century. Michael, a sprightly garrulous mustachioed gentleman in a neat blue overall jacket, who has been cutting hair here for thirty-two years, told me he took

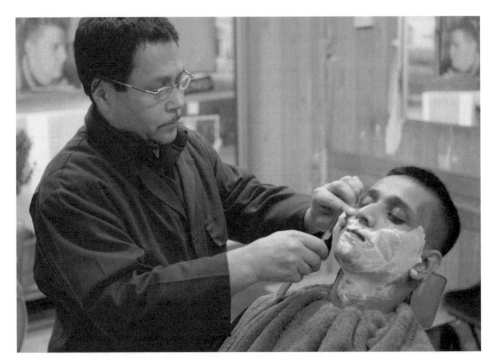

over from Maurice Pem, a Jewish barber, who was here for thirty-six years and whose unknown predecessor cut hair for at least forty years before that.

'All the time, I miss Istanbul,' revealed Michael, striking a pensive note, mid-haircut, gazing out at the low cloud in Stepney, as if he could see the minarets of the Blue Mosque emerging from the haze. 'The city is like a dream.' A moment of nostalgia before Michael declared himself an Anglophile. 'I love this country, the democracy – the country of equality and opportunities,' he said. Then, without a break in our conversation, he completed the haircut, unsheathing a ferocious cut-throat razor and tidying up the edges automatically before

instructing his amiable teenage son to lather up the young man swathed in a red towel, prior to a shave. I could not but admire the faith of this fellow in the chair, who never even blinked when Michael casually suggested his son might like to have a go with the razor to practise his shaving technique. I did not like to ask if it was appropriate to practise on customers with a cut-throat razor. If the young man had flinched, he might have lost his nose, and I could barely draw breath as Michael berated his son's clumsy attempts at scraping the stubble, causing the unfortunate apprentice to redden with frustration.

It was a great relief to all concerned when Michael took over from his son again, flashing a professional smile and gripping the young man's face firmly in one hand while using the other to skim the razor over his jaw with bold strokes – demonstrating, as if to an invisible lecture theatre, exactly how it should be done. With a skill his son will master one day, Michael achieved results almost instantly, pinching the customer's face and caressing his skin proudly. 'Look at that, as smooth as a baby's bottom!' he announced in unselfconscious triumph to the entire salon with a smirk, patting the young man's cheek with proprietorial affection.

CAPTAIN SHIV BANERJEE

JUSTICE OF THE PEACE

Human Life, Past Life

THIS IS SHIV BANERJEE – the captain at the wheel of his ship – on the long voyage that led from his birth in Kailash Ghosh Lane in Dhaka, East Bengal, in 1945, to Toynbee Hall in Commercial Street, Spitalfields, where he resides today. In fact, the accommodation block at the rear of Toynbee Hall has so many staircases opening on to galleries, with lines of neat front doors stretching in every direction, that it does have a certain nautical aspect to it, and on the upper terrace, where Shiv has his flat, there is even a metal rail just like that on a ship – except, when you peer over, you discover Gunthorpe Street below rather than the roaring ocean.

We met at the introduction of Muktha, waiter at Herb & Spice, from where it was a short hop down Commercial Street to Toynbee Hall, and as I walked through the courtyards with Shiv, other residents nodded

and waved in respectful acknowledgement, reinforcing my feeling that I was accompanying the captain of the vessel. So when I entered his quarters, it was no surprise to discover a model ship in the living room of his modest yet comfortably furnished flat. We had arrived at the chosen location for Captain Banerjee to tell me about his extraordinary journey.

'I was born in Kailash Ghosh Lane in Dhaka, and when I was two months old I was brought to New Delhi, where I lived in the government houses at Lake Square, designed by Edwin Lutyens. I'd never seen the sea when I applied to be a cadet, but I wanted to go to different places. I applied for the exam in 1962 and didn't get selected for interview – about 55,000 people applied for seventy-five places and they only interviewed 120. But I didn't give up and I studied civil engineering for a year before I was accepted on the *Dufferin*, the British Navy's cadet ship for Indians, Burmese, Ceylonese and Singaporeans.

'It was a lonely life but I learned to like it because I had never known anything better. I was sixteen years old and earning beyond what anyone in my family had ever earned before, and the uniform was very attractive to women too. I became an officer at twenty-one and when I went back to Lake Square and got out from the taxi, everyone would come and say, "Here is the hero!" Everyone was very proud of me and I was very proud of myself.

'In 1966, I visited Liverpool. It was wonderful. I thought, "All the white people will be there and all the important people will be there too." Going ashore was exciting, I had my first fish and chips and went out and saw the sights. At the Seaman's Club, *Top of the Pops* was on the television and I saw the Beatles. Everything excited me, nothing was depressing or bad. I came from a poor background and everything was free on board ship and I had money to spend on shore. It was one of the most exciting times in my life.

'Then, in 1972, I came to London to study for my master's ticket, so I could captain a ship – because if you had it from London, you were "Made in England" and you could work anywhere in the world. At Heathrow, I was asked a lot of questions and the official wasn't very polite. "Have you got enough money?" he asked me. "I've got 5,000 pounds in cash," I said. Then I took a taxi to Lancaster Gate and it was very expensive and I was pick-pocketed seventy-five pounds in the street on the first day. So I moved down to stay at Queen Victoria's Seamen's Rest in the East India Dock Road and went to study at the School of Navigation at Tower Hill.

'A priest in New Zealand once told me that Toynbee Hall in Commercial Street was the place to stay, so I went to find out more. They interviewed me and said I could stay for free for two nights and see how we got on. We all used to eat together then, it was very communal. I loved it. I said, "I'll stay here." And it was where I met my wife, who was a teacher at Christ Church School. This woman asked, "Can you teach me Bengali?" and I fell in love with her and didn't pass my exam. We moved in together to a flat in Sunley House, Toynbee Hall, at twelve pounds fifty per week, including heating, maintenance and service charge. Finally, in 1977, I passed my captain's exam and I told my wife, "I'll take you to sea." She said, "Either you stay here with me, or I change the locks on the door and get a new man." So I gave up my sea career, but I said, "Let's decide a few things. You are white and I am black. Our children will not know if they are black or white, so we will not have children." Next day, I went and had a vasectomy done and then I took her to sea for a year before we settled here. I came on land but I had no job.

'I became a volunteer for a year and a half, working at the Attlee Adventure Playground off Brick Lane, and then Donald Chesworth, Warden of Toynbee Hall, said, "I'll raise the money to pay you." In those days, the staff was entirely white. I went off to sea for six months to earn some money and he sent a cable to say I was offered the job of Volunteer Coordinator and Education Outreach Officer and I became the first black worker to be employed by Toynbee Hall. I launched an out-of-hours project for old people – if something went wrong at night, we would come and see to it – and I also worked with mentally and physically handicapped children. Toynbee Hall became my home. I decided it was my job to keep it neat and clean, although no one had given me that job. I was a proud person to keep this place clean.

'Then I joined the Inner London Education Authority as a social worker, but as I still did not have any qualification on land, I did a research diploma at the City Lit on barriers to education for Bangladeshi children. Next I worked in the homeless families' team. There were so many children out of school because their families were being housed in hotels. I negotiated with teachers to get them places in schools and I set up a homeless families' project in a church hall in Finsbury Park. Until then, the only entertainment for these people was making babies – sex and sex and sex, education was not in it.

'But I was getting tired, and John Profumo, CBE, Chairman of Toynbee Hall, took me under his wing and took me to the Reform Club, where I met the good and the great. And in 1984 he called me and said, "Do you want to be a magistrate?" I said, "I am not legally qualified. I only know about ship captain's law," but Lord Ponsonby, CEO of British Home Stores and a retired brigadier, said, "Put me down as your referee." They asked me to apply and I got it. I was the first Bengali-speaking justice of the peace.

'I consider language to be the basis of everything – knowledge of English language, both spoken and written. And I always felt that, for an individual, if they are to stay in this country, they have to know the language. In the past, people always said yes to everything, because they were not able to express their needs. I started to teach English to blind people and encouraged the families in the Finsbury Park homeless families' project to learn English together, because I still feel strongly that lack of education is the main barrier to progress.'

Shiv's voyage was guided by an instinctive moral compass, granting him a natural authority today, even though he refrains from asserting his status. Somehow, he discovered a sympathetic crossover from his life on board ship, with its respectfully structured society, to the civilian world – employing both his organisational skills and his sense of humanity too.

With quiet courtesy and dressing in undemonstrative formal clothes, Shiv has devoted himself to a life of usefulness. It is rare to meet someone as open as Shiv, a shrewd man with a clear conscience, who can speak without subtext and use plain words to tell you exactly what he means. Never cynical nor flippant, Captain Shiv Banerjee, Justice of the Peace, has an openhearted vocation to serve his people.

MR PUSSY IN WINTER

Animal Life

ON MIDWINTER'S NIGHT – the longest night of the year – Mr Pussy will not stir from the chimney corner. Warmed by the fire of burning pallets, he has no need of whisky to bring him solace through the dark hours. Instead he frazzles his brain in a heat-induced trance.

Outside in the streets, Spitalfields lies under snow, the paths are coated in sheet ice and icicles hang from the gutters, but this spectacle holds no interest for Mr Pussy. Like the cavemen of ancient times, his sole fascination is with the mesmerising dance of flames in the grate. And as the season descends towards its nadir in the plunging temperatures of the frozen byways, at home Mr Pussy falls into his own warm darkness of stupefaction.

Mr Pussy is getting old. The world is no longer new to him and his curiosity is tempered now by his love of sleeping. Once he was a brat in jet black, now he is a gentleman in a chenille velvet suit, and tufts of white hairs increasingly fleck his glossy pelt. Towards the end of summer, I noticed he was getting skinny, and then I discovered that his teeth had gone, which meant he could no longer crunch the hard biscuits that were always his delight. Extraordinarily, he made little protest at his starvation diet, even as he lost weight through lack of food. Now I fill his dish with biscuits and top it up with water, so that he may satisfy his hunger by supping the resulting slush. And through this simple accommodation – plus a supplement of raw meat – his weight

is restored to normal and he purrs in gratification while eating again.

Once Mr Pussy was a wild rover, ranging over the fields in Devon, disappearing for days on end and returning proudly with a dead rabbit in his mouth. Now he does not step beyond the end of the alley in Spitalfields and in these sub-zero temperatures goes outside only to do his necessary business. Sprinting up the stairs and calling impatiently outside the door of the living room, he is ever eager to return to the fireside and warm his cold toes afterwards, sore from scraping at the frost in the vain attempt to dig a hole in the frozen earth. Like a visionary poet, Mr Pussy has acquired a vivid internal life to insulate himself against the rigours of the world and, in the absence of sunlight, the fire provides his refuge, engendering a sublime reverie of peace and physical ease.

Yet Mr Pussy still loves to fight. If he hears cats screeching in the yard, he will race from the house to join the fray unless I can shut the door first and prevent him. And even when he has been injured and comes back leaking blood from huge wounds, he appears quite unconcerned. Only two small notches in his ears exist as permanent evidence of this violent tendency, although today I regularly check his brow for telltale scratches and recently he has acquired some deep bloody furrows that have caused swelling around his eyes. But I cannot stop him going out, even though it is a matter of concern to me that – as he ages and his reflexes lessen – he might get blinded in a fight one day, losing one of his soulful golden

bound. He can still bring in a live mouse from the garden when he pleases and delightedly crunch its skull between his jaws on the bedroom floor. If I work late into the night, he will still cry and tug on the bed sheets to waken me in the early morning to see the falling snow. When the fancy seizes him, he can be as sprightly as a kitten. Come the spring, he will be running up trees again, even if now – in the darkest depth of winter – he wants only to sleep by the fire.

Alone in the old house in Spitalfields, Mr Pussy is my sole companion, the perfect accomplice for a writer. When I take to my bed to keep warm while writing my stories, he is always there as the silent assistant, curled into a ball upon the sheepskin coverlet. As the years have gone by and Mr Pussy strays less from the house, I have grown accustomed to his constant presence. He has taught me that, rather than fear for his well-being, I need to embrace all the circumstances and seasons that life sends, just as he does.

eyes. Since he is blissfully unaware of this possibility, I must take consolation from his response when he could not eat, revealing that Mr Pussy has no expectations of life and consequently no fear of loss. His nature is to make his best accommodation to any exigency with grace.

And be assured, Mr Pussy can still leap up on to the kitchen counter in a single

MAURICE FRANKLIN
WOOD TURNER

Human Life, Past Life

IF YOU WERE to rise before dawn on Christmas Eve and walk down the empty Hackney Road past the dark shopfronts in the early morning, you would very likely see a mysterious glow emanating from the workshop at the rear of No. 45, where spindles for staircases are made. If you were to stop and press your face against the glass, peering further into the depths of the gloom, you would see a shower of wood chips flying magically into the air, illuminated by a single light, and falling like snow into the shadowy interior of the workshop where wood turner Maurice Franklin, who was born upstairs above the shop in 1920, has been working at his lathe since 1933, when he began his apprenticeship.

In the days when Maurice started out, Shoreditch was the centre of the furniture industry. But it has all gone long ago – except for Maurice, who has carried on regardless, working at his lathe. Now, at ninety-one years old, being in semi-retirement, Maurice comes in a few days each week, driving down from North Finchley in the early hours to work from four or five until eight or nine in the morning, whenever he fancies exercising his remarkable talent at wood turning.

Make no mistake, Maurice is a virtuoso. When rooms at Windsor Castle burned out a few years ago, the Queen asked Maurice to make a new set of spindles for her staircase and invited him to tea to thank him for it too. 'Did you grow up in the East End?' she enquired politely, and when Maurice nodded in modest confirmation of this, she extended her sympathy to him. 'That must have been hard,' she responded with an empathetic smile, although with characteristic frankness Maurice disagreed. 'I had a loving family,' he told her plainly. 'That's all you need for a happy childhood. You don't need palaces for that.'

Ofer Moses, who runs the Spindle Shop – in the former premises of Franklin and Sons – usually leaves a list for Maurice, detailing the work that is required, and when he returns next morning he finds the completed wood turning awaiting him, every piece perfectly achieved. But by then Maurice will already be gone, vanished like a shade of the night. So, in order to snatch a conversation with such an elusive character, a certain strategy was necessary which required Ofer's collaboration. Early one frosty morning recently, he waited outside the shop in his car until I arrived and then, once we had checked that there was a light glimmering inside the shop, he unlocked the door and we went in together to discover the source of the illumination. Sure enough, the wood chips were flying, accompanied by the purr of the motor that powered the lathe, and hunched over it was a figure in a blue jacket and black cap, liberally scattered with chips and sawdust. This was Maurice.

Unaware of our presence, he continued with his all-engaging task, and we stood mesmerised by the sight of the master at work, recognising that we were just in time to catch him as he finished off the last spindles to complete a pristine set. And then, as he placed the final spindle on the stack, Maurice looked up in surprise to see us standing there and a transformation came upon him, as with a twirl he removed his overall and cap, sending a shower of wood chips fluttering. The wood turner that we saw hunched over the lathe a moment before was no more and Maurice stood at his full height with arms outstretched, assuming a relaxed posture with easy grace, as he greeted us with a placid smile.

'This firm was the wood-turning champion of Britain in 1928,' he announced with a flourish. 'Samuel, my father, had been apprenticed in Romania and was in the Romanian army for two years before he came here at the beginning of the twentieth century, and then he served in the British army in the 14–18 war before he opened this place in 1920. He had been taught by the village wood worker in Romania. They made everything from cradles to coffins. All the boys used to sleep on a shelf under the bench then.'

Maurice told me he was one of a family of twelve – six boys and six girls – and he indicated the mark in the floor where the staircase once ascended to the quarters where they all lived. 'I started when I was thirteen. I've still got my indenture papers,' he informed me conscientiously, just in case I wanted to check the veracity of his claim. 'I took to it from the start. It's creative and at the end of the day you see what you've made. I'm proud of everything I do or I wouldn't do it.'

In spite of his remarkable age, Maurice's childhood world remains vivid to him. 'Here in Shoreditch, 90 per cent were Jewish and the ones that weren't were Jewish in their own way. Over in Hoxton, they'd take your tie off you when you arrived and sell it back to you when you left – but now you couldn't afford to go there. In 1925 you could buy a house in Boundary Street for 200 pounds, or you could put down a pound deposit and pay the rest off at three shillings a week. I was born here in 1920 and I went to Rochelle School – they won't remember me.'

The only time Maurice left his lathe was to go and fight in the Second World War, when, although he was offered war work making stretcher poles, he chose instead to enlist for Special Operations. Afterwards, Franklin and Sons expanded through acquiring the first automatic lathe from America, and opening a factory in Hackney Wick to mass-produce table legs. 'Eventually we closed it up because everyone was getting older, except me,' quipped Maurice with a tinge of melancholy. As the last of his generation now, he carries the stories of a world known directly only to a dwindling few.

Yet Maurice still enjoys a busy social calendar, giving frequent lectures about classical music – the other passion in his life. 'I especially like Verdi, Puccini and Rossini,' he declared, twinkling with bright-eyed enthusiasm, because having made chairs for the Royal Opera House he is a frequent visitor there. 'I like all music except Wagner. You'll never hear me listening to Wagner, because he was Hitler's favourite composer,' he added, changing tone and catching my eye to make a point. The comment led me to enquire if Maurice had ever gone back to Romania in search of his roots. 'I've

got no family there. They were all wiped out in the war. My father brought his close relatives over, but those that stayed ended up in Auschwitz,' he confided to me with a sombre grimace. 'Now you know why I wanted to go to war.'

And then, after we had shared a contemplative silence, Maurice's energy lifted again, pursuing a different thought. 'I remember the great yo-yo craze of the 1930s,' he said, his eyes meeting mine in excitement. 'We worked twenty-four hours a day.'

'What's the secret?' I asked Maurice, curious at his astonishing vitality, and causing him to break into a smile of wonderment at my question.

'All you've got to do is keep on living, and then you can do it. It isn't very difficult,' he said, spreading his arms demonstratively and shaking his head in disbelief at my obtuseness.

'Are you happy?' I queried, provocative in my eagerness to seize this opportunity of learning something about being a nonagenarian.

'I'll tell you why I am happy,' said Maurice with a grin of unqualified delight and raising one hand to count off his blessings. 'I've got a wonderful family and wonderful children. I've been successful and I've got an appetite for life, and I've eaten every day and slept every night.'

Maurice was on a roll now. 'I was going to write a book once,' he continued, 'but there's no time in this life. By the time you know how to live, it's over. This life is like a dress rehearsal, you just make it up as you go along. One life is not enough. Everyone should live twice.'

There was only one obvious question left to ask Maurice Franklin, so I asked it, and his response was automatic and immediate. 'Yes, I'd be a wood turner again,' he said, with absolute certainty.

ON CHRISTMAS NIGHT IN THE CITY

Night Life, Street Life

FORTIFIED BY A LATE SUPPER of lamb cutlets, I set out after eleven through the streets of Spitalfields just as some of the residents were making their way to Christ Church for the midnight service, but I did not join them. Instead I walked out into the City on Christmas Eve. As I passed through Brick Lane, the ever-optimistic curry touts were touting to an empty street and in Commercial Street a few stragglers who had been out for the night loitered, but I left them all behind as I entered the City of London, where there was no one. Passing through the deserted Leadenhall Market,

illuminated like a fairground, I slipped into the web of narrow alleys to emerge at the Bank of England. Here where the Bank, the Mansion House and the Royal Exchange face each other at this famous crossroads, the place was empty save for a lonely policeman patrolling outside the Bank of England.

I headed down to the river and as I crossed the footbridge above the dark water, with powerful currents churning in the depths below, I could enjoy the panorama of the vast city of empty rooms around me. Tonight, I was the sole rambler through its passages and byways, an explorer in the unknown territory of the familiar city, transformed by the complete absence of inhabitants. The sound of the gulls' cry registered as it had not before and birdsong followed me throughout my journey into the dark streets, in which for the first time ever I heard the echo of my own footsteps in the centre of London.

Yet just as I had befriended the emptiness, I came round a corner in Southwark to see the cathedral glowing with light and the tune of a carol blowing on the breeze. I stepped down to the cathedral door and discovered a candlelit service in progress. An usher saw me through the glass door and, although I kept a respectful distance, imbued with the generosity of the season, he could not resist coming outside to lead me in. Before I knew it, I was in the midst of the service and it was an overwhelming contrast to the cold dark streets to which I had acclimatised. But once the bishop had led the choir in procession through a haze of incense as the congregation sang 'O Come, All Ye Faithful', the service was over. So as quickly as I arrived, I was able to return to my wandering.

Hastening eastward along the Thames, I came to Tower Bridge, where I crossed and skirted around the Tower of London. In the absence of floodlighting, its grim austerity came to the fore, yet even though all the gates were shut for the night I could see a few of the residents' individual lights still burning within. From here I set out westward, along Cheapside and Cannon Street, where I came upon the fabled London Stone, built into an illuminated box in the wall, as I was passing on my way to St Paul's. Here also the floodlighting was off, allowing Wren's great cathedral to loom magnificently among the trees like some natural excrescence, a towering cliff of rock eroded into pinnacles.

Winding my way onwards along the Strand through the courtyards and alleys, I found myself in Lincoln's Inn Fields and had it to myself. And in homage to the writer most famous for his walks by night through London, I visited the Old Curiosity Shop. Already, the night was drawing on and I discovered a sense of urgency, walking on purposefully even though I did not know where I was going. At the Savoy I turned down Carting Lane, where I came upon one of just three people I saw suffering the misfortune of sleeping out that night, though equally I was also aware of many bundled up in dark clothing with backpacks walking slowly and keeping in the shadows. I could only presume that these people were walking all night in preference to sleeping in the frost.

I followed the Embankment along to Parliament Square, where there was no one apart from the anti-war protesters sleeping peacefully in their tents and statues of dead men standing around on plinths. Big Ben struck three in the morning and, without any traffic, I could sense the sound travelling around me, bouncing and reverberating off the stone buildings as I made my way up Whitehall. Coming to the end of Downing Street, two policemen with machine guns on duty behind the fortifications spotted me, the lone figure in the street,

and I realised they were focusing on me. Then, to my surprise, one waved, and so I returned the wave automatically and the atmosphere of unease was broken.

There were plenty of taxis for hire circling Trafalgar Square – they were the only traffic on the road by this time – but absurdly there were no customers to take them. Looking through Admiralty Arch, I espied Buckingham Palace tempting me, and I wanted to go walking around St James's Palace too, but weariness was also coming upon me. It was time to return home. I walked doggedly across Covent Garden, along Holborn and over Smithfield, then through the Barbican and so I found myself in Spitalfields again.

London was as still as the grave and there was a keen edge to the wind, yet I had kept warm by walking continuously. It was as though I had travelled through a dream – a dream of an empty city. Although I delighted in the privilege of having London to myself, it is an alien place with nobody in it, so I was eager to renounce my monopoly and give the city back to everyone else again, because I longed for the reassurance of my warm bed.

Already children were waking to unwrap parcels that had appeared mysteriously in the night, although I must confess I saw no evidence of nocturnal deliveries upon my walk. It was now four thirty on Christmas morning and as I approached my front door, even before I took out the key to place it in the lock, a cry of a certain cat was heard from just inside, where he had been waiting upon my return for all this time.

MY QUILT

ALL THE STORIES I have written this winter were written beneath this quilt, that I made a few years ago and which has special meaning for me. Once the snow began before Christmas, I retreated to my bed to work each day, abandoning my desk, which was disappearing under piles of paper, and taking consolation in the warmth and comfort under my quilt, as the ideal location to write. While the deep freeze overtook the city and snow whirled outside, I was happy there – secure in my private space, working through the long dark nights in Spitalfields.

This is the only quilt I have ever made and I make no claims for my ability as a stitcher, which is functional rather than demonstrating any special skill. Once I made a shirt that I sewed by hand, copying the pattern from one I already had, and it took me a week, with innumerable unpicking and resewing as I took the pieces apart and reassembled them until I achieved something wearable. It was a beautiful way to spend a week, sitting cross-legged sewing on the floor, and although I am proud of the shirt I made, I shall not attempt it again.

My quilt is significant because I made it to incarnate the memory of my mother, and as a means to manifest the warmth I drew from her, illustrating it with the lyrical imagery that I associate with her – something soft and rich in colour that I could enfold myself in, something that would be present in my daily life to connect me to my childhood, when I existed solely within the tender cocoon of my parents' affections. My sweetest memories are of being tucked up in bed as a child and of my parents lying beside me for ten minutes until I drifted off.

For several years, after the death of my father, I nursed my mother as she succumbed to the dementia that paralysed her, took away her nature, her mind, her faculties and eventually her life. It was an all-consuming task, both physically and emotionally, being a housewife, washing bed sheets constantly, cooking food, and feeding and tending to her as she declined slowly through months and years. And when it was over, at first I did not know what to do next.

One day, I saw a woollen tapestry at a market of a fisherman in a souwester. This sentimental image spoke to me, like a picture in a children's book, and evoked Cornwall, where my mother was born. It was made from a kit and entailed hours of skilful work, yet was on sale for a couple of pounds and so I bought it. At once, I discovered that there were lots of these tapestries around that no one wanted and I was drawn to collect them. Many were in stilted designs and crude colours, but it did not matter to me because I realised they look better the more you have, and it satisfied me to gather these unloved artefacts that had been created at the expense of so much labour and expertise, mostly – I suspected – by old women.

I have taught myself to be unsentimental about death itself, and I believe that human remains are merely remains – of no greater meaning than toenails or hair clippings. After their demise, the quality of a person does not reside within the body – and so I chose to have no tombstone for my parents and I shall not return to their grave.

Instead, through making a quilt, I found an active way to engage with my emotion at the loss of a parent and create something I can keep by me in fond remembrance for always.

I laid out the tapestries upon the floor and arranged them. When I realised I needed many more, I discovered there were hundreds for sale online. And soon they began to arrive in the mail every day. And the more I searched, the more discriminating I became, searching out the most beautiful and those with pictures which I could arrange to create a visual poem of all the things my mother loved – even the work of her favourite artists, Vermeer, Millet, Degas and Lowry, as well as animals, especially birds, and flowers, and the fishing boats and seascapes of her childhood beside the Cornish coast.

Over months, as the quilt came together, there were plenty of rejections and substitutions in the pursuit of my obsession to create the most beautiful arrangement possible. A room of the house was devoted to the quilt, where my cat, Mr Pussy, came to lie upon the fragments each day, to keep me company while I sat there alone for hours contemplating all the tapestries – shuffling them to discover the best juxtapositions of picture and colour, as each new arrival in the mail engendered different possibilities. The natural tones of the woollen dyes gave the quilt a rich luminous glow of colour and I was always aware of the hundreds of hours of work employed by those whose needlecraft was of a far greater quality than mine. After consideration, a soft lemon yellow velvet was sought out to line it, and a thin wadding was inserted to give it substance and warmth but not to be too heavy for a summer night.

It took me a year to make the quilt. From the first night, it has delighted me and I have slept beneath it ever since. I love to wake to see its colours and the pictures that I know so well, and it means so much to have the comfort of my beautiful quilt of memories of my mother to keep me warm and safe for the rest of my life.

NIGHT AT THE BRICK LANE BEIGEL BAKERY

Culinary Life, Night Life

NEW YEAR'S EVE is always the busiest night of the year at the Brick Lane Beigel Bakery. So I chose to spend a night accompanying Sammy Minzly, the manager of this peerless East End institution, to observe the activity through the early hours as the staff braced themselves for the rush. Yet even though this was a quiet night – relatively speaking – there was already helter-skelter in the kitchen when I arrived mid-evening to discover five bakers working at furious pace among clouds of steam to produce 3,000 beigels, as they do every day of the year between six at night and one in the morning.

At the centre of this tiny bakery which

occupies a lean-to at the rear of the shop, beigels boiled in a vat of hot water. From here, the glistening babies were scooped up in a mesh basket, doused mercilessly with cold water, then arranged neatly on to narrow wet planks named 'shebas', and inserted into the ovens by Stephen, the skinny garrulous baker who has spent his entire life on Brick Lane, working here in the kitchen since the age of fifteen. Between the ovens sat an ogre of a huge dough-making machine, mixing all the ingredients for the beigels, bread and cakes that are sold here. It was a cold night in Spitalfields, but it was sweltering here in the steamy atmosphere of the kitchen, where the speedy bakers exerted themselves to the limit, as they hauled great armfuls of dough out of the big metal basin in a hurry, plonking it down, kneading it vigorously, then chopping it up quickly and using scales to divide it into lumps sufficient to make twenty beigels – before another machine separated them into beigel-sized spongy balls of dough, ripe for transformation.

In the thick of this frenzied whirl of sweaty masculine endeavour – accompanied by the blare of the football on the radio, and raucous horseplay in different languages – stood Mr Sammy, a white-haired gentleman of diminutive stature, quietly taking the balls of dough and feeding them into the machine which delivers recognisable beigels on a conveyor belt at the other end, ready for immersion in hot water. In spite of the steamy hullabaloo in the kitchen, Mr Sammy carries an aura of calm, working at his own pace and, even at seventy-five years

old, he still pursues his labours all through the night, long after the bakers have departed to their beds. He has been working here since the beigel bakery opened at these premises in 1976, although he told me proudly that the Brick Lane Beigel Bakery superseded that of Lieberman's fifty-five years ago. Today it is celebrated as the most visible legacy of the Jewish culture that once defined Spitalfields.

Hovering at the entrance to the kitchen, I had only to turn my head to witness the counterpoint drama of the beigel shop, where hordes of hungry east Londoners line up all night, craving spiritual consolation in the form of beigels and hot salt beef. They come in sporadic waves, clubbers and party animals, insomniacs and sleepwalkers, hipsters and losers, street people and homeless people, cab drivers and firemen, police and dodgy dealers, working girls and binmen. Some can barely stand because they are so drunk, while others can barely keep their eyes open because they are so tired. Some can barely control their joy and others can barely conceal their misery. At times it was like the madhouse and at other times it was like the morgue. Irrespective, everyone at the beigel bakery keeps working, keeping the beigels coming, slicing them, filling them, counting them and sorting them. And the presiding spirit is Mr Sammy. Standing behind the counter, he checks every beigel personally to maintain quality control and tosses aside any that are too small or too toasted in unhesitating disdain.

As manager, Mr Sammy is the only one

whose work crosses both territories, moving back and forth all night between the kitchen and the shop, where he enjoys affectionate widespread regard from his customers. Every other person calls out 'Sammy!' or 'Mr Sammy' as they come through the door if he is in the shop – asking 'Where's Sammy?' if he is not, and wanting their beigels reheated in the oven as an excuse to step into the kitchen and enjoy a quiet word with him there. Only once did I find Mr Sammy resting, sitting peacefully on the salt bin in the empty kitchen in the middle of the night, long after all the bakers had left and the shop had emptied out. 'I'm getting lazy! I'm not doing nothing,' he exclaimed in alarmed self-recognition. 'I'd better do something, I'd better count some beigels.'

Later he boiled 150 eggs and peeled them, as he told me about Achmed, the cleaner, known as 'donkey' – 'because he can sleep anywhere' – whose arrival was imminent. 'He sleeps upstairs,' revealed Mr Sammy, pointing at the ceiling. 'He lives upstairs?' I enquired, looking up. 'No, he only sleeps there, but he doesn't like to pay rent, so he works as a cleaner,' explained Mr Sammy with an indulgent grin. Shortly after, when a doddery fellow arrived with frowsy eyes and sat eating a hot slice of cake from the oven, I gathered this was the gentleman in question. 'I peeled the eggs

for you,' Mr Sammy informed him encouragingly, a gesture that was reciprocated by 'donkey' with the merest nod. 'He's seventytwo,' Mr Sammy informed me later in a sympathetic whisper.

Witnessing the homeless man who came to collect a pound coin from Mr Sammy nightly and another of limited faculties who merely sought the reassurance of a regular handshake, I understood that, because it is always open, the Beigel Bakery exists as a touchstone for many people who have little else in life, and who come to acknowledge Mr Sammy as the one constant presence. With gentle charisma, Mr Sammy fulfils the role of spiritual leader and keeps the bakery

running smoothly too. After a busy Christmas week, he was getting low on bags for beigels and was concerned he had missed his weekly delivery from Paul Gardner because of the holiday. The morning was drawing near and I knew that Paul was opening that day for the first time after the break, so I elected to walk round to Gardners' Market Sundriesmen in Commercial Street. Sure enough, on the dot of six thirty, Paul arrived full of good humour to discover me and other customers waiting. The customers dispatched, Paul locked the shop again and we drove round to deliver the 25,000 to 30,000 brown paper bags that comprise the beigel shop's weekly order.

Mr Sammy's eyes lit up to see Paul carrying the packets of bags through the door in preparation for New Year's Eve and then, in celebration of the festive season, before I made my farewells and retired to my bed, I took advantage of the opportunity to photograph these two friends and long-term associates together – both representatives of traditional businesses that between them carry significant aspects of the history and identity of Spitalfields.

EXPLORE SPITALFIELDS
IN THE FOOTSTEPS OF THE
GENTLE AUTHOR

I OFFER THESE TWO WALKS AND A DETOUR as a guide to lead you
to some of the people and places in this book. Each of the walks may be
followed as it is given, or you can select from the destinations to make
your own path.

FROM LIVERPOOL STREET
TO LEILA'S

1. When you come out of Liverpool Street Station (see page 218) into Bishopsgate, cross the busy road and walk up New Street directly opposite, with the tall brick warehouses of the former East India Company to your right. Turn left at the Magpie into an alley which leads to an imposing gateway with a huge statue of a ram atop. Take courage and follow this alley as it narrows through twists and turns to left and right, between high walls, because it will deliver you to Spitalfields.

2. At the end of the alley, you will find yourself in Middlesex Street beside a yellow mural by Ben Eine (see page 255). If it is Sunday, the street will be crowded by the stalls of the famous Petticoat Lane Market (see page 105). Cross the road towards the tower opposite and enter Sandys Row on your left. Look out for a manhole cover, fifty yards to the right in the centre of the street, which has the Star of David at the centre of its design, a enigmatic reminder that this was once the Jewish quarter.

3. Here, in Sandys Row, among the echoey narrow streets at the edge of Spitalfields, you will find Spitalfields' last synagogue,

housed in a former Huguenot Chapel of 1766. If you ask for Jeremy Freedman – his ancestors first came to Spitalfields as tobacco dealers in the seventeenth century and his great-great-great-great-grandfather Alfred Freedman was one of those who founded this synagogue in 1854 – he may be persuaded to give you a tour.

4. Leading off to the right from Sandys Row is Artillery Passage. At the top you will discover Alexander Boyd, the tailor's shop, where you can drop in to meet master cutter Clive Phythian, who is always happy to show the work he has in hand.

5. Opposite Alexander Boyd, high on the wall at the corner of Artillery Passage, you will see one of the characteristic vertical arrows that mark a corner of the Artillery Ground created on this site by Henry VIII. Ahead of you is the former Sisters of Mercy night shelter, where you may still observe the worn steps at the entrance and read the words 'Men' and 'Women' above the doors. On the right are two of London's oldest shopfronts, built by Huguenot silk merchants in the rococo style, dating from the 1750s.

6. Turn left and walk down Artillery Lane. Those requiring a takeaway snack or cup of tea might like to continue on to the Mister City Sandwich Bar at No. 7, which is run by Roberto and Mirella Fiori and their son Daniele, with the assistance of Les Wilkes. Open from early, this tiny establishment is superior to the chains that surround it.

7. Otherwise, walk along Gun Street to emerge into Brushfield Street, with Christ Church, Spitalfields, in the distance to your right. The contrast is startling as you leave the domestic scale of the ancient streets to cross the open space between the twenty-first-century blocks of Norman Foster's Bishop's Square.

8. Cast your eyes down as you pass the entrance of Allen & Overy to view the medieval charnel house preserved under glass beneath your feet. It is all that survives of the leper hospital founded by Walter Brunus in 1197 which gave the place its name, St Mary's Hospital Fields, hence Spitalfields. Crossing these precincts, be aware that you are walking upon the site of a Roman cemetery and also of the garden where Nicholas Culpeper grew his herbs. Passing Bishop's Square, you come to Spital Square, where a similar leap of the imagination is required. The former board school and a few terraced houses are all that remain to remind us of this once grand old square.

9. Step across one block and you are in Folgate Street. Here Dennis Severs created his spellbinding time-capsule house at No. 18, where the sights, sounds, smells and the darkness of old London still linger. If you are not going to pay a visit, then peer through the lattice into the dining room on the ground floor and look down through the skylight into the cellar, where you might catch a glimpse of Madge, the cat, sleeping by the range (see page 133 and 290).

10. Walk up Elder Street, between terraces of tottering eighteenth-century houses. Look out for the flying freehold at No. 36 and the surreal eighteenth-century wood graining at No. 15 on the other side of the street.

11. Cross Commercial Street to enter Quaker Street and walk 100 yards past an imposing nineteenth-century railway warehouse to your left and a post-war public-housing development on your right, until you come upon Quaker Court, a small row of industrial units also on your right. The first of these is Crescent Trading, Spitalfields' last cloth warehouse (closed Saturday), where you will meet Philip Pittack and Martin White – the Mike and Bernie Winters of the rag trade – selling ends of runs of quality fabrics at bargain prices and delivering ceaseless repartee (see page 308).

12. Turn right along Quaker Street when you leave Crescent Trading with your bargain parcel of cloth under your arm. Within minutes you are in Brick Lane, the conduit of life in Spitalfields. Turn left and walk up the Lane. Look out for Pedley Street on your right, Spitalfields' smelliest alley but also where the East End's most vigorous fig trees flourish. If it is Sunday, this part of Brick Lane is a good place to stop and play carrom at the tables set up on the street for this purpose (see page 101).

13. Walk up Brick Lane to the crossroads with Sclater Street and Cheshire Street. On Sundays, this is an extraordinary chaotic spectacle, with stalls selling fresh fruit, Oriental slippers and cheap sunglasses to the crowds, while dealers peddle illegal tobacco, whispering, 'Cigarettes, tobacco!' under their breath. On the first Sunday of the month, the Pearly Kings and Queens (see page 301) stand at the corner of Cheshire Street, showing off their flamboyant outfits just to complete the crazy hullabaloo. Turn left into Sclater Street, but observe the corner building as you pass, a rare survivor of an eighteenth-century weaver's dwelling with a domestic workshop, indicated by the characteristic long windows on the second floor designed to admit maximum light.

14. During the week Sclater Street is empty but you may reliably discover Tom the Sailor and his dog, Matty, each morning at the tea stall upon the corner of Cygnet Street (see page 84). On Sundays, Sclater Street is the heart of the Brick Lane Market, with a maze of stalls upon the dirt yards on either side of the street buzzing with activity and lively business. At the far end, on the right, you will find Richard Lee, the longest-established stallholder, selling bicycle spares on the spot where his grandfather Henry William Lee began in 1880 (see page 222). Every Sunday I buy fruit and vegetables from the stall at the end of Sclater Street, and at certain times of the year you can carry off a box of ripe mangoes for a couple of pounds here.

15. Leave Sclater Street by following Cygnet Street back towards Brick Lane. This will deliver you to Des and Lorraine's junk shop, distinguished by Roa's crow painted on the door at 14 Bacon Street. Raise your eyes as you enter to view Des's incredible collection of old toys hanging from the ceiling. This is the last of the bona fide junk shops where real treasures are to be found. Ask Des to show you his authentic eighteenth-century mermaid from the South Seas.

16. Almost next door you will find ninety-six-year-old Charlie Burns (see page 271), who sits all day in his car outside his business, C. E. Burns & Sons, 16–22 Bacon Street, begun in this street by his grandfather John Burns in 1864. Pay your respects to the oldest man on Brick Lane and ask him about meeting Tom Mix, the famous cowboy of silent cinema. And, if you play your cards right, his sassy daughter Carol might take you into her shed and show you the family photos.

17. At Brick Lane, turn left and you are at Brick Lane Beigel Bakery (see page 403). This peerless East End institution, overseen by Sammy Minzly, never closes. Here the hungry hordes line up all night, craving spiritual consolation in the form of beigels and hot salt beef. Be sure to introduce yourself to Mr Sammy and ask him to show you the beigels boiling in the bakery at the rear. If he is not to be found, ask politely if you can have your beigel hot and, if you are lucky, you may be sent to the kitchen, where one of the bakers will pop your beigel in its bag straight into the oven while you wait.

18. At the Beigel Bakery, look out for Mick Taylor, a dandy, sitting on a doorstep nearby and offer to buy him a cup of tea. Known as 'the Sartorialist of Brick Lane', on account of his debonair dress sense and constantly changing outfits, Mick has been hanging around outside the Beigel Bakery for more than fifty years, becoming a star player in the street life that he loves so much.

19. Walk up to the top of Brick Lane where it meets the Bethnal Green Road. Cross this and walk up Redchurch Street to your left. There is a long-derelict terrace here with a couple of eighteenth-century weavers' dwellings. Once a notorious nineteenth-century slum when it was part of the Old Nichol and subsequently a centre of the cabinet-making trade, Redchurch Street has recently acquired a reputation as London's most fashionable street. Look out for people posing self-consciously to demonstrate their cool. Fifty yards along on your left is Malarky's lively frieze of characters with outsize carnival heads and little legs running along beneath. Pop into Labour and Wait on the corner of Turville Street to visit their Brush Museum and turn right at Club Row to admire Roa's huge squirrel. Further down Redchurch Street, in Ebor Street on the left, Ben Eine painted the words 'Anti Anti Anti Anti' down one side and 'Pro Pro Pro Pro' down the other.

20. Almost at the end of Redchurch Street, turn right up Boundary Street. Fifty yards along, on the left at the entrance to Boundary Passage, two French cannon from the Battle of Waterloo serve as bollards, with cannonballs welded into the ends. The upper room of the former Ship and Blue Ball on the corner here was where the notorious Great Train Robbery was planned. Walk further up Boundary Street until you come to Navarre Street on your right. To the left of this street is the Wargrave House, where you will find graffiti by children who lived in these streets and incised their names with nails in the 1950s. The names are at child height about halfway along the building. At first you may not see them, but once you have spotted one you will discover more. Look out for 'G Goldstein 1950 Age 12' and 'A Silkoff Wed 19 April 1950' (see page 116).

21. Continue up Boundary Street to Calvert Avenue, turn left and walk up to the junction with Shoreditch High Street, where you will find Syd's Coffee Stall (open Monday to Friday from early morning until 3 p.m.), which has served the people of Shoreditch since 1919. The first coffee stall to have electricity, in 1922, it is still hooked up to the adjoining lamp post and if you look underneath you can see the original road surface, because it has never moved in all this time (see page 234).

22. Cross Calvert Avenue and walk around the front of Shoreditch Church, completed by George Dance the Elder in 1740 – home to the famous bells of Shoreditch. If you can get inside to view the attractive unrestored interior, be sure to look for the monument to the Shakespearian actors up the stairs and the memorial for Dr Parkinson, who gave his name to the unfortunate affliction. The stocks in the entrance are an attraction too. 'Every church should have one,' the Rev. Turp declared to me, in pride at his historic whipping post. Scrutinise the door on the Clerk's House in the churchyard, which is reputed to come from the medieval church that stood here previously, once used by the actors who played at the first theatres nearby in the sixteenth century (see pages 136, 274 and 323).

23. Walk back down Calvert Avenue towards Arnold Circus at the centre of the Boundary Estate, begun in 1890 as the first social housing in Britain. Constructed of red brick in the Arts and Crafts style, and named after villages on the Thames, these handsome towering edifices resemble tithe barns and castles, with their steep pitched roofs and pleasantly irregular layout. The mound upon which the bandstand sits at the centre is composed of the rubble of the streets that once stood here, collectively known as the Old Nichol. Leila's Shop and Café (open Wednesday to Sunday) occupy the last two premises in Calvert Avenue beside the Circus (see page 382). Ask Leila McAlister to see the photograph that Joan Rose (née Raymond) brought her, taken in 1900, when the premises were owned by her grandfather Alfred Raymond and known as Raymond's (see pages 70 and 382). With baskets of fruit and vegetables stacked up outside, it does not look so different today. This is the ideal place to enjoy refreshment at the end of your walk and stock up on fresh produce to take home with you.

FROM PELLICCI'S TO
PETTICOAT LANE

1. What better way to set you up for a walk through Spitalfields than a hearty breakfast or lunch at E. Pellicci, London's most celebrated family-run café, at 332 Bethnal Green Road? Operating from behind a handsome primrose and chrome façade, into the third generation now and in business for over a century, Pellicci's welcomes everyone. Share a table with East Enders who have been coming since childhood to sit in the cosy, marquetry-lined interior and enjoy meals prepared every day by Maria Pellicci, justly known as the Meat Ball Queen of Bethnal Green (see page 40). Among the regular diners, look out for my friends Juke Box Jimmy, Rodney Archer (see page 231) and Myra Love, the Maori Princess (see page 310). If you ask Nevio or Anna Pellicci, or their cousin Toni, they will show you their celebrity album, with cheeky shots of Colin Farrell, Henry Cooper and Su Pollard skylarking behind the counter.

2. Turn left when you leave Pellicci's and cross the road to Squirries Street on your right. Fifty yards up, at No. 64, on the far side, you will see a steel shutter with a tiny glass panel. Wipe this grimy panel with your handkerchief and peer through into the yard of Hiller Bros, the last company to make wooden market barrows. Here you will see piles of old wheels and barrows where once there was a thriving trade.

3. Walk along the Bethnal Green Road, passing Attenborough Jewellers – the largest pawnbrokers in the East End – until you reach St Matthew's Row, then turn left. Walk down past George Dance's church of 1746 and you will come to Watch House, on the corner of Wood Close. Such was the threat from resurrectionists, taking bodies from this churchyard, that in 1792 it became necessary to appoint a watchman who was paid ten shillings and sixpence a week to be on permanent guard. The churchwarden who lives there today told me that the blunderbuss and rattle are still stored in this house.

4. Continuing down St Matthew's Row, you arrive at the Carpenter's Arms, on the corner of Cheshire Street, where I met Lennie Hamilton, the jewel thief (see page 329). Once a dodgy dive that the Kray twins bought for their mother, Violet, it has now been cleaned up lovingly by landlords Nigel Grocutt and Eric Le Novere, who offer the best selection of bottled beers in Spitalfields.

5. Turn right and walk down Cheshire Street, calling in to the Duke of Uke, Britain's only ukulele shop. Walk fifty yards until you reach the first alley on the left with a railway footbridge. Take this bridge and, if you are tall, enjoy the spectacular views over Spitalfields to the City, then descend on the far side to the Pedley Street Arch.

6. Graced by a profusion of graffiti and scattered with piles of burnt rubbish, the Pedley Street Arch retains its authentic insalubrious atmosphere – as described by Emanuel Litvinoff in *Journey Through a Small Planet*, recalling his childhood in Cheshire Street in the 1920s, 'The evil of the place was in its gloom, its putrid stench, in the industrial grime of half a century with which it was impregnated.'

7. Walking through the Pedley Street Arch, follow the viaduct around to the left, where you will find two huge birds painted by Roa, emerging from the brickwork constructed between 1836 and 1840 to bring the railway from Romford to Shoreditch. Turn and walk back towards Spitalfields, following the new East London Line for 100 yards until you can cross under a bridge. You will find yourself in Allen Gardens, the last field in Spitalfields and all that now exists to remind us that long ago there were orchards, market gardens and pleasure gardens here, where residents of the City of London once came to take rural walks.

8. Turn left in Allen Gardens and walk 100 yards to arrive at Spitalfields City Farm (open every day except Monday), an oasis of rural life in the East End, delivering farmyard sounds, of cockerels crowing and sheep bleating, along the street. Visit the pigs Holmes & Watson (see page 33), and you may be able to purchase some spinach and eggs if you are lucky (see page 99).

9. Leave the City Farm and turn right along Buxton Street. Walk towards the chimney with the word 'Truman' upon it until you reach Brick Lane, where the walls of the old brewery overshadow everything. Brewing on this site can be traced back to 1666, when Joseph Truman came to William Bucknall's Brewhouse in Brick Lane, and it continued until 1988, when the brewery was closed for good. Walking left down the Lane, you will discover the Brewer's House on your right and then the entrance to Dray Walk beyond. On Sundays, these atmospheric buildings house lively markets where you can buy all manner of interesting things from the people who make them.

10. Beyond the brewery, turn left from Brick Lane into Hanbury Street to view the mighty crane painted by Roa (see page 69). When he set out to paint a three-storey heron on the wall of a curry house here, Bengali people asked if it was a crane, which is a sacred bird for them, so Roa obligingly changed his heron into a crane.

11. Walk back along Hanbury Street to approach Commercial Street, cut through in

1851 to carry the trade from the London docks and still the primary conduit of traffic in Spitalfields. The market is ahead of you and the Golden Heart is to your left, but before you succumb to these attractions, cross Commercial Street and walk fifty yards right to enter Gardners' Market Sundriesmen, 149 Commercial Street, the oldest family business here (open Monday–Friday, 6.30 a.m.–2.30 p.m.). You cannot say you have been to Spitalfields until you have shaken hands with Paul Gardner, the fourth-generation paper bag seller (see page 51). Ask him to show you his great-grandfather's account books from the 1880s and buy a year's supply of cheap bin bags while you are there.

12. Double back to the Spitalfields Market, granted a charter by Charles I in 1638 'for the sale of flesh fowl and roots to be sold on Spittle Fields'. A large wholesale fruit and vegetable market existed here until 1991. Today's building is a hybrid, with an 1880s market hall by George Sherrin at one end and Norman Foster's new corporate offices at the other, telling you everything about the uneasy marriage between Spitalfields and the City of London. I recommend you visit on Thursday to explore the weekly Antiques Market, the best of its kind in London.

13. Facing the market across Commercial Street is the Golden Heart, our refuge from the toils and trials of life, where everyone delights to pay court upon Sandra Esqulant, the Queen of Spitalfields (see pages 68 and 336). Be sure to introduce yourself and ask to buy Sandra a drink in appreciation of her heroic dedication in keeping this pub open for us since 1979.

14. Almost next door at 94 Commercial Street is St John Bread and Wine. Every day I come here to buy a tasty brown sourdough loaf baked by baker and pastry chef Justin Piers Gellatly (see page 159), also famous for his doughnuts, custard tarts, treacle tarts, seed cakes, Eccles cakes and mince pies. Fergus Henderson's restaurant is a favourite place for breakfast, lunch and dinner too (see page 124).

15. Then pop in to visit Andrew Coram (see page 149) at 86 Commercial Street. I cannot walk past his antiques shop without directing my gaze to discover what is new here. Ask Andrew to show you the boar's tooth mounted in silver from the Thames Frost Fair of 1715.

16. Walk through Puma Court, where you can get a haircut or shave at Cleo's Barber Shop (see page 221). Kyriacos Cleovoulou (widely known as Cleo) opened up a tiny barber's shop in Puma Court that ran from 1962 until his death in 2005, and now his children, Stavroulla, Panayiotis and George, have reopened the salon to continue the family business.

17. At the end of Puma Court you are in Wilkes Street. Cross into Princelet Street, passing the house marked with a blue plaque where Anna Maria Garthwaite, the most famous eighteenth-designer of Spital-fields silk, lived (see page 333). Walk up Princelet Street to arrive in Brick Lane in the midst of the so-called Curry Mile – quite a spectacle, where umpteen touts will compete to charm you into their restaur-ants (see page 367). Stand for a moment to appreciate the fragrance of spices drifting on the breeze here. Many of these curry houses originated as canteens feeding Ben-gali men who came alone to work in the garment trade until they earned enough to bring their wives over. Gram Bangla at 68 Brick Lane (opposite Christ Church School) still serves authentic Bengali home cooking and owner Abdul Shahid will be happy to guide you through the menu. To your left, at 112 Brick Lane, you will find the Taj Stores, the oldest-established Bengali gro-cers, founded in 1936 by Abdul Jabbar and run today by his three nephews, Jamal, Junel and Joynal (see page 126). Definitely worth a tour around the aisles.

18. On the corner of Brick Lane and Four-nier Street is the Brick Lane Mosque, built as a Huguenot chapel in 1743, then in 1809 bought by the London Society for Promot-ing Christianity amongst the Jews. Later in the nineteenth century it became a syna-gogue, before being turned into a mosque in 1976 for the use of Bengali people with sermons in Sylheti.

19. Walk back along Fournier Street – the finest in Spitalfields, built speculatively in the early eighteenth century for wealthy silk merchants, with houses at subtly tipsy angles presenting an appealing balance of uniformity and difference. Those houses with spools hanging outside are former residences of Huguenot weavers. The usage of Fournier Street has followed the rise and fall of the neighbourhood over the cen-turies, with houses being subdivided into smaller dwellings, converted into factories and recently painstakingly restored to single dwellings again.

20. Note the painted sign 'COMMIT NO NUISANCE' as you round the corner, then ascend the steps of Nicholas Hawksmoor's towering masterpiece, Christ Church, Spital-fields, completed in 1729 and renovated in recent years (see page 315). Be sure to ad-mire the magnificent organ, once played by George Frederick Handel. If it is Tuesday, you will discover Stanley Rondeau there to greet you (see page 128). Stanley's great-great-great-great-great-great-grandfather Jean Rondeau was a Huguenot immigrant who came to Spitalfields in 1685 and his son John was Sexton here in 1761.

21. After leaving the church you might fancy a quick half in the Ten Bells on the corner of Fournier Street, where landlord and ten times Irish national fencing cham-pion, John Twomey, presides in a magnifi-cent nineteenth-century tiled barroom featuring a ceramic mural of 'Spitalfields in Olden Times'.

22. Back on Commercial Street, walk past Itchy Park next to the church, a sanctuary where for more than a century homeless people have slept upon the grass. Walk further down Commercial Street and take the crossing to Toynbee Street, where the ever popular Mama Thai sells noodles on the corner of Brune Street.

23. In Brune Street, you will discover the former Jewish Soup Kitchen, which opened in 1902 and even in the mid-1950s was still regularly feeding 1500 people a day. Actor and Spitalfields resident Harry Landis went there to receive charity as a child with his mother. He told me she used to break her loaf of bread in two and give half to the poor Christians waiting outside. The kitchen closed in 1992. At the end of Brune Street, turn left and walk down Bell Lane to Wentworth Street.

24. Almost as much of a familiar landmark in Spitalfields as the church or the market, Fred the chestnut seller has been standing at the corner of Bell Lane and Wentworth Street in his flat cap next to a can of hot coals on a barrow every Sunday, from October until spring each year, for over half a century (see page 24).

25. Wentworth Street is lined with shops selling 'wax', the richly coloured batik fabric of African design which has made this street such a destination and where today a troupe of magnificent women preside, each

one a shining goddess in her own universe. Call in to Novo Fashions on the corner of Leyden and Wentworth Streets, where Sheba will show her luxurious fabrics, or visit Franceskka Fabrics, one of the longest-established shops on Wentworth Street and ask Franceskka to tell you the story of how it all started (see page 105).

26. At the end of Wentworth Street you enter Middlesex Street, boundary with the City of London and location of the legendary Petticoat Lane Market. Today you can admire the alphabet which stretches the length of the street, painted on metal shutters by Ben Eine (see page 255), and the panels made of 6,000 bottle caps by Robson Cezar on the Bell at the corner of New Goulston Street (see page 226).

27. At the top of Middlesex Street, Ben Eine's shutters spell out the word 'HAPPY', indicating the entrance to Spitalfields from the City.

28. Walk around towards Whitechapel High Street to your left until you come to Tubby Isaac's Jellied Eel Stall at the junction with Goulston Street, run today by Paul Simpson, fourth generation in this legendary business founded in 1919, still selling the fresh seafood that was once the staple diet here (see page 131).

AN ESSENTIAL DETOUR

Everyone should make a detour to visit the site of William Shakespeare's first theatre at New Inn Yard, off Curtain Road, close by the junction with Great Eastern Street (see pages 137 and 323). Called simply the Theatre, it was built by James Burbage in 1576. Here Shakespeare worked as an actor, and *Romeo and Juliet* and an early version of *Hamlet* were first performed. A hundred yards away across Great Eastern Street, a small plaque in Hewett Street marks the site of the Curtain Theatre, which opened in 1577, where *Henry V* was first performed. These quiet, unremarkable streets are touching for their lack of the razzmatazz that you find at Bankside and in Stratford-upon-Avon, making them a more sympathetic location in which to contemplate the reality of William Shakespeare as a working writer in the midst of life.

ACKNOWLEDGEMENTS

In the creation of *Spitalfields Life*, I wish to thank the contributing photographers – Sarah Ainslie, Lucinda Douglas-Menzies, Jeremy Freedman, Phil Maxwell, Patricia Niven, Colin O'Brien and Martin Usborne. Also, Stefan Dickers of the Bishopsgate Institute who found so many old pictures, Walter Donohue who provided chickens, Leila McAlister who sent the vegetable boxes and Ros Niblett who gave her patronage.

Special acknowledgement is due to Andrew McCaldon who set up the interviews and co-ordinated my manuscript with scrupulous attention.

In the production of this book, I should like to express my gratitude to the illustrators, Mark Hearld, Lucinda Rogers and Rob Ryan, to the designers and typesetters, David Pearson and Nicky Barneby, to the copy editor, Lesley Levene, and especially to my magnificent publisher Elizabeth Hallett of Saltyard Books.

PICTURE ACKNOWLEDGEMENTS

Illustrators:

© Mark Hearld: Endpapers. Pages xviii–xx, 33, 56, 98, 134, 246, 268, 286, 398, 408.

© Lucinda Rogers: Page x Spitalfields rooftops looking west. Page 30 Commercial Street and Spitalfields Market. Page 82 Fournier Street from Christ Church. Page 162 Brick Lane with the Brick Lane Mosque minaret. Page 224 Sunday market stalls at Sclater Street. Page 340 The bandstand, Arnold Circus.

© Rob Ryan: *This Bell will Ring ...*

Contributing photographers:

© Sarah Ainslie: 6, 7, 8, 27, 28, 29, 48, 49, 50, 59, 170, 171, 172, 176, 226, 295, 296, 325, 327, 328, 348, 349, 384, 386.

© Lucinda Douglas-Menzies: 184.

© Jeremy Freedman: 25, 38, 39, 58, 74, 75, 92, 103 right, 106, 107, 121, 154, 155, 168, 169, 182, 187, 200 left, 223, 240, 241, 267, 293, 294, 313, 321 above, 342, 343, 351, 353, 368, 369, 381.

© Mark Jackson & Huw Davies: 62, 63, 64, 65, 66, 67.

© Phil Maxwell: 304, 336, 337.

© Patricia Niven: 17, 283, 284, 311, 393, 395.

© Martin Usborne: 344, 345, 346, 347.

INDEX

Literary Life

Market Life

Night Life